Unity 5.x Cookbook

Over 100 recipes exploring the new and exciting features
of Unity 5 to spice up your Unity skill set

Matt Smith

Chico Queiroz

BIRMINGHAM - MUMBAI

Unity 5.x Cookbook

First published: September 2015

Production reference: 1280915

Published by Packt Publishing Ltd.
Livery Place
35 Livery Street
Birmingham B3 2PB, UK.

ISBN 978-1-78439-136-2

www.packtpub.com

Credits

Authors

Matt Smith

Chico Queiroz

Reviewer

Brian Gatt

Tommaso Lintrami

Robert Ollington

Commissioning Editor

Edward Bowkett

Acquisition Editor

Vinay Argekar

Content Development Editor

Ajinkya Paranjpe

Technical Editor

Rohith Rajan

Copy Editor

Yesha Gangani

Project Coordinator

Harshal Ved

Proofreader

Safis Editing

Indexer

Rekha Nair

Graphics

Jason Monteiro

Production Coordinator

Aparna Bhagat

Cover Work

Aparna Bhagat

Contributor

Bryan Griffiths

Foreword

Not so long ago developing professional quality games meant licensing an expensive game engine (or writing one yourself) and hiring a small army of developers to use it. Today, game engines like Unity have democratized game development to the point where you can simply download the tools and start making the game of your dreams right away.

Well... kinda.

Having a powerful game creation tool is not the same thing as having the technical knowledge and skills to use it effectively. I've been developing games and game tools professionally for over 13 years. When I took the plunge into learning Unity development, I quickly found that there was a huge amount of online documentation, tutorials and forum answers available for Unity developers. This makes getting started with Unity development very easy. It's fantastic that this information is out there, but it can also be quite fragmented. A lot of the time the piece of the puzzle you are missing is buried 40 minutes into an hour-long tutorial video or on the 15th page of a long forum thread. The hours you spend looking for these nuggets of wisdom are time that would be better spent working on your game.

The beauty of the Unity 5.x Cookbook is that Matt and Chico have done the tedious legwork of finding this information for you and distilled it into a neat collection of easy to follow step-by-step recipes (and provided the scripts and complete working projects for you to download). Unity development covers a vast range of topics, so the authors have sensibly focused on those areas that almost all developers will encounter. If you're serious about developing great games and tools with Unity, then you'll need to master just the kinds of topics you'll find in this book.

Getting started with Unity development is free and easy. When you're ready to take your skills to the next level, this book is an easy and effective way to do it. It covers a great deal in its hundreds of pages, and if you can master even half of what's here you'll be well on the way to becoming a great Unity developer.

Chris Gregan
Founder & Developer
Fungus Ltd

http://www.fungusgames.com

About the Authors

Matt Smith is a computing academic from Dublin, Ireland. In 1983 Matt started computer programming (on a ZX80) and for his 'O-level' computing certificate (aged 16) he submitted 2 games for his programming project work. In 1985 Matt wrote the lyrics, and was a member of the band that played (and sang, sorry about that by the way) the music on the B-side of the audio cassette carrying the computer game Confuzion (`https://en.wikipedia.org/wiki/Confuzion`).

On a succession of scholarships he managed to spend almost 10 years as a full time student, gaining BA (Hons), then MSc then PhD degrees in computing and artificial intelligence. He then became a full-time lecturer. Having previously lectured full-time at Winchester University and London's Middlesex University, since 2002 he has been at the Institute of Technology Blanchardstown in Dublin (`http://www.itb.ie/`) where he is he is now senior lecturer in computing.

Some of his previous Irish–French student team games can be found and played at `http:// www.saintgermes.com` (thanks for continuing to host these Guillem!). Matt was one of the two technical experts for a recent multimedia European project for language and cultural student work mobility (`http://www.vocalproject.eu`).

He studies and teaches Taekwon-Do with his two children, having been awarded his first degree black belt in 2015 (he also runs his club's website at `http://www.maynoothtkd.com/`). He is trying to learn Irish, so he will understand the report cards from his children's Irish-speaking school. In occasional moments of free time he also tries to get better at playing the piano and classical guitar.

Matt is a documentation author for the Fungus open source interactive storytelling plugin for Unity (`http://www.fungusgames.com`). Matt also maintains a step-by-step open source introduction to Unity 2D and 3D game programming on his public Github pages (see `https://www.github.com/dr-matt-smith/gravity-guy2D`).

Matt's previous publications include a chapter in *Serious Games and Edutainment Applications* (*Springer 2011*, ISBN: 1447121600), and contributions and editing of several music education and artificial intelligence books.

Thanks to my family for all their support. Thanks also to my students, who continue to challenge and surprise me with their enthusiasm for multimedia and game development. Thanks also to the editors, reviewers, readers and students who provided feedback and suggestions on how to improve the first edition and drafts of this new edition.

A special mention to my parents in England, and my wife's Aunty Maureen in County Mayo – here's another book for the family-authored bookshelves.

Finally, I would like to dedicate this book to my wife Sinéad and my children Charlotte and Luke.

Chico Queiroz is a digital media designer from Rio de Janeiro, Brazil. Chico started his career back in 2000, soon after graduating in Communications/Advertising (PUC-Rio), working with advergames and webgames using Flash and Director at LocZ Multimedia, where he contributed to the design and development of games for clients, such as Volkswagen and Parmalat, along with some independent titles.

Chico has a master's degree in Digital Game Design (University for the Creative Arts, UK). His final project was exhibited at events and festivals such as *London Serious Games Showcase* and *FILE*. Chico has also published articles for academic conferences and websites such as http://www.gameology.org, http://www.gamasutra.com, and http://www.gamecareerguide.com.

He curated and organized an exhibition held at SBGames 2009, which explored the connections between video games and art. SBGames is the annual symposium of the Special Commission of Games and Digital Entertainment of the Computing Brazilian Society.

Chico currently works as a digital designer at the Tecgraf/PUC-Rio Institute for Technical-Scientific Software Development, where he, among other responsibilities, uses Unity to develop interactive presentations and concept prototypes for interactive visualization software. He also works as a lecturer at PUC-Rio, teaching undergraduate design students 3D modeling and technology/CG for games, in which Unity is used as the engine for the students' projects. Additionally, Chico is a PhD student in design at the same institution.

I would like to thank my friends, family, and all who have made this book possible and helped me along the way. Special thanks to:

Carl Callewaert and Jay Santos, from Unity, for their help with the Unity beta access and explanations of Unity 5 capabilities; Morten, Anthony, and Robertas, at Unity QA, for their help and support during beta testing; and Aras Pranckevicius, for his illuminating work on Unity's new shader system.

The editors and technical reviewers from Packt, who have made this book much better through their observations and advice.

All my coworkers from Tecgraf/PUC-Rio. Marcelo Gattass, the director, for his continuing support and Eduardo Thadeu Corseuil, my manager, for giving me the opportunity to use Unity in our interactive projects.

All my students and colleagues from the PUC-Rio Art & Design Department. Special mentions to Rejane Spitz, my PhD tutor and the coordinator of the Electronic Art Lab (LAE); Maria das Graças Chagas and my supervisor, João de Sá Bonelli, for his encouragement; and everyone at LAE (especially Axel, Clorisval, Leo, Levy, Pedro, Renan, and Wesley), for the constant exchange of ideas.

Jon Weinbren, from the UK's National Film and Television School, for constantly encouraging his former MA student.

Stefano Corazza and Chantel Benson, from Mixamo, for their extended support.

Wes McDermott, from Allegorithmic, for his excellent material on physically-based rendering.

Gabriel Williams, from ProCore3D, for his help with ProBuilder.

Aaron Brown, from PlaydotSound.com, for his decibel to float calculator.

Fachhochschule Würzburg-Schweinfurt MSc student Christian Petry, for his NormalMap-Online service.

Every reader who gave us feedback on *Unity 4.x Cookbook, Packt Publishing*.

Finally, I would like to dedicate this book to my wife, Ana, and my daughters, Alice and Olivia. Thank you for all your love and support.

About the Reviewers

Brian Gatt is a software developer who holds a bachelor's degree in computer science and Artificial Intelligence from the University of Malta, and a master's degree in computer games and entertainment from Goldsmiths, University of London. Having initially dabbled with OpenGL at university, he has since developed an interest in graphics programming. In his spare time, he likes to keep up with what the latest graphics APIs have to offer, native C++ programming, and game development techniques.

Tommaso Lintrami started with programming on a Commodore VIC-20 back in 1982 when he was nine.

He is a multimedia and a game director, game designer, web and game developer. He has 17 years of work experience in many IT companies, starting initially as a web developer.

Tomasso later shifted to the video game industry, multimedia interactive installations and dedicated software development, home and industrial automation.

Robert Ollington is a lecturer in the Discipline of Information and Communication Technology, School of Engineering and ICT, University of Tasmania, Australia. His research is in the fields of Reinforcement Learning, ANNs, Robotics and Sensing, and Games (Graphics and Physics). His teaching includes units in programming, game design and game production.

www.PacktPub.com

Support files, eBooks, discount offers, and more

For support files and downloads related to your book, please visit www.PacktPub.com.

Did you know that Packt offers eBook versions of every book published, with PDF and ePub files available? You can upgrade to the eBook version at www.PacktPub.com and as a print book customer, you are entitled to a discount on the eBook copy. Get in touch with us at service@packtpub.com for more details.

At www.PacktPub.com, you can also read a collection of free technical articles, sign up for a range of free newsletters and receive exclusive discounts and offers on Packt books and eBooks.

https://www2.packtpub.com/books/subscription/packtlib

Do you need instant solutions to your IT questions? PacktLib is Packt's online digital book library. Here, you can search, access, and read Packt's entire library of books.

Why subscribe?

- Fully searchable across every book published by Packt
- Copy and paste, print, and bookmark content
- On demand and accessible via a web browser

Free access for Packt account holders

If you have an account with Packt at www.PacktPub.com, you can use this to access PacktLib today and view 9 entirely free books. Simply use your login credentials for immediate access.

Table of Contents

Preface

Game development is a broad and complex task. It is an interdisciplinary field, covering subjects as diverse as artificial intelligence, character animation, digital painting, and sound editing. All these areas of knowledge can materialize as the production of hundreds (or thousands!) of multimedia and data assets. A special software application—the game engine—is required to consolidate all of these assets into a single product.

Game engines are specialized pieces of software, which used to belong to an esoteric domain. They were expensive, inflexible, and extremely complicated to use. They were for big studios or hardcore programmers only. Then along came Unity.

Unity represents the true democratization of game development. It is an engine and multimedia editing environment that is user-friendly and versatile. It has free and Pro versions; the latter includes even more features. As we write this preface, Unity offers deployment to:

- **Mobile**: Android, iOS, Windows Phone, and BlackBerry
- **Web**: WebGL
- **Desktop**: PC, Mac, and Linux platforms
- **Console**: PS4, PS3, Xbox One, XBox 360, PlayStation Mobile, PlayStation Vita, and Wii U
- **Virtual Reality (VR)/Augmented Reality (AR)**: Oculus Rift and Gear VR

Today, Unity is used by a diverse community of developers all around the world. Some are students and hobbyists, but many are commercial organizations, ranging from garage developers to international studios, who use Unity to make a huge number of games — some you might have already played on one platform or another.

This book provides over 100 Unity game development recipes. Some recipes demonstrate Unity application techniques for multimedia features, including working with animations and using preinstalled package systems. Other recipes develop game components with C# scripts, ranging from working with data structures and data file manipulation, to artificial intelligence algorithms for computer-controlled characters.

If you want to develop quality games in an organized and straightforward way, and want to learn how to create useful game components and solve common problems, then both Unity and this book are for you.

What this book covers

Chapter 1, Core UI – Messages, Menus, Scores, and Timers, is filled with UI (User Interface) recipes to help you increase the entertainment and enjoyment value of your games through the quality of the interactive visual elements. You'll learn a wide range of UI techniques, including updatable text and images, directional radars, countdown timers, and custom mouse cursors.

Chapter 2, Inventory GUIs, shows you how many games involve the player-collecting items, such as keys to open doors, ammo for weapons, or choosing from a selection of items, such as from a collection of spells to cast. The recipes in this chapter offer a range of text and graphical solutions for displaying inventory status to the player, including whether they are carrying an item or not, or the maximum number of items they are able to collect.

Chapter 3, 2D Animation, includes powerful 2D animation and physics features. In this chapter, we present recipes to help you understand the relationships between the different animation elements in Unity, exploring both the movement of different parts of the body and the use of sprite-sheet image files that contain sequences of sprite frames pictures.

Chapter 4, Creating Maps and Materials, contains recipes that will give you a better understanding of how to use maps and materials with Unity 5's new Physically Based Shaders, whether you are a game artist or not. It is a great resource for exercising your image editing skills.

Chapter 5, Using Cameras, explains recipes covering techniques for controlling and enhancing your game's camera. This chapter will present interesting solutions to work with both single and multiple cameras.

Chapter 6, Lights and Effects, offers a hands-on approach to a number Unity's lighting system features, such as cookie textures, Reflection maps, Lightmaps, Light and Reflection probes, and Procedural Skyboxes. Also, it demonstrates the use of Projectors.

Chapter 7, Controlling 3D Animations, focuses on character animation, and demonstrates how to take advantage of Unity's animation system — Mecanim. It covers a range of subjects from basic character setup to procedural animation and ragdoll physics.

Chapter 8, Positions, Movement and Navigation for Character GameObjects, presents a range of directional recipes for computer-controlled objects and characters, which can lead to games with a richer and more exciting user experience. Examples of these recipes include spawn points, checkpoints, and waypoints. It also includes examples that make groups of objects flock together, and the use of Unity NavMeshes for automated path-finding over terrains and around obstacles.

Chapter 9, Playing and Manipulating Sounds, is dedicated to making sound effects and soundtrack music in your game more interesting. The chapter demonstrates how to manipulate sound during runtime through the use of scripts, Reverb Zones, and Unity's new Audio Mixer.

Chapter 10, Working with External Resource Files and Devices, throws light on how external data can enhance your game in ways such as adding renewable content and communicating with websites. The chapter also includes recipes on automating your builds with Unity Cloud, and how to structure your projects, so they can be easily backed up using online version control systems such as GitHub.

Chapter 11, Improving Games with Extra Features and Optimization, provides several recipes with ideas for adding extra features to your game (such as adding slow motion and securing online games). Many other recipes in this chapter provide examples of how to investigate and potentially improve the efficiency and performance of your game's code.

Chapter 12, Editor Extensions, provides several recipes for enhancing design-time work in the Unity Editor. Editor Extensions are scripting and multimedia components, that allows working with custom text, UI presentation of the game parameters, data in the Inspector and Scene panels, and custom menus and menu items. These can facilitate workflow improvements, thus allowing game developers to achieve their goals quicker and easier.

What you need for this book

All you need is a copy of Unity 5.x, which can be downloaded for free from `http://www.unity3d.com`.

If you wish to create your own image files for the recipes in *Chapter 4, Creating Maps and Materials*, you will also need an image editor, such as Adobe Photoshop, which can be found at `http://www.photoshop.com`, or GIMP, which is free and can be found at `http://www.gimp.org`.

Who this book is for

This book is for anyone who wants to explore a wide range of Unity scripting and multimedia features, and find ready-to-use solutions for many game features. Programmers can explore multimedia features, and multimedia developers can try their hand at scripting.

From intermediate to advanced users, from artists to coders, this book is for you, and everyone on your team!

It is intended for everyone who has the basics of using Unity, and a little programming knowledge in C#.

Sections

In this book, you will find several headings that appear frequently.

To give clear instructions on how to complete a recipe, we use these sections as follows:

Getting ready

This section tells you what to expect in the recipe, and describes how to set up any software, or any preliminary settings required for the recipe.

How to do it...

This section contains the steps required to follow the recipe.

How it works...

This section usually consists of a detailed explanation of what happened in the previous section.

There's more...

This section consists of additional information about the recipe in order to make the reader more knowledgeable about the recipe.

See also

This section provides helpful links to other useful information for the recipe.

Conventions

In this book, you will find a number of text styles that distinguish between different kinds of information. Here are some examples of these styles and an explanation of their meaning.

Code words in text, folder names, filenames, file extensions, pathnames, and user input are shown as follows: " For this recipe, we have prepared the font that you need in a folder named `Fonts` in the `1362_01_01` folder."

URLs are shown as follows: Learn more about the Unity UI on their manual pages at `http://docs.unity3d.com/Manual/UISystem.html`.

A block of code is set as follows:

```
void Start (){
  textClock = GetComponent<Text>();
}

void Update (){
  DateTime time = DateTime.Now;
  string hour = LeadingZero( time.Hour );
  string minute = LeadingZero( time.Minute );
  string second = LeadingZero( time.Second );

  textClock.text = hour + ":" + minute + ":" +
second;
  }
```

New terms and important words are shown in bold. Words that you see on the screen, for example, in menus or dialog boxes, appear in the text like this: "In the **Hierarchy** panel, add a **UI | Text** GameObject to the scene – choose menu: **GameObject | UI | Text**."

 Warnings or important notes appear in a box like this.

 Tips and tricks appear like this.

Reader feedback

Feedback from our readers is always welcome. Let us know what you think about this book—what you liked or disliked. Reader feedback is important for us as it helps us develop titles that you will really get the most out of.

To send us general feedback, simply e-mail `feedback@packtpub.com`, and mention the book's title in the subject of your message.

If there is a topic that you have expertise in and you are interested in either writing or contributing to a book, see our author guide at `www.packtpub.com/authors`.

Customer support

Now that you are the proud owner of a Packt book, we have a number of things to help you to get the most from your purchase.

Downloading the example codes and color images

All the files you need to complete the recipes in the book can be downloaded from: `https://github.com/dr-matt-smith/unity-5-cookbook-codes`.

The downloadable codes are fully commented, and completed Unity projects for each recipe are also provided. In addition you'll also find a folder containing the color images for each chapter in this repository.

Errata

Although we have taken every care to ensure the accuracy of our content, mistakes do happen. If you find a mistake in one of our books—maybe a mistake in the text or the code—we would be grateful if you could report this to us. By doing so, you can save other readers from frustration and help us improve subsequent versions of this book. If you find any errata, please report them by visiting `http://www.packtpub.com/submit-errata`, selecting your book, clicking on the **Errata Submission Form** link, and entering the details of your errata. Once your errata are verified, your submission will be accepted and the errata will be uploaded to our website or added to any list of existing errata under the Errata section of that title.

To view the previously submitted errata, go to `https://www.packtpub.com/books/content/support` and enter the name of the book in the search field. The required information will appear under the **Errata** section.

Piracy

Piracy of copyrighted material on the Internet is an ongoing problem across all media. At Packt, we take the protection of our copyright and licenses very seriously. If you come across any illegal copies of our works in any form on the Internet, please provide us with the location address or website name immediately so that we can pursue a remedy.

Please contact us at copyright@packtpub.com with a link to the suspected pirated material.

We appreciate your help in protecting our authors and our ability to bring you valuable content.

Questions

If you have a problem with any aspect of this book, you can contact us at questions@packtpub.com, and we will do our best to address the problem.

1
Core UI – Messages, Menus, Scores, and Timers

In this chapter, we will cover:

- ▶ Displaying a "Hello World" UI text message
- ▶ Displaying a digital clock
- ▶ Displaying a digital countdown timer
- ▶ Creating a message that fades away
- ▶ Displaying a perspective 3D text message
- ▶ Displaying an image
- ▶ Creating UI Buttons to move between scenes
- ▶ Organizing images inside panels and changing panel depths via buttons
- ▶ Displaying the value of an interactive UI Slider
- ▶ Displaying a countdown timer graphically with a UI Slider
- ▶ Displaying a radar to indicate the relative locations of objects
- ▶ Creating UIs with the Fungus open-source dialog system
- ▶ Setting custom mouse cursor images
- ▶ Input Fields component for text entry
- ▶ Toggles and radio buttons via Toggle Groups

Introduction

A key element contributing to the entertainment and enjoyment of most games is the quality of the visual experience, and an important part of this is the **User Interface** (**UI**). UI elements involve ways for the user to interact with the game (such as buttons, cursors, text boxes, and so on), as well as ways for the game to present up-to-date information to the user (such as the time remaining, current health, score, lives left, or location of enemies). This chapter is filled with UI recipes to give you a range of examples and ideas for creating game UIs.

The big picture

Every game is different, and so this chapter attempts to fulfill two key roles. The first aim is to provide step-by-step instructions on how to create a wide range of the **Unity 5** UI elements and, where appropriate, associate them with game variables in code. The second aim is to provide a rich illustration of how UI elements can be used for a variety of purposes, so that you can get good ideas about how to make the Unity 5 UI set of controls deliver the particular visual experience and interactions for the games that you are developing.

The basic UI elements can provide static images and text to just make the screen look more interesting. By using scripts, we can change the content of these images and text objects, so that the players' numeric scores can be updated, or we can show stickmen images to indicate how many lives the player has left, and so on. Other UI elements are interactive, allowing users to click on buttons, choose options, enter text, and so on. More sophisticated kinds of UI can involve collecting and calculating data about the game (such as percentage time remaining or enemy hit damage; or the positions and types of key GameObjects in the scene, and their relationship to the location and orientation of the player), and then displaying these values in a natural, graphical way (such as progress bars or radar screens).

Core GameObjects, components, and concepts relating to Unity UI development include:

- **Canvas**: Every UI element is a child to a **Canvas**. There can be multiple **Canvas** GameObjects in a single scene. If a **Canvas** is not already present, then one will automatically be created when a new UI GameObject is created, with that UI object childed to the new **Canvas** GameObject.

- **EventSystem**: An **EventSystem** GameObject is required to manage the interaction events for UI controls. One will automatically be created with the first UI element.

- **Panel**: UI objects can be grouped together (logically and physically) with UI **Panels**. **Panels** can play several roles, including providing a GameObject parent in the **Hierarchy** for a related group of controls. They can provide a visual background image to graphically relate controls on the screen, and they can also have scripted resize and drag interactions added, if desired.

- **Visual UI** controls: The visible UI controls themselves include **Button**, **Image**, **Text**, **Toggle**, and so on.

- **Interaction UI** controls: These are non-visible components that are added to GameObjects; examples include Input Field and Toggle Group.

- The **Rect Transform** component: UI GameObjects can exist in a different space from that of the 2D and 3D scenes, which cameras render. Therefore, UI GameObjects all have the special **Rect Transform** component, which has some different properties to the scene's GameObject **Transform** component (with its straightforward *X/Y/Z* position, rotation, and scale properties). Associated with **Rect Transforms** are pivot points (reference points for scaling, resizing, and rotations) and anchor points. Read more about these core features below.

- **Sibling Depth**: The bottom-to-top display order (what appears on the top of what) for a UI element is determined initially by their sequence in the **Hierarchy**. At designtime, this can be manually set by dragging GameObjects into the desired sequence in the **Hierarchy**. At runtime, we can send messages to the **Rect Transforms** of GameObjects to dynamically change their **Hierarchy** position (and therefore, the display order), as the game or user interaction demands. This is illustrated in the *Organizing images inside panels and changing panel depths via buttons* recipe in this chapter.

The following diagram shows how there are four main categories of UI controls, each in a **Canvas** GameObject and interacting via an **EventSystem** GameObject. UI Controls can have their own **Canvas**, or several UI controls can be in the same **Canvas**. The four categories are: static (display-only) and interactive UI controls, non-visible components (such as ones to group a set of mutually exclusive radio buttons), and C# script classes to manage UI control behavior through logic written in the program code. Note that UI controls that are not a child or descendent of a **Canvas** will not work properly, and interactive UI controls will not work properly if the **EventSystem** is missing. Both the **Canvas** and **EventSystem** GameObjects are automatically added to the Hierarchy as soon as the first UI GameObject is added to a scene.

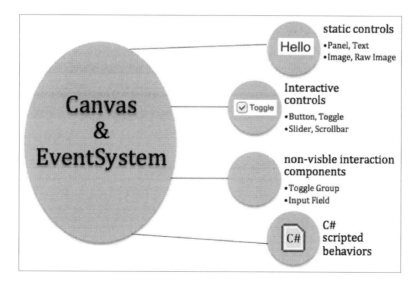

UI **Rect Transforms** represents a rectangular area rather than a single point, which is the case for scene GameObject **Transforms**. **Rect Transforms** describe how a UI element should be positioned and sized relatively to its parent. **Rect Transforms** have a width and height that can be changed without affecting the local scale of the component. When the scale is changed for the **Rect Transform** of a UI element, then this will also scale font sizes and borders on sliced images, and so on. If all four anchors are at the same point, then resizing the **Canvas** will not stretch the **Rect Transform**. It will only affect its position. In this case, we'll see the **Pos X** and **Pos Y** properties, and the **Width** and **Height** of the rectangle. However, if the anchors are not all at the same point, then **Canvas** resizing will result in a stretching of the element's rectangle. So instead of the **Width**, we'll see the values for **Left** and **Right**—the position of the horizontal sides of the rectangle to the sides of the **Canvas**, where the **Width** will depend on the actual **Canvas** width (and the same for **Top/Bottom/Height**).

Unity provides a set of preset values for pivots and anchors, making the most common values very quick and easy to assign to an element's **Rect Transform**. The following screenshot shows the 3 x 3 grid that allows you quick choices about left, right, top, bottom, middle, horizontal, and vertical values. Also, the extra column on the right offers horizontal stretch presets, and the extra row at the bottom offers vertical stretch presets. Using the *SHIFT* and *ALT* keys sets the pivot and anchors when a preset is clicked.

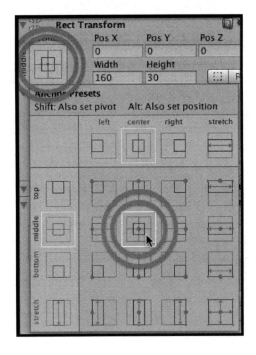

The Unity manual provides a very good introduction to the **Rect Transform.** In addition, Ray Wenderlich's two-part Unity UI web tutorial also presents a great overview of the **Rect Transform**, pivots, and anchors. Both parts of Wenderlich's tutorial make great use of animated GIFs to illustrate the effect of different values for pivots and anchors:

- ▸ `http://docs.unity3d.com/Manual/UIBasicLayout.html`
- ▸ `http://www.raywenderlich.com/78675/unity-new-gui-part-1`

There are three **Canvas** render modes:

- ▸ **Screen Space – Overlay**: In this mode, the UI elements are displayed without any reference to any camera (there is no need for any **Camera** in the scene). The UI elements are presented in front of (overlaying) any sort of camera display of the scene contents.

- ▸ **Screen Space – Camera**: In this mode, the **Canvas** is treated as a flat plane in the frustum (viewing space) of a **Camera** scene —where this plane is always facing the camera. So, any scene objects in front of this plane will be rendered in front of the UI elements on the **Canvas**. The **Canvas** is automatically resized if the screen size, resolution, or camera settings are changed.

- ▸ **World Space**: In this mode, the **Canvas** acts as a flat plane in the frustum (viewing space) of a **Camera** scene—but the plane is not made to always face the **Camera**. How the **Canvas** appears is just as with any other objects in the scene, relative to where (if anywhere) in the camera's viewing frustum the **Canvas** plane is located and oriented.

In this chapter, we have focused on the **Screen Space – Overlay** mode. But all these recipes can equally be used with the other two modes as well.

Be creative! This chapter aims to act as a launching pad of ideas, techniques, and reusable **C#** scripts for your own projects. Get to know the range of Unity UI elements, and try to work smart. Often, a UI element exists with most of the components that you may need for something in your game, but you may need to adapt it somehow. An example of this can be seen in the recipe that makes a UI Slider non-interactive, instead using it to display a red-green progress bar for the status of a countdown timer. See this in the *Displaying a countdown timer graphically with a UI Slider* recipe.

Displaying a "Hello World" UI text message

The first traditional problem to be solved with a new computing technology is often to display the *Hello World* message. In this recipe, you'll learn to create a simple UI Text object with this message, in large white text with a selected font, and in the center of the screen.

Getting ready

For this recipe, we have prepared the font that you need in a folder named `Fonts` in the `1362_01_01` folder.

How to do it...

To display a **Hello World** text message, follow these steps:

1. Create a new Unity 2D project.

2. Import the provided `Fonts` folder.

3. In the **Hierarchy** panel, add a **UI | Text** GameObject to the scene – choose menu: **GameObject | UI | Text**. Name this GameObject **Text-hello**.

> Alternatively, use the **Create** menu immediately below the **Hierarchy** tab, choosing menu: **Create | UI | Text**.

4. Ensure that your new **Text-hello** GameObject is selected in the **Hierarchy** panel. Now, in the **Inspector**, ensure the following properties are set:

   - **Text** set to read `Hello World`
   - **Font** set to `Xolonium-Bold`
   - **Font size** as per your requirements (large—this depends on your screen—try `50` or `100`)
   - **Alignment** set to horizontal and vertical center
   - **Horizontal** and **Vertical Overflow** set to `Overflow`
   - **Color** set to white

The following screenshot shows the **Inspector** panel with these settings:

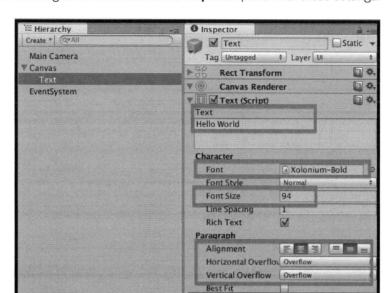

5. Now, in the **Rect Transform**, click on the **Anchor Presets** square icon, which should result in several rows and columns of preset position squares appearing. Hold down *SHIFT* and *ALT* and click on the center one (row **middle** and column **center**).

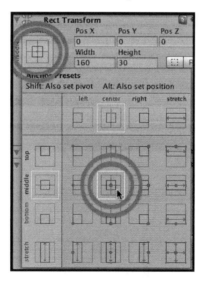

6. Your **Hello World** text will now appear, centered nicely in the **Game** panel.

How it works...

You have added a new **Text-hello** GameObject to a scene. A parent **Canvas** and UI **EventSystem** will also have been automatically created.

You set the text content and presentation properties, and use the **Rect Transform** anchor presets to ensure that whatever way the screen is resized, the text will stay horizontally and vertically centered.

There's more...

Here are some more details that you don't want to miss.

Styling substrings with Rich Text

Each separate UI **Text** component can have its own color, size, boldness styling, and so on. However, if you wish to quickly add some highlighting style to a part of a string to be displayed to the user, the following are examples of some of the HTML-style markups that are available without the need to create separate UI **Text** objects:

- Embolden text with the "b" markup: `I am <b>bold</b>`
- Italicize text with the "i" markup: `I am <i>italic</i>`
- Set the text color with hex values or a color name: `I am <color=green>green text</color>`, but `I am <color=#FF0000>red</color>`

 Learn more from the Unity online manual **Rich Text** page at: `http://docs.unity3d.com/Manual/StyledText.html`.

Displaying a digital clock

Whether it is the real-world time, or perhaps an in-game countdown clock, many games are enhanced by some form of clock or timer display. The most straightforward type of clock to display is a string composed of the integers for hours, minutes, and seconds, which is what we'll create in this recipe.

The following screenshot shows the kind of clock we will be creating in this recipe:

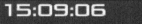

Getting ready

For this recipe, we have prepared the font that you need in a folder named Fonts in the 1362_01_01 folder.

How to do it...

To create a digital clock, follow these steps:

1. Create a new Unity 2D project.

2. Import the provided Fonts folder.

3. In the **Hierarchy** panel, add a **UI | Text** game object to the scene named **Text-clock**.

4. Ensure that GameObject **Text-clock** is selected in the **Hierarchy** panel. Now, in **Inspector**, ensure that the following properties are set:

    ❑   **Text** set to read as time goes here (this placeholder text will be replaced by the time when the scene is running.)

    ❑   **Font type** set to Xolonium Bold

    ❑   **Font Size** set to 20

    ❑   **Alignment** set to horizontal and vertical center

    ❑   **Horizontal** and **Vertical Overflow** settings set to **Overflow**

    ❑   **Color** set to white

5. Now, in the **Rect Transform**, click on the **Anchor Presets** square icon, which will result in the appearance of several rows and columns of preset position squares. Hold down *SHIFT* and *ALT* and click on the **top** and column **center** rows.

6. Create a folder named Scripts and create a C# script class called ClockDigital in this new folder:

```csharp
using UnityEngine;
using System.Collections;

using UnityEngine.UI;
using System;

public class ClockDigital : MonoBehaviour {
  private Text textClock;

  void Start (){
    textClock = GetComponent<Text>();
  }
```

```
void Update (){
  DateTime time = DateTime.Now;
  string hour = LeadingZero( time.Hour );
  string minute = LeadingZero( time.Minute );
  string second = LeadingZero( time.Second );

  textClock.text = hour + ":" + minute + ":" +
second;
  }

  string LeadingZero (int n){
    return n.ToString().PadLeft(2, '0');
  }
}
```

7. With GameObject **Text-clock** selected in the **Hierarchy** panel, drag your
    `ClockDigital` script onto it to add an instance of this script class as a component
    to GameObject **Text-clock**, as shown in the following screenshot:

8. When you run the scene, you will now see a digital clock, showing hours, minutes,
    and seconds, at the top-center part of the screen.

How it works...

You added a **Text** GameObject to a scene. You have added an instance of the `ClockDigital`
C# script class to that GameObject.

Notice that as well as the standard two C# packages (`UnityEngine` and `System.`
`Collections`) that are written by default for every new script, you have added the `using`
statements for two more C# script packages, `UnityEngine.UI` and `System`. The UI package
is needed, since our code uses UI `Text` object; and the `System` package is needed, since it
contains the `DateTime` class that we need to access the clock on the computer where our
game is running.

There is one variable, `textClock`, which will be a reference to the `Text` component, whose text content we wish to update in each frame with the current time in hours, minutes, and seconds.

The `Start()` method (executed when the scene begins) sets the `textClock` variable to be a reference to the `Text` component in the GameObject, to which our scripted object has been added.

 Note that an alternative approach would be to make `textClock` a `public` variable. This will allow us to assign it via drag-and-drop in the **Inspector** panel.

The `Update()` method is executed in every frame. The current time is stored in the `time` variable, and strings are created by adding leading zeros to the number values for the hours, minutes, and seconds properties of variable `time`.

This method finally updates the `text` property (that is, the letters and numbers that the user sees) to be a string, concatenating the hours, minutes, and seconds with colon separator characters.

The `LeadingZero(...)` method takes as input an integer and returns a string of this number with leading zeros added to the left, if the value was less than 10.

There's more...

There are some details that you don't want to miss.

The Unity tutorial for animating an analogue clock

Unity has published a nice tutorial on how to create 3D objects, and animate them through C# script to display an analogue clock at `https://unity3d.com/learn/tutorials/modules/beginner/scripting/simple-clock`.

Displaying a digital countdown timer

This recipe will show you how to display a digital countdown clock shown here:

`Countdown seconds remaining = 25`

Getting ready

This recipe adapts the previous one. So, make a copy of the project for the previous recipe, and work on this copy.

For this recipe, we have prepared the script that you need in a folder named `Scripts` in the `1362_01_03` folder.

How to do it...

To create a digital countdown timer, follow these steps:

1. In the **Inspector** panel, remove the scripted component, `ClockDigital`, from GameObject **Text-clock**.

2. Create a `DigitalCountdown` C# script class containing the following code, and add an instance as a scripted component to GameObject **Text-clock**:

```
using UnityEngine;
using System.Collections;
using UnityEngine.UI;
using System;

public class DigitalCountdown : MonoBehaviour {
   private Text textClock;

   private float countdownTimerDuration;
   private float countdownTimerStartTime;

   void Start (){
     textClock = GetComponent<Text>();
     CountdownTimerReset(30);
   }

   void Update (){
     // default - timer finished
     string timerMessage = "countdown has finished";
     int timeLeft = (int)CountdownTimerSecondsRemaining();

     if(timeLeft > 0)
        timerMessage = "Countdown seconds remaining = " +
LeadingZero( timeLeft );

     textClock.text = timerMessage;
   }

   private void CountdownTimerReset (float delayInSeconds){
     countdownTimerDuration = delayInSeconds;
     countdownTimerStartTime = Time.time;
   }

   private float CountdownTimerSecondsRemaining (){
      float elapsedSeconds = Time.time -
countdownTimerStartTime;
```

```
        float timeLeft = countdownTimerDuration -
    elapsedSeconds;
        return timeLeft;
    }

    private string LeadingZero (int n){
        return n.ToString().PadLeft(2, '0');
    }
}
```

3. When you run the scene, you will now see a digital clock counting down from 30. When the countdown reaches zero, the message **countdown has finished** will be displayed.

How it works...

You added a **Text** GameObject to a scene. You have added an instance of the DigitalCountdown C# script class to that GameObject.

There is one variable, textClock, which will be a reference to the Text component, whose text content we wish to update in each frame with a time remaining message (or a timer complete message). Then, a call is made to the CountdownTimerReset (...) method, passing an initial value of 30 seconds.

The Start() method (executed when the scene begins) sets the textClock variable to find the Text component in the GameObject where our scripted object has been added.

The Update() method is executed in every frame. This method initially sets the timerMessage variable to a message, stating that the timer has finished (the default message to display). Then the seconds remaining are tested to be greater than zero. And if so, then the message variable has its contents changed to display the integer (whole) number of the seconds remaining in the countdown—retrieved from the CountdownTimerSecondsRemaining() method. This method finally updates the text property (that is, the letters and numbers that the user sees) to be a string with a message about the remaining seconds.

The CountdownTimerReset (...) method records the number of seconds provided, and the time the method was called.

The CountdownTimerSecondsRemaining() method returns an integer value of the number of seconds remaining.

Creating a message that fades away

Sometimes, we want a message to display just for a certain time, and then fade away and disappear, which will appear as shown in this screenshot:

Getting ready

This recipe adapts the first recipe in this chapter, so make a copy of that project to work on for this recipe.

For this recipe, we have prepared the script that you need in a folder named `Scripts` in the `1362_01_04` folder.

How to do it...

To display a text message that fades away, follow these steps:

1. Import the provided C# script class called `CountdownTimer`.

2. Ensure that GameObject **Text-hello** is selected in the **Hierarchy** tab. Then, attach an instance of the `CountdownTimer` C# script class as a component of this GameObject.

3. Create a C# script class, `FadeAway`, containing the following code, and add an instance as a scripted component to the GameObject **Text-hello**:

```
using UnityEngine;
using System.Collections;
using UnityEngine.UI;

public class FadeAway : MonoBehaviour {
  private CountdownTimer countdownTimer;
  private Text textUI;
  private int fadeDuration = 5;
  private bool fading = false;

  void Start (){
    textUI = GetComponent<Text>();
    countdownTimer = GetComponent<CountdownTimer>();
```

```
      StartFading(fadeDuration);
   }

   void Update () {
     if(fading){
       float alphaRemaining =
countdownTimer.GetProportionTimeRemaining();
       print (alphaRemaining);
       Color c = textUI.material.color;
       c.a = alphaRemaining;
       textUI.material.color = c;

       // stop fading when very small number
       if(alphaRemaining < 0.01)
         fading = false;
     }
   }

   public void StartFading (int timerTotal){
     countdownTimer.ResetTimer(timerTotal);
     fading = true;
   }
}
```

4. When you run the scene, you will now see that the message on the screen slowly fades away, disappearing after 5 seconds.

How it works...

An instance of the provided `CountdownTimer` script class was added as a component to the GameObject **Text-hello**.

You added to the GameObject **Text-hello** an instance of the scripted class, `FadeAway`. The `Start()` method caches references to the `Text` and `CountdownTimer` components in the `countdownTimer` and `textUI` variables. Then, it calls the `StartFading(...)` method, passing in the number 5, so that the message will have faded to invisible after 5 seconds.

The `StartFading(...)` method starts this timer scripted component to countdown to the given number of seconds. It also sets the `fading` Boolean flag variable to `true`.

The `Update()` method, in each frame, tests if the `fading` variable is `true`. If it is true, then the alpha (transparency) component of the color of the **Text-hello** object is set to a value between 0.0 and 1.0, based on the proportion of the time remaining in the `CountdownTimer` object. Finally, if the proportion of time remaining is less than a very small value (0.01), then the `fading` variable is set to `false` (to save the processing work since the text is now invisible).

Displaying a perspective 3D text message

Unity provides an alternative way to display text in 3D via the `TextMesh` component. While this is really suitable for a text-in-the-scene kind of situation (such as billboards, road signs, and generally wording on the side of 3D objects that might be seen close up), it is quick to create, and is another way of creating interesting menus or instructions scenes, and the like.

In this recipe, you'll learn how to create a scrolling 3D text, simulating the famous opening credits of the movie **Star Wars**, which looks something like this:

Getting ready

For this recipe, we have prepared the fonts that you need in a folder named `Fonts`, and the text file that you need in a folder named `Text`, in the `1362_01_04` folder.

How to do it...

To display perspective 3D text, follow these steps:

1. Create a new Unity 3D project (this ensures that we start off with a **Perspective** camera, suitable for the 3D effect that we want to create).

 If you need to mix 2D and 3D scenes in your project, you can always manually set any camera's **Camera Projection** property to **Perspective** or **Orthographic** via the **Inspector** panel.

2. In the **Hierarchy** panel, select the **Main Camera** item, and, in the **Inspector** panel, set its properties as follows: **Camera Clear Flags** to **solid color**, **Field of View** to **150**. Also set the **Background color** to black.

3. Import the provided `Fonts` folder.

4. In the **Hierarchy** panel, add a **UI | Text** game object to the scene – choose menu: **GameObject | UI | Text**. Name this GameObject as `Text-star-wars`. Set its **Text Content** as Star Wars (with each word on a new line). Then, set its **Font** to `Xolonium Bold`, and its **Font Size** to `50`. Use the anchor presets in **Rect Transform** to position this UI **Text** object at the top center of the screen.

5. In the **Hierarchy** panel, add a **3D Text** game object to the scene – choose menu: **GameObject | 3D Object | 3D Text**. Name this GameObject `Text-crawler`.

6. In the **Inspector** panel, set the **Transform** properties for GameObject **Text-crawler** as follows: **Position** (`0, -300, -20`), **Rotation** (`15, 0, 0`).

7. In the **Inspector** panel, set the **Text Mesh** properties for GameObject **Text-crawler** as follows:

   ❑ Paste the content of the provided text file, `star_wars.txt`, into **Text**.

   ❑ Set **Offset Z** = `20`, **Line Spacing** = `0.8`, and **Anchor** = Middle center

   ❑ Set **Font Size** = `200`, **Font** = `SourceSansPro-BoldIt`

8. When the scene is made to run, the Star Wars story text will now appear nicely squashed in 3D perspective on the screen.

How it works...

You have simulated the opening screen of the movie *Star Wars*, with a flat UI **Text** object title at the top of the screen, and 3D **Text Mesh** with settings that appear to be disappearing into the horizon with 3D perspective 'squashing'.

There's more...

There are some details that you don't want to miss.

We have to make this text crawl like it does in the movie

With a few lines of code, we can make this text scroll in the horizon just as it does in the movie. Add the following C# script class, `ScrollZ`, as a component to GameObject **Text-crawler**:

```
using UnityEngine;
using System.Collections;

public class ScrollZ : MonoBehaviour {
  public float scrollSpeed = 20;

  void Update () {
    Vector3 pos = transform.position;
    Vector3 localVectorUp = transform.TransformDirection(0,1,0);
    pos += localVectorUp * scrollSpeed * Time.deltaTime;
    transform.position = pos;
  }
}
```

In each frame via the `Update()` method, the position of the 3D text object is moved in the direction of this GameObject's local up-direction.

Where to learn more

Learn more about 3D Text and Text Meshes in the Unity online manual at `http://docs.unity3d.com/Manual/class-TextMesh.html`.

 NOTE: An alternative way of achieving perspective text like this would be to use a Canvas with render mode World Space.

Displaying an image

There are many cases where we wish to display an image onscreen, including logos, maps, icons, splash graphics, and so on. In this recipe, we will display an image at the top of the screen, and make it stretch to fit whatever width that the screen is resized to.

The following screenshot shows Unity displaying an image:

Getting ready

For this recipe, we have prepared the image that you need in a folder named Images in the 1362_01_06 folder.

How to do it...

To display a stretched image, follow these steps:

1. Create a new Unity 3D project.

    3D projects will, by default, import images as a **Texture**, and 2D projects will import images as **Sprite (2D and UI)**. Since we're going to use a **RawImage** UI component, we need our images to be imported as textures.

2. Set the Game panel to a 400 x 300 size. Do this via menu: **Edit | Project Settings | Player**. Ensure that the **Resolution | Default is Full Screen** setting check is unchecked, and the width/height is set to 400 x 300. Then, in the **Game** panel, select **Stand Alone (400 x 300)**. This will allow us to test the stretching of our image to a width of 400 pixels.

3. Import the provided folder, which is called `Images`. In the **Inspector** tab, ensure that the `unity5_learn` image has **Texture Type** set to **Texture**. If it does not, then choose **Texture** from the drop-down list, and click on the **Apply** button. The following screenshot shows the **Inspector** tab with the **Texture** settings:

4. In the **Hierarchy** panel, add a **UI | RawImage** GameObject to the scene named **RawImage-unity5**.

 If you wish to *prevent* the distortion and stretching of an image, then use the UI **Sprite** GameObject instead, and ensure that you check the **Preserve Aspect** option, in its **Image (Script)** component, in the **Inspector** panel.

5. Ensure that the GameObject **RawImage-unity5** is selected in the **Hierarchy** panel. From your **Project** folder (`Images`), drag the `unity5_learn` image into the **Raw Image (Script)** public property **Texture**. Click on the **Set Native Size** button to preview the image before it gets stretched, as shown:

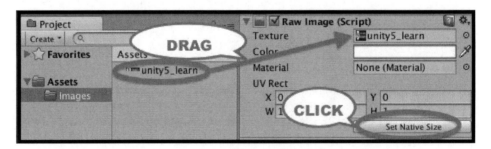

6. Now, in **Rect Transform**, click on the **Anchor Presets** square icon, which will result in several rows and columns of preset position squares appearing. Hold down *SHIFT* and *ALT* and click on the **top row** and the **stretch column**.

7. The image will now be positioned neatly at the top of the **Game** panel, and will be stretched to the full width of 400 pixels.

How it works...

You have ensured that an image has **Texture Type** set to **Texture**. You added a **UI RawImage** control to the scene. The **RawImage** control has been made to display the `unity5_learn` image file.

The image has been positioned at the top of the **Game** panel, and using the anchor and pivot presets, it has made the image stretch to fill the whole width, which we set to 400 pixels via the **Player** settings.

There's more...

There are some details that you don't want to miss:

Working with Sprites and UI Image components

If you simply wish to display non-animated images, then **Texture** images and UI **RawImage** controls are the way to go. However, if you want more options on how an image should be displayed (such as tiling, and animation), then the UI **Sprite** control should be used instead. This control needs image files to be imported as the **Sprite (2D and UI) type**.

Once an image file has been dragged into the UI **Image** control's **Sprite** property, additional properties will be available, such as **Image Type**, options to preserve aspect ratio, and so on.

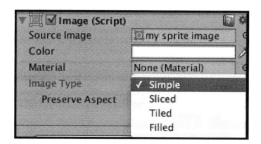

See also

An example of tiling a Sprite image can be found in the *Revealing icons for multiple object pickups by changing the size of a tiled image* recipe in *Chapter 2, Inventory GUIs*.

Creating UI Buttons to move between scenes

As well as scenes where the player plays the game, most games will have menu screens, which display to the user messages about instructions, high scores, the level they have reached so far, and so on. Unity provides the UI **Buttons** to make it easy to offer users a simple way to indicate their choice of action on such screens.

In this recipe, we'll create a very simple game consisting of two screens, each with a button to load the other one, similar to the following screenshot:

How to do it...

To create a button-navigable multi-scene game, follow these steps:

1. Create a new Unity 2D project.

2. Save the current (empty) scene, naming it **page1**.

3. Add a UI **Text** object positioned at the top center of the scene, containing text `Main Menu / (page 1)` in a large font size.

4. Add a UI **Button** to the scene positioned in the middle center of the screen. In the **Hierarchy** panel, click on the show children triangle to display the UI **Text** child of this button GameObject. Select the **Text** button-child GameObject, and in the **Inspector** panel for the **Text** property of the **Text (Script)** component, enter the button text called `goto page 2`, as shown here:

5. Add the current scene to the build, choosing menu: **File | Build Settings…**. Then, click on the **Add Current** button so that the **page1** scene becomes the first scene on the list of **Scenes in the Build**.

> We cannot tell Unity to load a scene that has not been added to the list of scenes in the build. We use the `Application.LoadLevel(…)` code to tell Unity to load the scene name (or numeric index) that is provided.

6. Create a C# script class, `MenuActions`, containing the following code, and add an instance as a scripted component to the **Main Camera**:

```csharp
using UnityEngine;
using System.Collections;

public class MenuActions : MonoBehaviour {
  public void MENU_ACTION_GotoPage(string sceneName){
    Application.LoadLevel(sceneName);
  }
}
```

7. Ensure that the **Button** is selected in the **Hierarchy** and click on the plus sign "**+**" button at the bottom of the **Button (Script)** component, in the **Inspector view**, to create a new **OnClick** event handler for this button.

8. Drag the **Main Camera** from the **Hierarchy** over the **Object** slot—immediately below the menu saying **Runtime Only**. This means that when the **Button** receives an **OnClick** event, we can call a public method from a scripted object inside the **Main Camera**.

9. Now, select the **MENU_ACTION_GotoPage()** method from the **MenuActions** drop-down list (initially showing **No Function**). Type page2 (the name of the scene we want to be loaded when this button is clicked) in the text box, below the method's drop-down menu. This **page2** string will be passed to the method when the button receives an **OnClick** event message, as shown here:

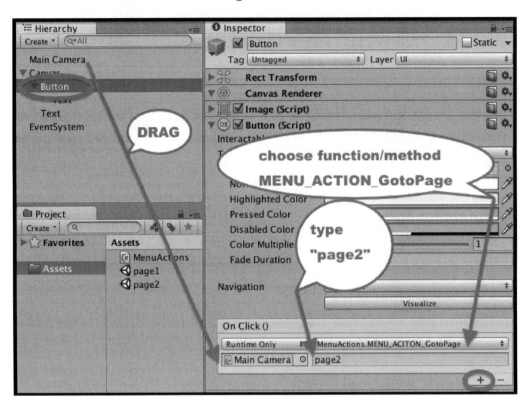

10. Save the current scene, create a new empty scene, and then save this new scene as **page2**.

11. Follow the similar steps for this scene. Add a **UI Text** GameObject, displaying the text **Instructions / (page 2)** in a large font size. Add a UI **Button,** showing the **goto page 1 text.**

12. Add the current scene to the build (so now, both **page1** and **page2** will be listed in the build).

13. Add an instance of MenuActions script class to the **Main Camera**.

14. Select the **Button** in the **Hierarchy** panel, and add an **On Click** event handler, which will pass the **MENU_ACTION_GotoPage()** method the string **page1** (the name of the scene we want to be loaded when this button is clicked).

15. Save the scene.

16. When you run the **page1 scene,** you will be presented with your **Main Menu** text and a button, which when clicked, makes the game load the **page2 scene**. On scene **page2,** you'll have a button to take you back to **page1**.

How it works...

You have created two scenes, and added both of them to the game build. Each scene has a button, which when clicked (when the game is playing), makes Unity load the (named) other scene. This is made possible because when each button is clicked, it runs the MENU_ ACTION_GotoPage(...) method from the scripted MenuActions component inside the **Main Camera**. This method inputs a text string of the name of the scene to be loaded, so that the button in the **page1 scene** gives the string name of **page2** as the scene to be loaded, and vice versa.

When a UI **Button** is added to the **Hierarchy** panel, a child UI **Text** object is also automatically created, and the content of the **Text** property of this UI **Text** child is the text that the user sees on the button.

There's more...

There are some details that you don't want to miss.

Visual animation for the button mouse-over

There are several ways in which we can visually inform the user that the button is interactive when they move their mouse cursor over it. The simplest is to add a color tint that will appear when the mouse is over the button—this is the default **Transition**. With the **Button** selected in the **Hierarchy**, choose a tint color (for example, red), for the **Highlighted Color** property of the **Button (Script)** component, in the **Inspector** tab, as shown here:

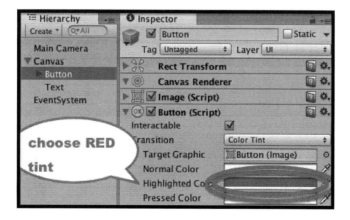

Another form of visual **Transition** to inform the user of an active button is **Sprite Swap**. In this case, properties for different images for **Targeted/Highlighted/Pressed/Disabled** are available in the **Inspector** tab. The default **Targeted Graphic** is the built-in Unity **Button (image)** – this is the grey rounded rectangle default when GameObjects buttons are created. Dragging in a very different-looking image for the **Highlighted Sprite** is an effective alternative to set a color hint. We have provided a `rainbow.png` image with the project for this recipe that can be used for the **Button** mouse over **Highlighted Sprite**. The following screenshot shows the button with this rainbow background image:

Animating button properties on mouse over

Finally, animations can be created for dynamically highlighting a button to the user, for example, a button might get larger when the mouse is over it, and then it might shrink back to its original size when the mouse pointer is moved away. These effects are achieved by choosing the **Animation** option for the **Transition** property, and by creating an animation controller with triggers for the **Normal**, **Highlighted**, **Pressed** and **Disabled** states. To animate a button for enlargement when the mouse is over it (the highlighted state), do the following:

1. Create a new Unity 2D project.

2. Create a button.

3. In the **Inspector Button (Script)** component, set the **Transition** property to **Animation**.

4. Click the **Auto Generate Animation** button (just below the **Disabled Trigger** property) for the **Button (Script)** component, as shown here:

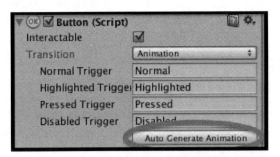

5. Save the new controller by naming it **button-animation-controller**.

6. Ensure that the **Button** GameObject is selected in the **Hierarchy**. Then, in the **Animation** panel, select the **Highlighted** clip from the drop-down menu, as shown here:

7. In the **Animation** panel, click on the red **record** circle button, and then click on the **Add Property** button, choosing to record changes to the **Rect Transform | Scale** property.

8. Two key frames will have been created, delete the second one at **1:00** (since we don't want a "bouncing" button), as shown in the following screenshot .

9. Select the first key frame at **0:00** (the only one now!). Then, in the **Inspector** view, set the *X* and *Y* scale properties of the **Rect Transform** component to (1.2, 1.2).

10. Finally, click on the red **record** circle button for the second time to end the recording of the animation changes.

11. Save and run your scene, and you will see that the button smoothly animates to get larger when the mouse is over it, and then smoothly returns to its original size when the mouse is moved away.

The following web pages offer video and web-based tutorials on UI animations:

▶ The Unity button transitions tutorial is available at:

```
http://unity3d.com/learn/tutorials/modules/beginner/ui/ui-
transitions
```

▶ Ray Wenderlich's tutorial (part 2), including the button animations, is available at:

```
http://www.raywenderlich.com/79031/unity-new-gui-tutorial-
part-2
```

Organizing images inside panels and changing panel depths via buttons

UI **Panels** are provided by Unity to allow UI controls to be grouped and moved together, and also to visually group elements with an **Image** background (if desired). The **sibling depth** is what determines which UI elements will appear above or below others. We can see the sibling depth explicitly in the **Hierarchy**, since the top-to-bottom sequence of UI GameObjects in the **Hierarchy** sets the sibling depth. So, the first item has a depth of 1, the second has a depth of 2, and so on. The UI GameObjects with larger sibling depths (further down the **Hierarchy**) appear above the UI GameObjects with lower sibling depths.

In this recipe, we'll create three UI panels, each showing a different playing card image. We'll also add four triangle arrangement buttons to change the display order (move to bottom, move to top, move up one, and move down one).

Getting ready

For this recipe, we have prepared the images that you need in a folder named Images in the 1362_01_08 folder.

How to do it...

To create the UI **Panels** whose layering can be changed by the user-clicking buttons, follow these steps:

1. Create a new Unity 2D project.
2. Create a new UI **Panel** named Panel-jack-diamonds. Position it in the middle-center part of the screen, and size it 200 pixels wide by 300 pixels high. Uncheck the **Image (Script)** component for this panel (since we don't want to see the default semi-transparent rectangular grey background image of a panel).

3. Create a new UI **Image**, and child this image to **Panel-jack-diamonds**.

4. Position the **Panel-jack-diamonds** image at center-middle, and size it to 200 x 300. Drag the **Jack-of-diamonds** playing card image into the **Source Image** property, for the **Image (Script)** component in the **Inspector** tab.

5. Create a UI **Button** named **Button-move-to-front**. Child this button to **Panel-jack-diamonds**. Delete the **Text** child GameObject of this button (since we'll use an icon to indicate what this button does).

6. Size the **Button-move-to-front** button to 16 x 16, and position it top-center of the player card image, so that it can be seen at the top of the playing card. Drag the `icon_move_to_front` arrangement triangle icon image into the **Source Image** property, for the **Image (Script)** component, in the **Inspector** view.

7. Ensure that the **Button-move-to-front** button is selected in the **Hierarchy**. Then, click on the plus sign (**+**) at the bottom of the **Button (Script)** component, in the **Inspector** view to create a new **OnClick** event handler for this button.

8. Drag **Panel-jack-diamonds** from the **Hierarchy** over the **Object** slot (immediately below the menu saying **Runtime Only**).

9. Now, select the **RectTransform.SetAsLastSibling** method from the drop-down function list (initially showing **No Function**).

This means that when the **Button** receives an **OnClick** event, the **RectTransform** of the **Panel** will be sent the **SetAsLastSibling** message – this will move the **Panel** to the bottom of the GameObjects in the **Canvas**, and therefore will move this **Panel** in front of all other GameObjects in the **Canvas**.

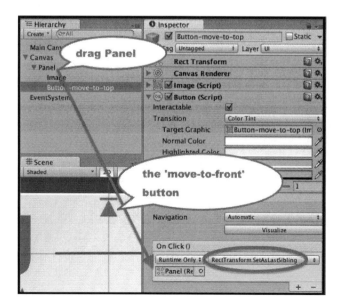

10. Repeat *step 2*; create a second **Panel** with a move-to-front button. Name this second Panel **Panel-2-diamonds**, then move and position it slightly to the right of **Panel-jack-diamonds**, allowing both the move-to-front buttons to be seen.

11. Save your scene and run the game. You will be able to click the move-to-front button on either of the cards to move that card's panel to the front. If you run the game with the Game panel not maximized, you'll actually see the panels changing order in the list of the children of the **Canvas** in the **Hierarchy**.

How it works...

You've created two UI **Panels**, each panel containing an image of a playing card and a button whose action will make its parent panel move to the front. The button's action illustrates how the **OnClick** function does not have to be the calling of a public method of a scripted component of an object, but it can be sending a message to one of the components of the targeted GameObject—in this instance we send the **SetAsLastSibling** message to the **RectTransform** of the **Panel** in which the **Button** is located.

There's more...

There are some details that you don't want to miss.

Moving up or down by just one position, using scripted methods

While the Rect Transform offers a useful **SetAsLastSibling** (move to front) and **SetAsFirstSibling** (move to back), and even **SetSiblingIndex** (if we knew exactly what position in the sequence to type in), there isn't a built-in way to make an element move up or down, just a single position in the sequence of GameObjects in the **Hierarchy** panel. However, we can write two straightforward methods in C# to do this, and we can add buttons to call these methods, providing full control of the top-to-bottom arrangement of the UI controls on the screen. To implement four buttons (move-to-front/move-to-back/up one/down one), do the following:

1. Create a C# script class called `ArrangeActions`, containing the following code, and add an instance as a scripted component to each of your **Panels**:

```
using UnityEngine;
using UnityEngine.UI;
using UnityEngine.EventSystems;
using System.Collections;

public class ArrangeActions : MonoBehaviour {
   private RectTransform panelRectTransform;
```

```
void Start(){
  panelRectTransform = GetComponent<RectTransform>();
}

public void MoveDownOne(){
   print ("(before change) " + GameObject.name + "
sibling index = " + panelRectTransform.GetSiblingIndex());

   int currentSiblingIndex =
panelRectTransform.GetSiblingIndex();
   panelRectTransform.SetSiblingIndex( currentSiblingIndex
- 1 );

   print ("(after change) " + GameObject.name + " sibling
index = " + panelRectTransform.GetSiblingIndex());
  }

public void MoveUpOne(){
   print ("(before change) " + GameObject.name + "
sibling index = " + panelRectTransform.GetSiblingIndex());

   int currentSiblingIndex =
panelRectTransform.GetSiblingIndex();
   panelRectTransform.SetSiblingIndex( currentSiblingIndex
+ 1 );

   print ("(after change) " + GameObject.name + " sibling
index = " + panelRectTransform.GetSiblingIndex());
  }
}
```

2. Add a second button to each card panel, this time, using the arrangement triangle icon image called icon_move_to_front, and set the **OnClick** event function for these buttons to **SetAsFirstSibling**.

3. Add two further buttons to each card panel with the up and down triangle icon images: icon_down_one and icon_up_one. Set the **OnClick** event handler function for the down-one buttons to call the MoveDownOne() method, and set the functions for the up-one buttons to call the MoveUpOne() method.

4. Copy one of the panels to create a third card (this time showing the Ace of diamonds). Arrange the three cards so that you can see all four buttons for at least two of the cards, even when those cards are at the bottom (see the screenshot at the beginning of this recipe).

5. Save the scene and run your game. You will now have full control over the layering of the three card panels.

Displaying the value of an interactive UI Slider

This recipe illustrates how to create an interactive UI **Slider**, and execute a C# method each time the user changes the **Slider value**.

How to do it...

To create a UI Slider and display its value on the screen, follow these steps:

1. Create a new 2D project.

2. Add a UI Text GameObject to the scene with a Font size of 30 and placeholder text such as `slider value here` (this text will be replaced with the slider value when the scene starts).

3. In the **Hierarchy** panel, add a **UI | Slider** game object to the scene—choose the menu: **GameObject | UI | Slider**.

4. In the **Inspector** tab, modify settings for the **Rect Transform** to position the slider on the top-middle part of the screen and the text just below it.

5. In the **Inspector** tab, set the **Min Value** of the slider to 0, the **Max Value** to 20, and check the **Whole Numbers** checkbox, as shown here:

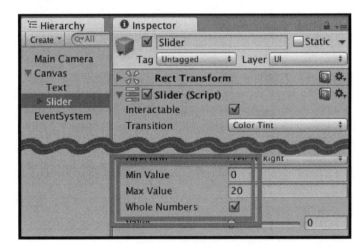

6. Create a C# script class called `SliderValueToText`, containing the following code, and add an instance as a scripted component to the GameObject called **Text**:

```
using UnityEngine;
using System.Collections;
using UnityEngine.UI;

public class SliderValueToText : MonoBehaviour {
  public Slider sliderUI;
  private Text textSliderValue;

  void Start (){
    textSliderValue = GetComponent<Text>();
    ShowSliderValue();
  }

  public void ShowSliderValue () {
    string sliderMessage = "Slider value = " +
sliderUI.value;
    textSliderValue.text = sliderMessage;
  }
}
```

7. Ensure that the **Text** GameObject is selected in the **Hierarchy**. Then, in the **Inspector** view, drag the **Slider** GameObject into the public **Slider UI** variable slot for the `Slider Value To Text (Script)` scripted component, as shown here:

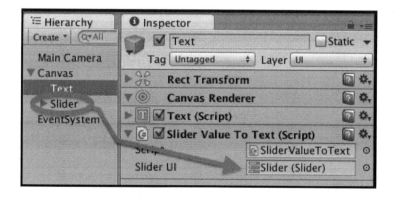

8. Ensure that the **Slider** GameObject is selected in the **Hierarchy**. Then, in the **Inspector** view, drag the **Text** GameObject into the public **None (Object)** slot for the **Slider (Script)** scripted component, in the section for **On Value Changed (Single)**.

> You have now told Unity to which object a message should be sent each time the slider is changed.

9. From the drop-down menu, select **SliderValueToText** and the `ShowSliderValue()` method, as shown in the following screenshot. This means that each time the slider is updated, the `ShowSliderValue()` method, in the scripted object, in GameObject **Text** will be executed.

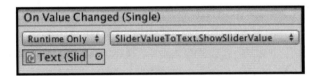

10. When you run the scene, you will now see a slider. Below it, you will see a text message in the `Slider value = <n>` form.

11. Each time the slider is moved, the text value shown will be (almost) instantly updated. The values should range from `0` (the leftmost of the slider) to `20` (the rightmost of the slider).

> The update of the text value on the screen probably won't be instantaneous, as in happening in the same frame as the slider value is moved, since there is some computation involved in the slider deciding that an **On Value Changed** event message needs to be triggered, and then looking up any methods of objects that are registered as event handlers for such an event. Then, the statements in the object's method need to be executed in sequence. However, this should all happen within a few milliseconds, and should be sufficiently fast enough to offer the user a satisifyingly responsive UI for interface actions such as changing and moving this slider.

How it works...

You have added to the **Text** GameObject a scripted instance of the `SliderValueToText` class.

The `Start()` method, which is executed when the scene first runs, sets the variable to be a reference to the **Text** component inside the **Slider** item. Next, the `ShowSliderValue()` method is called, so that the display is correct when the scene begins (the initial slider value is displayed).

This contains the `ShowSliderValue()` method, which gets the value of the slider. It updates the text displayed to be a message in the form: `Slider value = <n>`.

You created a **UI Slider** GameObject, and set it to be whole numbers in the 0-20 range.

You added to the **UI Slider** GameObject's list of **On Value Changed** event listeners the `ShowSliderValue()` method of the `SliderValueToText` scripted component. So, each time the slider value changes, it sends a message to call the `ShowSliderValue()` method, and so the new value is updated on the screen.

Displaying a countdown timer graphically with a UI Slider

There are many cases where we wish to inform the player of the proportion of time remaining, or at the completion of some value at a point in time, for example, a loading progress bar, the time or health remaining compared to the starting maximum, how much the player has filled up their water bottle from the fountain of youth, and so on. In this recipe, we'll illustrate how to remove the interactive 'handle' of a **UI Slider**, and change the size and color of its components to provide us with an easy-to-use, general purpose progress/proportion bar. In this recipe, we'll use our modified slider to graphically present to the user how much time remains for a countdown timer.

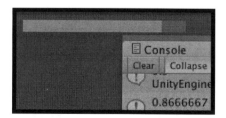

Getting ready

This recipe adapts the previous one. So, make a copy of the project for the previous recipe, and work on this copy to follow this recipe.

For this recipe, we have prepared the script and images that you need in the folders named `Scripts` and `Images` in the `1362_01_10` folder.

How to do it...

To create a digital countdown timer with a graphical display, follow these steps:

1. Delete the **Text** GameObject.

2. Import the `CountdownTimer` script and the `red_square` and `green_square` images to this project.

3. Ensure that the **Slider** GameObject is selected in the **Hierarchy** tab.

4. Deactivate the **Handle Slide Area** child GameObject (by unchecking it)

5. You'll see the "drag circle" disappear in the **Game** panel (the user will not be dragging the slider, since we want this slider to be display-only), as shown in the following screenshot:

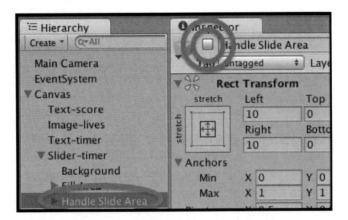

6. Select the **Background** child:

   ❑ Drag the `red_square` image into the **Source Image** property of the **Image (Script)** component in the **Inspector** view

7. Select the **Fill** child:

   ❑ Drag the `green_square` image into the **Source Image** property of the **Image (Script)** component in the **Inspector** tab

8. Select the **Fill Area** child:

    ❏ In the **Rect Transform** component, use the **Anchors** preset position of **left-middle**

    ❏ Set **Width** to 155 and **Height** to 12, as shown here:

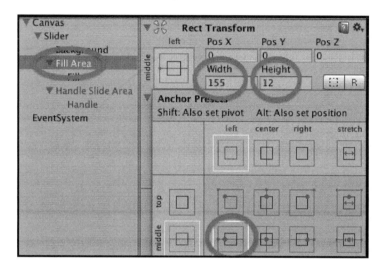

9. Ensure that the **Slider** GameObject is selected in the **Hierarchy**. Then, attach an instance of C# script class called CountdownTimer as a component of this GameObject.

10. Create a C# script class called SliderTimerDisplay containing the following code, and add an instance as a scripted component to the **Slider** GameObject:

```
using UnityEngine;
using System.Collections;
using UnityEngine.UI;

public class SliderTimerDisplay : MonoBehaviour {
  private CountdownTimer countdownTimer;
  private Slider sliderUI;
  private int startSeconds = 30;

  void Start (){
    SetupSlider();
    SetupTimer();
  }

  void Update () {
    sliderUI.value =
countdownTimer.GetProportionTimeRemaining();
```

```
            print (countdownTimer.GetProportionTimeRemaining());
        }

        private void SetupSlider (){
            sliderUI = GetComponent<Slider>();
            sliderUI.minValue = 0;
            sliderUI.maxValue = 1;
            sliderUI.wholeNumbers = false;
        }

        private void SetupTimer (){
            countdownTimer = GetComponent<CountdownTimer>();
            countdownTimer.ResetTimer(startSeconds);
        }
    }
```

11. Run your game and you will see the slider move with each second, revealing more and more of the red background to indicate the time remaining.

How it works...

You hid the **Handle Slide Area** child so that **Slider** is for display only, and cannot be interacted with by the user. The **Background** color of the **Slider** was set to red, so that, as the counter goes down, more and more red is revealed—warning the user that the time is running out. The **Fill** of the **Slider** was set to green, so that the proportion remaining is displayed in green (the more green it becomes, the larger the value of the slider/timer).

An instance of the provided CountdownTimer script class was added as a component to the Slider. The ResetTimer (...) method records the number of seconds provided and the time the method was called. The GetProportionRemaining() method returns a value from 0.0-1.0, representing the proportion of the seconds remaining (1.0 being all seconds, 0.5 half the seconds, and 0.0 meaning that no seconds are left).

You have added to the **Slider** GameObject an instance of the SliderTimerDisplay scripted class. The Start() method calls the SetupSlider() and SetupTimer() methods.

The SetupSlider() method sets the sliderUI variable to be a reference to the **Slider** component, and sets up this slider mapped to float (decimal) values between 0.0 and 1.0.

The SetupTimer() method sets the countdownTimer variable to be a reference for the **CountdownTimer** component, and starts this timer scripted component to count down from 30 seconds.

In each frame, the Update() method sets the slider value to the float returned by calling the GetProportionRemaining() method from the running timer.

Try to work with floats between 0.0-1.0 whenever possible.

Integers could have been used, setting the Slider min to 0 and max to 30 (for 30 seconds). However, changing the total number of seconds would then also require the Slider settings to be changed. In most cases working with a float proportion between 0.0 and 1.0 is the more general-purpose and reusable approach to adopt.

Displaying a radar to indicate the relative locations of objects

A radar displays the locations of other objects relative to the player, usually based on a circular display, where the center represents the player, and each graphical 'blip' indicates how far away and what relative direction objects are to the player. Sophisticated radar displays will display different categories of objects with different colored or shaped 'blip' icons.

In the screenshot, we can see 2 red square 'blips', indicating the relative position of the 2 red cube GameObjects tagged Cube near the player, and a yellow circle 'blip' indicating the relative position of the yellow sphere GameObject tagged Sphere. The green circle radar background image gives the impression of an aircraft control tower radar or something similar.

Getting ready

For this recipe, we have prepared the images that you need in a folder named Images in 1362_01_11.

How to do it...

To create a radar to show the relative positions of the objects, follow these steps:

1. Create a new 3D project by importing the following standard assets:

    -   **Environment**
    -   **Characters**
    -   **Cameras**

2. Create a terrain by navigating to the **Create | 3D Object | Terrain** menu.

3. Size the terrain 20 x 20, positioned at (-10, 0, -10)—so that its center is at (0, 0, 0), as shown in the following figure:

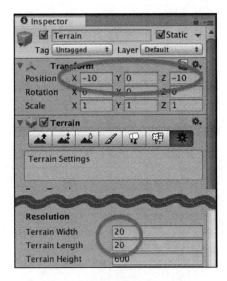

4. Texture paint your terrain with the **SandAlbedo** option, as shown here:

5. From the **Standard Assets** folder in the **Project** panel, drag the prefab **ThirdPersonController** into the scene and position it at (0, 1, 0).

6. Tag this **ThirdPersonController** GameObject called **Player**.

7. Remove the **Main Camera** GameObject.

8. From the **Standard Assets** folder in the **Project** panel, drag the prefab **Multi-PurposeCameraRig** into the scene.

9. With **Multi-PurposeCameraRig** selected in the **Hierarchy**, drag the **ThirdPersonController** GameObject into the **Target** property of the **Auto Cam (Script)** public variable in the **Inspector** tab, as shown in the following screenshot:

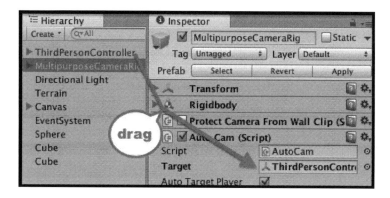

10. Import the provided folder known as `Images`.

11. In the **Hierarchy** panel, add a **UI | RawImage** GameObject to the scene named **RawImage-radar**.

12. Ensure that the **RawImage-radar** GameObject is selected in the **Hierarchy** panel. From your **Project** `Images` folder, drag the `radarBackground` image into the **Raw Image (Script)** public property **Texture**.

13. Now, in **Rect Transform** position **RawImage-radar** at the top-left part using the **Anchor Presets** item. Then set the width and height to 200 pixels.

14. Create another new UI **RawImage** named **RawImage-blip**. Assign the `yellowCircleBlackBorder` texture. Tag the **Blip** GameObject.

15. In the **Project** panel, create a new empty prefab named **blip-sphere**, and drag the **RawImage-blip** GameObject into this prefab to store all its properties.

16. Now, change the texture of **RawImage-blip** to `redSquareBlackBorder`.

17. In the Project panel, create a new empty prefab named **blip-cube**, and drag the **RawImage-blip** GameObject into this prefab to store all its properties.

18. Delete the **RawImage-blip** GameObject from the **Hierarchy** panel.

19. Create a C# script class called `Radar`, containing the following code, and add an instance as a scripted component to the **RawImage-radar** GameObject:

```csharp
using UnityEngine;
using System.Collections;
using UnityEngine.UI;

public class Radar : MonoBehaviour{
  public float insideRadarDistance = 20;
  public float blipSizePercentage = 5;

  public GameObject rawImageBlipCube;
  public GameObject rawImageBlipSphere;

  private RawImage rawImageRadarBackground;
  private Transform playerTransform;
  private float radarWidth;
  private float radarHeight;
  private float blipHeight;
  private float blipWidth;

  void Start (){
    playerTransform =
GameObject.FindGameObjectWithTag("Player").transform;
    rawImageRadarBackground = GetComponent<RawImage>();

    radarWidth =
rawImageRadarBackground.rectTransform.rect.width;
    radarHeight =
rawImageRadarBackground.rectTransform.rect.height;

    blipHeight = radarHeight * blipSizePercentage/100;
    blipWidth = radarWidth * blipSizePercentage/100;
  }

  void Update (){
    RemoveAllBlips();
    FindAndDisplayBlipsForTag("Cube", rawImageBlipCube);
    FindAndDisplayBlipsForTag("Sphere", rawImageBlipSphere);
  }

  private void FindAndDisplayBlipsForTag(string tag,
GameObject prefabBlip){
    Vector3 playerPos = playerTransform.position;
```

```
      GameObject[] targets =
GameObject.FindGameObjectsWithTag(tag);

      foreach (GameObject target in targets) {
        Vector3 targetPos = target.transform.position;
        float distanceToTarget = Vector3.Distance(targetPos,
playerPos);
        if( (distanceToTarget <= insideRadarDistance) ){
          Vector3 normalisedTargetPosiiton =
NormalisedPosition(playerPos, targetPos);
          Vector2 blipPosition =
CalculateBlipPosition(normalisedTargetPosiiton);
          DrawBlip(blipPosition, prefabBlip);
        }
      }
    }

    private void RemoveAllBlips(){
      GameObject[] blips =
GameObject.FindGameObjectsWithTag("Blip");
      foreach (GameObject blip in blips)
        Destroy(blip);
    }

    private Vector3 NormalisedPosition(Vector3 playerPos,
Vector3 targetPos){
      float normalisedyTargetX = (targetPos.x -
playerPos.x)/insideRadarDistance;
      float normalisedyTargetZ = (targetPos.z -
playerPos.z)/insideRadarDistance;
      return new Vector3(normalisedyTargetX, 0,
normalisedyTargetZ);
    }

    private Vector2 CalculateBlipPosition(Vector3 targetPos){
      // find angle from player to target
      float angleToTarget = Mathf.Atan2(targetPos.x,
targetPos.z) * Mathf.Rad2Deg;

      // direction player facing
      float anglePlayer = playerTransform.eulerAngles.y;

      // subtract player angle, to get relative angle to
object
      // subtract 90
```

```
      // (so 0 degrees (same direction as player) is UP)
      float angleRadarDegrees = angleToTarget - anglePlayer
- 90;

      // calculate (x,y) position given angle and distance
      float normalisedDistanceToTarget = targetPos.magnitude;
      float angleRadians = angleRadarDegrees * Mathf.Deg2Rad;
      float blipX = normalisedDistanceToTarget *
Mathf.Cos(angleRadians);
      float blipY = normalisedDistanceToTarget *
Mathf.Sin(angleRadians);

      // scale blip position according to radar size
      blipX *= radarWidth/2;
      blipY *= radarHeight/2;

      // offset blip position relative to radar center
      blipX += radarWidth/2;
      blipY += radarHeight/2;

      return new Vector2(blipX, blipY);
   }

   private void DrawBlip(Vector2 pos, GameObject
blipPrefab){
      GameObject blipGO =
(GameObject)Instantiate(blipPrefab);
      blipGO.transform.SetParent(transform.parent);
      RectTransform rt =
blipGO.GetComponent<RectTransform>();
      rt.SetInsetAndSizeFromParentEdge(RectTransform.Edge.Left,
pos.x, blipWidth);
      rt.SetInsetAndSizeFromParentEdge(RectTransform.Edge.Top,
pos.y, blipHeight);
   }
}
```

20. Create two cubes—tagged **Cube**, textured with a red image called **icon32_square_red**. Position each away from the player's character.

21. Create a sphere—tagged **Sphere**, textured with a red image called **icon32_square_yellow**. Position this away from the cubes and the player's character.

22. Run your game. You will see two red squares and one yellow circle on the radar, showing the relative positions of the red cubes and yellow sphere. If you move too far away, then the blips will disappear.

This radar script scans 360 degrees all around the player, and only considers straight line distances in the X-Z plane. So, the distances in this radar are not affected by any height difference between the player and target GameObjects. The script can be adapted to ignore targets whose height is more than some threshold different to the player's height. Also, as presented, this recipe radar sees through everything, even if there are obstacles between the player and the target. The recipe can be extended to not show obscured targets through the user of the ray-casting techniques. See the Unity scripting reference for more details about ray-casting at `http://docs.unity3d.com/ScriptReference/Physics.Raycast.html`.

How it works...

A radar background is displayed on the screen. The center of this circular image represents the position of the player's character. You have created two prefabs; one for red square images to represent each red cube found within the radar distance, and one for yellow circles to represent yellow sphere GameObjects.

The `Radar` C# script class has been added to the radar UI Image GameObject. This class defines four public variables:

- `insideRadarDistance`: This value defines the maximum distance that an object may be from the player to still be included on the radar (objects further than this distance will not be displayed on the radar).

- `blipSizePercentage`: This public variable allows the developer to decide how large each 'blip' will be, as a proportion of the radar's image.

- `rawImageBlipCube` and `rawImageBlipSphere`: These are references to the prefab UI **RawImages** that are to be used to visually indicate the relative distance and position of cubes and spheres on the radar.

Since there is a lot happening in the code for this recipe, each method will be described in its own section.

The Start() method

The `Start()` method caches a reference to the **Transform** component of the player's character (tagged as **Player**). This allows the scripted object to know about the position of the Player's character in each frame. Next, the width and height of the radar image are cached—so, the relative positions for 'blips' can be calculated, based on the size of this background radar image. Finally, the size of each blip (width and height) is calculated, using the `blipSizePercentage` public variable.

The Update() method

The `Update()` method calls the `RemoveAllBlips()` method, which removes any old **RawImage** UI GameObjects of cubes and spheres that might currently be displayed.

Next, the `FindAndDisplayBlipsForTag(...)` method is called twice. First, for the objects tagged **Cube**, to be represented on the radar with the `rawImageBlipCube` prefab and then again for objects tagged **Sphere**, to be represented on the radar with the `rawImageBlipSphere` prefab. As you might expect, most of the hard work for the radar is to be performed by the `FindAndDisplayBlipsForTag(...)` method.

The FindAndDisplayBlipsForTag(...) method

This method inputs two parameters: the string tag for the objects to be searched for; and a reference to the **RawImage** prefab to be displayed on the radar for any such tagged objects within the range.

First, the current position of the player's character is retrieved from the cached player transform variable. Next, an array is constructed, referring to all GameObjects in the scene that have the provided tag. This array of GameObjects is looped through, and for each GameObject, the following actions are performed:

- The position of the target GameObject is retrieved
- The distance from this target position to the player's position is calculated, and if this distance is within the range (less than or equal to `insideRadarDistance`), then three steps are now required to get the blip for this object to appear on the radar:
  - The normalized position of the target is calculated by calling `NormalisedPosition(...)`
  - The position of the blip on the radar is then calculated from this normalized position by calling `CalculateBlipPosition(...)`
  - Finally, the **RawImage** blip is displayed by calling `DrawBlip(...)` and passing the blip position and the reference to the **RawImage** prefab that is to be created there

The NormalisedPosition(...) method

The `NormalisedPosition(...)` method inputs the player's character position and the target GameObject position. It has the goal of outputting the relative position of the target to the player, returning a Vector3 object with a triplet of *X*, *Y*, and *Z* values. Note that since the radar is only 2D, we ignore the *Y* value of target GameObjects. So, the *Y* value of the Vector3 object returned by this method will always be 0. So, for example, if a target was at exactly the same location as the player, the returned *X*, *Y*, *Z* Vector3 object would be (0, 0, 0).

Since we know that the target GameObject is no further from the player's character than `insideRadarDistance`, we can calculate a value in the -1 ... 0 ... +1 range for the *X* and *Z* axis by finding the distance on each axis from the target to the player, and then dividing it by `insideRadarDistance`. An *X* value of -1 means that the target is fully to the left of the player (at a distance that is equal to `insideRadarDistance`), and +1 means it is fully to the right. A value of 0 means that the target has the same *X* position as the player's character. Likewise, for -1 ... 0 ... +1 values in the *Z-axis* (this axis represents how far, in front or behind us an object, is located, which will be mapped to the vertical axis in our radar).

Finally, this method constructs and returns a new Vector3 object, with the calculated *X* and *Z* normalized values, and a *Y* value of zero.

The normalized position

A *normalized* value is one that has been simplified in some way, so the context has been abstracted away. In this recipe, what we are interested in is where an object is relative to the player. So, our normal form is to get a value of the *X* and *Z* position of a target in the -1 to +1 range for each axis. Since we are only considering GameObject within out `insideRadarDistance` value, we can map these normalized target positions directly onto the location of the radar image in our UI.

The CalculateBlipPosition(...) method

First, we calculate `angleToTarget`: the angle from (0, 0, 0) to our normalized target position.

Next, we calculate `anglePlayer`: the angle the player's character is facing. This recipe makes use of the **yaw** angle of the rotation, which is the rotation about the *Y-axis*—that is, the direction that a character controller is facing. This can be found in the *Y* component of a GameObject's `eulerAngles` component of its transform. You can imagine looking from above and down at the character controller, and see what direction they are facing—this is just what we are trying to display graphically with the compass.

Our desired radar angle (the `angleRadarDegrees` variable) is calculated by subtracting the player's direction angle from the angle between target and player, since a radar displays the relative angle from the direction that the player is facing, to the target object. In mathematics, an angle of zero indicates an *east* direction. To correct this, we need to also subtract 90 degrees from the angle.

The angle is then converted into radians, since this is required for the Unity trigonometry methods. We then multiply the $Sin()$ and $Cos()$ results by our normalized distances to calculate the *X* and *Y* values respectively (see the following figure):

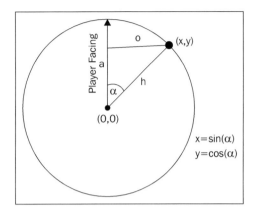

Our final position values need to be expressed as pixel lengths, relative to the center of the radar. So, we multiply our $blipX$ and $blipY$ values by half the width and the height of the radar; note that we multiply only with half the width, since these values are relative to the center of the radar.

 Note: In this figure, alpha is the angle between player and target object, 'a' is the adjacent side, 'h' is the hypotenuse and 'o' is the side opposite the angle.

We then add half the width and height of the radar image to the $blipX/Y$ values. So, these values are now positioned relative to the center.

Finally a new **Vector2** object is created and returned, passing back these final calculated *X* and *Y* pixel values for the position of our blip icon.

The DrawBlip() method

The $DrawBlip()$ method takes the input parameters of the position of the blip (as a $Vector2$ *X*, *Y* pair), and the reference to the **RawImage** prefab to be created at that location on the radar.

A new GameObject is created from the prefab, and is parented to the radar GameObject (of which the scripted object is also a component). A reference is retrieved to the **Rect Transform** of the new **RawImage** GameObject that has been created for the 'blip'. Calls to the Unity **RectTransform** method, $SetInsetAndSizeFromParentEdge(...)$, result in the blip GameObject being positioned at the provided horizontal and vertical locations over the radar image, regardless of where in the **Game** panel the background radar image has been located.

Creating UIs with the Fungus open-source dialog system

Rather than constructing your own UI and interactions from scratch each time, there are plenty of UI and dialogue systems available for Unity. One powerful, free, and open source dialog system is called **Fungus**, which uses a visual flowcharting approach to dialog design.

In this recipe, we'll create a very simple, two-sentence dialogue, to illustrate the basics of Fungus. The following screenshot shows the Fungus-generated dialog for the first sentence ('**Hello, how are you**') and the interactive button (a triangle inside a circle) the user clicks to progress to the next piece of dialog (in the bottom-right part of the rectangle).

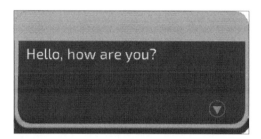

How to do it...

To create a two-sentence dialog using Fungus, follow these steps:

1. Download the latest version of the Fungus **unitypackage** from the FungusGames website `http://www.fungusgames.com/`.

2. Create a new Unity 2D project.

3. Import the Fungus **unitypackage** by navigating to **Assets | Import Package | Custom Package...**, and then navigating to your downloaded file location.

4. Create a new Fungus **Flowchart** GameObject by choosing menu: **Tools | Fungus | Create | Flowchart**.

5. Display and dock the Fungus **Flowchart** window panel by choosing menu: **Tools | Fungus | Flowchart Window**.

6. There will be a block in the **Flowchart** Window. Click on this block to select it (a green border appears around the block to indicate that it is selected), and then in the **Inspector** panel, change the name of this block to **Start**, as shown in the following screenshot:

7. Each **Block** in a Flowchart follows a sequence of commands. So, we are now going to create a sequence of commands to display two sentences to the user when the game runs.

The sequence of **Commands** in a **Block**

Each **Block** in a **Flowchart** follows a sequence of **Commands**, so to display two sentences to the user when the game runs, we need to create a sequence of two **Say** commands in the **Inspector** panel properties for our **Block**.

8. Ensure that the **Start** block is still selected in the **Flowchart** panel. Now, click on the plus **+'** button at the bottom section of the **Inspector** panel to display the menu of **Commands**, and select the **Narrative | Say** command, as shown here:

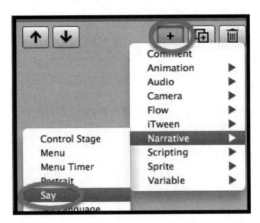

9. Since we only have one command for this block, that command will automatically be selected (highlighted green) in the top-half part of the **Inspector** view. The bottom half of the **Inspector** view presents the properties for the currently selected **Command**, as shown in the following screenshot. In the bottom-half part of the **Inspector** view, for the **Story Text** property, enter the text of the question that you wish to be presented to the user: How are you today?

10. Now, create another **Say Command**, and type the following for its **Story Text** property: Very well thank you.

11. When you run the game, the user will first be presented with the **How are you today?** text (hearing a clicking noise as each letter is *typed* on screen). After the user clicks on the 'continue' triangle button (at the bottom-right part of the dialog window), they will then be presented with the second sentence: **Very well thank you.**

How it works...

You have created a new Unity project, and imported the Fungus asset package, containing the Fungus Unity menus, windows and commands, and also the example projects.

You have added a **Fungus Flowchart** to your scene with a single **Block** that you have named **Start**. Your block starts to execute when the game begins (since the default for the first block is to be executed upon receiving the **Game Started** event).

In the **Start** block, you added a sequence of two **Say Commands**. Each command presents a sentence to the user, and then waits for the continue button to be clicked before proceeding to the next **Command**.

As can be seen, the Fungus system handles the work of creating a nicely presented panel to the user, displaying the desired text and continue button. Fungus offers many more features, including menus, animations, control of sounds and music, and so on, details of which can be found by exploring their provided example projects, and their websites:

- ▶ `http://fungusgames.com/`
- ▶ `https://github.com/FungusGames/Fungus`

Setting custom mouse cursor images

Cursor icons are often used to indicate the nature of the interaction that can be done with the mouse. Zooming, for instance, might be illustrated by a magnifying glass. Shooting, on the other hand, is usually represented by a stylized target. In this recipe, we will learn how to implement custom mouse cursor icons to better illustrate your gameplay—or just to escape the Windows, OSX, and Linux default GUI. The following screenshot shows a custom magnifying glass mouse cursor when the use's mouse pointer hovers over a **Button**:

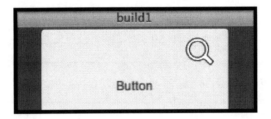

Getting ready

For this recipe, we have prepared the images that you'll need in a folder named `IconsCursors` in the `1362_01_13` folder.

How to do it...

To make a custom cursor appear when the mouse is over a GameObject, follow these steps:

1. Create a new Unity 2D project.
2. Add a **Directional Light** item to the scene by navigating to **Create | Light | Directional light**.
3. Add a 3D **Cube** to the scene, scaled to (5, 5, 5). Because it was created as a 2D project the cube will appear as a grey square in the **Game** panel (2D projects have an orthographic camera, so we won't see perspective effects).

4. Import the provided folder called `IconsCursors`.

 Ensure that each image in this folder has been imported as **Texture Type Cursor**. If they are not, then select this type for each image and click on the **Apply** button in the **Inspector** view.

5. Create a C# script class called `CustomCursorPointer`, containing the following code, and add an instance as a scripted component to the **Cube** GameObject:

```csharp
using UnityEngine;
using System.Collections;

public class CustomCursorPointer : MonoBehaviour {
  public Texture2D cursorTexture2D;

  private CursorMode cursorMode = CursorMode.Auto;
  private Vector2 hotSpot = Vector2.zero;

  public void OnMouseEnter() {
    SetCustomCursor(cursorTexture2D);
  }

  public void OnMouseExit() {
    SetCustomCursor(null);
  }

  private void SetCustomCursor(Texture2D curText){
    Cursor.SetCursor(curText, hotSpot, cursorMode);
  }
}
```

 Event methods `OnMouseEnter()` and `OnMouseExit()` have been purposely declared as `public`. This will allow these methods to also be called from UI GameObjects when they receive the `OnPointerEnterExit` events.

6. With the **Cube** item selected in the **Hierarchy** panel, drag the `CursorTarget` image into the public **Cursor Texture 2D** variable slot in the **Inspector** panel for the **Customer Cursor Pointer (Script)** component.

7. Save the current scene, and add it to the **Build**.

 You will not be able to see the custom cursors in the Unity Editor. You must build your game application, and you'll see the custom cursors when you run the build app.

8. Build your project. Now, run your built application, and when the mouse pointer moves over the grey square of the **Cube**, it will change to the custom `CursorTarget` image that you chose.

How it works...

You have added a scripted object to a cube that will tell Unity to change the mouse pointer when an **OnMouseEnter** message is received—that is, when the user's mouse pointer moves over the part of the screen where the cube is being rendered. When an **OnMouseExit** event is received (the users mouse pointer is no longer over the cube part of the screen), the system is told to go back to the operating system default cursor. This event should be received within a few milliseconds of the user's mouse exiting from the collider.

There's more...

There are some details that you don't want to miss.

Custom cursors for mouse over UI controls

Unity 5 UI controls do not receive the **OnMouseEnter** and **OnMouseExit** events. They can respond to the **PointerEnter/Exit** events, but this requires adding the **Event Trigger** components. To change the mouse pointer when the mouse moves over a UI element, do the following:

1. Add a UI **Button** to the scene.

2. Add an instance of the C# script class called `CustomCursorPointer` to the button.

3. With **Button** selected in the **Hierarchy panel**, drag the `CursorZoom` image into the public **Cursor Texture 2D** variable slot in the **Inspector** panel for the **Customer Cursor Pointer (Script)** component.

4. In the **Inspector** view, add an **Event Triggers** component to the **Button**. Choose menu: **Add Component | Event | Event Trigger**.

5. Add a **Pointer Enter** event to your **Event Trigger** component, click on the plus (**+**) button to add an event handler slot, and drag the **Button** GameObject into the **Object** slot.

6. From the **Function** drop-down menu, choose **CustomCursorPointer** and then choose the **OnMouseEnter** method.

> We have added an Event Handler so that when the **Button** receives a **Pointer Enter** (mouse over) event, it will execute the **OnMouseEnter()** method of the **CustomCursorPointer** scripted object inside the **Button**.

7. Add a **Pointer Exit** event to your **Event Trigger** component, and make it call the OnMouseExit() method from **CustomCursorPointer** when this event is received.

8. Save the current scene.

9. Build your project. Now, run your built application and when the mouse pointer moves over the **Button,** it will change to the custom CursorZoom image that you chose.

Input Fields component for text entry

While many times we just wish to display non-interactive text messages to the user, there are times (such as name entry for high scores) where we wish that the user was able to enter text or numbers into our game. Unity provides the **Input Field** UI component for this purpose. In this recipe, we'll create a simple text input UI by making use of the default Button image and text GameObjects, and we'll add a script to respond to each new value of the input field.

> You can, of course, create a working text input quicker than this recipe's method by choosing menu: **Create | UI | Input Field**, which creates a GameObject containing an Input Field component, child text, and placeholder GameObjects, as shown in the following screenshot. However, by following the steps in this recipe, you'll learn the interrelationships between the different interface elements, because you'll be creating these connections manually from the deconstructed parts of the UI Button GameObject.

Name: Enter name...

How to do it...

To create a promoted text input box to the user with faint placeholder text, follow these steps:

1. Create a new Unity 2D project.

2. In the **Inspector** view, change the background of the **Main Camera** to solid white.

3. Add a **UI Button** to the scene. Delete the **Button (Script)** component of the **Button** GameObject (since it won't be a button, it will be an interactive text input by the time we are finished with it!).

4. Rename the **Text** child GameObject of the **Button** component to **Text-placeholder**. Uncheck the **Rich Text** option, change the text to **Enter name...**, change the **Alignment** in **Left** and **Top**, and in the **Rect Transform**, set **Left** to 4 and **Top** to 7.

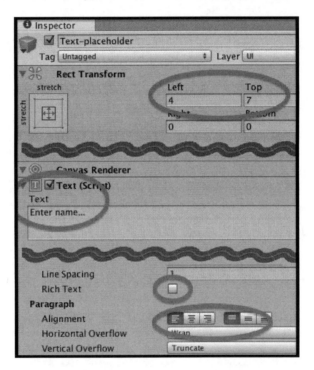

5. Duplicate **Text-placeholder by** naming the copy **Text-prompt**. Change the **Text** of this GameObject to **Name:**, and set its **Left** position to -50.

6. Duplicate **Text-placeholder** again, naming this new copy **Text-input**. Delete all of the content of the **Text** property of this new GameObject.

7. Select **Text-placeholder** in the **Hierarchy,** and we will now make the placeholder text mostly transparent. Set the **A** (alpha) **Color** value of the **Text (Script)** component of this GameObject to a value that is about a quarter of its maximum value (e.g. 64).

8. Select **Text-input** in the **Hierarchy,** and add an **Input Field** component by choosing menu: **Add Component | UI | Input Field**.

9. Drag the **Text-input** GameObject into the **Text Component** property of **Input Field**, and drag the **Text-placeholder** GameObject into the **Placeholder** property.

10. Save and run your scene. You now have a working text input UI for your user. When there is no text content, the faint placeholder text will be displayed. As soon as any characters have been typed, the placeholder will be hidden and the characters typed will appear in black text. Then, if all the characters are deleted, the placeholder will appear again.

How it works...

The core of interactive text input in Unity is the responsibility of the **Input Field** component. This needs a reference to a UI **Text** GameObject. To make it easier to see where the text can be typed, we have made use of the default rounded rectangle image that Unity provides when a **Button** GameObject is created. **Buttons** have both an **Image** component and a **Text** child GameObject. So, two items that we need can be acquired very easily by creating a new **Button,** and simply by removing the **Button (Script)** component.

There are usually three **Text** GameObjects involved with the user text input: the static prompt text (in our recipe, for example, the **Name:** text); then the faint placeholder text, reminding users where and what they should type; and finally the text object (with the font and color settings and so on) that is actually displayed to the user, showing the characters as they type.

At runtime, a **Text-Input Input Caret** GameObject is created—displaying the blinking vertical line to inform the user where their next letter will be typed. Note that the **Content Type** of the **Input Field (Script)**, in the **Inspector**, can be set to several specific types of text input, including e-mail addresses, integer or decimal numbers only, or the password text (where an asterisk is displayed for each entered character).

There's more...

There are some details that you don't want to miss.

Executing a C# method to respond each time the user changes the input text content

Having interactive text on the screen isn't of much use unless we can retrieve the text entered to use in our game logic, and we may need to know each time the user changes the text content and act accordingly.

To add code and events to respond each time the text content has been changed by the user, do the following:

1. Add an instance of the C# script class called `DisplayChangedTextContent` to the **Text-input** GameObject:

```csharp
using UnityEngine;
using System.Collections;
using UnityEngine.UI;

public class DisplayChangedTextContent : MonoBehaviour {
  private InputField inputField;

  void Start(){
    inputField = GetComponent<InputField>();
  }

  public void PrintNewValue (){
    string msg = "new content = '" + inputField.text + "'";
    print (msg);
  }
}
```

2. Add an **End Edit (String)** event to the list of event handlers for the **Input Field (Script)** component. Click on the plus (**+**) button to add an event handler slot, and drag the **Text-input** GameObject into the **Object** slot.

3. From the **Function** drop-down menu, choose **DisplayChangedTextContent** and then choose the **PrintNewValue** method.

4. Save and run the scene. Each time the user types in new text and then presses *Tab* or *Enter*, the **End Edit** event will fire, and you'll see a new content text message printed in the **Console** window by our script, as shown in the following screenshot:

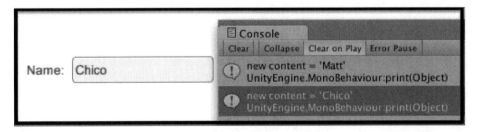

Toggles and radio buttons via Toggle Groups

Users make choices, and often, these choices are either to have one of two available options (for example, sound on or off), or sometimes to choose one of several possibilities (for example, difficulty level easy/medium/hard). Unity UI **Toggles** allows users to turn options on and off; and when combined with **Toggle Groups**, they restrict choices to one of the group of items. In this recipe, we'll first explore the basic **Toggle**, and a script to respond to a change in values. Then in the *There's More* section, we'll extend the example to illustrate **Toggle Groups**, and styling these with round images to make them look more like traditional radio buttons.

The following screenshot shows how the button's status changes are logged in the **Console** panel when the scene is running:

Getting ready

For this recipe, we have prepared the images that you'll need in a folder named UI Demo Textures in the 1362_01_15 folder.

How to do it...

To display an on/off UI Toggle to the user, follow these steps:

1. Create a new Unity 2D project.

2. In the **Inspector** panel, change the **Background** color of the **Main Camera** to white.

3. Add **UI Toggle** to the scene.

4. Enter First Class as **Text** for the **Label** child GameObject of the **Toggle** GameObject.

5. Add an instance of the C# script class called ToggleChangeManager to the **Toggle** GameObject:

```
using UnityEngine;
using System.Collections;
using UnityEngine.UI;
```

```
public class ToggleChangeManager : MonoBehaviour {
  private Toggle toggle;

  void Start () {
    toggle = GetComponent<Toggle>();
  }

  public void PrintNewToggleValue(){
    bool status = toggle.isOn;
    print ("toggle status = " + status);
  }
}
```

6. With the **Toggle** GameObject selected, add an **On Value Changed** event to the list of event handlers for the **Toggle (Script)** component, click on the plus (+) button to add an event handler slot, and drag **Toggle** into the **Object** slot.

7. From the **Function** drop-down menu, choose **ToggleChangeManager** and then choose the **PrintNewToggleValue** method.

8. Save and run the scene. Each time you check or uncheck the **Toggle** GameObject, the **On Value Changed** event will fire, and you'll see a new text message printed into the Console window by our script, stating the new Boolean true/false value of the **Toggle**.

How it works...

When you create a Unity UI **Toggle** GameObject, it comes with several child GameObjects automatically—**Background**, **Checkmark**, and the text **Label**. Unless we need to style the look of a **Toggle** in a special way, all that is needed is simply to edit the text **Label** so that the user knows what option or feature that this **Toggle** is going to turn on/off.

The C# scripted class called ToggleChangeManager's method called Start() gets a reference to the **Toggle** component in the GameObject, where the script instance is located. When the game is running, each time the user clicks on the **Toggle** to change its value, an **On Value Changed** event is fired. We then register the PrintNewToggleValue() method, which is supposed to be executed when such an event occurs. This method retrieves, and then prints out to the **Console** panel the new Boolean true/false value of the **Toggle**.

There's more...

There are some details that you don't want to miss.

Adding more Toggles and a Toggle Group to implement mutually-exclusive radio buttons

The Unity UI **Toggles** are also the base components, if we wish to implement a group of mutually-exclusive options in the style of radio buttons. To create such a group of related choices, do the following:

1. Import the `UI Demo Textures` folder into the project.

2. Remove the C# script class `ToggleChangeManager` component from the **Toggle** GameObject.

3. Rename the **Toggle** GameObject as **Toggle-easy**.

4. Change the **Label** text to **Easy**, and tag this GameObject with a new tag called **Easy**.

5. Select the **Background** child GameObject of **Toggle-easy**, and in the **Image (Script)** component, drag the `UIToggleBG` image into the **Source Image** property.

6. Ensure that the **Is On** property of the **Toggle (Script)** component is checked, and then select the **Checkmark** child GameObject of **Toggle-easy**. In the **Image (Script)** component, drag the `UIToggleButton` image into the **Source Image** property.

> Of the three choices (easy, medium, and hard) that we'll offer to the user, we'll set the easy option to be the one that is supposed to be initially selected. Therefore, we need its **Is On** property to be checked, which will lead to its 'checkmark' image being displayed.
>
> To make these **Toggles** look more like radio buttons, the background of each is set to the circle image of `UIToggleBG`, and the checkmark (which displays the **Toggles** that are on) is filled with the circle image called `UIToggleButton`.

7. Duplicate the **Toggle-easy** GameObject, naming the copy **Toggle-medium**. Set its **Rect Transform** property **Pos Y** to `-25` (so, this copy is positioned below the easy option), and uncheck the **Is On** property of the **Toggle (Script)** component. Tag this copy with a new tag called **Medium**.

8. Duplicate the **Toggle-medium** GameObject, naming the copy **Toggle-hard**. Set its **Rect Transform** property **Pos Y** to `-50` (so this copy is positioned below the medium option). Tag this copy with a new tag called **Hard**.

9. Add an instance of the C# script class called `RadioButtonManager` to the **Canvas** GameObject:

```
using UnityEngine;
using System.Collections;
using UnityEngine.UI;

public class RadioButtonManager : MonoBehaviour {
  private string currentDifficulty = "Easy";
```

```
public void PrintNewGroupValue(Toggle sender){
  // only take notice from Toggle just swtiched to On
  if(sender.isOn){
    currentDifficulty = sender.tag;
    print ("option changed to = " + currentDifficulty);
  }
 }
}
```

10. With the **Toggle-easy** GameObject selected, add an **On Value Changed** event to the list of event handlers for the **Toggle (Script)** component. Click on the plus (**+**) button to add an event handler slot, and drag the **Canvas** GameObject into the Object slot.

11. From the **Function** drop-down menu, choose **RadioButtonManager**, and then choose the **PrintNewGroupValue** method. In the **Toggle** parameter slot, which is initially None (Toggle), drag the **Toggle-easy** GameObject.

12. Do the same for the **Toggle-medium** and **Toggle-hard** GameObjects—so each **Toggle** object calls the PrintNewGroupValue(...) method of a C# scripted component called RadioButtonManager in the **Canvas** GameObject, passing itself as a parameter.

13. Save and run the scene. Each time you check one of the three radio buttons, the **On Value Changed** event will fire, and you'll see a new text message printed into the **Console** window by our script, stating the tag of whichever **Toggle** (radio button) was just set to true (**Is On**).

14. The following screenshot shows how the value corresponding to the selected radio button is logged to the **Console** panel when the scene is running:

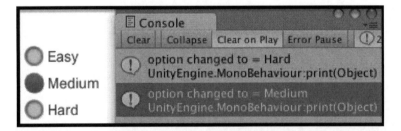

Conclusion

In this chapter, we have introduced recipes demonstrating a range of Unity 5 UI components, and illustrated how the same components can be used in different ways (such as an interactive slider being used to display the status of a countdown timer). One set of UI components in many games are those that communicate to the user what they are carrying (or yet to pick up). We have dedicated another chapter in this book to inventories in *Chapter 2, Inventory GUIs*, which provides many inventory recipes and additional UI controls, such as adding interactive scroll bars.

Here are some suggestions for further reading, tutorials, and resources to help you continue your learning of UI development in Unity:

- Learn more about the Unity UI on manual pages at `http://docs.unity3d.com/Manual/UISystem.html`.

- Work through the Unity UI tutorial videos at `https://unity3d.com/learn/tutorials/topics/user-interface-ui`.

- Ray Wenderlich's great tutorial on Unity UI development at `http://www.raywenderlich.com/78675/unity-new-gui-part-1`.

- Unity's documentation pages about designing UI for multiple resolutions: `http://docs.unity3d.com/Manual/HOWTO-UIMultiResolution.html`.

Games need fonts in a style to match the gameplay and theme. Here are some of the sources of free personal/commercial fonts suitable for many games:

- All the fonts at FontSquirrel are 100% free for commercial use. They are available at `http://www.fontsquirrel.com/`.

- See each font for individual license at the DaFont website. Many people ask for a donation if these are used for commercial purposes. For more information, check out `http://www.dafont.com/xolonium.font`.

- See each font for individual licenses available on the Naldz Graphics blog at `http://naldzgraphics.net/textures/`.

- 1001 Free Fonts (for personal use) are available at `http://www.1001freefonts.com/index.php`.

2
Inventory GUIs

In this chapter, we will cover the following topics:

- ▶ Creating a simple 2D mini-game – SpaceGirl
- ▶ Displaying single object pickups with carrying and not-carrying text
- ▶ Displaying single object pickups with carrying and not-carrying icons
- ▶ Displaying multiple pickups of the same object with text totals
- ▶ Displaying multiple pickups of the same object with multiple status icons
- ▶ Revealing icons for multiple object pickups by changing the size of a tiled image
- ▶ Displaying multiple pickups of different objects as a list of text via a dynamic List<> of PickUp objects
- ▶ Displaying multiple pickups of different objects as text totals via a dynamic Dictionary<> of PickUp objects and "enum" pickup types
- ▶ Generalizing multiple icon displays using UI Grid Layout Groups (with scrollbars!)

Introduction

Many games involve the player collecting items or choosing from a selection of items. Examples could be collecting keys to open doors, collecting ammo for weapons, choosing from a collection of spells to cast, and so on.

The recipes in this chapter offer a range of solutions for displaying to the player whether they are carrying an item or not, if they are allowed more than one of an item, and how many they have.

The big picture

The two parts of software design for implementing inventories relate to, first, how we choose to represent the data about inventory items (that is, the data types and structures to store the data) and, secondly, how we choose to display information about inventory items to the player (the UI: User Interface).

Also, whilst not strictly inventory items, player properties such as lives left, health, or time remaining can also be designed around the same concepts that we present in this chapter.

We need to first think about the nature of different inventory items for any particular game:

- Single items:
    - Example(s): the only key for a level, our suit of magic armor
    - Data type: bool (true/false)
    - UI: nothing (if not carried) or text/image to show being carried
        - Or perhaps text saying "no key"/"key", or two images, one showing an empty key outline and the second showing a full color key
        - If we wish to highlight to the player that there is an option to be carrying this item

- Continuous item:
    - Example(s): time left, health, shield strength
    - Data type: float (for example, 0.00–1.00) or integer scale (for example, 0% .. 100%)
    - UI: text number or image progress bar/pie chart

- Two or more of same item
    - Example(s): lives left, or number of arrows or bullets left
    - Data type: int (whole numbers)
    - UI: text count or images

- Collection of related items
    - Example(s): keys of different colors to open correspondingly colored doors, potions of different strength with different titles
    - Data structure: a struct or class for the general item type (for example, class Key (color/cost/doorOpenTagString), stored as an array or List<>
    - UI: text list or list/grid arrangement of icons

- ▸ Collection of different items
  - ❑ Example(s): keys, potions, weapons, tools—all in the same inventory system
  - ❑ Data structure: List<> or Dictionary<> or array of objects, which can be instances of different class for each item type

Each of the above representations and UI display methods are illustrated by the recipes in this chapter.

Creating a simple 2D mini-game – SpaceGirl

This recipe presents the steps to create the 2DSpaceGirl mini-game, on which all the recipes of this chapter are based.

Getting ready

For this recipe, we have prepared the images you need in a folder named Sprites in the 1362_02_01 folder. We have also provided the completed game as a Unity package in this folder named Simple2DGame_SpaceGirl.

How to do it...

To create the simple 2D mini-game *Space Girl* follow these steps:

1. Create a new, empty 2D project.
2. Import supplied folder Sprites into your project.

3. Convert each sprite image to be of type **Sprite (2D and UI)**. To do this, select the sprite in the **Project** panel, then, in the **Inspector**, change choose **Sprite (2D and UI)** from the drop-down menu **Texture Type**, and click on the **Apply** button, as shown in the following screenshot:

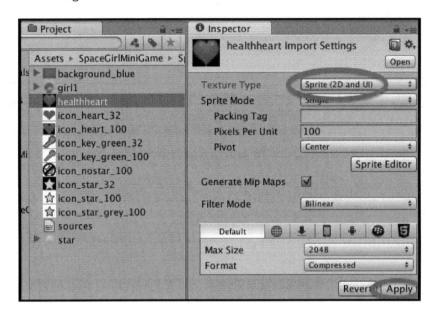

4. Set the Unity Player screen size to 800 x 600: choose the **Edit | Project Settings | Player** menu, then for option **Resolution and Presentation** uncheck Default is Full Screen, and set the width to 800 and height to 600, as shown in the following screenshot:

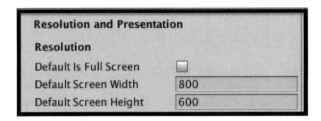

5. Select the **Game** panel; if not already chosen, then choose **Standalone (800 x 600)** from the drop-down menu, as shown in the following screenshot:

6. Display the **Tags & Layers** properties for the current Unity project. Choose menu **Edit | Project Settings | Tags and Layers**. Alternatively, if you are already editing a GameObject, then you can select the **Add Layer...** menu from the **Layer** drop-down menu at the top of the **Inspector** panel, as shown in the following screenshot:

7. The **Inspector** should now being displaying the **Tags & Layers** properties for the current Unity project. Use the expand/contract triangle tools to contract **Tags** and **Layers**, and to expand **Sorting Layers**.

8. Use the plus sign **+** button to add two new sorting layers, as shown in the following screenshot: first, add one named **Background**, and next, add one named **Foreground**. The sequence is important, since Unity will draw items in layers further down this list on top of items earlier in the list.

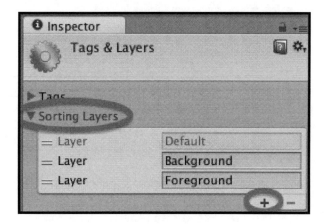

9. Drag the sprite background-blue from the **Project** panel (folder Sprites) into either the **Game** or **Hierarchy** panel to create a GameObject for the current scene.

10. Set the **Sorting Layer** of GameObject background-blue to **Background** (in the **Sprite Renderer** component).

11. Drag sprite star from the **Project** panel (folder Sprites) into either the **Game** or **Hierarchy** panel to create a GameObject for the current scene.

12. In the **Inspector** panel, add a new tag **Star** by selecting the **Add Tag...** option from the **Tag** drop-down menu at the top of the **Inspector** panel, as shown in the following screenshot:

13. Apply the **Star** tag to GameObject star in the **Hierarchy** scene.

14. Set the **Sorting Layer** of GameObject star to **Foreground** (in the **Sprite Renderer** component).

15. Add to GameObject star a Box Collider 2D (**Add Component | Physics 2D | Box Collider 2D**) and check its Is Trigger, as shown in the following screenshot:

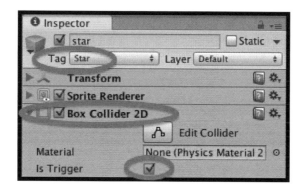

16. Drag sprite `girl1` from the **Project** panel (folder `Sprites`) into either the **Game** or **Hierarchy** panel to create a GameObject for the player's character in the current scene. Rename this GameObject `player-SpaceGirl`.

17. Set the **Sorting Layer** of GameObject `player-SpaceGirl` to **Foreground** (in the **Sprite Renderer** component).

18. Add to GameObject `player-SpaceGirl` a Box Collider 2D (**Add Component | Physics 2D | Box Collider 2D**).

19. Add to GameObject `player-SpaceGirl` a RigidBody 2D (**Add Component | Physics 2D | Rigid Body 2D**). Set its **Gravity Scale** to zero (so it isn't falling down the screen due to simulated gravity), as shown in the following screenshot:

20. Create a new folder for your scripts named `Scripts`.

21. Create the following C# Script `PlayerMove` (in folder `Scripts`) and add an instance as a component to GameObject `player-SpaceGirl` in the **Hierarchy**:

```
using UnityEngine;
using System.Collections;

public class PlayerMove : MonoBehaviour {
  public float speed = 10;
  private Rigidbody2D rigidBody2D;

  void Awake(){
    rigidBody2D = GetComponent<Rigidbody2D>();
  }

  void FixedUpdate(){
    float xMove = Input.GetAxis("Horizontal");
    float yMove = Input.GetAxis("Vertical");

    float xSpeed = xMove * speed;
    float ySpeed = yMove * speed;

    Vector2 newVelocity = new Vector2(xSpeed, ySpeed);

    rigidBody2D.velocity = newVelocity;
  }
}
```

22. Save the scene (name it **Main Scene** and save it into a new folder named `Scenes`).

How it works...

You have created a player character in the scene, with its movement scripted component `PlayerMove`. You have also created a star GameObject (a pickup), tagged `Star` and with a 2D box collider that will trigger a collision when the player's character hits it. When you run the game, the `player-SpaceGirl` character should move around using the *W A S D*, arrow keys, or joystick. Currently, nothing will happen if the `player-SpaceGirl` character hits a star since that has yet to be scripted.

You have added a background (GameObject `background-blue`) to the scene, which will be behind everything since it is in the rearmost sorting layer **Background**. Items you want to appear in front of this background (the player's character and the star so far) are placed on sorting layer **Foreground**. Learn more about Unity tags and layers at `http://docs. unity3d.com/Manual/class-TagManager.html`.

Displaying single object pickups with carrying and not-carrying text

Often the simplest inventory situation is to display text to tell players if they are carrying a single item (or not).

Getting ready

This recipe assumes that you are starting with the project `Simple2Dgame_SpaceGirl` setup from the first recipe in this chapter. So, either make a copy of that project or do the following:

1. Create a new, empty 2D project.

2. Import the `Simple2Dgame_SpaceGirl` package.

3. Open scene **Scene1** (in the `Scenes` folder).

4. Set the Unity Player screen size to 800 x 600 (see the previous recipe for how to do this) and select this resolution in the **Game** panel the drop-down menu.

5. Convert each sprite image to be of type **Sprite (2D and UI)**. In the **Inspector,** choose **Sprite (2D and UI)** from drop-down menu **Texture Type**, and click on the **Apply** button.

For this recipe, we have prepared the font you need in a folder named `Fonts` in the `1362_02_02` folder.

How to do it...

To display text to inform the user about the status of carrying a single object pickup, follow these steps:

1. Start with a new copy of mini-game `Simple2Dgame_SpaceGirl`.

2. Add a UI **Text** object (**Create | UI | Text**). Rename it `Text-carrying-star`. Change its text to `Carrying star: false`.

3. Import the provided `Fonts` folder into your project.

4. In the **Inspector** panel, set the font of `Text-carrying-star` to **Xolonium-Bold** (folder `Fonts`), and set its color to yellow. Center the text horizontally and vertically, and set its **Height** to 50, and set the **Font Size** to 32, as shown in the following screenshot:

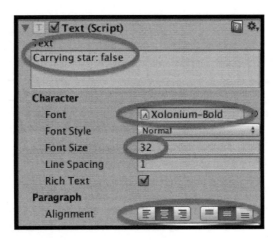

5. In its **Rect Transform** component, set its **Height** to 50, as shown in the next screenshot:

6. Edit its **Rect Transform**, and while holding down *SHIFT* and *ALT* (to set pivot and position), choose the top-stretch box, as shown in the following screenshot:

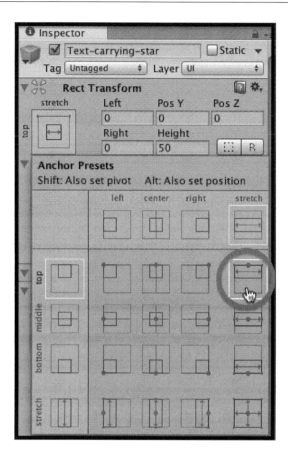

7. Your text should now be positioned at the middle top of the **Game** panel, and its width should stretch to match that of the whole panel, as shown in the next screenshot:

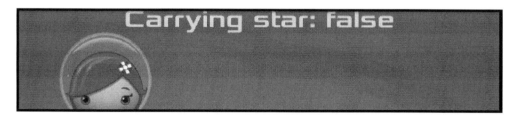

8. Add the following C# Script `Player` to GameObject `player-SpaceGirl` in the **Hierarchy**:

```
using UnityEngine;
using System.Collections;
using UnityEngine.UI;

public class Player : MonoBehaviour {
  public Text starText;
  private bool carryingStar = false;

  void Start(){
    UpdateStarText();
  }

  void OnTriggerEnter2D(Collider2D hit){
    if(hit.CompareTag("Star")){
      carryingStar = true;
      UpdateStarText();
      Destroy(hit.gameObject);
    }
  }

  private void UpdateStarText(){
    string starMessage = "no star :-(";
    if(carryingStar) starMessage = "Carrying star :-)";
    starText.text = starMessage;
  }
}
```

9. From the **Hierarchy** view, select the GameObject `player-SpaceGirl`. Then, from the **Inspector**, access the **Player (Script)** component and populate the **Star Text** public field with UI **Text** object `Text-carrying-star`, as shown in the following screenshot:

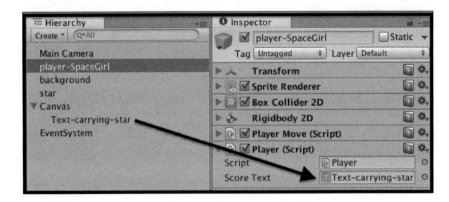

10. When you play the scene, after moving the character into the star, the star should disappear, and the onscreen UI **Text** message should change to **Carrying star :-)** , as shown in the following screenshot:

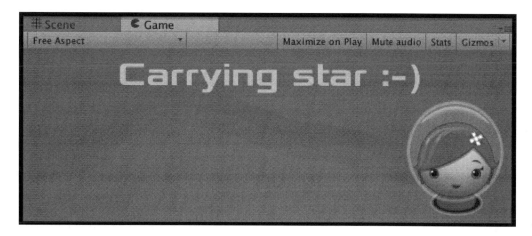

How it works...

The Text variable starText is a reference to the UI **Text** object Text-carrying-star. The bool variable carryingStar represents whether or not the player is carrying the star at any point in time; it is initialized to false.

The UpdateStarText() method copies the contents of the starMessage string to the text property of starText. The default value of this string tells the user that the player is not carrying the star, but an if statement tests the value of carryingKey, and, if that is true, then the message is changed to inform the player that they are carrying the star.

Each time the player's character collides with any object that has its **Is Trigger** set to true, an OnTriggerEnter2D() event message is sent to both objects involved in the collision. The OnTriggerEnter2D() message is passed a parameter that is the Collider2D component inside the object just collided with.

Our player's OnTriggerEnter2D() method tests the tag string of the object collided with to see if it has the value **Star**. Since the GameObject **star** we created has its trigger set, and has the tag **Star**, the if statement inside this method will detect a collision with **star** and complete three actions: it sets the Boolean variable carryingStar to true, it calls the method UpdateStarText(), and it destroys the GameObject it has just collided with (in this case, **star**).

NOTE: Boolean variables are often referred to as **flags.**

The use of a bool (true/false) variable to represent whether some feature of the game state is true or false is very common. Programmers often refer to these variables as flags. So, programmers might refer to the `carryingStar` variable as the star-carrying flag.

When the scene begins, via the `Start()` method, we call the `UpdateStarText()` method; this ensures that we are not relying on text typed into the UI **Text** object `Text-carrying-star` at design time, but that the UI seen by the user is always set by our run-time methods. This avoids problems where the words to be displayed to the user are changed in code and not in the **Inspector** panel—which leads to a mismatch between the onscreen text when the scene first runs and after it has been updated from a script.

A golden rule in Unity game design is to **avoid duplicating content in more than one place**, and, therefore, we avoid having to maintain two or more copies of the same content. Each duplicate is an opportunity for maintenance issues when some, but not all, copies of a value are changed.

Maximizing use of prefabs is another example of this principle in action. This is also know as the DRY principal - Do Not Repeat Yourself.

There's more...

Some details you don't want to miss:

The separation of view logic

A game design pattern (best practice approach) called the **Model-View-Controller** pattern (**MVC**) is to separate the code that updates the UI from the code that changes player and game variables such as score and inventory item lists. Although this recipe has only one variable and one method to update the UI, well structured game architectures scale up to cope with more complex games, so it is often worth the effort of a little more code and an extra script class, even at this game-beginning stage, if we want our final game architecture to be well structured and maintainable.

To implement the separation of view pattern for this recipe, we need to do the following:

1. Add the following C# Script `PlayerInventoryDisplay` to GameObject `player-SpaceGirl` in the **Hierarchy**:

```
using UnityEngine;
using System.Collections;
using UnityEngine.UI;
```

```
public class PlayerInventoryDisplay : MonoBehaviour
{
  public Text starText;

  public void OnChangeCarryingStar(bool carryingStar){
    string starMessage = "no star :-(";
    if(carryingStar) starMessage = "Carrying star :-)";
    starText.text = starMessage;
  }
}
```

2. From the **Hierarchy** view, select the GameObject `player-SpaceGirl`. Then, from the **Inspector**, access the `PlayerInventoryDisplay` **(Script)** component and populate the **Score Text** public field with the UI **Text** object `Text-carrying-star`.

3. Remove the existing C# Script component `Player` and replace it with this C# Script `PlayerInventory` containing the following (simplified) code:

```
using UnityEngine;
using System.Collections;

public class PlayerInventory : MonoBehaviour {
  private PlayerInventoryDisplay playerInventoryDisplay;
  private bool carryingStar = false;

  void Start(){
     playerInventoryDisplay = GetComponent<PlayerInventoryDispl
ay>();
    playerInventoryDisplay.OnChangeCarryingStar(carryingStar);
  }

  void OnTriggerEnter2D(Collider2D hit){
    if(hit.CompareTag("Star")){
      carryingStar = true;
    playerInventoryDisplay.OnChangeCarryingStar(carryingStar);
      Destroy(hit.gameObject);
    }
  }
}
```

As can be seen, the `PlayerInventory` script class no longer has to maintain a link to the UI **Text** or worry about changing the text property of that UI component—all that work is now the responsibility of the `PlayerInventoryDisplay` script. When the Player instance component detects a collision with the star, after changing the `carryingStar` bool flag's value to `true`, it just calls the `OnChangeCarryingStar()` method of the `PlayerInventoryDisplay` component.

The result is that the code for the script class `PlayerInventory` concentrates on the player collision and status variables, while the code for the script class `PlayerInventoryDisplay` handles the communication to the user. Another advantage of this design pattern is that the method in which the information is communicated to the user via the UI can be changed (for example, from text to an icon), without any change to the code in script class `Player`.

> Note: There is no difference in the experience of the player, and all the changes are to improve the architectural structure of our game code.

Displaying single object pickups with carrying and not-carrying icons

Graphic icons are an effective way to inform the player that they are carrying an item. In this recipe, if no star is being carried, a grey-filled icon in a blocked-off circle is displayed; then, after the star has been picked up, a yellow-filled icon is displayed, as shown in the following screenshot.

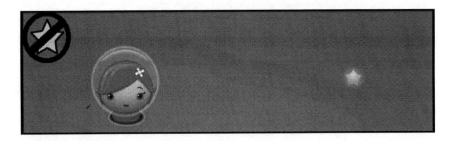

In many cases, icons are clearer (they don't require reading and thinking about) and can also be smaller onscreen than text messages for indicating player status and inventory items.

Getting ready

This recipe assumes that you are starting with the project `Simple2Dgame_SpaceGirl` setup from the first recipe in this chapter.

How to do it...

To toggle carrying and not-carrying icons for a single object pickup, follow these steps:

1. Start with a new copy of the mini-game `Simple2Dgame_SpaceGirl`.

2. In the **Hierarchy** panel, add a new UI **Image** object (**Create | UI | Image**). Rename it `Image-star-icon`.

3. Select `Image-star-icon` in the **Hierarchy** panel.

4. From the **Project** panel, drag the sprite **icon_nostar_100** (folder `Sprites`) into the **Source Image** field in the **Inspector** (in the **Image (Script)** component).

5. Click on the **Set Native Size** button for the **Image** component. This will resize the UI **Image** to fit the physical pixel width and height of sprite file **icon_nostar_100**, as shown in the following screenshot:

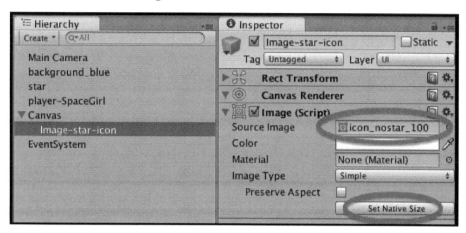

6. Now, we will position our icon at the **top** and **left** of the **Game** panel. Edit the UI **Image's Rect Transform** component, and while holding down *SHIFT* and *ALT* (to set pivot and position), choose the top-left box. The UI **Image** should now be positioned at the top left of the **Game** panel, as shown in the following screenshot:

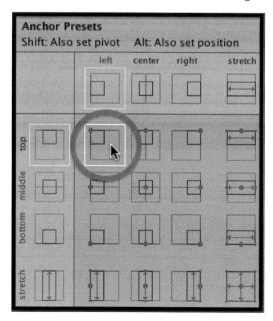

7. Add the following C# Script `Player` to GameObject `player-SpaceGirl` in the **Hierarchy**:

```
using UnityEngine;
using System.Collections;
using UnityEngine.UI;

public class Player : MonoBehaviour {
  public Image starImage;
  public Sprite iconStar;
  public Sprite iconNoStar;
  private bool carryingStar = false;

  void OnTriggerEnter2D(Collider2D hit){
    if(hit.CompareTag("Star")){
      carryingStar = true;
      UpdateStarImage();
      Destroy(hit.gameObject);
    }
  }

  private void UpdateStarImage(){
    if(carryingStar)
      starImage.sprite = iconStar;
    else
      starImage.sprite = iconNoStar;
  }
}
```

8. From the **Hierarchy** view, select the GameObject `player-SpaceGirl`. Then, from the **Inspector**, access the **Player (Script)** component and populate the **Star Image** public field with UI **Image** object `Image-star-icon`.

9. Now, populate the **Icon Star** public field from the **Project** panel with sprite `icon_star_100` and populate the **Icon No Star** public field from the **Project** panel with sprite `icon_nostar_100`, as shown in the following screenshot:

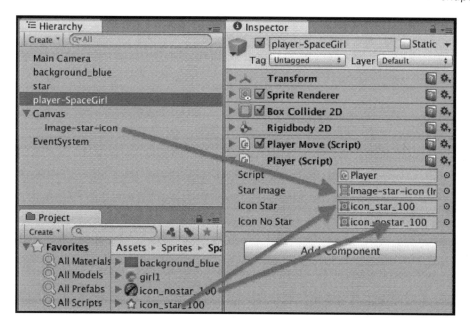

10. Now when you play the scene, you should see the no star icon (a grey-filled icon in a blocked-off circle) at the top left until you pick up the star, at which point it will change to show the carrying star icon (yellow-filled star).

How it works...

The Image variable starImage is a reference to the UI **Image** object Image-star-icon. Sprite variables iconStar and iconNoStar are references to the Sprite files in the **Project** panel—the sprites to tell the player whether or not a star is being carried. The bool variable carryingStar represents internally as program data whether or not the player is carrying the star at any point in time; it is initialized to false.

Much of the logic for this recipe is the same as the previous one. Each time the UpdateStarImage() method is called, it sets the UI **Image** to the sprite that corresponds to the value of bool variable carryingsStar.

Displaying multiple pickups of the same object with text totals

When several items of the same type have been picked up, often the simplest way to convey what is being carried to the user is to display a text message showing the numeric total of each item type being carried, as shown in the following screenshot. In this recipe, the total number of stars collected is displayed using a UI **Text** object.

Getting ready

This recipe assumes you are starting with project `Simple2Dgame_SpaceGirl` setup from the first recipe in this chapter. The font you need can be found in folder `1362_02_02`.

How to do it...

To display inventory total text for multiple pickups of same type of object, follow these steps:

1. Start with a new copy of the mini-game `Simple2Dgame_SpaceGirl`.

2. Add a UI **Text** object (**Create | UI | Text**). Rename it `Text-carrying-star`. Change its text to **stars = 0**.

3. Import the provided `Fonts` folder into your project.

4. In the **Inspector** panel, set the font of `Text-carrying-star` to **Xolonium-Bold** (folder `Fonts`) and set its color to yellow. Center the text horizontally and vertically, and set its **Font Size** to `32`.

5. In its **Rect Transform** component, set its **Height** to `50`. Edit its **Rect Transform**, and while holding down *SHIFT* and *ALT* (to set pivot and position), choose the top-stretch box. Your text should now be positioned at the middle top of the **Game** panel, and its width should stretch to match that of the whole panel.

6. Add the following C# Script `Player` to GameObject `player-SpaceGirl` in the **Hierarchy**:

```csharp
using UnityEngine;
using System.Collections;
using UnityEngine.UI;

public class Player : MonoBehaviour {
  public Text starText;
  private int totalStars = 0;

  void Start(){
    UpdateStarText();
  }

  void OnTriggerEnter2D(Collider2D hit){
    if(hit.CompareTag("Star")){
      totalStars++;
      UpdateStarText();
      Destroy(hit.gameObject);
    }
  }

  private void UpdateStarText(){
    string starMessage = "stars = " + totalStars;
    starText.text = starMessage;
  }
}
```

7. From the **Hierarchy** view, select the GameObject `player-SpaceGirl`. Then, from the **Inspector**, access the **Player (Script)** component and populate the **Star Text** public field with UI **Text** object `Text-carrying-star`.

8. Select the GameObject `star` in the **Hierarchy** panel and make three more copies of this GameObject.

 Note: Use keyboard shortcut *CTRL + D* (Windows) or *CMD + D* (Mac) to quickly duplicate GameObjects.

9. Move these new GameObject to different parts of the screen.

10. Play the game—each time you pick up a star, the total should be displayed in the form **stars = 2**.

How it works...

The Text variable starText is a reference to the UI **Text** object Text-carrying-star. The int variable totalStars represents how many stars have been collected so far; it is initialized to zero.

In the OnTriggerEnter2D() method, the totalStars counter is incremented by 1 each time the player's character hits an object tagged **Star**. The collided star GameObject is destroyed and a call is made to the UpdateStarText() method.

The UpdateStarText() method updates the text content of UI **Text** object Text-carrying-star with text string stars = concatenated with the integer value inside variable totalStars to display the updated total number of stars to the user.

Displaying multiple pickups of the same object with multiple status icons

If there is a small, fixed total number of an item to be collected rather than text totals, an alternative effective UI approach is to display placeholder icons (empty or greyed out pictures) to show the user how many of the item remain to be collected, and each time an item is picked up, a placeholder icon is replaced by a full color collected icon.

In this recipe, we use grey-filled star icons as the placeholders and yellow-filled star icons to indicate each collected star, as shown in the following screenshot.

Since our UI code is getting a little more complicated, this recipe will implement the MVC design pattern to separate the view code from the core player logic (as introduced at the end of recipe *Displaying single object pickups with carrying and not-carrying text*).

Getting ready

This recipe assumes that you are starting with the project Simple2Dgame_SpaceGirl setup from the first recipe in this chapter.

How to do it...

To display multiple inventory icons for multiple pickups of same type of object, follow these steps:

1. Start with a new copy of the mini-game `Simple2Dgame_SpaceGirl`.

2. Add the following C# Script `Player` to GameObject `player-SpaceGirl` in the **Hierarchy**:

```
using UnityEngine;
using System.Collections;
using UnityEngine.UI;

public class Player : MonoBehaviour {
  private PlayerInventoryDisplay playerInventoryDisplay;
  private int totalStars = 0;

  void Start(){
    playerInventoryDisplay = GetComponent<PlayerInventoryDispl
ay>();
  }

  void OnTriggerEnter2D(Collider2D hit){
    if(hit.CompareTag("Star")){
      totalStars++;
    playerInventoryDisplay.OnChangeStarTotal(totalStars);
      Destroy(hit.gameObject);
    }
  }
}
```

3. Select GameObject `star` in the **Hierarchy** panel and make three more copies of this GameObject (Windows *CTRL + D* / Mac *CMD + D*).

4. Move these new GameObject to different parts of the screen.

5. Add the following C# Script `PlayerInventoryDisplay` to the GameObject `player-SpaceGirl` in the **Hierarchy:**

```
using UnityEngine;
using System.Collections;
using UnityEngine.UI;

public class PlayerInventoryDisplay : MonoBehaviour
{
  public Image[] starPlaceholders;
```

```
public Sprite iconStarYellow;
public Sprite iconStarGrey;

public void OnChangeStarTotal(int starTotal){
    for (int i = 0;i < starPlaceholders.Length; ++i){
    if (i < starTotal)
        starPlaceholders[i].sprite = iconStarYellow;
      else
        starPlaceholders[i].sprite = iconStarGrey;
    }
  }
}
```

6. Select the **Canvas** in the **Hierarchy** panel and add a new UI Image object (**Create | UI | Image**). Rename it Image-star0.

7. Select Image-star0 in the **Hierarchy** panel.

8. From the **Project** panel, drag the sprite icon_star_grey_100 (folder Sprites) into the **Source Image** field in the **Inspector** for the **Image** component.

9. Click on the **Set Native Size** button for this for the **Image** component. This will resize the UI **Image** to fit the physical pixel width and height of sprite file icon_star_grey_100.

10. Now we will position our icon at the **top** and **left** of the **Game** panel. Edit the UI **Image's Rect Transform** component, and while holding down *SHIFT* and *ALT* (to set pivot and position), choose the top-left box. The UI **Image** should now be positioned at the top left of the **Game** panel.

11. Make three more copies of Image-star0 in the **Hierarchy** panel, naming them Image-star1, Image-star2, and Image-star3.

12. In the **Inspector** panel, change the **Pos X** position (in the **Rect Transform** component) of Image-star1 to 100, of Image-star2 to 200, and of Image-star3 to 100, as shown in the following screenshot:

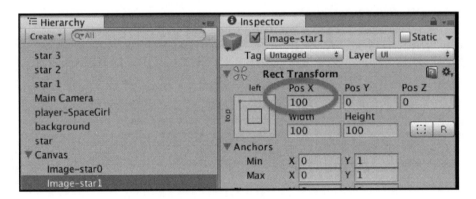

13. From the **Hierarchy** view, select the GameObject `player-SpaceGirl`. Then, from the **Inspector**, access the **Player Inventory Display (Script)** component and set the **Size** property of public field **Star Playholders** to 4.

14. Next, populate the **Element 0/1/2/3** array values of public field **Star Playholders** with UI **Image** objects `Image-star0/1/2/3`.

15. Now, populate the **Icon Star Yellow** and **Icon Star Grey** public fields from the **Project** panel with sprite `icon_star_100` and `icon_star_grey_100`, as shown in the following screenshot:

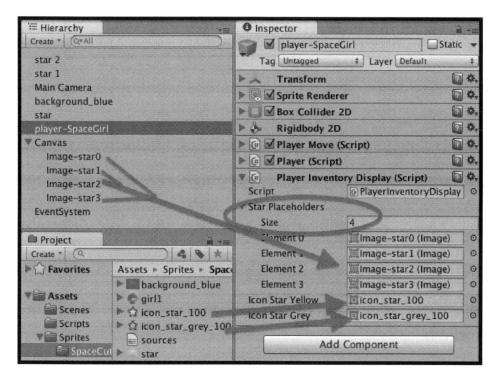

16. Now, when you play the scene, you should see the sequence of four grey placeholder star icons initially, and each time you collide with a star, the next icon at the top should turn yellow.

How it works...

Four UI **Image** objects `Image-star0/1/2/3` have been created at the top of the screen, initialized with the grey placeholder icon. The grey and yellow icon sprite files have been resized to be 100 x 100 pixels, making their arrangement horizontal positioning at design time easier, since their positions are (0,0), (100, 0), (200, 0), and (300,0). In a more complicated game screen, or one where real estate is precious, the actual size of the icons would probably be smaller and whatever the game graphic designer decides.

The int variable totalStars represents how many stars have been collected so far; it is initialized to zero. The PlayerInventoryDisplay variable playerInventory is a reference to the scripted component that manages our inventory display—this variable is set when the scene begins to run in the Start() method.

In the OnTriggerEnter2D() method, the totalStars counter is incremented by 1 each time the player's character hits an object tagged **Star**. As well as destroying the hit GameObject, the OnChangeStarTotal(...) method of the PlayerInventoryDisplay component is called, passing the new star total integer.

The OnChangeStarTotal(...) method of script class PlayerInventoryDisplay has references to the four UI **Images**, and loops through each item in the array of Image references, setting the given number of Images to yellow, and the remaining to grey. This method is public, allowing it to be called from an instance of script class Player.

As can be seen, the code in script class Player is still quite straightforward since we have moved all of the inventory UI logic to its own class, PlayerInventory.

Revealing icons for multiple object pickups by changing the size of a tiled image

Another approach that could be taken to show increasing numbers of images is to make use of tiled images. The same visual effect as in the previous recipe can also be achieved by making use of a tiled grey star image of width 400 (showing four copies of the grey star icon), behind a tiled yellow star image, whose width is 100 times the number of stars collected. We'll adapt the previous recipe to illustrate this technique.

Getting ready

This recipe follows on from the previous recipe in this chapter.

How to do it...

To display grey and yellow star icons for multiple object pickups using tiled images, follow these steps:

1. Make a copy of your work for the previous recipe.
2. In the **Hierarchy** panel, remove the four Image-star0/1/2/3 UI **Images** in the **Canvas**.
3. Select the **Canvas** in the **Hierarchy** panel and add a new UI **Image** object (**Create | UI | Image**). Rename it Image-stars-grey.
4. Select Image-stars-grey in the **Hierarchy** panel.

5. From the **Project** panel, drag sprite `icon_star_grey_100` (folder `Sprites`) into the **Source Image** field in the **Inspector** (in the **Image (Script)** component).

6. Click on the **Set Native Size** button for this for the **Image** component. This will resize the UI **Image** to fit the physical pixel width and height of sprite file **star_empty_icon.**

7. Now we will position our icon at the **top** and **left** of the **Game** panel. Edit the UI **Image's Rect Transform** component, and while holding down *SHIFT* and *ALT* (to set pivot and position), choose the top-left box. The UI **Image** should now be positioned at the top left of the **Game** panel.

8. In the **Inspector** panel, change the **Width** (in the **Rect Transform** component) of `Image-stars-grey` to 400. Also, set the **Image Type** (in the **Image (Script)** component) to **Tiled**, as shown in the following screenshot:

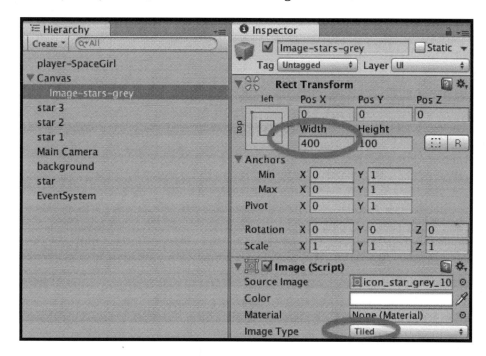

9. Make a copy of `Image-stars-grey` in the **Hierarchy** panel, naming the copy `Image-stars-yellow`.

10. With `Image-stars-yellow` selected in **Hierarchy** panel, from the **Project** panel, drag the sprite `icon_star_100` (folder `Sprites`) into the **Source Image** field in the **Inspector** (in the **Image (Script)** component).

11. Set the width of `Image-stars-yellow` to 0 (in the **Rect Transform** component). So, now we have the yellow stars tiled image above the grey tiled image, but since its width is zero, we don't see any of the yellow stars yet.

12. Replace the existing C# Script `PlayerInventoryDisplay` with the following code:

```
using UnityEngine;
using System.Collections;
using UnityEngine.UI;

public class PlayerInventoryDisplay : MonoBehaviour
{
   public Image iconStarsYellow;

   public void OnChangeStarTotal(int starTotal){
      float newWidth = 100 * starTotal;
      iconStarsYellow.rectTransform.SetSizeWithCurrentAnchors(RectTr
ansform.Axis.Horizontal, newWidth);
   }
}
```

13. From the **Hierarchy** view, select the GameObject `player-SpaceGirl`. Then, from the **Inspector**, access the **Player Inventory Display (Script)** component and populate the **Icons Stars Yellow** public field with UI **Image** object `Image-stars-yellow`.

How it works...

UI **Image** `Image-stars-grey` is a tiled image, wide enough (400px) for grey sprite **icon_star_grey_100** to be shown four times. UI **Image** `Image-stars-yellow` is a tiled image, above the grey one, initially with width set to zero, so no yellow stars can be seen.

Each time a star is picked up, a call is made to the `OnChangeStarTotal(...)` method of the script class `PlayerInventoryDisplay`, passing the new integer number of stars collected. By multiplying this by the width of the yellow sprite image (100px), we get the correct width to set for UI **Image** `Image-stars-yellow` so that the corresponding number of yellow stars will now be seen by the user. Any stars that remain to be collected will still be seen as the grey stars that are not yet covered up.

The actual task of changing the width of UI **Image** `Image-stars-yellow` is completed by calling the `SetSizeWithCurrentAnchors(...)` method. The first parameter is the axis, so we pass constant `RectTransform.Axis.Horizontal` so that it will be the width that is changed. The second parameter is the new size for that axis—so we pass a value that is 100 times the number of stars collected so far (variable `newWidth`).

Displaying multiple pickups of different objects as a list of text via a dynamic List<> of PickUp objects

When working with different kinds of pickups, one approach is to use a C# **List** to maintain a flexible-length data structure of the items currently in the inventory. In this recipe, we will show you how, each time an item is picked up, a new object is added to such a **List** collection. An iteration through the **List** is how the text display of items is generated each time the inventory changes. We introduce a very simple `PickUp` script class, demonstrating how information about a pickup can be stored in a scripted component, extracted upon collision, and stored in our **List**.

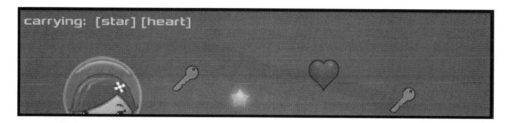

Getting ready

This recipe assumes that you are starting with the project `Simple2Dgame_SpaceGirl` setup from the first recipe in this chapter. The font you need can be found in the `1362_02_02` folder.

How to do it...

To display inventory total text for multiple pickups of different object types, follow these steps:

1. Start with a new copy of the mini-game `Simple2Dgame_SpaceGirl`.

2. Edit the tags, changing tag **Star** to **Pickup**. Ensure that the `star` GameObject now has the tag **Pickup**.

3. Add the following C# Script `PickUp` to GameObject `star` in the **Hierarchy**:

```
using UnityEngine;
using System.Collections;

public class PickUp : MonoBehaviour {
  public string description;
}
```

4. In the **Inspector,** change the description property of component **Pick Up (Script)** of GameObject `star` to the text `star`, as shown in the following screenshot:

5. Select the GameObject `star` in the **Hierarchy** panel and make a copy of this GameObject, renaming the copy `heart`.

6. In the **Inspector,** change the description property of component **Pick Up (Script)** of GameObject `heart` to the text `heart`. Also, drag from the **Project** panel (folder `Sprites`) image **healthheart** into the Sprite property of GameObject `heart`. The player should now see the heart image on screen for this pickup item.

7. Select the GameObject `star` in the **Hierarchy** panel and make a copy of this GameObject, renaming the copy `key`.

8. In the **Inspector,** change the description property of component **Pick Up (Script)** of GameObject `key` to the text `key`. Also, drag from the **Project** panel (folder **Sprites**) image **icon_key_green_100** into the **Sprite** property of GameObject `key`. The player should now see the key image on screen for this pickup item.

9. Make another one or two copies of each pickup GameObject and arrange them around the screen, so there are two or three each of star, heart, and key pickup GameObjects.

10. Add the following C# Script `Player` to GameObject `player-SpaceGirl` in the **Hierarchy**:

```
using UnityEngine;
using System.Collections;
using UnityEngine.UI;
using System.Collections.Generic;

public class Player : MonoBehaviour {
  private PlayerInventoryDisplay playerInventoryDisplay;
  private List<PickUp> inventory = new List<PickUp>();

  void Start(){
    playerInventoryDisplay = GetComponent<PlayerInventoryDispl
ay>();
```

```
    playerInventoryDisplay.OnChangeInventory(inventory);
  }

  void OnTriggerEnter2D(Collider2D hit){
    if(hit.CompareTag("Pickup")){
      PickUp item = hit.GetComponent<PickUp>();
      inventory.Add( item );
      playerInventoryDisplay.OnChangeInventory(inventory);
      Destroy(hit.gameObject);
    }
  }
}
```

11. Add a UI **Text** object (**Create | UI | Text**). Rename it `Text-inventory-list`. Change its text to **the quick brown fox jumped over the lazy dog the quick brown fox jumped over the lazy dog,** or another long list of nonsense words, to test the overflow settings you change in the next step.

12. In the **Text (Script)** component, ensure that **Horizontal Overflow** is set to **Wrap,** and set **Vertical Overflow** to **Overflow**—this will ensure that the text will wrap onto a second or third line (if needed) and not be hidden if there are lots of pickups.

13. In the **Inspector** panel, set its font to **Xolonium-Bold** (folder `Fonts`) and set its color to yellow. For the **Alignment** property, center the text horizontally and ensure that the text is top aligned vertically, and set the **Font Size** to 28 and choose a yellow text **Color.**

14. Edit its **Rect Transform** and set its **Height** to `50`. Then, while holding down *SHIFT* and *ALT* (to set pivot and position), choose the top-stretch box. The text should now be positioned at the middle top of the **Game** panel, and its width should stretch to match that of the whole panel.

15. Your text should now appear at the top of the game panel.

16. Add the following C# Script `PlayerInventoryDisplay` to GameObject `player-SpaceGirl` in the **Hierarchy**:

```
using UnityEngine;
using System.Collections;
using UnityEngine.UI;
using System.Collections.Generic;

public class PlayerInventoryDisplay : MonoBehaviour
{
  public Text inventoryText;

  public void OnChangeInventory(List<PickUp> inventory){
    // (1) clear existing display
```

```
            inventoryText.text = "";

            // (2) build up new set of items
            string newInventoryText = "carrying: ";
            int numItems = inventory.Count;
            for(int i = 0; i < numItems; i++){
              string description = inventory[i].description;
              newInventoryText += " [" + description+ "]";
            }

            if(numItems < 1) newInventoryText = "(empty inventory)";

            // (3) update screen display
            inventoryText.text = newInventoryText;
        }
    }
```

17. From the **Hierarchy** view, select the GameObject player-SpaceGirl. Then, from the **Inspector**, access the **Player Inventory Display (Script)** component and populate the **Inventory Text** public field with the UI **Text** object Text-inventory-list.

18. Play the game—each time you pick up a star or key or heart, the updated list of what you are carrying should be displayed in the form **carrying: [key] [heart]**.

How it works...

In the script class Player, the variable inventory is a C# **List<>**. This is a flexible data structure, which can be sorted, searched, and dynamically (at run time, when the game is being played) have items added to and removed from it. The <PickUp> in pointy brackets means that variable inventory will contain a list of PickUp objects. For this recipe, our PickUp class just has a single field, a string description, but we'll add more sophisticated data items in PickUp classes in later recipes.

When the scene starts, the Start() method of script class Player gets a reference to the PlayerInventoryDisplay scripted component and also initializes variable inventory to be a new, empty C# List of PickUp objects. When the OnColliderEnter2D(...) method detects collisions with items tagged Pickup, the PickUp object component of the item hit is added to our inventory list. A call is also made to the OnChangeInventory(...) method of playerInventoryDisplay to update out inventory display to the player, passing the updated inventory **List** as a parameter.

The script class playerInventoryDisplay has a public variable, linked to the UI **Text** object Text-inventory-list. The OnChangeInventory(...) method first sets the UI text to empty, and then loops through the inventory list, building up a string of each items description in square brackets ([key], [heart], and so on). If there were no items in the list, then the string is set to the text (empty inventory). Finally, the text property of the UI **Text** object Text-inventory-list is set to the value of this string representation of what is inside variable inventory.

There's more...

Some details you don't want to miss:

Order items in the inventory list alphabetically

It would be nice to alphabetically sort the words in the inventory list—both for neatness and consistency (so, in a game, if we pick up a key and a heart, it will look the same regardless of which order), but also so that items of the same type will be listed together, so we can easily see how many of each item we are carrying.

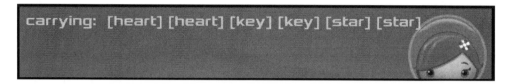

To implement the alphabetic sorting of the items in the inventory list, we need to do the following:

1. Add the following C# code to the beginning of method OnChangeInventory(...) in the script class PlayerInventoryDisplay:

    ```csharp
    public void OnChangeInventory(List<PickUp> inventory){
        inventory.Sort(
            delegate(PickUp p1, PickUp p2){
                return p1.description.CompareTo(p2.description);
            }
        );

        // rest of the method as before …
    }
    ```

2. You should now see all the items listed in alphabetic sequence. This C# code takes advantage of the List.Sort (...) method, a feature of collections whereby each item can be compared to the next, and they are swapped if in the wrong order (if the CompareTo (...) methods returns false).

Displaying multiple pickups of different objects as text totals via a dynamic Dictionary<> of PickUp objects and "enum" pickup types

While the previous recipe worked fine, any old text might have been typed into the description for a pickup or perhaps mistyped (**star, Sstar, starr**, and so on). A much better way of restricting game properties to one of a predefined (enumerated) list of possible values is to use C# enums. As well as removing the chance of mistyping a string, it also means that we can write code to appropriately deal with the predefined set of possible values. In this recipe, we will improve our general purpose `PickUp` class by introducing three possible pickup types (Star, Heart, and Key), and write inventory display code that counts the number of each type of pickup being carried and displays these totals via a UI **Text** object on screen. We also switch from using a **List** to using a **Dictionary**, since the Dictionary data structure is designed specifically for key-value pairs, perfect for associating a numeric total with an enumerated pickup type.

Getting ready

This recipe follows on from the previous recipe in this chapter.

How to do it...

To display multiple pickups of different objects as text totals via a dynamic `Dictionary`, follow these steps:

1. Make a copy of your work for the previous recipe.

2. Replace the content of script class `PickUp` with the following code:

```
using UnityEngine;
using System.Collections;

public class PickUp : MonoBehaviour {
    public enum PickUpType {
```

```
      Star, Key, Heart
  }

  public PickUpType type;
}
```

3. Replace the content of script class `Player` with the following code:

```
using UnityEngine;
using System.Collections;
using UnityEngine.UI;
using System.Collections.Generic;

public class Player : MonoBehaviour {
  private InventoryManager inventoryManager;

  void Start(){
    inventoryManager = GetComponent<InventoryManager>();
  }

  void OnTriggerEnter2D(Collider2D hit){
    if(hit.CompareTag("Pickup")){
      PickUp item = hit.GetComponent<PickUp>();
      inventoryManager.Add( item );
      Destroy(hit.gameObject);
    }
  }
}
```

4. Replace the content of script class `PlayerInventoryDisplay` with the following code:

```
using UnityEngine;
using System.Collections;
using UnityEngine.UI;
using System.Collections.Generic;

public class PlayerInventoryDisplay : MonoBehaviour {
  public Text inventoryText;
  private string newInventoryText;

  public void OnChangeInventory(Dictionary<PickUp.PickUpType, int>
inventory){
    inventoryText.text = "";

    newInventoryText = "carrying: ";
```

```
      int numItems = inventory.Count;

      foreach(var item in inventory){
        int itemTotal = item.Value;
        string description = item.Key.ToString();
        newInventoryText += " [ " + description + " " + itemTotal +
" ]";
      }

      if(numItems < 1) newInventoryText = "(empty inventory)";

      inventoryText.text = newInventoryText;
    }
  }
```

5. Add the following C# Script `InventoryManager` to the GameObject `player-SpaceGirl` in the **Hierarchy**:

```
using UnityEngine;
using System.Collections;
using System.Collections.Generic;

public class InventoryManager : MonoBehaviour {
  private PlayerInventoryDisplay playerInventoryDisplay;
  private Dictionary<PickUp.PickUpType, int> items = new
Dictionary<PickUp.PickUpType, int>();

  void Start(){
    playerInventoryDisplay = GetComponent<PlayerInventoryDispl
ay>();
    playerInventoryDisplay.OnChangeInventory(items);
  }

  public void Add(PickUp pickup){
    PickUp.PickUpType type = pickup.type;
    int oldTotal = 0;
    if(items.TryGetValue(type, out oldTotal))
      items[type] = oldTotal + 1;
    else
      items.Add (type, 1);

    playerInventoryDisplay.OnChangeInventory(items);
  }
}
```

6. In the **Hierarchy** (or **Scene**) panel, select each pickup GameObject in turn, and choose from the drop-down menu its corresponding **Type** in the **Inspector** panel. As you can see, public variables that are of an `enum` type are automatically restricted to the set of possible values as a combo-box drop-down menu in the **Inspector** panel.

7. Play the game. First, you should see a message on screen stating the inventory is empty, and then as you pick up one or more items of each pickup type, you'll see text totals of each type you have collected.

How it works...

Each pickup GameObject in the scene has a scripted component of class `PickUp`. The `PickUp` object for each `Pickup` GameObject has a single property, a pickup type, which has to be one of the enumerated set of `Star, Key, Heart`. The `Player` script class gets a reference to the `InventoryManager` component via its `Start()` method, and each time the player's character collides with a pickup GameObject, it calls the `Add(...)` method of the inventory manager, passing the `PickUp` object of the object collided with.

In this recipe, the inventory being carried by the player is being represented by a C# `Dictionary`. In this case, we have in script class `InventoryManager` a dictionary of key-value pairs, where the key is one of the possible `PickUp.PickUpType` enumerated values, and the value is an integer total of how many of that type of pickup is being carried. Each `InventoryItemTotal` object has just two properties: a `PickUp` type and an integer total. This extra layer of the `InventoryManager` has been added between script class `Player` and `PlayerInventoryDisplay` to both separate the `Player` behavior from how the inventory is internally stored and to prevent the `Player` script class from becoming too large and attempting to handle too many different responsibilities.

C# dictionaries provide a `TryGetValue(...)` method, which receives parameters of a key and is passed a reference to a variable the same data type as the value for the `Dictionary`. When the `Add(...)` method of the inventory manager is called, the type of the `PickUp` object is tested to see if a total for this type is already in `Dictionary items`. If an item total is found inside the `Dictionary` for the given type, then the value for this item in the `Dictionary` is incremented. If no entry is found for the given type, then a new element is added to the `Dictionary` with a total of 1.

The last action of the Add (...) method is to call the OnChangeInventory (...) method of the PlayerInventoryDisplay scripted component of the player's GameObject to update the text totals displayed on screen. This method in PlayerInventoryDisplay iterates through the Dictionary, building up a string of the type names and totals, and then updates the text property of the UI Text object with the string showing the inventory totals to the player.

Learn more about using C# lists and dictionaries in Unity in the Unity Technologies tutorial at https://unity3d.com/learn/tutorials/modules/intermediate/scripting/lists-and-dictionaries.

Generalizing multiple icon displays using UI Grid Layout Groups (with scrollbars!)

The recipes in this chapter up to this point have been hand-crafted for each situation. While this is fine, more general and automated approaches to inventory UIs can sometimes save time and effort but still achieve visual and usability results of equal quality. In the next recipe, we will begin to explore a more engineered approach to inventory UIs by exploiting the automated sizing and layouts offered by Unity 5's Grid Layout Group component.

Getting ready

This recipe assumes that you are starting with the project Simple2Dgame_SpaceGirl setup from the first recipe in this chapter. The font you need can be found in the 1362_02_02 folder.

How to do it...

To display grey and yellow star icons for multiple object pickups using UI grid layout groups, follow these steps:

1. Start with a new copy of the mini-game Simple2Dgame_SpaceGirl.
2. In the **Hierarchy** panel, create a UI Panel Panel-background (**Create | UI | Panel**).

3. Let's now position `Panel-background` at the **top** of the **Game** panel, stretching the horizontal width of the canvas. Edit the UI **Image's Rect Transform** component, and while holding down *SHIFT* and *ALT* (to set pivot and position), choose the top-stretch box.

4. The panel will still be taking up the whole game window. So, now in the **Inspector** panel, change the **Height** (in the **Rect Transform** component) of `Panel-background` to 100, as shown in the following screenshot:

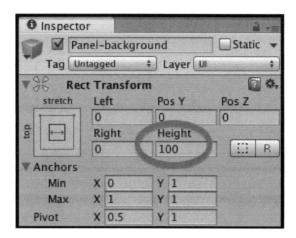

5. Add a UI **Text** object (**Create | UI | Text**), rename it `Text-inventory`, and change its text to **Inventory**.

6. In the **Hierarchy** panel, child this UI Text object to panel `Panel-background`.

7. In the **Inspector** panel, also set the font of `Text-inventory` to **Xolonium-Bold** (the `Fonts` folder). Center the text horizontally, top align the text vertically, set its **Height** to 50, and set the **Font Size** to 23.

8. Edit the **Rect Transform** of `Text-inventory`, and while holding down *SHIFT* and *ALT* (to set pivot and position), choose the top-stretch box. The text should now be positioned at the middle top of the **UI Panel** `Panel-background` and its width should stretch to match that of the whole panel.

9. Select the **Canvas** in the **Hierarchy** panel and add a new UI Panel object (**Create | UI | Image**). Rename it `Panel-slot-grid`.

10. Position `Panel-slot-grid` at the **top** of the **Game** panel, stretching the horizontal width of the canvas. Edit the UI **Image's Rect Transform** component, and while holding down *SHIFT* and *ALT* (to set pivot and position), choose the top-stretch box.

11. In the **Inspector** panel, change the **Height** (in the **Rect Transform** component) of `Panel-slot-grid` to `80` and set its **Top** to `20` (so it is below UI **Text** GameObject `Text-inventory`).

12. With the panel `Panel-slot-grid` selected in the **Hierarchy** panel, add a grid layout group component (**Add Component | Layout | Grid Layout Group**). Set **Cell Size** to `70 x 70` and **Spacing** to `5 x 5`. Also, set the **Child Alignment** to **Middle Center** (so our icons will have even spacing at the far left and right), as shown in the following screenshot:

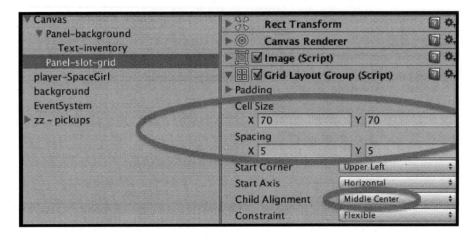

13. With the panel `Panel-slot-grid` selected in the **Hierarchy** panel, add a mask (script) component (**Add Component | UI | Mask**). Uncheck the option **Show Mask Graphic**. Having this mask component means that any overflow of our grid will NOT be seen by the user—only content within the image area of the panel `Panel-slot-grid` will ever be visible.

14. Add to your **Canvas** a UI **Image** object (**Create | UI | Image**). Rename it `Image-slot`.

15. In the **Hierarchy** panel, child UI **Image** object `Image-slot` to panel `Panel-slot-grid`.

16. Set the **Source Image** of `Image-slot` to the Unity provided **Knob** (circle) image, as shown in the following screenshot:

17. Since `Image-slot` is the only UI object inside `Panel-slot-grid`, it will be displayed (sized 70 x 70) in center in that panel, as shown in the following screenshot:

18. Each image slot will have a yellow star child image and a grey star child image. Let's create those now.

19. Add to your **Canvas** a UI **Image** object (**Create | UI | Image**). Rename it `Image-star-yellow`.

20. In the **Hierarchy** panel, child UI **Image** object `Image-star-yellow` to image `Image-slot`.

21. Set the **Source Image** of `Image-star-yellow` to the `icon_star_100` image (in folder `Sprites`).

22. Now we will set our yellow star icon image to fully fill its parent `Image-slot` by stretching horizontally and vertically. Edit the UI **Image's Rect Transform** component, and while holding down *SHIFT* and *ALT* (to set pivot and position), choose the bottom right option to fully **stretch** horizontally and vertically. The UI **Image** `Image-star-yellow` should now be visible in the middle of the `Image-slot` circular **Knob** image, as shown in the following screenshot:

23. Duplicate `Image-star-yellow` in the **Hierarchy** panel, naming the copy `Image-star-grey`. This new GameObject should also be a child of `Image-slot`.

24. Change the **Source Image** of `Image-star-grey` to the `icon_star_grey_100` image (in folder `Sprites`). At any time, our inventory slot can now display nothing, a yellow star icon, or a grey star icon, depending on whether `Image-star-yellow` and `Image-star-grey` are enabled or not: we'll control this through the inventory display code later in this recipe.

25. In the **Hierarchy** panel, ensure that `Image-slot` is selected, and add the C# Script `PickupUI` with the following code:

```
using UnityEngine;
using System.Collections;

public class PickupUI : MonoBehaviour {
  public GameObject starYellow;
  public GameObject starGrey;

  void Awake(){
    DisplayEmpty();
  }

  public void DisplayYellow(){
    starYellow.SetActive(true);
    starGrey.SetActive(false);
  }

  public void DisplayGrey(){
    starYellow.SetActive(false);
    starGrey.SetActive(true);
  }
```

```
public void DisplayEmpty(){
  starYellow.SetActive(false);
  starGrey.SetActive(false);
  }
}
```

26. With the GameObject `Image-slot` selected in the **Hierarchy** panel, drag each of its two children `Image-star-yellow` and `Image-star-grey` into their corresponding **Inspector** panel **Pickup UI** slots **Star Yellow** and **Star Grey**, as shown in the following screenshot:

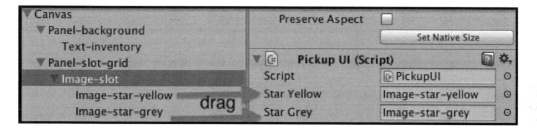

27. In the **Hierarchy** panel, make nine duplicates of `Image-slot` in the **Hierarchy** panel; they should automatically be named `Image-slot 1 .. 9`. See the following screenshot to ensure the Hierarchy of your Canvas is correct—the parenting of `Image-slot` as a child of `Image-slot-grid`, and the parenting of `Image-star-yellow` and `Image-star-grey` as children of each `Image-slot` is very important.

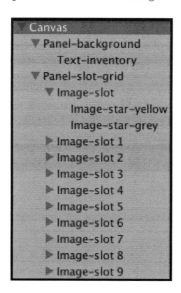

28. In the **Hierarchy** panel, ensure that `player-SpaceGirl` is selected, and add the C# script `Player` with the following code:

```
using UnityEngine;
using System.Collections;
using UnityEngine.UI;

public class Player : MonoBehaviour {
  private PlayerInventoryModel playerInventoryModel;

  void Start(){
    playerInventoryModel = GetComponent<PlayerInventoryModel>();
  }

  void OnTriggerEnter2D(Collider2D hit){
    if(hit.CompareTag("Star")){
      playerInventoryModel.AddStar();
      Destroy(hit.gameObject);
    }
  }
}
```

29. In the **Hierarchy** panel, ensure that `player-SpaceGirl` is selected, and add the C# script `PlayerInventoryModel` with the following code:

```
using UnityEngine;
using System.Collections;

public class PlayerInventoryModel : MonoBehaviour {
  private int starTotal = 0;
  private PlayerInventoryDisplay playerInventoryDisplay;

  void Start(){
    playerInventoryDisplay = GetComponent<PlayerInventoryDispl
ay>();
    playerInventoryDisplay.OnChangeStarTotal(starTotal);
  }

  public void AddStar(){
    starTotal++;
    playerInventoryDisplay.OnChangeStarTotal(starTotal);
  }
}
```

30. In the **Hierarchy** panel, ensure that `player-SpaceGirl` is selected, and add the C# script `PlayerInventoryDisplay` with the following code:

```
using UnityEngine;
using System.Collections;
using UnityEngine.UI;

public class PlayerInventoryDisplay : MonoBehaviour
{
  const int NUM_INVENTORY_SLOTS = 10;
  public PickupUI[] slots = new PickupUI[NUM_INVENTORY_SLOTS];

  public void OnChangeStarTotal(int starTotal){
    for(int i = 0; i < NUM_INVENTORY_SLOTS; i++){
      PickupUI slot = slots[i];
      if(i < starTotal)
        slot.DisplayYellow();
      else
        slot.DisplayGrey();
    }
  }
}
```

31. With GameObject `player-SpaceGirl` selected in the **Hierarchy** panel, drag the ten `Image-slot` GameObjects into their corresponding locations in the **Player Inventory Display (Script)** component array **Slots**, in the **Inspector** panel, as shown in the following screenshot:

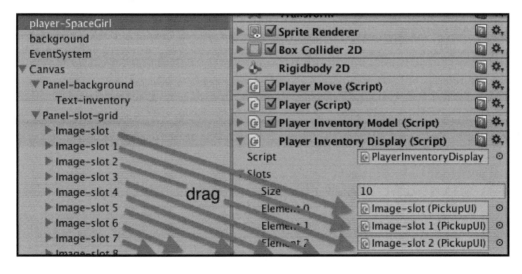

32. Save the scene and play the game. As you pick up stars, you should see more of the grey stars change to yellow in the inventory display.

How it works...

We have created a simple panel (`Panel-background`) and text at the top of the game canvas—showing a greyish background rectangle and text "Inventory". We created a small panel inside this area (`Panel-slot-grid`), with a grid layout group component, which automatically sizes and lays out the 10 `Image-slot` GameObjects we created with the knob (circle) source image. By adding a mask component to `Panel-slot-grid`, we ensure that no content will overflow outside of the rectangle of the source image for this panel.

Each of the 10 `Image-slot` GameObjects that are children of `Panel-slot-grid` contains a yellow star image and a grey star image. Also, each `Image-slot` GameObjects has a script component `PickupUI`. The `PickupUI` script offers three public methods, which will show just the yellow star image, just the grey star image, or neither (so, an empty knob circle image will be seen).

Our player's character GameObject `player-SpaceGirl` has a very simple basic `Player` script—this just detected collisions with objects tagged `Star`, and when this happens, it removes the star GameObject collided with and calls the `AddStar()` method to its `playerInventoryModel` scripted component. The `PlayerInventoryModel` C# script class maintains a running integer total of the number of stars added to the inventory. Each time the `AddStar()` method is called, it increments (adds 1) to this total, and then calls the `OnChangeStarTotal(...)` method of scripted component `playerInventoryDisplay`. Also, when the scene starts, an initial call is made to the `OnChangeStarTotal(...)` method so that the UI display for the inventory is set up to show that we are initially carrying no stars.

The C# script class `PlayerInventoryDisplay` has two properties: one is a constant integer defining the number of slots in our inventory, which for this game we set to 10, and the other variable is an array of references to `PickupUI` scripted components—each of these is a reference to the scripted component in each of the 10 `Image-slot` GameObjects in our `Panel-slot-grid`. When the `OnChangeStarTotal(...)` method is passed the number of stars we are carrying, it loops through each of the 10 slots. While the current slot is less than our star total, a yellow star is displayed, by the calling of the `DisplayYellow()` method of the current slot (`PickupUI` scripted component). Once the loop counter is equal to or larger than our star total, then all remaining slots are made to display a grey star via the calling of method `DisplayGrey()`.

This recipe is an example of the **low coupling** of the MVC design pattern. We have designed our code to not rely or make too many assumptions about other parts of the game so that the chances of a change in some other part of our game breaking our inventory display code are much smaller. The display (view) is separated from the logical representation of what we are carrying (model), and changes to the model are made by public methods called from the player (controller).

Note: It might seem that we could make our code simpler by assuming that slots are always displaying grey (no star) and just changing one slot to yellow each time a yellow star is picked up. But this would lead to problems if something happens in the game (for example, hitting a black hole or being shot by an alien) that makes us drop one or more stars. C# script class `PlayerInventoryDisplay` makes no assumptions about which slots may or may not have been displayed grey or yellow or empty previously—each time it is called, it ensures that an appropriate number of yellow stars are displayed, and all other slots are displayed with grey stars.

There's more...

Some details you don't want to miss:

Add a horizontal scrollbar to the inventory slot display

We can see 10 inventory slots now—but what if there are many more? One solution is to add a scroll bar so that the user can scroll left and right, viewing 10 at a time, as shown in the following screenshot. Let's add a horizontal scroll bar to our game. This can be achieved without any C# code changes, all through the Unity 5 UI system.

To implement a horizontal scrollbar for our inventory display, we need to do the following:

1. Increase the height of `Panel-background` to 130 pixels.

2. In the **Inspector** panel, set the **Child Alignment** property of component **Grid Layout Group (Script)** of `Panel-slot-grid` to Upper Left. Then, move this panel to the right a little so that the 10 inventory icons are centered on screen.

3. In the **Hierarchy** panel, duplicate Image-slot 9 three more times so that there are now 13 inventory icons in `Panel-slot-grid`.

4. In the **Scene** panel, drag the right-hand edge of panel `Panel-slot-grid` to make it wide enough so that all 13 inventory icons fit horizontally—of course the last three will be off screen, as shown in the following screenshot:

5. Add a UI **Panel** to the **Canvas** and name it `Panel-scroll-container`, and tint it red by setting the **Color** property of its **Image (Script)** component to red.

6. Size and position `Panel-scroll-container` so that it is just behind our `Panel-slot-grid`. So, you should now see a red rectangle behind the 10 inventory circle slots.

7. In the **Hierarchy** panel, drag `Panel-slot-grid` so that it is now childed to `Panel-scroll-container`.

8. Add a UI **Mask** to `Panel-scroll-container` so now you should only be able to see the 10 inventory icons that fit within the rectangle of this red-tinted panel.

 Note: You may wish to temporarily set this mask component as inactive so that you can see and work on the unseen parts of `Panel-slot-grid` if required.

9. Add a UI **Scrollbar** to the **Canvas** and name it `Scrollbar-horizontal`. Move it to be just below the 10 inventory icons, and resize it to be the same width as the red-tinted `Panel-scroll-container`, as shown in the following screenshot:

10. Add a UI **Scroll Rect** component to `Panel-scroll-container`.

11. In the **Inspector** panel, drag `Scrolbar-horizontal` to the Horizontal Scrollbar property of the **Scroll Rect** component of `Panel-scroll-container`.

12. In the **Inspector** panel, drag `Panel-slot-grid` to the Content property of the **Scroll Rect** component of `Panel-scroll-container`, as shown in the following screenshot:

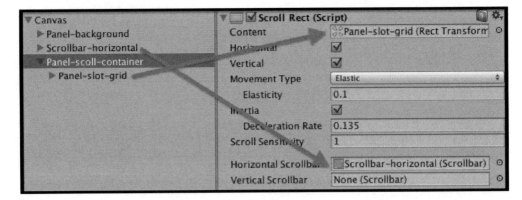

13. Now, ensure the **mask** component of `Panel-scroll-container` is set as active so that we don't see the overflow of `Panel-slot-grid` and uncheck this **mask** components option to **Show Mask Graphic** (so that we don't see the red rectangle any more).

You should now have a working scrollable inventory system. Note that the last three new icons will just be empty circles, since the inventory display script does not have references to, or attempt to make, any changes to these extra three slots; so the script code would need to be changed to reflect every additional slot we add to `Panel-slot-grid`.

The automation of PlayerInventoryDisplay getting references to all the slots

There was a lot of dragging slots from the **Hierarchy** panel into the array for the scripted component `PlayerInventoryDisplay`. This takes a bit of work (and mistakes might be made when dragging items in the wrong order or the same item twice). Also, if we change the number of slots, then we may have to do this all over again or try to remember to drag more slots if we increase the number, and so on. A better way of doing things is to make the first task of the script class `PlayerInventoryDisplay` when the scene begins to create each of these `Image-slot` GameObjects as a child of `Panel-slot-grid` and populate the array at the same time.

To implement the automated population of our scripted array of PickupUI objects for this recipe, we need to do the following:

1. Create a new folder named `Prefabs`. In this folder, create a new empty prefab named `starUI`.

2. From the **Hierarchy** panel, drag the GameObject `Image-slot` into your new empty prefab named `starUI`. This prefab should now turn blue, showing it is populated.

3. In the **Hierarchy** panel, delete GameObject `Image-slot` and all its copies `Image-slot 1 - 9`.

4. Replace C# Script `PlayerInventoryDisplay` in GameObject `player-SpaceGirl` with the following code:

```
using UnityEngine;
using System.Collections;
using UnityEngine.UI;

public class PlayerInventoryDisplay : MonoBehaviour
{
  const int NUM_INVENTORY_SLOTS = 10;
  private PickupUI[] slots = new PickupUI[NUM_INVENTORY_SLOTS];
  public GameObject slotGrid;
  public GameObject starSlotPrefab;

  void Awake(){
```

```
for(int i=0; i < NUM_INVENTORY_SLOTS; i++){
  GameObject starSlotGO = (GameObject)
  Instantiate(starSlotPrefab);
  starSlotGO.transform.SetParent(slotGrid.transform);
  starSlotGO.transform.localScale = new Vector3(1,1,1);
  slots[i] = starSlotGO.GetComponent<PickupUI>();
  }
}

public void OnChangeStarTotal(int starTotal){
  for(int i = 0; i < NUM_INVENTORY_SLOTS; i++){
  PickupUI slot = slots[i];
    if(i < starTotal)
      slot.DisplayYellow();
    else
      slot.DisplayGrey();
  }
}
}
```

5. With GameObject `player-SpaceGirl` selected in the **Hierarchy** panel, drag the GameObject `Panel-slot-grid` into **Player Inventory Display (Script)** variable **Slot grid**, in the **Inspector** panel.

6. With GameObject `player-SpaceGirl` selected in the **Hierarchy** panel, drag from the **Project** panel prefab `starUI` into **Player Inventory Display (Script)** variable **Star Slot Prefab**, in the **Inspector** panel, as shown in the following screenshot:

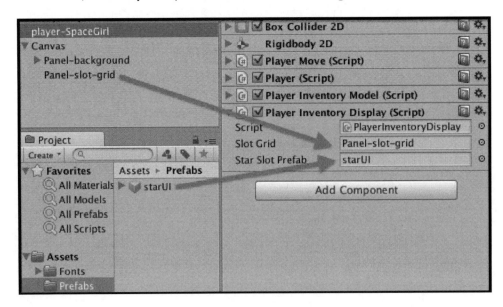

The public array has been made private and no longer needs to be populated through manual drag-and-drop. When you run the game, it will play just the same as before, with the population of the array of images in our inventory grid panel now automated. The `Awake()` method creates new instances of the prefab (as many as defined by constant `NUM_INVENTORY_SLOTS`) and immediately childed them to `Panel-slot-grid`. Since we have a grid layout group component, their placement is automatically neat and tidy in our panel.

Note: The scale property of the transform component of GameObjects is reset when a GameObject changes its parent (to maintain relative child size to parent size). So, it is a good idea to always reset the local scale of GameObjects to (1,1,1) immediately after they have been childed to another GameObject. We do this in the `for`-loop to `starSlotGO` immediately following the `SetParent(...)` statement.

Note that we use the `Awake() method` for creating the instances of the prefab in `PlayerInventoryDispay` so that we know this will be executed before the `Start()` method in `PlayerInventoryModel`—since no `Start()` method is executed until all `Awake()` methods for all GameObjects in the scene have been completed.

Automatically changing the grid cell size based on the number of slots in inventory

Consider a situation where we wish to change the number of slots. Another alternative to using scrollbars is to change the cell size in the **Grid Layout Group** component. We can automate this through code so that the cell size is changed to ensure that `NUM_INVENTORY_SLOTS` will fit along the width of our panel at the top of the canvas.

To implement the automated resizing of the **Grid Layout Group** cell size for this recipe, we need to do the following:

▶ Add the following method `Start()` to the C# Script `PlayerInventoryDisplay` in GameObject `player-SpaceGirl` with the following code:

```
void Start(){
    float panelWidth = slotGrid.GetComponent<RectTransform>().rect.
width;
    print ("slotGrid.GetComponent<RectTransform>().rect = " +
slotGrid.GetComponent<RectTransform>().rect);

    GridLayoutGroup gridLayoutGroup = slotGrid.GetComponent<GridLayo
utGroup>();
    float xCellSize = panelWidth / NUM_INVENTORY_SLOTS;
    xCellSize -= gridLayoutGroup.spacing.x;
```

```
        gridLayoutGroup.cellSize = new Vector2(xCellSize, xCellSize);
    }
```

We write our code in the `Start()` method, rather than adding to code in the `Awake()` method, to ensure that the **RectTransform** of GameObject `Panel-slot-grid` has finished sizing (in this recipe, it stretches based on the width of the **Game** panel). While we can't know the sequence in which **Hierarchy** GameObjects are created when a scene begins, we can rely on the Unity behavior that every GameObject sends the `Awake()` message, and only after all corresponding `Awake()` methods have finished executing all objects, and then sends the `Start()` message. So, any code in the `Start()` method can safely assume that every GameObject has been initialized.

The above screenshot shows the value of `NUM_INVENTORY_SLOTS` having been changed to 15, and the cell size, having been corresponding, changed, so that all 15 now fit horizontally in our panel. Note that the spacing between cells is subtracted from the calculated available with divided by the number of slots (`xCellSize -= gridLayoutGroup.spacing.x`) since that spacing is needed between each item displayed as well.

Add some help methods to the Rect Transform script class

If we wish to further change, say, the `RectTransform` properties using code, we can add extension methods by creating a file containing special static methods and using the special "this" keyword. See the following code that adds `SetWidth(...)`, `SetHeight(...)`, and `SetSize(...)` methods to the `RectTransform` scripted component:

```
using UnityEngine;
using System;
using System.Collections;

public static class RectTransformExtensions
{
  public static void SetSize(this RectTransform trans, Vector2
newSize) {
    Vector2 oldSize = trans.rect.size;
    Vector2 deltaSize = newSize - oldSize;
    trans.offsetMin = trans.offsetMin - new Vector2(deltaSize.x *
trans.pivot.x, deltaSize.y * trans.pivot.y);
```

```
      trans.offsetMax = trans.offsetMax + new Vector2(deltaSize.x * (1f
 - trans.pivot.x), deltaSize.y * (1f - trans.pivot.y));
   }

   public static void SetWidth(this RectTransform trans, float newSize)
 {
      SetSize(trans, new Vector2(newSize, trans.rect.size.y));
   }

   public static void SetHeight(this RectTransform trans, float
 newSize) {
      SetSize(trans, new Vector2(trans.rect.size.x, newSize));
   }
 }
```

Unity C# allows us to add these extensions methods by declaring `static void` methods whose first argument is in the form this `<ClassName> <var>`. The method can then be called as a built-in method defined in the original class.

All we would need to do is create a new C# script class file `RectTransformExtensions` in the folder **Scripts** in the **Project** panel, containing the above code. In fact, you can find a whole set of useful extra `RectTransform` methods (on which the above is an extract) created by OrbcreationBV, and it is available online at `http://www.orbcreation.com/orbcreation/page.orb?1099`.

Conclusion

In this chapter, we introduced recipes demonstrating a range of C# data representations for inventory items and a range of Unity UI interface components to display the status and contents of player inventories at run time.

Inventory UI needs good quality graphical assets for a high quality result. Some sources of assets that you might wish to explore include the following sites:

- The graphics for our SpaceGirl mini game are from the Space Cute art by Daniel Cook; he generously publishes lots of 2D art for game developers to use:
  - `http://www.lostgarden.com/`
  - `http://www.lostgarden.com/search?q=planet+cute`
- Sethbyrd—lots of fun 2D graphics:
  - `http://www.sethbyrd.com/`
- Royalty-free art for 2D games:
  - `http://www.gameart2d.com/freebies.html`

3
2D Animation

In this chapter, we will cover:

- ▸ Flipping a sprite horizontally
- ▸ Animating body parts for character movement events
- ▸ Creating a 3-frame animation clip to make a platform continually animate
- ▸ Making a platform start falling once stepped-on using a Trigger to move animation from one state to another
- ▸ Creating animation clips from sprite sheet sequences

Introduction

Unity 5 builds on the introduction of powerful 2D features in the Mecanim animation system and the 2D physics system that were introduced in Unity 4.6 late 2014. In this chapter, we present a range of recipes to introduce the basics of 2D animation in Unity 5, and help you understand the relationships between the different animation elements.

The big picture

In Unity 2D animations can be created in several different ways – one way is to create many images, each slightly different, which frame-by-frame give the appearance of movement. A second way to create animations is by defining keyframe positions for individual parts of an object (for example, the arms, legs, feet, head, eyes, and so on), and getting Unity to calculate all the in-between positions when the game in running.

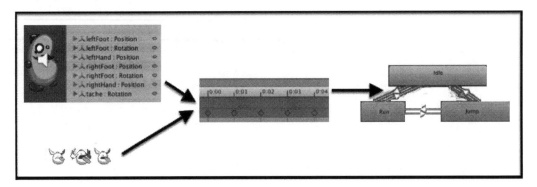

Both sources of animations become **Animation Clips** in the Animation panel. Each **Animation Clip** then becomes a **State** in the **Animator Controller State Machine**. We then define under what conditions a GameObject will **Transition** from one animation state (clip) to another.

Flipping a sprite horizontally

Perhaps the simplest 2D animation is a simple flip, from facing left to facing right, or facing up to facing down, and so on. In this recipe we'll add a cute bug sprite to the scene, and write a short script to flip its horizontal direction when the *Left* and *Right* arrow keys are pressed.

Getting ready

For this recipe, we have prepared the image you need in a folder named Sprites in folder 1362_03_01.

How to do it...

To flip an object horizontally with arrow key presses, follow these steps:

1. Create a new Unity 2D project.

2. Import the provided image EnemyBug.png.

3. Drag an instance of the red **Enemy Bug** image from the **Project | Sprites** folder into the scene. Position this GameObject at (0, 0, 0) and scale to (2, 2, 2).

4. Add an instance of C# script class BugFlip as a component to your **Enemy Bug** GameObject:

```
using UnityEngine;
using System.Collections;

public class BugFlip : MonoBehaviour {
  private bool facingRight = true;

  void Update() {
    if (Input.GetKeyDown(KeyCode.LeftArrow) && facingRight)
      Flip ();
    if (Input.GetKeyDown(KeyCode.RightArrow) && !facingRight)
      Flip();
  }

  void Flip (){
    // Switch the way the player is labelled as facing.
    facingRight = !facingRight;

    // Multiply the player's x local scale by -1.
    Vector3 theScale = transform.localScale;
    theScale.x *= -1;
    transform.localScale = theScale;
  }
}
```

5. When you run your scene, pressing the *Left* and *Right* arrow keys should make the bug face left or right correspondingly.

How it works...

The C# class defines a Boolean variable `facingRight`, which stores a `true/false` value corresponding to whether or not the bug is facing right or not. Since our bug sprite is initially facing right, then we set the initial value of `facingRight` to true to match this.

Method `Update()`, every frame, checks to see if the *Left* or *Right* arrow keys have been pressed. If the *Left* arrow key is pressed and the bug is facing right, then method `Flip()` is called, likewise if the *Right* arrow key is pressed and the bug is facing left (that is, facing right is false), again method `Flip()` is called.

Method `Flip()` performs two actions, the first simply reverses the true/false value in variable `facingRight`. The second action changes the **+/-** sign of the X-value of the `localScale` property of the transform. Reversing the sign of the `localScale` results in the 2D flip that we desire. Look inside the `PlayerControl` script for the **BeanMan** character in the next recipe – you'll see exactly the same `Flip()` method being used.

Animating body parts for character movement events

In this recipe, we'll learn to animate the hat of the Unity bean-man character in response to a jump event.

Getting ready

For this recipe, we have prepared the files you need in folder `1362_03_02`.

How to do it...

To animate body parts for character movement events, follow these steps:

1. Create a new Unity 2D project.

2. Import the provided package `BeanManAssets`, by choosing menu: **Assets | Import Package | Custom Package ...**, and then click the **Import** button to import all these assets into your **Project** panel.

3. Increase the size of the **Main Camera** to `10`.

4. Let's setup the 2D gravity setting for this project – we'll use the same setting as from Unity's 2D platform tutorial, a setting of Y= `-30`. Set 2D gravity to this value by choosing menu: **Edit | Project Settings | Physics 2D**, and then at the top change the Y value to `-30`.

5. Drag an instance of the BeanMan **character2D** from the **Project | Prefabs** folder into the scene. Position this GameObject at (0, 3, 0).

6. Drag an instance of the sprite **platformWallBlocks** from the **Project | Sprites** folder into the scene. Position this GameObject at (0, -4, 0).

7. Add a **Box Collider 2D** component to GameObject **platformWallBlocks** by choosing menu: **Add Component | Physics 2D | Box Collider 2D**.

8. We now have a stationary platform that the player can land upon, and walk left and right on. Create a new **Layer** named **Ground**, and assign GameObject **platformWallBlocks** to this new layer, as shown in the following screenshot. Pressing the *Space* key when the character is on the platform will now make him jump.

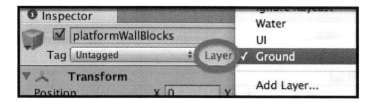

9. Currently the BeanMan character is animated (arms and legs moving) when we make him jump. Let's remove the Animation clips and Animator controller and create our own from scratch. Delete folders Clips and Controllers from **Project | Assets | PotatoMan2DAssets | Character2D | Animation**, as shown:

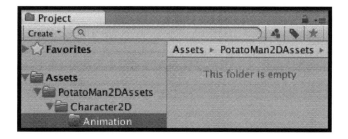

10. Let's create an Animation clip (and its associated Animator controller) for our hero character. In the Hierarchy panel select GameObject **hero**. Ensuring GameObject **character2D** is selected in the **Hierarchy**, open the **Animation** panel, and ensure it is in **Dope Sheet** view (this is the default).

11. Click the empty dropdown menu in the **Animation** panel (next to the greyed out word `Samples`), and choose menu item **[Create New Clip]**:

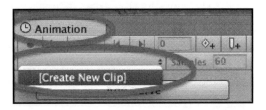

12. Save the new clip in the **Character2D | Animation** folder, naming it as **character-beanman-idle**. You've now created an Animation clip for the 'idle' character state (which is not animated).

 Your final game may end up with tens, or even hundreds, of animation clips. Make things easy to search by prefixing the names of clips with object type, name, and then description of the animation clip.

13. Looking at the **Character2D | Animation** folder in the Project panel you should now see both the Animation clip you have just created (**character-beanman-idle**) and also a new Animator controller, which has defaulted to the name of your GameObject **character2D**:

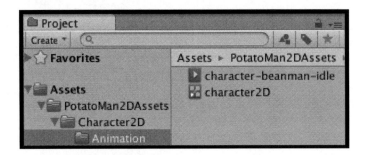

14. Ensuring GameObject **character2D** is selected in the **Hierarchy**, open the **Animator** panel and you'll see the State Machine for controlling the animation of our character. Since we only have one Animation clip (**character-beanman-idle**) then upon entry the State Machine immediately enters this state.

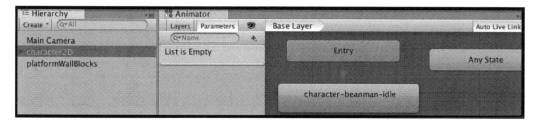

15. Run your scene – since the character is always in the 'idle' state, we see no animation yet when we make it jump.

16. Now we'll create a 'jump' Animation clip which animates the hat. Click the empty dropdown menu in the **Animation** panel (next to the greyed out word 'Samples'), and create a new clip in your **Animation** folder, naming it **character-beanman-jump**.

17. Click button **Add Property**, and chose **Transform | Position** of the **hat** child object, by clicking its '**+**' plus-sign button. We are now recording changes to the (X, Y, Z) position of GameObject **hat** in this animation clip:

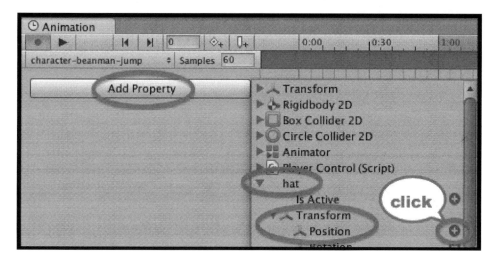

18. You should now see 2 'keyframes' at 0.0 and at 1.0. These are indicated by diamonds in the **Timeline** area in the right-hand-section of the **Animation** panel.

19. Click to select the first keyframe (at time 0.0). Now in the **Scene** panel move the hat up and left a little, away from the head. You should see that all three X, Y, Z values have a red background in the **Inspector** – this is to inform you that the values of the **Transform** component are being recorded in the animation clip:

20. Since 1 second is perhaps too long for our jump animation, drag the second keyframe diamond to the left to a time of 0.5.

21. We now need to define when the character should Transition from the 'idle' state to the 'jump' state. In the **Animator** panel select state **character-beanman-idle**, and create a transition to the state **character-beanman-jump** by right-mouse-clicking and choosing menu Make Transition, then drag the transition arrow to state **character-beanman-jump**, as shown:

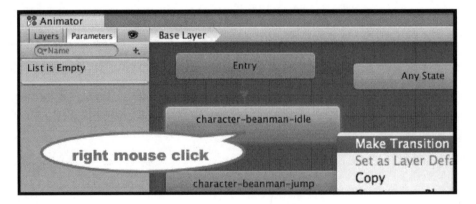

22. Now let's add a Trigger parameter named 'Jump', by clicking on the add parameter plus-sign "**+**" button at the top-left of the **Animator** panel, choosing **Trigger**, and typing the name **Jump**:

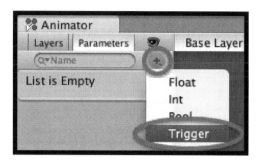

23. We can now define the properties for when our character should **Transition** from idle to jump. Click the Transition arrow to select it, and set the following 4 properties in the **Inspector** panel:

   ❏ **Has Exit Time**: uncheck

   ❏ **Transition Duration**: 0.01

   ❏ **Interruption State**: Current State

   ❏ **Conditions**: Add Jump (click plus-sign '+' button at bottom)

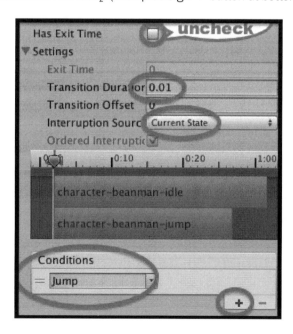

24. Save and run your scene. Once the character has landed on the platform and you press the *SPACE* key to jump, you'll now see the character's hat jump away from his head, and slowly move back. Since we haven't added any transition to ever leave the Jump state, this Animation clip will loop, so the hat keeps on moving even when the jump is completed.

25. In the Animator panel select state **character-beanman-jump** and add a new Transition back to state **character-beanman-idle**. Select this Transition arrow and in the Inspector panel sets its properties as follows:

   ❑ **Has Exit Time**: (leave as checked)

   ❑ **Exit time**: 0.5 (this needs to be the same time value as the second keyfame of our Jump animation clip)

   ❑ **Transition Duration**: 0.01

   ❑ **Interruption State**: Current State

26. Save and run your scene. Now when you jump the hat should animate once, after which the character immediately returns to its Idle state.

How it works...

You have added an Animation controller State Machine to GameObject **character2D**. The two Animation clips you created (idle and jump) appear as States in the Animator panel. You created a Transition from Idle to Jump when the 'Jump' Trigger parameter is received by the State Machine. You created a second Transition, which transitions back to the Idle state after waiting 0.5 seconds (the same duration between the 2 keyframes in our Jump Animation clip).

Note that the key to everything working for the bean-man character is that when we make the character jump with the *SPACE* key, then code in the PlayerControl C# scripted component of GameObject **character2D**, as well as making the sprite move upwards on screen, also sends a SetTrigger(...) message to the Animator controller component, for the **Trigger** named **Jump**.

The difference between a **Boolean** Parameter and a **Trigger** is that a **Trigger** is temporality set to True and once the SetTrigger(...) event has been 'consumed' by a state transition it automatically returns to being False. So Triggers are useful for actions we wish to do once and then revert to a previous state. A **Boolean** Parameter is a variable, which can have its value set to true/or False at different times during the game, and so different Transitions can be created to fire depending on the value of the variable at any time. Note that **Boolean** parameters have to have their values explicitly set back to False with a SetBool(...).

The following screenshot highlights the line of code that sends the `SetTrigger(...)` message:

```
PlayerControl.cs
No selection
69        // If the player should jump...
70        if(jump)
71        {
72            // Set the Jump animator trigger parameter.
73            anim.SetTrigger("Jump");
74
75            // Add a vertical force to the player.
```

State Machines for animations of a range of motions (running/walking/jumping/falling/dying and so on.) will have more states and transitions. The Unity-provided bean-man character has a more complex **State Machine**, and more complex animations (of hands and feet, and eyes and hat and so on, for each **Animation** clip), which you may find useful to explore.

Learn more about the Animation view on the Unity Manual web pages at `http://docs.unity3d.com/Manual/AnimationEditorGuide.html`.

Creating a 3-frame animation clip to make a platform continually animate

In this recipe, we'll make a wooden-looking platform continually animate, moving upwards and downwards. This can be achieved with a single, 3-frame, animation clip (starting at top, position at bottom, top position again).

Getting ready

This recipe builds on the previous one, so make a copy of that project, and work on the copy for this recipe.

How to do it...

To create a continually moving animated platform, follow these steps:

1. Drag an instance of the sprite **platformWoodBlocks** from the **Project | Sprites** folder into the scene. Position this GameObject at (-4, -5, 0), so that these wood blocks are neatly to left, and slightly below, the wall blocks platform.

2. Add a Box Collider 2D component to GameObject **platformWoodBlocks** so that the player's character can stand on this platform too. Choose menu: **Add Component | Physics 2D | Box Collider 2D**.

3. Create a new folder named `Animations`, in which to store the animation clip and controller we'll create next.

4. Ensuring GameObject **platformWoodBlocks** is still selected in the **Hierarchy**, open an **Animation** panel, and ensure it is in **Dope Sheet** view (this is the default).

5. Click the empty dropdown menu in the **Animation** panel (next to the greyed out word 'Samples'), and choose menu item **[Create New Clip]**.

6. Save the new clip in your **Animations** folder, naming it '**platform-wood-moving-up-down**'.

7. Click button **Add Curve**, and chose **Transform** and the click the '**+**' plus-sign by **Position**. We are now recording changes to the (X, Y, Z) position of GameObject **platformWoodBlocks** in this animation clip.

8. You should now see 2 'keyframes' at 0.0 and at 1.0. These are indicated by diamonds in the **Timeline** area in the right-hand-section of the **Animation** panel.

9. We need 3 keyframes, with the new one at **2:00** seconds. Click at **2:00** in the Timeline along the top of the **Animation** panel, so that the red line for the current playhead time is at time 2:00. Then click diamond+ button to create a new keyframe at the current playhead time:

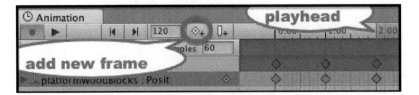

10. The first and third keyframes are fine – they record the current height of the wood platform at Y= - 5. We need to make the middle keyframe record the height of the platform at the top of its motion, and Unity in-betweening will do all the rest of the animation work for us. Select the middle keyframe (at time 1:00), by clicking on either diamond at time 1:00 (they should both turn blue, and the red playhead vertical line should move to 1:00, to indicate the middle keyframe is being edited).

11. Now in the **Inspector** change the Y position of the platform to 0. You should see that all three X, Y, Z values have a red background in the **Inspector** – this is to inform you that the values of the **Transform** component are being recorded in the animation clip.

12. Save and run your scene. The wooden platform should now be animating continuously, moving smoothly up and down the positions we setup.

How it works...

You have added an animation to GameObject **platformWoodBlocks**. This animation contains three keyframes. A keyframe represents the values of properties of the object at a point in time. The first keyframe stores a Y-value of -4, the second keyframe a Y-value of 0, and the final keyframe -4 again. Unity calculates all the in-between values for us, and the result is a smooth animation of the Y-position of the platform.

 Note: If we wanted to duplicate the moving platform, first we'd need to create a new, empty GameObject named movingBlockParent, and then parent platformWoodBlocks to this GameObject. Duplicating GameObject movingBlockParent would then allow us to create more moving blocks in our scene. If we simply duplicated platformWoodBlocks directly, then when the scene runs each duplicate would be animated back to the location of the original animation frames (that is, all copies would be positioned and moving in the original location).

Making a platform start falling once stepped-on using a Trigger to move animation from one state to another

In many cases we don't wish an animation to begin until some condition has been met, or some event occurred. In these cases a good way to organize the Animator Controller is to have two animation states (clips) and a Trigger on the Transition between the clips. We use code to detect when we wish the animation to start playing, and at that time we send the Trigger message to the Animation Controller, causing the transition to start.

In this recipe we'll create a water platform block in our 2D platform game; such blocks will begin to slowly fall down the screen as soon as they have been stepped on, and so the player must keep on moving otherwise they'll fall down the screen with the blocks too! It looks as shown in the following screenshot:

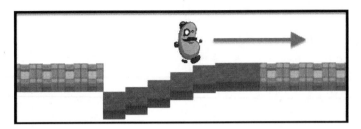

Getting ready

This recipe builds on the previous one, so make a copy of that project, and work on the copy for this recipe.

How to do it...

To construct an animation that only plays once a Trigger has been received, follow these steps:

1. In the **Hierarchy** create an **Empty** GameObject named **water-block-container**, positioned at (2.5, -4, 0). This empty GameObject will allow us to make duplicates of animated Water Blocks that will animate relative to their parent GameObject position.

2. Drag an instance of the sprite **Water Block** from the **Project | Sprites** folder into the scene and child it to GameObject **water-block-container**. Ensure the position of your new child GameObject **Water Block** is (0, 0, 0), so that it appears neatly to right of the wall blocks platform, as shown in the following screenshot:

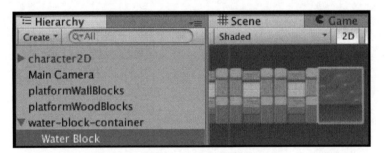

3. Add a **Box Collider 2D** component to child GameObject **Water Block**, and set the layer of this GameObject to **Ground**, so that the player's character can stand and jump on this water block platform.

4. Ensuring child GameObject **Water Block** is selected in the **Hierarchy**, open an **Animation** panel, then create a new clip named **platform-water-up**. saving it in your `Animations` folder.

5. Click button **Add Curve**, and chose **Transform** and **Position**.

6. Delete the second keyframe at time **1:00**. You have now completed the creation of the water block up animation clip.

7. Create a second Animation clip, named **platform-water-down**. Again, click button **Add Curve**, and chose **Transform** and **Position**, and delete the second keyframe at time **1:00**.

8. With the first keyframe at time **0:00** selected, set the Y-value of the GameObjects Transform Position to `-5`. You have now completed the creation of the water block down animation clip, so you can click the red record button to stop recording.

9. You may have noticed that as well as the up/down **Animation Clips** that you created, another file was created in your `Animations` folder, an **Animator Controller** named **Water Block**. Select this file and open the **Animator** panel, to see and edit the State Machine diagram:

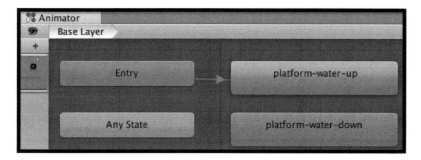

10. Currently, although we created 2 animation clips (states), only the **Up** state is ever active. This is because when the scene begins (Entry) the object will immediately go in state **platform-water-up**, but since there are no transition arrows from this state to **platform-water-down**, then at present the **Water Block** GameObject will always be in its **Up** state.

11. Ensure state **platform-water-up** is selected (it will have a blue border around it), and create a Transition (arrow) to state **platform-water-down**, by choosing **Make Transition** from the **mouse-right-click** menu.

12. If you run the scene now, the default **Transition** settings are that after 0.9 seconds the **Water Blocks** will transition into their **Down** state. We don't want this – we only want them to animate downwards after the player has walked onto them. So create a **Trigger** named **Fall**, by choosing the **Parameters** tab in the **Animator** panel, clicking the plus '**+**' button and selecting **Trigger**, and then selecting **Fall**.

13. Do the following to create our Trigger:

□ In the **Animator** panel select the **Transition**

□ In the **Inspector** panel uncheck the **Has Exit Time** option

□ In the **Inspector** panel drag the Transition end time to **2:00** seconds (so the Water Block slowly Transitions to its Down state over a period of 2 seconds)

□ In the **Inspector** panel click the plus '**+**' button to add a **Condition**, which should automatically suggest the only possible condition parameter, which is our **Trigger Fall**.

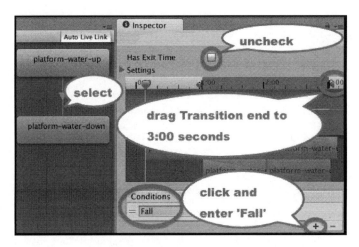

14. We now need to add a collider trigger just above the Water Block, and add C# script behavior to send the **Animator Controller Trigger** when the player enters the collider. Ensuring child GameObject **Water Block** is selected, add a (second) **2D Box Collider**, with a Y-Offset of **1**, and tick its **Is Trigger** checkbox:

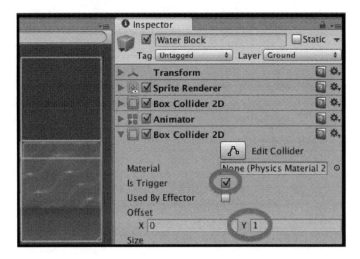

15. Add an instance of C# script class `WaterBlock` as a component to your **Water Block** child GameObject:

```csharp
using UnityEngine;
using System.Collections;

public class WaterBlock : MonoBehaviour {
  private Animator animatorController;

  void Start(){
    animatorController = GetComponent<Animator>();
  }

  void OnTriggerEnter2D(Collider2D hit){
    if(hit.CompareTag("Player")){
      animatorController.SetTrigger("Fall");
    }
  }
}
```

16. Make 6 more copies of GameObject **water-block-container**, with X positions increasing by 1 each time, that is, `3.5`, `4.5`, `5.5`, and so on.

17. Run the scene, and as the player's character runs across each water block they will start falling down, so he had better keep running!

How it works...

You created a two-state **Animator Controller** state machine. Each state was an **Animation Clip**. You created a **Transition** from the **Water Block** Up state to its Down state that will take place when the Animator Controller received a Fall Trigger message. You created a **Box Collider 2D** with a **Trigger**, so that scripted component WaterBlock could be detected when the player (tagged **Player**) enters its collider, and at that point send the **Fall** Trigger message to make the **Water Block** GameObject start gently Transitioning into its Down state further down the screen.

Learn more about the Animator Controllers on the Unity Manual web pages at `http://docs.unity3d.com/Manual/class-AnimatorController.html`.

Creating animation clips from sprite sheet sequences

The traditional method of animation involved hand-drawing many images, each slightly different, which displayed quickly frame-by-frame to give the appearance of movement. For computer game animation, the term Sprite Sheet is given to the image file that contains one or more sequences of sprite frames. Unity provides tools to breakup individual sprite images in large sprite sheet files, so that individual frames, or sub-sequences of frames can be used to create Animation Clips that can become States in Animator Controller State Machines. In this recipe, we'll import and break up an open source monster sprite sheet into three animation clips for Idle, Attack, and Death that looks as shown:

Getting ready

For all the recipes in this chapter, we have prepared the sprite images you need in folder `1362_03_05`. Many thanks to Rosswet Mobile for making these sprites available as Open Source at: `http://www.rosswet.com/wp/?p=156`.

How to do it...

To create an animation from a sprite sheet of frame-by-frame animation images, follow these steps:

1. Create a new Unity 2D project.

2. Import the provided image `monster1`.

3. With image `monster1` selected in the **Project** panel, change its **Sprite** mode to **Multiple** in the **Inspector**, then open the **Sprite Editor** panel by clicking button **Sprite Editor**.

4. In the **Sprite Editor** open the **Slice** dropdown dialog, set the **Type** to **Grid**, set the grid **Pixel Size** to **64x64**, and then click the **Slice** button. Finally, click the **Apply** button in the bar at the top right of the **Sprite Editor** panel):

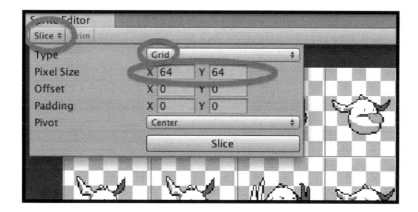

5. In the **Project** panel you can now click the expand triangle button center-right on the sprite, and you'll see all the different child frames for this sprite.

6. Create a folder named `Animations`.

7. In your new folder, create an **Animator Controller** named **monster-animator**.

8. In the scene create a new **Empty** GameObject named **monster1** (at position 0, 0, 0), and drag your **monster-animator** into this GameObject.

9. With GameObject **monster1** selected in the **Hierarchy**, open up the **Animation** panel, and create a new **Animation Clip** named **Idle**.

10. Select image `monster1` in the **Project** panel (in its expanded view), and select and drag the first 5 frames (frames 0-4) into the **Animation** panel. Change the sample rate to 12 (since this animation was created to run at 12-frames per second).

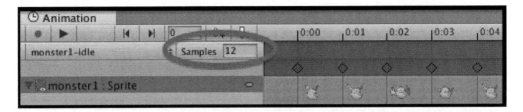

11. If you look at the State Chart for **monster-animator**, you'll see it has a default state (clip) named monster-idle.

12. When you run your scene you should now see the **monster1** GameObject animating in its monster-idle state. You may wish to make the Main Camera size a bit smaller, since these are quite small sprites.

How it works...

Unity's Sprite Editor knows about sprite sheets, and once the correct grid size has been entered it treats the items in each grid square inside the sprite sheet image as an individual image, or frame, of the animation. You selected sub-sequences of sprite animation frames and added them into several **Animation Clips**. You had added an **Animation Controller** to your GameObject, and so each **Animation Clip** appears as a state in the **Animation Controller State Machine**.

You can now repeat the process, creating an **Animation Clip** monster-attack with frames 8-12, and a third clip monster-death with frames 15-21. You would then create Triggers and **Transitions** to make the monster GameObject transition into the appropriate **states** as the game is played.

Learn more about the Unity Sprite Editor from the Unity video tutorials at `https://unity3d.com/learn/tutorials/modules/beginner/2d/sprite-editor`.

Conclusion

In this chapter, we have introduced recipes demonstrating the animation system for 2D game elements. The bean-man 2D character is from the Unity 2D Platformer, which you can download yourself from the Unity asset store. That project is a good place to see lots more examples of 2D game and animation techniques (`www.assetstore.unity3d.com/en/#!/content/11228`).

Here are some links for useful resources and sources of information to explore these topics further:

- Unity 2D Platformer (where the BeanMan character came from):

  `https://www.assetstore.unity3d.com/en/#!/content/11228`

- The platform sprites are from Daniel Cook's Planet Cute game resources:

  `http://www.lostgarden.com/2007/05/dancs-miraculously-flexible-game.html`

- Creating a basic 2D platformer game:

  `https://www.unity3d.com/learn/tutorials/modules/beginner/live-training-archive/creating-a-basic-platformer-game`

- Hat Catch 2D game tutorial:

  `https://www.unity3d.com/learn/tutorials/modules/beginner/live-training-archive/2d-catch-game-pt1`

- Unity games from a 2D perspective video:

  `https://www.unity3d.com/learn/tutorials/modules/beginner/live-training-archive/introduction-to-unity-via-2d`

- A fantastic set of modular 2D characters with a free Creative Commons license from 'Kenny'. These assets would be perfect for animating body parts in a similar way to the bean-man example in this chapter and in the Unity 2D platformer demo:

  `http://kenney.nl/assets/modular-characters`

4

Creating Maps and Materials

In this chapter, we will cover the following topics:

- ▸ Creating a basic material with Standard Shader (Specular setup)
- ▸ Adapting a basic material from Specular setup to Metallic
- ▸ Applying Normal maps to a material
- ▸ Adding Transparency and Emission maps to a material
- ▸ Highlighting materials at mouse-over
- ▸ Adding Detail maps to a material
- ▸ Fading the transparency of a material
- ▸ Playing videos inside a scene

Introduction

Unity 5 introduces in new **Physically-Based Shaders**. Physically-Based Rendering is a technique that simulates the appearance of materials based on how the light reacts with that material (more specifically, the *matter* from which that material is made) in the real world. Such a technique allows for more realistic and consistent materials. So, your creations in Unity should look better than ever. Creating materials in Unity has also become more efficient now. Once you have chosen between the available workflows (**Metallic** or **Specular setup**; we'll get back to that later), there is no longer the need to browse the drop-down menus in search of specific features, as Unity optimizes the shader for the created material, removing unnecessary code for unused properties once the material has been set up and the texture maps have been assigned.

For a deep understanding of Physically-Based Rendering, we recommend you to take a look at *The Comprehensive PBR Guide*, written by Wes McDermott from Allegorithmic, freely available in two volumes at `http://www.allegorithmic.com/pbr-guide`. Allegorithmic's guide contains invaluable information on PBR theory and techniques, having been a fundamental reference for this chapter. A great resource that we'd recommend you take a look at is *Mastering Physically Based Shading in Unity 5* by Renaldas Zioma (Unity), Erland Körner (Unity), and Wes McDermott (Allegorithmic), available at `http://www.slideshare.net/RenaldasZioma/unite2014-mastering-physically-based-shading-in-unity-5`.

Another resource is *Physically Based Shading in Unity* by Aras Pranckevičius (Unity), available at `http://aras-p.info/texts/files/201403-GDC_UnityPhysicallyBasedShading_notes.pdf`.

Creating and saving texture maps

The visual aspects of a material can be modified through the use of textures. In order to create and edit image files, you will need an image editor such as Adobe Photoshop (the industry standard, and has its native format supported by Unity), GIMP, and so on. In order to follow the recipes in this chapter, it's strongly recommended that you have access to a few pieces of software like these.

When saving texture maps, especially the ones that have an Alpha Channel, you might want to choose an adequate file format. **PSD**, Photoshop's native format, is practical for preserving the original artwork in many layers. The PNG format is also a great option, but please note that Photoshop doesn't handle PNG's Alpha channel independently of the transparency, possibly compromising the material's appearance. Also, PNG files don't support layers. For this chapter, we will often use the TIF format for three main reasons: (a) it's open to those not using Photoshop; (b) it uses layers; (c) it preserves the Alpha Channel information. The file size is significantly greater than in PSDs and PNGs, so feel free to save your work as PSDs (if you have Photoshop) or PNGs (if you don't need layers and, if using Photoshop, Alpha Channels).

Finally, a word of advice - although it's possible to manually create texture maps for our materials by using the traditional image editing software, new tools such as Allegorthmic's Substance Painter and Bitmap2Material make this work much more efficient, complete, and intuitive, complementing the traditional texture-making process or replacing it altogether - in a similar way to what zBrush and Mudbox did for 3D modeling. For design professionals, we strongly recommend at least trying such tools. Note, however, that products from Allegorithmic won't make use of Unity's Standard Shader, relying on the **substance** files (which are natively supported by Unity).

The big picture

To understand the new Standard Shaders, it's a good idea to know the workflows, their properties, and how they affect the material's appearance. There are, however, many possible ways to work with materials - texture map requirements, for instance, might change from engine to engine, or from one tool to another. Presently, Unity supports two different workflows: one based on Specular, and another based on Metallic values. Although both workflows share similar properties (such as Normal, Height, Occlusion, and Emission), they differ in the way the diffuse color and reflectance properties are set up.

Specular workflow

Unity's Standard Shader (Specular setup) uses Albedo and Specular/Smoothness maps, combining them to create some of the material's aspect—mainly its color and reflectance qualities. The following shows the difference between Albedo and Smoothness maps:

- **Albedo**: This is the material's diffused color. Plainly and simply, this is how you usually describe the appearance of the material (the British flag is red, white and blue; Ferrari's logo is a black horse in a yellow setting; some sunglasses' lenses are semi-transparent gradients, and more). This description, however, can be deceptive. Purely metallic objects (such as aluminum, chrome, gold, and others) should have black as their diffuse color. Their colors, as we perceive them, have originated from their specular channel. Non-metallic objects (plastic, wood, and even painted or rusted metal), on the other hand, do have very distinct diffuse colors. Texture maps for the Albedo property feature RGB channels for colors and (optionally) an Alpha Channel for transparency.

- **Specular/Smoothness**: This refers to the shininess of the material. Texture maps make use of RGB channels for specular color (which informs hue and intensity), and Alpha Channel for smoothness/gloss (dark values for less shiny surfaces and blurred reflections; light/white values for shiny, mirror-like appearance). It is important to note that non-metallic objects feature neutral, very dark specular colors (with plastic, for instance, you should work with a grey value around 59). Metallic objects, on the other hand, feature very light values, and are also a bit yellowish in hue.

To illustrate such concepts, we have created a battery object (shown below), featuring brushed metal caps and a plastic body. Observe how each map contributes to the final result:

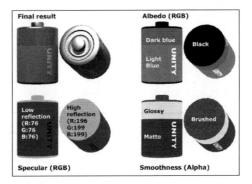

The metallic workflow

Unity's default Standard Shader combines Albedo and Metallic/Glossiness maps to create the color and reflectance qualities of the material. The following are the differences:

- **Albedo**: As in the Specular workflow, this is the material's diffuse color; how you would describe the material. However, Albedo maps for the Metallic workflow should be configured in a slightly different way than ones for Specular workflow. This time around, the perceived diffuse color of metallic materials (grey for iron, yellow/ orange for golden, and so on) have to be present in the Albedo map. Again, Albedo maps feature RGB channels for the colors and (optionally) an Alpha channel for transparency.

- **Metallic/Smoothness**: This refers to how metallic the material looks. Metallic texture maps make use of the Red channel for the Metallic value (black for non-metallic and white for metallic materials that are not painted or rusted) and the Alpha Channel for smoothness (in a similar way to the Specular workflow). Please note that Metallic maps do not include any information on hue, and in these cases the yellow-ish nature of the metallic gloss should be applied to the Albedo map.

To reproduce the battery that illustrated the Specular workflow by using the Metallic workflow, maps would have to be recreated as follows:

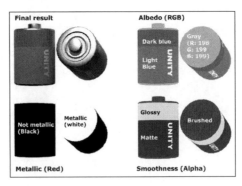

You might have noticed that we've used white to convey a metallic object. Technically, since only the Red channel is relevant, we could have used red (R: 255, G: 0, B: 0), yellow (R: 255, G: 255, B: 0) or, for that matter, any color that has a red value of 255.

Other material properties

It's also worth mentioning that Unity's Standard Shaders support other maps such as:

- **Normal maps**: The normal map adds detailed bumpiness into the material, simulating a more complex geometry. For instance, the internal ring on the positive (top) node of the battery that illustrated shader workflows is not modeled in the 3D object's geometry, but rather created through a simple normal map.

- **Occlusion maps**: A greyscale map is used to simulate the dark sections of an object under ambient light. Usually, it is used to emphasize joints, creases, and other details of geometry.

- **Height maps**: These add a displacement effect, giving the impression of depth without the need for complex geometry.

- **Emission maps**: These add color emitted by the material, as if self-illuminated, such as fluorescent surfaces or LCDs. Texture maps for Emission feature RGB channels for color.

Unity samples and documentation

Before you start, it might be a good idea to read Unity's documentation on textures. It can be found online at `http://unity3d.com/support/documentation/Manual/Textures.html`.

Finally, Unity has put together a great resource for those looking for some pointers regarding how to set up maps for a variety of materials: the **Shader Calibration Scene**, which can be downloaded (for free) from the Unity Asset Store. It is a fantastic collection, featuring sample materials (both Metallic and Specular setup) for wood, metal, rubber, plastic, glass, skin, mud, and much more.

Creating a basic material with Standard Shader (Specular setup)

In this recipe, we will learn how to create a basic material using the new Standard Shader (Specular Setup), an Albedo map, and a Specular/Smoothness map. The material will feature both metallic and non-metallic parts, with various smoothness levels.

Getting ready

Two files have been prepared to support this recipe: a 3D model (in FBX format) of a battery, and an UVW template texture (in PNG format) to guide us when creating the diffuse texture map. 3D models and UVW templates can be made with 3D modeling software, such as 3DS MAX, Maya, or Blender. All necessary files are available in the `1362_04_01` folder.

How to do it...

To create a basic material, follow these steps:

1. Import the `battery.FBX` and `uvw_template.png` files to your project.

2. Place the **battery** model in the scene by dragging it from the **Assets** folder, in the **Project** view, to the **Hierarchy** view. Select it on the **Hierarchy** view and make sure, via the **Transform** component on the **Inspector** view, that it is positioned at **X: 0, Y: 0, Z: 0**.

3. Now, let's create a Specular/Smoothness map for our object. Open the image file called `uvw_template.png` in your image editor (we'll use Adobe Photoshop to illustrate the next steps). Note that the image file has only a single layer, mostly transparent, containing the UVW mapping templates that we will use as guidelines for our specular map.

4. Create a new layer and place it beneath the one with the guidelines. Fill the new layer with dark gray (**R: 56, G: 56, B: 56**). The guidelines will be visible at the top of the solid black fill:

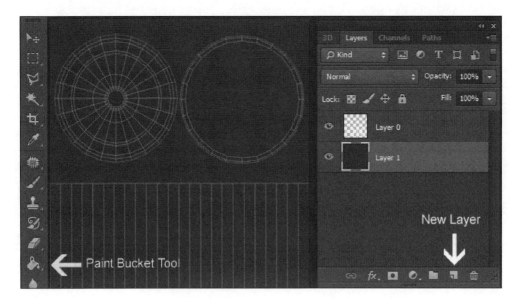

5. Create a new layer and select the upper section of the image (the one with the circles). Then, fill that area with a slightly hued light gray (**R: 196**, **G: 199**, **B: 199**):

 The RGB values for our specular map are not arbitrary: Physically-Based Shading takes out most of the guesswork from the mapping process, replacing it with the research for references. In our case, we have used colors based on the reflectance values of iron (the slightly hued light gray) and plastic (the dark gray). Check out the chapter's conclusion for a list of references.

6. Use the text elements in white to add a brand, size, and positive/negative indicators to the battery body. Then, hide the guidelines layer.

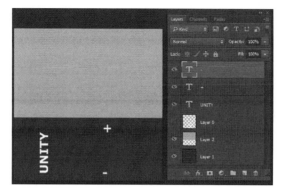

7. Select all your layers and organize them into a group (in Photoshop, this can be done by clicking on the drop-down menu in the **Layers** window and navigating to **Window | New Group from Layers...**). Name the new group `Specular`:

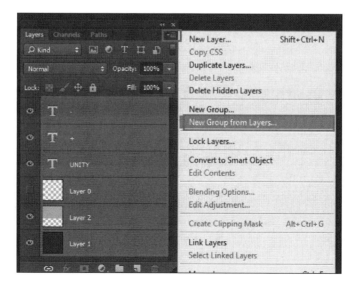

8. Duplicate the `Specular` group (in the **Layers** window, right-click on the group's name and select **Duplicate Group...**). Name the duplicated group `Smoothness`.

9. Hide the `Smoothness` group. Then, expand the `Specular` group and hide all text layers:

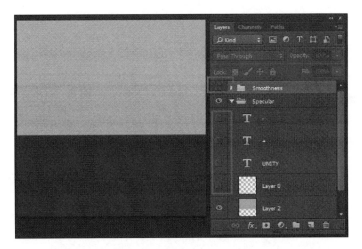

10. Unhide the `Smoothness` group, and hide the `Specular` group. Select the dark gray layer. Then, make an area selection around the upper region of the battery body, and fill it with light gray (**R: 220**, **G: 220**, **B: 220**). Rescale and rearrange the **Text** layers if needed:

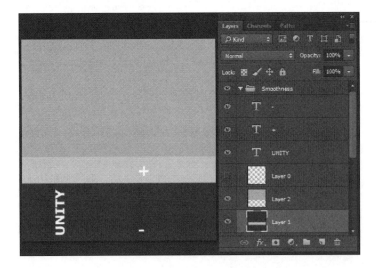

11. Duplicate the layer that contains the gray fill for the upper section of the image (the one that went over the circles).

12. To add a brushed quality to this material, add a **Noise** filter to the duplicated layer (in Photoshop, this can be done by navigating to **Filter | Noise | Add Noise...**). Use **50%** as the **Amount** and set **Monochromatic** to `true`. Then, apply a **Motion Blur** filter (**Filter | Blur | Motion Blur...**) using **30 Pixels** as the **Distance**.

13. Duplicate the `Smoothness` group. Then, select the duplicated group and merge it into a single layer (on the **Layers** window, right-click on the group's name and select **Merge Group**).

14. Select the merged layer, use the *CTRL + A* key combination to select the entire image, and copy it using the *CTRL + C* keys:

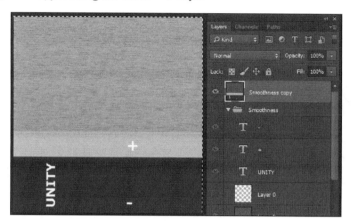

15. Hide the merged layer and the `Smoothness` group. Then, unhide the `Specular` group.

16. In your image editor, access the image channels window (in Photoshop, this can be done by navigating to **Window | Channels**). Create a **New Channel**. This will be our **Alpha** Channel.

17. Paste the image that you previously copied (from the merged layer) in to the **Alpha** Channel. Then, set all channels as `visible`:

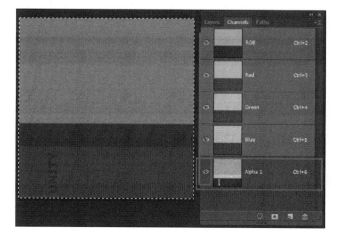

18. Save your image in the Project's **Assets** folder as `Battery_specular`, either in Photoshop format (PSD) or TIF format.

19. Now, let's work on the Albedo map. Save a copy of `Battery_specular` as `Battery_albedo`. Then, from the **Channels** window, delete the **Alpha** Channel.

20. From the **Layers** window, hide the `Smoothness copy` merged layer, and unhide the `Smoothness` group. Finally, expand the `Smoothness` group, and hide the layer where the **Noise** filter was applied:

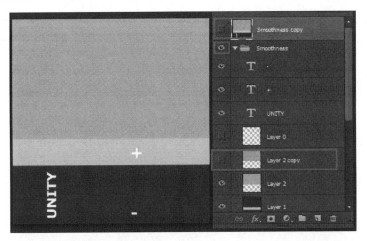

21. Change the color of the upper rectangle to black. Then, change the light gray area to dark red (**R: 204**, **G: 0**, **B: 0**), and the dark gray to red (**R: 255**, **G: 0**, **B: 0**). Rename the group `Albedo` and save the file:

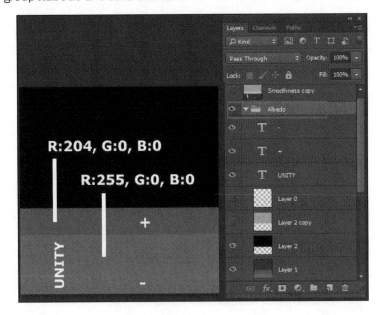

22. Go back to Unity and make sure that both files were imported. Then, from the **Project** view, create a new **Material**. Name it `Battery_MAT`.

 An easy way to create new materials is to access the **Project** view, click on the **Create** drop-down menu, and choose **Material**.

23. Select `Battery_MAT`. From the **Inspector** view, change the Shader to **Standard (Specular setup),** and make sure that the rendering mode is set to **Opaque**.

24. Set `Battery_specular` as the **Specular** map, and `Battery_albedo` as the **Albedo** map for `Battery_MAT`.

25. Drag the `Battery_MAT` material from the **Project** view and drop it into the **battery** object in the **Hierarchy** view:

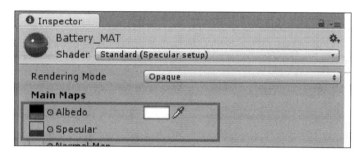

26. Drag the `Battery_MAT` material from the **Project** view and, in the **Hierarchy** view, drop it into the **battery** object:

How it works...

Ultimately, the visual aspect of the battery is a combination of three properties of its material: Specular, Smoothness, and Albedo.

To compose the dark red part of the plastic body, for instance, we have mixed the following:

- ▸ **The Specular** map (RGB): Very dark grey specularity (for non-metallic appearance)
- ▸ **The Smoothness** (the Alpha channel of the Specular map): Light gray (for a glossy aspect)
- ▸ **The Albedo** map: Dark red (for a dark red color)

The light red portion, on the other hand, combines the following:

- ▸ **The Specular** map (RGB): That same dark grey specular
- ▸ **The Smoothness** (the Alpha Channel of the Specular map): Dark gray (for a matte aspect)
- ▸ **The Albedo** map: Red (for a red color)

Finally, the brushed metal used for the top and bottom covers combines the following:

- ▸ **The Specular** map (RGB): Light grey (for a metallic aspect)
- ▸ **The Smoothness** (the Alpha Channel of the Specular map): A blurred grey noise pattern (for a brushed aspect)
- ▸ **The Albedo** map: Black (for a red color)

Regarding how the image layers are structured, it's good practice to organize your layers into groups named after the property that they are related to. As texture maps get more diversified, it can be a good idea to keep a file that contains all the maps for quick reference and consistency.

There's more...

A few things you should have in mind when working with Albedo maps are as follows.

Setting the texture type for an image file

Since image files can be used for several purposes within Unity (texture maps, GUI textures, cursors, and more), it's a good idea to check if the right **Texture Type** is assigned to your file. This can be done by selecting the image file in the **Project** view, and in the **Inspector** view by using the drop-down menu to select the right **Texture Type** (in this case, `Texture`). Please note that other settings can be adjusted, such as **Wrap Mode**, **Filter Mode**, and **Maximum Size**. This last parameter is very useful if you want to keep your texture maps small in size for your game, while still being able to edit them in full size.

Combining the map with color

When editing a material, the color picker to the right of the **Albedo** map slot, on the **Inspector** view, can be used to select the material's color, in case there is no texture map. If a texture map is being used, the selected color will be multiplied to the image, allowing variations on the material's color hue.

Adapting a basic material from Specular setup to Metallic

For a better understanding of the differences between Metallic and Specular workflows, we will modify the Albedo and Specular/Smoothness maps that are used on a Specular setup material, in order to adapt them to the Metallic workflow. The material to be generated will feature both metallic and non-metallic parts, with various smoothness levels.

Getting ready

For this recipe, we have prepared a Unity package containing a battery model and its original material (made with Standard Shader—Specular setup). The package includes two image files for the original Albedo and Specular/Smoothness maps which, throughout the recipe, should be adapted for use with the Metallic setup. The package is available in the `1362_04_02` folder.

How to do it...

To create a basic material, follow these steps:

1. Import the `battery_prefab` Unity package into a new project.

2. From the **Project** view, select the **battery_prefab** element. Then, from **Inspector**, access its material (named **Battery_MAT**) and change its **Shader** to **Standard** (as opposed to its current shader—**Standard (Specular setup)**.

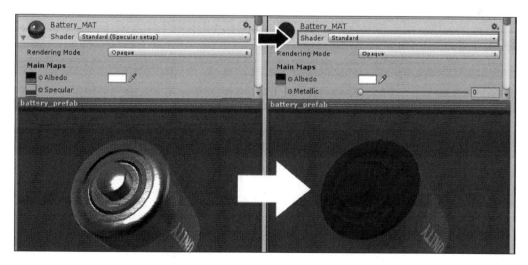

3. From the **Project** view, find the `Battery_specular` map and rename it `Battery_metallic`. Open it in your image editor (we'll use Adobe Photoshop to illustrate the following steps).

4. Find the layer group named **Specular** and rename it **Metallic**. Then, fill the light gray layer (named **Layer 2**, in the **Metallic** group) with white (**R: 255, G: 255, B: 255**), and the dark gray layer (named **Layer 1**, in the **Metallic** group) with black (**R: 0, G: 0, B: 0**). Save the file:

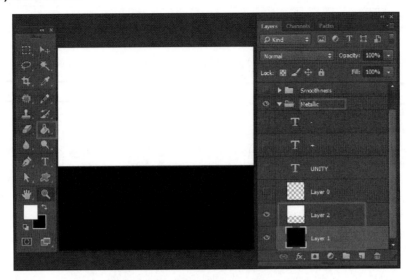

5. Go back to Unity. From the **Inspector** view, set the modified **Battery_metallic** map as the **Metallic** map of the **Battery_MAT** material. Also, set **None** as the **Albedo** map for that material. This will give you an idea of how the material is coming along:

6. Now, let's adjust the Albedo texture map. From the **Project** view, locate the `Battery_albedo` map and open it in your image editor. Then, use the **Paint Bucket** tool to fill the black area of **Layer 2**, in the **Albedo** group, with light gray (R: 196, G: 199, B: 199). Save the file:

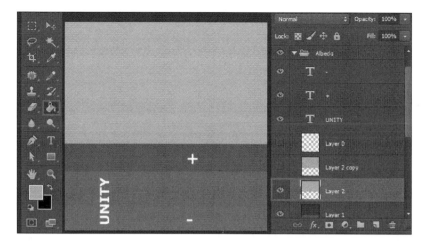

7. Go back to Unity. From the **Inspector** view, set the modified **Battery_albedo** map as the **Albedo** map of the **Battery_MAT** material.

Your material is ready, combining visual properties based on the different maps that you have edited and assigned.

How it works...

The visual aspect of the battery is a combination of three properties of its material: Metallic, Smoothness, and Albedo.

To compose the dark red part of the plastic body, for instance, we have mixed the following:

- **The Metallic** map (RGB): Black (for a non-metallic appearance)
- **The Smoothness** (the Alpha Channel of a Metallic map): Light gray (for a glossy appearance)
- **The Albedo** map: Dark red (for a dark red color)

The light red portion, on the other hand, combines the following:

▸ **The Metallic** map (RGB): Black

▸ **The Smoothness** (the Alpha Channel of the Metallic map): dark gray (for a matte appearance)

▸ **Albedo** map: red (for a red color)

Finally, the brushed metal used for the top and bottom covers combines the following:

▸ **The Metallic** map (RGB): white (for a metallic aspect)

▸ **The Smoothness** (the Alpha Channel of the Metallic map): blurred grey noise pattern (for a brushed appearance);

▸ **Albedo** map: light grey (for an iron-like appearance)

Remember to organize your layers in to groups named after the property that they are related to.

Applying Normal maps to a material

Normal maps are generally used to simulate complex geometry that would be too expensive, in terms of computer processing, to be actually represented by the 3D polygons during the game's runtime. Oversimplifying, Normal maps fake complex geometry on low-definition 3D meshes. These maps can be generated either by projecting high-definition 3D meshes onto low-poly ones (a technique usually referred to as *baking*), or, as will be the case for this recipe, from another texture map.

Getting ready

For this recipe, we will prepare two texture maps: the **Heightmap** and the **Normal map**. The former will be made from simple shapes in an image editor. The latter will be automatically processed from the Heightmap. Although there are a number of tools that can be used to generate Normal maps (see the *There is more* section of this chapter for a list of resources), we will use a free online tool, Windows and Mac compatible, to generate our texture. Developed by Christian Petry, the **NormalMap Online** feature can be accessed at `http://cpetry.github.io/NormalMap-Online/`.

To help you with this recipe, it's been provided a Unity package, containing a prefab made of a 3D object and its material; and also an UVW template texture (in PNG format) to guide you when creating the diffuse texture map. All the files are in the `1362_04_03` folder.

How to do it...

To apply a Normal map to a material, follow these steps:

1. Import the `1362_04_03.unitypackage` file to your project. Select the `batteryPrefab` object from the **Assets** | `1362_04_03` folder, in the **Project** view. After comparing it with some reference photos, inform yourself about the features that should be reproduced by the Normal map: (**A**) a bumpy ring at the top; and (**B**) some circular creases at the bottom, shown in the following image:

2. In an image editor, open `uvw_template.png`. Create a new layer, fill it with grey (RGB: 128), and position it below the pre-existing layer as shown:

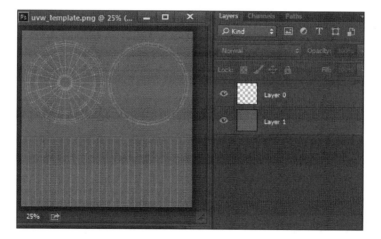

3. On a separate layer, draw a white circle centered on the battery's top. Then, on another layer, draw a black circle, centered on the battery's bottom, as shown below:

4. If you have used vector shapes to make the circles, rasterize their layers (in Adobe Photoshop, right-click on the layer's name and select the **Rasterize Layer** option from the context menu).

5. Blur the white circle (in Photoshop, this can be done by navigating to **Filter | Blur | Gaussian Blur...**). Use **4,0** pixels as the **Radius**.

6. Hide the UVW template layer and save the image as `Battery_height.png`.

7. If you want to convert the Heightmap directly from Unity, import it to your project. Select it from the **Project** view and, from the **Inspector** view, change its **Texture Type** to **Normal map**. Check the **Create from Grayscale** option, adjust **Bumpiness** and **Filtering** as you like, and click on **Apply** to save the changes:

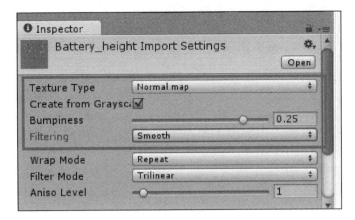

8. To convert your Heightmap externally, access the website at `http://cpetry.github.io/NormalMap-Online/`. Then, drag the `HEIGHT_battery.png` file to the appropriate image slot. Feel free to play with the **Strength**, **Level** and **Blur/Sharp** parameters:

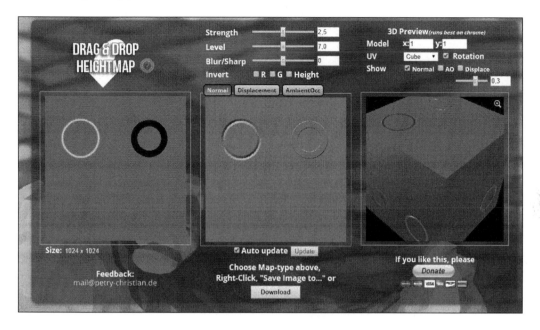

9. Save the resulting Normal map as `Battery_normal.jpg` and add it to your Unity project.

10. In Unity, select `Battery_normal` from the **Project** view. Then, from the **Inspector** view, change its **Texture Type** to **Normal**, leaving the **Create from Grayscale** box unchecked. Click on **Apply** to save the changes:

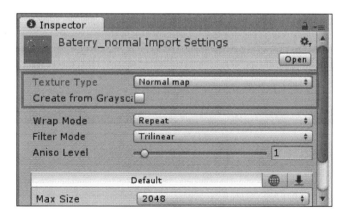

11. In the **Project** view, select `batteryPrefab`. Then, in the **Inspector** view, scroll down to the **Material** component, and assign `Battery_normal` to the **Normal Map** slot. To adjust its intensity and direction, change its value to `-0.35`:

How it works...

The **Normal** map was calculated from the grey values on the **Heightmap**, where the lighter tones were interpreted as recesses (applied to the top of the battery), and the darker tones as bulges (applied to the bottom). Since the desired output was actually the opposite, it was necessary to adjust the Normal map to a negative value (`-0.35`). Another possible solution to the issue would have been to redraw the Heightmap and switch the colors for the white and black circles.

There's more...

If you wish to explore Normal mapping beyond the limitations of NormalMap Online, there is an ever-growing list of full-featured software that can produce Normal maps (and much more). Here are some resources that you might want to check out:

▶ *CrazyBump* is a standalone tool for Windows and Mac, which is available at `http://www.crazybump.com`

▶ *nDo* is a Photoshop plugin by Quixel (Windows only), available at `http://quixel.se/ndo`

- ▶ *GIMP normalmap Plugin*, available for Windows only, is available at `http://code.google.com/p/gimp-normalmap/`
- ▶ *NVIDIA Texture Tools for Adobe Photoshop*, available for Windows only, is available at `http://developer.nvidia.com/nvidia-texture-tools-adobe-photoshop`
- ▶ *Bitmap2Material* is an amazing texture generating tool from Allegorithmic, which is available at `http://www.allegorithmic.com/`

Adding Transparency and Emission maps to a material

The **Emission** property can be used to simulate a variety of self-illuminated objects, from the LEDs of mobile displays to futuristic Tron suits. **Transparency**, on the other hand, can make the diffuse color of a material more or less visible. In this recipe, you will learn how to configure these properties to produce a toy's cardboard packaging that features a plastic case and glow-in-the-dark text.

Getting ready

For this recipe, we have prepared a Unity package containing a prefab made of a 3D object, its material, and its respective diffused texture map (in PNG format). All files are in the `1362_04_04` folder.

How to do it...

To add transparency and color emissions to a material, follow these steps:

1. Import `TransparencyEmission.unitypackage` to your project. Select the `DIFF_package` texture from the `Assets` folder, in the **Project** view. Then, open it in your image editor.

2. First, we will add transparency to the image by deleting the white areas around the package (and the hang hole). Make a selection of those areas (in Photoshop, this can be done with the **Magic Wand** Tool).

3. Make sure you unlock the **Background** layer by clicking on the lock icon, to the left of the layer's name, as shown below:

4. Delete the previously-made selection (this can be done in Photoshop by pressing the *Delete* key). The background of the image should be transparent, as shown below. Save the file:

5. Back in Unity, in the **Assets** folder, expand the **packagePrefab** list and select the **PackageCard** object. Now, in the **Inspector** view, scroll down to the **Material** component and change its **Rendering Mode** to **Cutout**, and adjust its **Alpha Cutoff** to 0.9:

 Choosing **Cutout** means that your material can be either invisible or fully visible, not allowing for semi-transparency. The **Alpha Cutoff** is used to get rid of unwanted pixels around the transparent borders.

6. From the expanded **packagePrefab**, select the **PackagePlastic** object. In the **Inspector** view, scroll down to the **Material** component and change its **Rendering Mode** to **Transparent**. Then, use the **Diffuse** color picker to change the color's **RGB** values to 56, and **Alpha** to 25. Also, change the **Smoothness** level to 0.9:

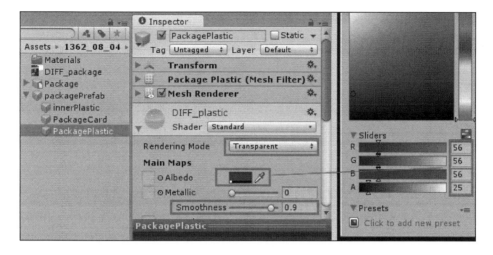

7. Now that we have taken care of our transparency needs, we need to work on the **Emission** map. From the **Assets** folder, duplicate the `DIFF_package` texture, rename it `EMI_package`, and open it in your image editor.

8. Select all the characters from the **Ms. Laser** inscription and the green star (in Photoshop, this can be done with the Magic Wand tool, keeping the *Shift* key pressed while selecting multiple areas).

9. Copy and paste your selection into a new layer. Then, select it and apply a Noise filter to it (in Photoshop, this can be done by navigating to **Filter | Noise | Add Noise...**). Use **50%** as the value.

10. Create a new layer and, using a tool such as the **Paint Bucket**, fill it with black (R: 0, G: 0, B: 0). Place this black layer beneath the one with the colored elements.

11. Flatten your image (in Photoshop this can be done by navigating to **Layer | Flatten Image**) and save your file:

12. Back in Unity, in the **Assets** folder, expand **packagePrefab** and select the **PackageCard** object. Now, in the **Inspector** view, scroll down to the **Material** component and assign the `EMI_package` texture to its **Emission** slot. Then, change the **Emission** color slot to white (**R**: 255; **G**: 255; **B**: 255), and turn down its intensity to `0.25`, as shown in the following screenshot. Also, change its **GI** option to **None**, so that its glow won't be added to the Lightmaps or influence the illumination in real time:

13. Place an instance of the **packagePrefab** in your scene and check out the results. Your material is ready:

How it works...

Unity is able to read four channels of a texture map: R (Red), G (Green), B (Blue) and A (Alpha). When set to `Transparent` or Cutout, the Alpha channel of the diffuse texture map sets the transparency of the material according to each pixel's brightness level (the **Cutout** mode will not render semi-transparency—only fully visible or invisible pixels). You might have noticed that we didn't add an Alpha channel—this is because Photoshop exports the PNG's Alpha map, based on its transparency. To help you visualize the Alpha map, the `1362_04_04` folder contains a `DIFF_packageFinal.TIF` file featuring an Alpha map that works exactly in the same way as the PNG file that we have generated:

Regarding the Emission texture map, Unity assigns its RGB colors to the material, combining them with the appropriate color selection slot, and also allowing adjustments to the intensity of that Emission.

There's more...

Let look at a little more information on Transparency and Emission.

Using texture maps with Transparent Mode

Please note that you can use a bitmap texture for the **Diffuse** map in the **Transparent** render mode. In this case, RGB values will be interpreted as the Diffuse color, while the Alpha will be used to determine that pixel's transparency (in this case, semi-transparent materials are allowed).

Avoiding issues with the semi-transparent objects

You might have noticed that the plastic case was made from two objects (**PackagePlastic** and **innerPlastic**). This was done to avoid z-sorting problems, where faces are rendered in front of other geometry when they should be behind it. Having multiple meshes instead of a single one allows these faces to be correctly sorted for rendering. Materials in the `Cutout` mode are not affected by this problem, though.

Emitting light over other objects

The **Emission** value can be used to calculate the material's light projection over other objects when using Lightmaps.

Highlighting materials at mouse over

Changing the color of an object at runtime can be a very effective way of letting players know that they can interact with it. This is very useful in a number of game *genres*, such as puzzles and point-and-click adventures, and it can also be used to create 3D user interfaces.

Getting ready

For this recipe, we'll use objects created directly in Unity. Alternatively, you can use any 3D model you like.

How to do it...

To highlight a material at mouse-over, follow these steps:

1. Create a new 3D project, and add a **Cube** to the scene (from the **Hierarchy** view, navigate to **Create | 3D Object | Cube**).

2. From the **Project** view, click the **Create** drop-down menu and choose **Material**. Name it `HighlightMaterial`.

3. Select **HighlightMaterial**, and, from the **Inspector** view, change its **Albedo** color to gray (R: 135, G: 135, B: 135), its **Emission** intensity to 1, as shown in the screenshot below, and it's **Emission** color to R: 1, G: 1, **B**: 1:

4. Assign **HighlightMaterial** to the **Cube** that you previously created.

5. From the **Project** view, click on the **Create** drop-down menu and choose **C# Script**. Rename it `HighlightObject` and open it in your editor.

6. Replace everything with the following code:

```
using UnityEngine;
using System.Collections;
public class HighlightObject : MonoBehaviour{
    private Color initialColor;
    public bool noEmissionAtStart = true;
    public Color highlightColor = Color.red;
    public Color mousedownColor = Color.green;

    private bool mouseon = false;
```

```
    private Renderer myRenderer;

    void Start() {
      myRenderer = GetComponent<Renderer>();
      if (noEmissionAtStart)
      initialColor = Color.black;
      else
      initialColor = myRenderer.material.GetColor("_EmissionColor");
    }

    void OnMouseEnter(){
      mouseon = true;
      myRenderer.material.SetColor("_
EmissionColor", highlightColor);
    }

    void OnMouseExit(){
      mouseon = false;
      myRenderer.material.SetColor("_EmissionColor",initialColor);
    }

    void OnMouseDown(){
      myRenderer.material.SetColor("_EmissionColor",
mousedownColor);
    }

    void OnMouseUp(){
      if (mouseon)
      myRenderer.material.SetColor("_EmissionColor",
highlightColor);
      else
      myRenderer.material.SetColor("_EmissionColor", initialColor);
    }
}
```

7. Save your script and attach it to the **Cube**.

8. Select the **Cube**, and, in the **Inspector** view, set the **Highlight Color** and **Mousedown Color** values to any colors that you would like:

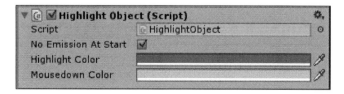

9. If you are using the script with your own imported 3D mesh, please make sure you add a **Collider** component to your object.

10. Test the scene. The **Cube** will be highlighted red when the mouse is over it (and green when clicked on).

How it works...

The cube is automatically sent the mouse enter/exit/down/up events as the user moves the mouse pointer over and away from the part of the screen where the cube is visible. Our script adds a behavior to the cube when these events are detected. The `Start()` method gets a reference to the `Renderer` component of the GameObject that the script has been added to, and stores it in the variable `myRenderer` (note that 'renderer' already has a meaning in Unity so it is not appropriate as a private variable name for this script). The Boolean variable called `mouseon` records whether or not the mouse pointer is currently over the object. When the mouse button is released, we use the `mouseon` variable to decide whether to change the cube back to its initial color (`mouseon` FALSE, so the mouse pointer is away from the cube), or back to its highlight color (`mouseon` TRUE, so the mouse pointer is over the cube).

The reason we needed to change the material's original **Emission** color to ultra, dark gray is that leaving it black would have caused Unity to optimize the Shader by removing the **Emission** property from the material. Our script wouldn't have worked if this had happened.

There's more...

You can achieve other interesting results by changing the other properties of your material (by changing the `_EmissionColor` script to `_Color` or `"_SpecularColor`, for instance). For a full list of properties, select your material, and, in the **Inspector** view, click on the **Edit** button, at the side of the **Shader** drop-down menu.

Adding Detail maps to a material

When creating a large object, there is not only the desire to texture it as a whole, but also to add details that can make it look better at closer distances. To overcome the need for gigantic texture maps, the use of Detail maps can make a real difference. In this recipe, we will add Detail maps to a rocket toy by applying a Detail mask and a Detail Normal map. In our case, we want to add a textured quality (and a stripe pattern) to the green plastic, except in the region where there is a battery compartment and the toy's logo:

Getting ready

For this recipe, we have prepared a Unity package, containing the prefab for a rocket toy. The prefab includes the 3D model and a material, featuring a Diffuse map and a Normal map (made from a Heightmap). The file can be found in the `1362_04_06` folder.

How to do it...

To add the Detail maps to your object, follow these steps:

1. Import the `rocket.unitypackage` file into your project. Then, select the prefab named `rocketToy` from the **Assets** folder, in the **Project** view, and place it in your scene.

2. From the **Hierarchy** view, expand the **rocketToy** GameObject and select its child called **rocketLevel1**. Then, scroll down the **Inspector** view to the **Material** component. Observe that it uses the `DIFF_ship` texture as the **Diffuse** map. Duplicate this file and rename the new copy `COPY_ship`.

3. Open `COPY_ship` in your image editor. Select all the solid green pixels around the logo and battery compartment (in Photoshop, this can be done with the Magic Wand tool, keeping the *Shift* key pressed while selecting multiple areas):

4. Keeping your selection active, access the image **Channels** window (in Photoshop, this can be done by navigating to **Window | Channels**). Click on **New Channel**. This will be our **Alpha** channel:

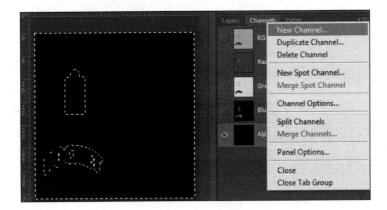

5. Hide the **Red**, **Green** and **Blue** channels. Select the **Alpha** channel and paint the selection white. Then, select the area of the battery compartment and paint it grey (R, G and B: 100):

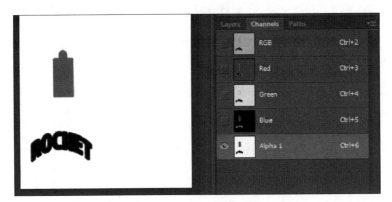

6. Save it in the TIFF format as MASK_ship.TIF, in the Assets folder. Make sure that you include **Alpha Channels**:

7. Now that we have the mask, let's create a diffuse map for our detail. In your image editor, create a new image with the following dimensions: **width**: 64, and **height**: 64.

8. Fill the new image with grey (R, G and B: `128`). Then, use shapes or rectangular fills to create a dark grey (R, G, and B: `100`) horizontal line that is about 16 pixels tall:

9. Save the image as `DIFF_detail`.`PNG` in the `Assets` folder.

10. Create a new 64 x 64 image. Use a **Gradient** tool to create a black and white **Radial Gradient** (in Photoshop, this can be done with the **Gradient** Tool in **Radial** mode):

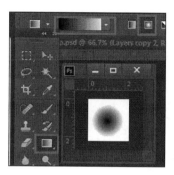

11. Save the image as `HEIGHT_detail`.`PNG` in the `Assets` folder.

12. Go back to Unity. From the `Assets` folder, select `HEIGHT_detail`. Then, from the **Inspector** view, change its **Texture Type** to **Normal map**, check the **Create from Grayscale** option, adjust **Bumpiness** to `0.25`, and set **Filtering** to `smooth`. Click on **Apply** to save the changes:

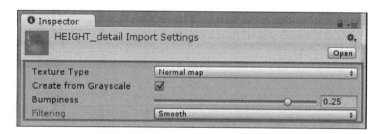

13. From the **Hierarchy** view, expand the **rocketToy** GameObject and select its child called **rocketLevel1**. Then, scroll down the **Inspector** view to the **Material** component. Assign `MASK_ship` to the **Detail Mask** slot; `DIFF_detail` as **Secondary Maps | Detail Diffuse x 2**; and `HEIGHT_detail` as **Secondary Maps | Normal Map**. Also, turn the **Normal Map** intensity down to `0.6`.

14. In the **Secondary Maps** section, change the **Tiling** values to **X**: 200, and **Y**: 50. You might notice that the pattern is not seamless. This is because we are using the same **UV Set** from our **Diffuse** texture. However, the object has been assigned to two different **UV channels** (back when it was being modeled). While UV channel 1 contains the mapping for our **Diffuse** map, UV channel 2 uses a basic cylindrical mapping. We need to change the **Secondary Maps** section's **UV Set** from **UV0** to **UV1**. The Detail map for your material is ready:

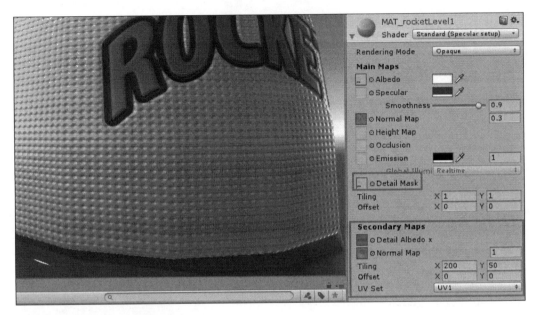

How it works...

When in use, **Secondary Maps** are blended onto the material's primary **Diffuse** and **Normal** maps (that's why our object is green even after the **Detail Diffuse** is applied: the grey tones are superimposed on the original **Diffuse** texture). By using a **Detail Mask**, the artist defines which areas of the object should be affected by Secondary Maps. This is great for customization, and also for creating nuances (like the semi-bumped battery compartment in our example).

Another helpful feature is the possibility of using a separate UV channel for Details maps and Tiling. Besides adding variation to texture mapping, this allows us to paint the details that can be perceived even at a very close distance by dramatically enhancing the visual quality of our objects.

Fading the transparency of a material

In this recipe, we will create an object that, once clicked, fades out and disappears. However, the script will be flexible enough to allow us adjust the initial and final alpha values. Plus, we will have the option of making the object self-destructible when turned invisible.

How to do it...

Follow these steps:

1. Add a **Sphere** to your scene by accessing the **GameObject | 3D Object | Sphere** menu.

2. Select the **Sphere** and make sure it has a collider (if you are using a custom 3D object, you might have to add a collider through the **Components | Physics** menu).

3. Create a new material. The easiest way to do that is to access the **Project** view, click the **Create** drop-down menu, and choose **Material**.

4. Rename your new material. For this example, let's call it `Fade_MAT`.

5. Select your material. From the **Inspector** view, use the drop-down menu to change its **Rendering Mode** to **Fade**:

 The **Fade** rendering mode is specifically designed for situations like this. Other rendering modes, such as Transparent, will fade turn the Albedo color transparent, but not the specular highlights nor the reflections, in which case the object will still be visible.

6. Apply the **FadeMaterial** to **Sphere** by dragging it from the **Project** view into the **Sphere** Game Object name in the **Hierarchy** view.

7. From the **Project** view, click the **Create** drop down menu and choose **C# Script**. Rename it as `FadeMaterial` and open it in your editor.

8. Replace your script with the code below:

```
using UnityEngine;
using System.Collections;
public class FadeMaterial : MonoBehaviour {
  public float fadeDuration = 1.0f;
  public bool useMaterialAlpha = false;
  public float alphaStart = 1.0f;
  public float alphaEnd = 0.0f;
  public bool destroyInvisibleObject = true;
  private bool isFading = false;
  private float alphaDiff;
  private float startTime;
  private Renderer rend;
  private Color fadeColor;

  void Start () {
    rend = GetComponent<Renderer>();
    fadeColor = rend.material.color;

    if (!useMaterialAlpha) {
      fadeColor.a = alphaStart;
    } else {
      alphaStart = fadeColor.a;
    }

    rend.material.color = fadeColor;
    alphaDiff = alphaStart - alphaEnd;
  }

  void Update () {
    if(isFading){
      var elapsedTime = Time.time - startTime;

      if(elapsedTime <= fadeDuration){
        var fadeProgress = elapsedTime / fadeDuration;
        var alphaChange = fadeProgress * alphaDiff;
        fadeColor.a = alphaStart - alphaChange;
        rend.material.color = fadeColor;
      } else {
        fadeColor.a = alphaEnd;
        rend.material.color = fadeColor;

        if(destroyInvisibleObject)
          Destroy (gameObject);
```

```
        isFading = false;
      }
    }
  }

  void OnMouseUp(){
    FadeAlpha();
  }

  public void FadeAlpha(){
    isFading = true;
    startTime = Time.time;
  }
}
```

9. Save your script and apply it to the **Sphere** Game.

10. Play your scene and click on the **Sphere** to see it fade away and self-destruct.

How it works...

Since the opaqueness of the material using a transparent Shader is determined by the alpha value of its main color, all we need to do in order to fade it is changing that value over a given amount of time. This transformation is expressed, in our script, on the following lines of code:

```
var fadeProgress = elapsedTime / fadeDuration;
var alphaChange = fadeProgress * alphaDiff;
fadeColor.a = alphaStart - alphaChange;
rend.material.color = fadeColor;
```

There's more...

You could call the `FadeAlpha` function in other circumstances (such as a `Rigidbody` collision, for instance). In fact, you could even call it from another Game Object's script by using the `GetComponent` command. The script would be something like:

```
GameObject.Find("Sphere").GetComponent<FadeMaterial>().FadeAlpha();
```

Playing videos inside a scene

TV sets, projectors, monitors.... If you want complex animated materials in your level, you can play video files as texture maps. In this recipe, we will learn how to apply a video texture to a cube. We will also implement a simple control scheme that plays or pauses the video whenever that cube is clicked on.

Getting ready

Unity imports video files through Apple Quicktime. If you don't have it installed in your machine, please download it at `http://www.apple.com/quicktime/download/`.

Also, if you need a video file to follow this recipe, please use the `videoTexture.mov` included in the folder `1632_04_08`.

How to do it...

Follow these steps:

1. Add a cube to the scene through the **GameObject** | **3D Object** | **Cube** menu.

2. Import the provided `videoTexture.mov` file.

3. From the **Project** view, use the **Create** drop-down menu to create a new **Material**. Rename it `Video_MAT` and, from the **Inspector** view, change its **Shader** to **Unlit/Texture**:

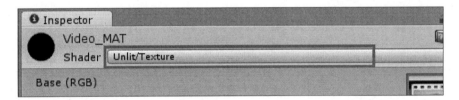

4. Apply `videoTexture` to the texture slot of `Video_MAT` by dragging it from the **Project** view into the appropriate slot.

5. Apply the `Video_MAT` to the **Cube** you have previously created.

6. Expand `videoTexture` on the **Project** view to reveal its correspondent **Audio Clip**. Then, apply that audio clip to the **Cube** (you can do it by dragging it from the **Project** view to the **Cube** in the **Hierarchy** view, or a **Scene** view).

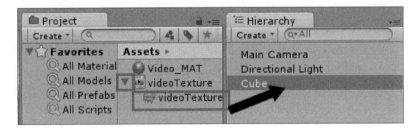

7. Select the **Cube**. Make sure there is a **Collider** component visible from the **Inspector** view. In case there isn't one, add it via the **Component | Physics | Box Collider** menu. Colliders are needed for mouse collision detection.

8. Now we need to create a script for controlling the movie texture and associated audio clip. From **Project** view, use the **Create** drop-down menu to add a **C# Script**. Name it PlayVideo.

9. Open the script and replace it with the following code:

```csharp
using UnityEngine;
using System.Collections;

[RequireComponent(typeof(AudioSource))]

public class PlayVideo : MonoBehaviour {

  public bool loop = true;
  public bool playFromStart = true;
  public MovieTexture video;
    public AudioClip audioClip;
  private AudioSource audio;

  void Start () {
    audio = GetComponent<AudioSource> ();

    if (!video)
      video = GetComponent<Renderer>().material.mainTexture as
MovieTexture;

    if (!audioClip)
        audioClip = audio.clip;

    video.Stop ();
    audio.Stop ();
    video.loop = loop;
    audio.loop = loop;

    if (playFromStart)
      ControlMovie ();
  }

  void OnMouseUp(){
    ControlMovie ();
  }
```

```
      public void ControlMovie(){

        if(video.isPlaying){
          video.Pause();
          audio.Pause();
        } else {
          video.Play();
          audio.Play();
        }
      }
    }
```

10. Save your script and attach it to the **Cube**.

11. Test your scene. You should be able to see the movie being played in the cube face, and also pause/play it by clicking on it.

How it works...

By default, our script makes the movie texture play in loop mode. There is, however, a Boolean variable than can be changed through the **Inspector** panel, where it is represented by a check box. Likewise, there is a check box that can be used to prevent the movie from playing when the level starts.

There's more...

There are some other movie texture commands and parameters that can be played with. Don't forget to check out Unity's scripting guide at `http://docs.unity3d.com/ Documentation/ScriptReference/MovieTexture.html`.

Conclusion

This chapter has covered a number of techniques used to create, often manually and sometimes automatically, texture maps that are capable of giving distinctive features to materials. Hopefully, you are now more confident about working with Unity's new Physically-Based Shading, which is capable of understanding differences between available workflows, is aware of the role of each material property, and is ready to make better-looking materials for your games. We have also explored ways of changing the properties of materials during runtime by accessing an object's material via script.

Resources

Physically-Based Rendering is a complex (and current) topic, so it's a good idea to study it a bit by familiarizing yourself with the tools and concepts behind it. To help you with this task, we have included a non-exhaustive list of resources below that you should take a look at.

References

Here's a list of interesting, detailed material on Physically-Based Rendering (within and outside Unity):

- *The Comprehensive PBR Guide Volumes 1 and 2* by Wes McDermott (Allegorithmic), available at `http://www.allegorithmic.com/pbr-guide`. This guide takes an in-depth look at the practical and theoretical aspects of PBR, including great analysis of possible workflows.

- *Mastering Physically Based Shading in Unity 5* by Renaldas Zioma (Unity), Erland Körner (Unity), and Wes McDermott (Allegorithmic), is available at `http://www.slideshare.net/RenaldasZioma/unite2014-mastering-physically-based-shading-in-unity-5`. This is a detailed presentation about using PBS in Unity. Originally presented at the Unite 2014 conference, it contains some out-of-date information, but, nevertheless, it is still worth taking a look at.

- *Physically Based Shading in Unity 5* by Aras Pranckevičius, from Unity, is available at `http://aras-p.info/texts/talks.html`. Slides and notes from a presentation on the subject are given at the GDC.

- *Tutorial: Physically Based Rendering, And You Can Too!* by Joe "EarthQuake" Wilson is available at `http://www.marmoset.co/toolbag/learn/pbr-practice`. It is a great overview from the makers of **Marmoset Toolbag** and **Skyshop**.

- *Polycount PBR Wiki*, which is available at `http://wiki.polycount.com/wiki/PBR`, is a list of resources compiled by the Polycount community.

Tools

This is a new generation of texturing software for you to check out, in case you haven't yet:

- *Substance Painter* is a 3D painting application from Allegorithmic. It is available at `http://www.allegorithmic.com/products/substance-painter`. Again, it's worth mentioning that Allegorithmic products won't make use of Unity's Standard Shader, relying instead on substance files that are natively supported by Unity.

- *Bitmap2Material* creates full-featured materials (including normal maps, specular maps, and more) from a single bitmap image. Also, it is from Allegorithmic, and it is available at `http://www.allegorithmic.com/products/bitmap2material`.

> ▶ *Quixel DDO* is a plugin for creating PBR-ready textures in Adobe Photoshop. From Quixel, it is available at `http://www.quixel.se/ddo`.

> ▶ *Quixel NDO* is a plugin for creating Normal maps in Adobe Photoshop. From Quixel, it is available at `http://www.quixel.se/ndo`.

> ▶ *Mari* is a 3D painting tool from The Foundry. It is available at `http://www.thefoundry.co.uk/products/mari/`.

5
Using Cameras

In this chapter, we will cover:

- ▶ Creating a picture-in-picture effect
- ▶ Switching between multiple cameras
- ▶ Making textures from screen content
- ▶ Zooming a telescopic camera
- ▶ Displaying a mini-map
- ▶ Creating an in-game surveillance camera

Introduction

As developers, we should never forget to pay attention to the cameras. After all, they are the windows through which our players see our games. In this chapter, we will take a look at interesting ways of using cameras that enhance the player's experience.

The big picture

Cameras can be customized in many ways:

- ▶ They can exclude objects on specific layers from rendering
- ▶ They can be set to render in **Orthographic** mode (that is, without perspective)
- ▶ They can have their **Field of View** (**FOV**) manipulated to simulate a wide angle lens
- ▶ They can be rendered on top of other cameras or within specific areas of the screen
- ▶ They can be rendered onto Textures

The list goes on.

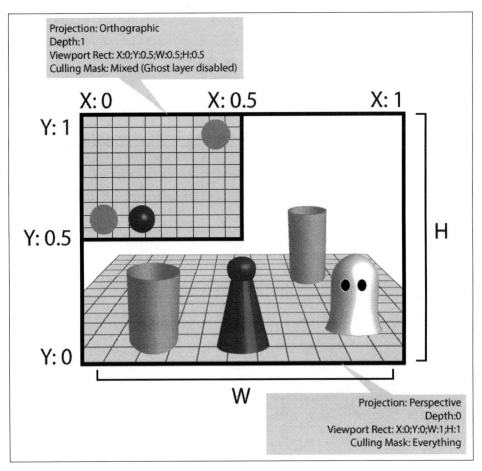

Two simultaneous camera views

Note that throughout this chapter you will notice that some recipes feature a camera rig that follows the player's third-person character. That rig is the **Multipurpose Camera Rig**, originally available from Unity's sample assets, which can be imported into your projects by navigating to **Assets | Import Package | Camera**. To make things easier, we organized the `MultipurposeCamera` Unity Package containing it as a prefab, which can be found in the `1362_05_codes` folder.

Creating a picture-in-picture effect

Having more than one viewport displayed can be useful in many situations. For example, you may want to show simultaneous events going on in different locations, or you may want to have a separate window for hot-seat multiplayer games. Although you can do this manually by adjusting the **Normalized Viewport Rect** parameters on your camera, this recipe includes a series of extra preferences to make it more independent from the user's display configuration.

Getting ready

For this recipe, we have prepared the `BasicScene` Unity package, containing a scene named `BasicScene`. The package is in the `1362_05_codes` folder.

How to do it...

To create a picture-in-picture display, just follow these steps:

1. Import the `BasicScene` package into your Unity Project.

2. From the **Project** view, open the **BasicScene** level. This is a basic scene featuring an animated character and some extra geometry.

3. Add a new **Camera** to the scene through the **Create** drop-down menu on top of the **Hierarchy** view (**Create | Camera**).

4. Select the camera you have created and, from the **Inspector** view, change its **Depth** to **1**, as shown in the following screenshot:

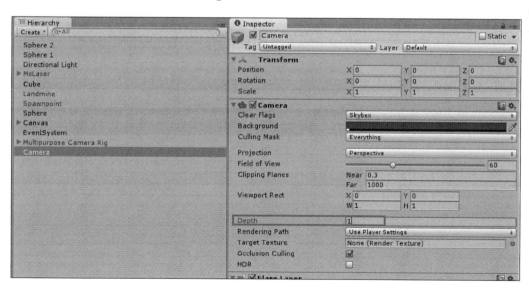

5. From the **Project** view, create a new **C# Script** file and rename it `PictureInPicture`.

6. Open your script and replace everything with the following code:

```csharp
using UnityEngine;

public class PictureInPicture: MonoBehaviour {
  public enum hAlignment{left, center, right};
  public enum vAlignment{top, middle, bottom};
  public hAlignment horAlign = hAlignment.left;
  public vAlignment verAlign = vAlignment.top;
  public enum UnitsIn{pixels, screen_percentage};
  public UnitsIn unit = UnitsIn.pixels;
  public int width = 50;
  public int height= 50;
  public int xOffset = 0;
  public int yOffset = 0;
  public bool  update = true;
  private int hsize, vsize, hloc, vloc;

  void Start (){
    AdjustCamera ();
  }

  void Update (){
    if(update)
    AdjustCamera ();
  }

  void AdjustCamera(){
    int sw = Screen.width;
    int sh = Screen.height;
    float swPercent = sw * 0.01f;
    float shPercent = sh * 0.01f;
    float xOffPercent = xOffset * swPercent;
    float yOffPercent = yOffset * shPercent;
    int xOff;
    int yOff;
    if(unit == UnitsIn.screen_percentage){
      hsize = width * (int)swPercent;
      vsize = height * (int)shPercent;
      xOff = (int)xOffPercent;
      yOff = (int)yOffPercent;
    } else {
      hsize = width;
```

```
    vsize = height;
    xOff = xOffset;
    yOff = yOffset;
  }

  switch (horAlign) {
    case hAlignment.left:
    hloc = xOff;
    break;
    case hAlignment.right:
    int justfiedRight = (sw - hsize);
    hloc = (justfiedRight - xOff);
    break;
    case hAlignment.center:
    float justifiedCenter = (sw * 0.5f) - (hsize * 0.5f);
    hloc = (int)(justifiedCenter - xOff);
    break;
  }

  switch (verAlign) {
    case vAlignment.top:
    int justifiedTop = sh - vsize;
    vloc = (justifiedTop - (yOff));
    break;
    case vAlignment.bottom:
    vloc = yOff;
    break;
    case vAlignment.middle:
    float justifiedMiddle = (sh * 0.5f) - (vsize * 0.5f);
    vloc = (int)(justifiedMiddle - yOff);
    break;
  }

  GetComponent<Camera>().pixelRect = new
Rect(hloc,vloc,hsize,vsize);
  }
}
```

 In case you haven't noticed, we are not achieving percentages by dividing numbers by 100, but rather multiplying them by 0.01. The reason behind this is that computer processors are faster at multiplying than dividing.

7. Save your script and attach it to the camera you previously created.

8. Uncheck the new camera's **Audio Listener** component and change some of the **PictureInPicture** parameters: change **Hor Align** to `right`, **Ver Align** to `top`, and **Unit** to `pixels`. Leave **XOffset** and **YOffset** as 0, change **Width** to 400 and **Height** to 200, as shown here:

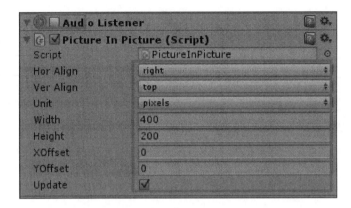

9. Play your scene. The new camera's viewport should be visible in the top-right corner of the screen, as shown below:

How it works...

In this example, we added a second camera in order to display the scene from a different point of view. The second camera's relative viewport was originally placed on top of the **Main Camera**'s viewport, hence taking up all of the screen space.

The `PictureInPicture` script changes the camera's **Normalized Viewport Rect**, thus resizing and positioning the viewport according to the user's preferences.

First, it reads user preferences for the component (dimensions, alignment, and offset for the PiP viewport) and converts dimensions in screen percentage to pixels.

Later, from the `if(unit == UnitsIn.screen_percentage) {` conditional, the script calculates two of the viewport Rect parameters (width and height) according to the user's selection.

Later on, to **switch** statements to adjust the other two viewport Rect parameters (horizontal and vertical location) according to the total screen dimensions, PiP viewport dimension, vertical/horizontal alignment, and offset.

Finally, a line of code tells the camera to change the location and dimensions of the camera's **Viewport Rect**:

```
GetComponent<Camera>().pixelRect = new
Rect(hloc,vloc,hsize,vsize);
```

There's more...

The following are some aspects of your picture-in-picture that you could change:

Making the picture-in-picture proportional to the screen's size

If you change the **Unit** option to `screen_percentage`, the viewport size will be based on the actual screen's dimensions instead of pixels.

Changing the position of the picture-in-picture

The **Ver Align** and **Hor Align** options can be used to change the viewport's vertical and horizontal alignment. Use them to place it where you wish.

Preventing the picture-in-picture from updating on every frame

Leave the **Update** option unchecked if you don't plan to change the viewport position in running mode. Also, it's a good idea to leave it checked when testing and uncheck it once the position has been decided and set up.

See also

▸ The *Displaying a mini-map* recipe in this chapter

Switching between multiple cameras

Choosing from a variety of cameras is a common feature in many genres: racing, sports, tycoon/strategy, and many others. In this recipe, you will learn how to give players the ability to choose from many cameras by using their keyboards.

Getting ready

For this recipe, we have prepared the `BasicScene` Unity package containing a scene named `BasicScene`. The package is in the `1362_05_codes` folder.

How to do it...

To implement switchable cameras, follow these steps:

1. Import the `BasicScene` package into a new **Project**.

2. From the **Project** view, open the **BasicScene** level. This is a basic scene featuring an animated character and some extra geometry.

3. Add two more cameras to the scene through the **Create** drop-down menu on top of the **Hierarchy** view (**Create | Camera**). Rename them `cam1` and `cam2`.

4. Change the `cam2` camera's position and rotation so that it won't be identical to `cam1`.

5. Create an **Empty** GameObject by navigating to the **Create** drop-down menu on top of the **Hierarchy** view (**Create | Create Empty**). Then, rename it `Switchboard`.

6. From the **Inspector** view, disable the **Camera** and **Audio Listener** components of both `cam1` and `cam2`. Also, set their **Tags** as **MainCamera**, as shown:

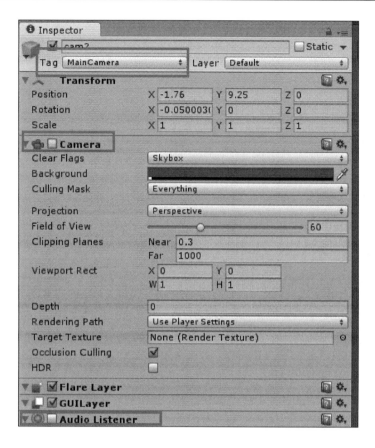

7. From the **Project** view, create a new **C# Script** file. Rename it `CameraSwitch` and open it in your editor.

8. Open your script and replace everything with the following code:

```
using UnityEngine;

public class CameraSwitch : MonoBehaviour {
  public GameObject[] cameras;
  public string[] shortcuts;
  public bool  changeAudioListener = true;
  void  Update (){
    if (Input.anyKeyDown) {
      for (int i=0; i<cameras.Length; i++) {
        if (Input.GetKeyDown (shortcuts [i]))
          SwitchCamera (i);
      }
    }
```

```
}

void  SwitchCamera (int indexToSelect){
   for (int i = 0; i<cameras.Length; i++){
      // test whether current array index matches camera to make
active
         bool cameraActive = (i == indexToSelect);
         cameras[i].GetComponent<Camera>().enabled = cameraActive;

      if (changeAudioListener)
            cameras[i].GetComponent<AudioListener>().enabled =
cameraActive;
      }
   }
}
```

9. Attach `CameraSwitch` to the `Switchboard` GameObject.

10. From the **Inspector** view, set both the **Cameras** and **Shortcuts** sizes to 3. Then, drag and populate the **Cameras** slots with the cameras from the scene (including the **Main Camera**, within the **Multipurpose Camera Rig | Pivot** GameObject) Then, type 1, 2, and 3 into the **Shortcuts** text fields, as shown in the next screenshot:

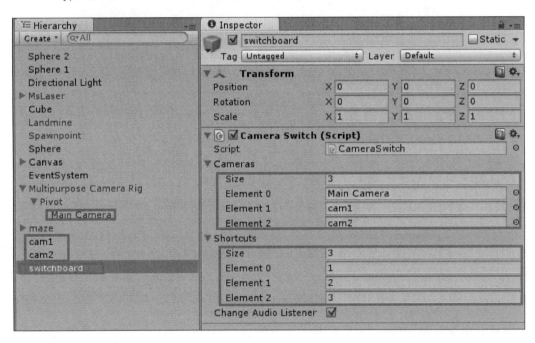

11. Play your scene and test your cameras by pressing *1*, *2*, and *3* on the keyboard.

How it works...

The script is very straightforward. First, it compares the key being pressed to the list of shortcuts. If the key is indeed included on a list of shortcuts, it is passed on to the `SwitchCamera` function, which, in turn, goes through a list of cameras, enables the one associated with the shortcut that was received, and also enables its **Audio Listener**, in case the **Change Audio Listener** option is checked.

There's more...

Here are some ideas about how you could try twisting this recipe a bit.

Using a single-enabled camera

A different approach to the problem would be keeping all secondary cameras disabled and assigning their position and rotation to the main camera via a script (you would need to make a copy of the main camera and add it to the list, in case you wanted to save its **Transform** settings).

Triggering the switch from other events

Also, you can change your camera from other GameObjects' scripts by using a line of code such as the one given here:

```
GameObject.Find("Switchboard").GetComponent("CameraSwitch").Switch
Camera(1);
```

See also

▸ The *Creating an in-game surveillance camera* recipe in this chapter

Making textures from screen content

If you want your game or player to take in-game snapshots and apply them as textures, this recipe will show you how. This can be very useful if you plan to implement an in-game photo gallery or display a snapshot of a past key moment at the end of a level (racing games and stunt simulations use this feature a lot). For this particular example, we will take a snapshot from within a framed region of the screen and print it on the top-right corner of the display.

Getting ready

For this recipe, we have prepared the `BasicScene` Unity package, containing a scene named `BasicScene`. The package is in the `1362_05_codes` folder.

How to do it...

To create textures from screen content, follow these steps:

1. Import the `BasicScene` package into a new **Project**.

2. From the **Project** view, open the **BasicScene** level. This is a basic scene featuring an animated character and some extra geometry. It also features a **Canvas** for UI elements.

3. Create an **UI Image** GameObject from the **Create** drop-down menu on top of the **Hierarchy** view (**Create | UI | Image**). Please note that it will be created as a child of the **Canvas** GameObject. Then, rename it `frame`.

4. From the **Inspector** view, find the **Image (Script)** component of the **frame** GameObject and set `InputFieldBackground` as its **Source Image**. This is a sprite that comes bundled with Unity, and it's already sliced for resizing purposes.

5. Now, from the **Inspector** view, change **Rect Transform** to the following values: **Anchors | Min | X**: 0.25, **Y**: 0.25; **Anchors | Max | X**: 0.75, **Y**: 0.75; **Pivot | X**: 0.5, **Y**: 0.5; **Left**: 0; **Top**: 0; **Pos Z**: 0; **Right**: 0; **Bottom**: 0.

6. From the **Image (Script)** component, uncheck the **Fill Center** option, as shown below:

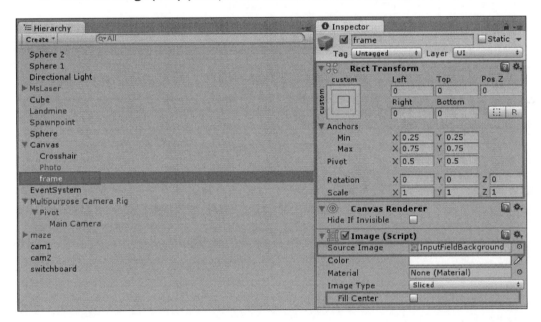

7. Create an **UI Raw Image** GameObject from the **Create** drop-down menu on top of the **Hierarchy** view (**Create | UI | RawImage**). Please note that it will be created as a child of the **Canvas** GameObject. Then, rename it `Photo`.

8. From the **Inspector** view, find the **Raw Image (Script)** component of the **Photo** GameObject and set None as its **Texture**. Also, from the top of the **Inspector** view, disable the **Photo** GameObject by unchecking the box on the side of its name.

9. Now, from the **Inspector** view, change the **Rect Transform** to the following values: **Width**: 1; **Height**: 1; **Anchors | Min | X**: 0, **Y**: 1; **Anchors | Max | X**: 0, **Y**: 1; **Pivot | X**: 0, **Y**: 1; **Pos X**: 0; **Pos Y**: 0; **Pos Z**: 0 as shown in the following screenshot:

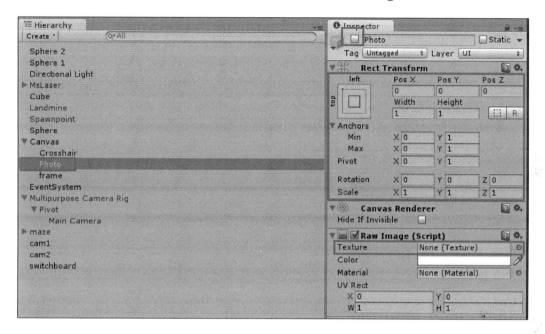

10. We need to create a script. In the **Project** view, click on the **Create** drop-down menu and choose **C# Script**. Rename it ScreenTexture and open it in your editor.

11. Open your script and replace everything with the following code:

```
using UnityEngine;
using UnityEngine.UI;
using System.Collections;

public class ScreenTexture : MonoBehaviour {
  public GameObject photoGUI;
  public GameObject frameGUI;
  public float ratio = 0.25f;

  void  Update (){
    if (Input.GetKeyUp (KeyCode.Mouse0))
```

```
            StartCoroutine(CaptureScreen());
    }

    IEnumerator  CaptureScreen (){
      photoGUI.SetActive (false);
      int sw = Screen.width;
      int sh = Screen.height;
      RectTransform frameTransform =
frameGUI.GetComponent<RectTransform> ();
      Rect framing = frameTransform.rect;
      Vector2 pivot = frameTransform.pivot;
      Vector2 origin = frameTransform.anchorMin;
      origin.x *= sw;
      origin.y *= sh;
      float xOffset = pivot.x * framing.width;
      origin.x += xOffset;
      float yOffset = pivot.y * framing.height;
      origin.y += yOffset;
      framing.x += origin.x;
      framing.y += origin.y;
      int textWidth = (int)framing.width;
      int textHeight = (int)framing.height;
      Texture2D texture = new
Texture2D(textWidth,textHeight);
      yield return new WaitForEndOfFrame();
      texture.ReadPixels(framing, 0, 0);
      texture.Apply();
      photoGUI.SetActive (true);
      Vector3 photoScale = new Vector3 (framing.width *
ratio, framing.height * ratio, 1);
      photoGUI.GetComponent<RectTransform> ().localScale =
photoScale;
      photoGUI.GetComponent<RawImage>().texture = texture;
    }
}
```

12. Save your script and apply it to the **Main Camera** GameObject within the
    Multipurpose Camera Rig | Pivot GameObject.

13. In the **Inspector** view, find the **Screen Texture** component and populate the fields **Photo GUI** and **Frame GUI** with the GameObjects **Photo** and **frame** respectively:

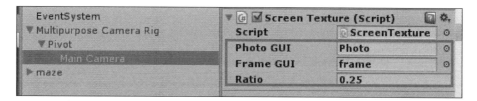

14. Play the scene. You will be able to take a snapshot of the screen (and have it displayed in the top-left corner at a quarter of the original size) by clicking the mouse button, as shown in the following screenshot:

How it works...

First, we created a GUI frame from which to take a snapshot and a GUI element onto which to apply the texture. Then, we applied a script to the **Main Camera** to capture the screen content and apply a new texture to it.

The script creates a new texture and captures the left mouse button being pressed, whereupon it starts a coroutine to calculate a Rect area, copy screen pixels from that area, and apply them to a texture to be displayed by the **photo** GUI element, which is also resized to fit the texture.

The size of the Rect is calculated from the screen's dimensions and the frame's **Rect Transform** settings, particularly its Pivot, Anchors, Width, and Height. The screen pixels are then captured by the `ReadPixels()` command, and applied to the texture, which is then applied to the **Raw Image** photo, which is resized to meet the desired ratio between the photo size and the original pixels.

There's more...

Apart from displaying the texture as a GUI element, you can use it in other ways.

Applying your texture to a material

You can apply your texture to an existing object's material by adding a line similar to `GameObject.Find("MyObject").renderer.material.mainTexture = texture;` to the end of the `CaptureScreen` function.

Using your texture as a screenshot

You can encode your texture as a PNG image file and save it. Check out Unity's documentation on this feature at `http://docs.unity3d.com/Documentation/ScriptReference/Texture2D.EncodeToPNG.html`.

See also

> ► The Saving screenshots from the game recipe in Chapter 10, Working with the External Resource Files and Devices

Zooming a telescopic camera

In this recipe, we will create a telescopic camera that zooms in whenever the left mouse button is pressed. This can be very useful, for instance, if we have a sniper in our game.

Getting ready...

For this recipe, we have prepared the `BasicScene` Unity package, containing a scene named `BasicScene`. The package is in the `1362_05_codes` folder.

How to do it...

To create a telescopic camera, follow these steps:

1. Import the `BasicScene` package into a new **Project**.

2. From the **Project** view, open the **BasicScene** level. This is a basic scene featuring an animated character and some extra geometry.

3. Import Unity's **Effects** package by navigating to **Assets | Import Package | Effects.**

4. Select the **Main Camera** GameObject within the **Multipurpose Camera Rig | Pivot** GameObject and apply the **Vignette** image effect (by navigating to **Component | Image Effects | Camera | Vignette and Chromatic Aberration**).

5. We need to create a script. In the **Project** view, click on the **Create** drop-down menu and choose **C# Script**. Rename it `TelescopicView` and open it in your editor.

6. Open your script and replace everything with the following code:

```
using UnityEngine;
using System.Collections;
using UnityStandardAssets.ImageEffects;

public class TelescopicView : MonoBehaviour{
  public float zoom = 2.0f;
  public float speedIn = 100.0f;
  public float speedOut = 100.0f;
  private float initFov;
  private float currFov;
  private float minFov;
  private float addFov;
  private VignetteAndChromaticAberration v;
  public float vMax = 10.0f;

  void Start(){
    initFov = Camera.main.fieldOfView;
    minFov = initFov / zoom;
    v = this.GetComponent<VignetteAndChromaticAberration>()
as VignetteAndChromaticAberration;
  }
  void Update(){
    if (Input.GetKey(KeyCode.Mouse0))
      ZoomView();
    else
      ZoomOut();
    float currDistance = currFov - initFov;
    float totalDistance = minFov - initFov;
    float vMultiplier = currDistance / totalDistance;
    float vAmount = vMax * vMultiplier;
    vAmount = Mathf.Clamp (vAmount,0,vMax);
    v.intensity = vAmount;
  }

  void ZoomView(){
    currFov = Camera.main.fieldOfView;
```

```
            addFov = speedIn * Time.deltaTime;

        if (Mathf.Abs(currFov - minFov) < 0.5f)
            currFov = minFov;
        else if (currFov - addFov >= minFov)
            currFov -= addFov;

        Camera.main.fieldOfView = currFov;
    }

    void ZoomOut(){
        currFov = Camera.main.fieldOfView;
        addFov = speedOut * Time.deltaTime;

        if (Mathf.Abs(currFov - initFov) < 0.5f)
            currFov = initFov;
        else if (currFov + addFov <= initFov)
            currFov += addFov;

        Camera.main.fieldOfView = currFov;
    }
}
```

7. Save your script and apply it to the **Main Camera** GameObject within the
    Multipurpose Camera Rig | Pivot GameObject.

8. Play the level. You should see an animated vignette effect in addition to the zooming:

How it works...

The zooming effect is actually caused by changes to the value of the camera's **Field Of View** (**FOV**) property; small values result in closer views of a smaller area, while high values enlarge the FOV.

The `TelescopicView` script changes the camera's field of view by subtracting from it whenever the left mouse button is pressed. It also adds to the FOV value when the mouse button is *not* being held, until it reaches its original value.

The zoom limit of the FOV can be deduced from the code `minFov = initFov / zoom;`. This means that the minimum value of the FOV is equal to its original value divided by the zoom amount. For instance, if our camera features, originally, a FOV of 60, and we set the **Telescopic View Zoom** amount to 2.0, the minimum FOV allowed will be 60/2 = 30. The difference is shown in the following two screenshots:

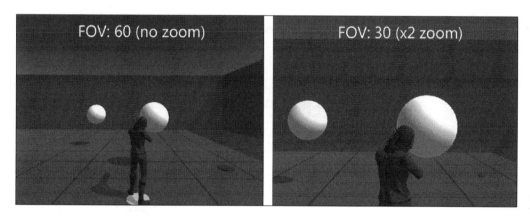

There's more...

You can also add a variable to control the **Blur Vignette** level of the **Vignette** image effect.

Displaying a mini-map

In many games, a broader view of the scene can be invaluable for navigation and information. Mini-maps are great for giving players that extra perspective that they may need when in first- or third-person mode.

Getting ready...

For this recipe, we have prepared the `BasicScene` Unity Package, containing a scene named `BasicScene`. You will also need to import three image files named `Compass.png`, `compassMarker.png`, and `compassMask.png`. All files are available in the `1362_05_05` folder.

How to do it...

To create a mini-map, follow these steps:

1. Import the `BasicScene` package into a new **Project**. Also, import the provided png files. Open the **BasicScene** level.

2. From the **Project** view, select the `Compass`, `compassMarker`, and `compassMask` texture files. Then, from the **Inspector**, change their **Texture Type** to **Sprite (2D and UI)**, leaving the **Sprite Mode** as **Single** and the **Pivot** at **Center**. Click on **Apply** to confirm the changes, as shown in the following screenshot:

3. From the **Hierarchy** view, create a new **UI Panel** object (**Create | UI | Panel**). It will be created as a child of the UI **Canvas** GameObject. Rename it `MiniMap`. Then, from the **Inspector** view, set its alignment to **Top/Right**, change both the **Width** and **Height** to `256`, and its **Pos X** and **Pos Y** fields to `-128`. Also, populate the **Source Image** field, within the **Image** component, with the **compassMask** sprite, adjusting the **Color** field by bringing **Alpha** up to `255`, as shown in the following screenshot:

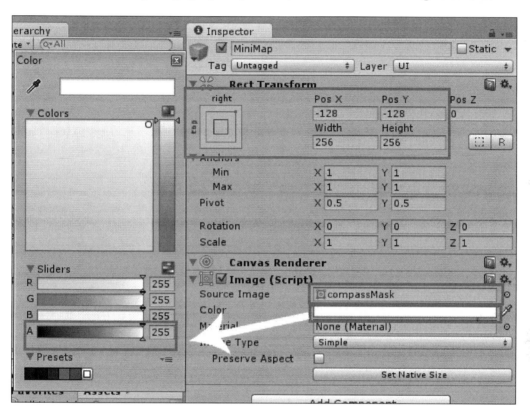

4. Add a **Mask** component to **MiniMap** (from the main menu, select **Component | UI | Mask**). Then, from the **Inspector** view, find the **Mask** component and uncheck **Show Mask Graphic** (it will become invisible, serving as a mask for the mini-map).

5. Select the **MsLaser** GameObject (which is the player's character), and, from the top of the **Inspector** view, access the **Layer** drop-down menu. Select **Add Layer...** and then name a **User Layer** Player, as shown in the following screenshot:

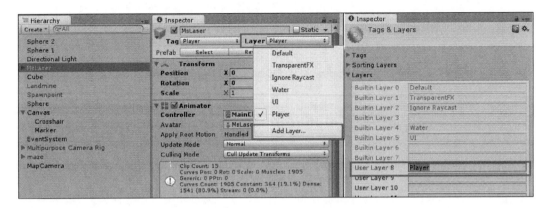

6. Select the **MsLaser** character again, and, from the **Layer** drop-down menu, select **Player**:

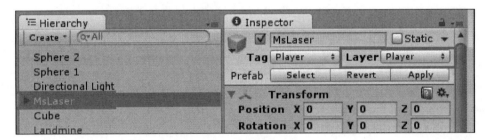

7. From the **Project** view, create a new **Render Texture** and name it Map_Render. Then, from **Inspector**, change its size to 256 x 256.

8. From the **Hierarchy** view, create a new camera (**Create | Camera**) and rename it MapCamera. From the **Inspector** view, change its parameters as follows (shown in the screenshot that will follow):

   ❑ **Clear Flags**: Depth Only

   ❑ **Culling Mask**: Mixed... (unselect **Player**)

   ❑ **Projection**: Orthographic

   ❑ **Depth**: 1 (or higher)

   ❑ **Target Texture**: Map_Render

   ❑ Also, uncheck the camera's **Audio Listener** component

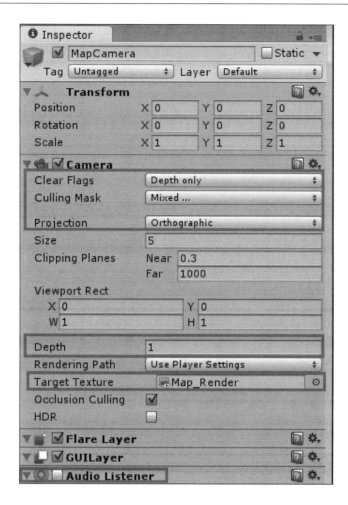

9. From the **Hierarchy** view, right-click on **MiniMap** and navigate to **UI | Raw Image** to create a child UI element. Name it `MapTexture`. Then, from the **Inspector** view, populate the **Texture** field with the `Map_Render` texture and click on the **Set Native Size** button, as shown in the following screenshot:

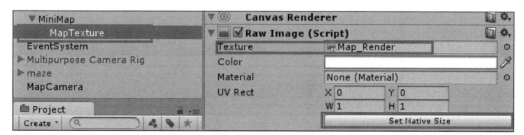

10. Now, right-click on **MiniMap** and navigate to **UI | Image** to create another child element. Name it `Compass`. Then, from the **Inspector** view, populate the **Source Image** field with the `Compass` image and click on the **Set Native Size** button.

11. Once again, right-click on **MiniMap** and navigate to **UI | Image** to add another child element. Name it `Marker`. Then, from the **Inspector** view, populate the **Source Image** field with the `compassMarker` image and click on the **Set Native Size** button.

12. From the **Project** view, create a new **C# Script** and name it `MiniMap`. Open it and replace everything with the following code:

```
using UnityEngine;
using UnityEngine.UI;
using System.Collections;

public class MiniMap : MonoBehaviour
{
  public Transform target;
  public GameObject marker;
  public GameObject mapGUI;
  public float height = 10.0f;
  public float distance = 10.0f;
  public bool rotate = true;
  private Vector3 camAngle;
  private Vector3 camPos;
  private Vector3 targetAngle;
  private Vector3 targetPos;
  private Camera cam;

  void Start(){
    cam = GetComponent<Camera> ();
    camAngle = transform.eulerAngles;
    targetAngle = target.transform.eulerAngles;
    camAngle.x = 90;
    camAngle.y = targetAngle.y;
    transform.eulerAngles = camAngle;
  }

  void Update(){
    targetPos = target.transform.position;
    camPos = targetPos;
```

```
camPos.y += height;
transform.position = camPos;
cam.orthographicSize = distance;
Vector3 compassAngle = new Vector3();
compassAngle.z = target.transform.eulerAngles.y;

if (rotate) {
  mapGUI.transform.eulerAngles = compassAngle;
  marker.transform.eulerAngles = new Vector3();
} else {
  marker.transform.eulerAngles = -compassAngle;
}

  }
}
```

13. Save the script and attach it to **MapCamera**. Then, from the **Inspector** view, change the parameters of the **Mini Map** component as follows (shown in the screenshot that will follow):

   ❑ **Target**: MsLaser

   ❑ **Marker**: Marker (the UI element previously created)

   ❑ **Map GUI**: MiniMap (the UI panel previously created)

   ❑ **Height**: 10

   ❑ **Distance**: 10

   ❑ **Rotate**: Checked

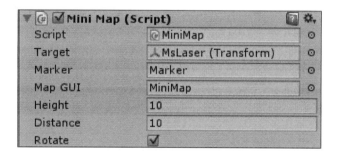

14. Play the scene. You should be able to see the mini-map functioning in the top-right corner of the screen:

How it works...

The main element of the mini-map is a texture, used as a GUI element, rendered from an orthographic camera that follows the player from a top-down perspective. Some necessary adjustments were made to **MapCamera**:

- ► Changing its **Projection** mode to **Orthographic** (to make it two-dimensional)
- ► Excluding the **Player** tag from its **Culling Mask** (to make the character's model invisible to the camera)
- ► Disabling its **Audio Listener** (so it won't conflict with the main camera)

The mini-map was embellished with a compass frame and a marker indicating the player's position. All these GUI elements were parented by a **Panel** that also functioned as a **Mask** to the visual elements. Finally, a script was created, serving three purposes: configuring preferences for the **Camera** (such as the area covered), repositioning the **Camera** at runtime according to the player's transform settings, and rotating the appropriate UI elements.

There's more...

If you want to experiment more with your mini-map, read on.

Covering a wider or narrower area

The range of the mini-map is given by the **Distance** parameter. A higher value will result in coverage of a wider area, as the **MiniMap** class uses the same value as the viewport size of the orthographic camera.

Changing the map's orientation

The mini-map, by default, is set to rotate as the player changes direction. Should you want it to be static, uncheck the **Rotate** option to make the **Marker** rotate instead.

Adapting your mini-map to other styles

You can easily modify this recipe to make a top or isometric view of a racing game circuit map. Just position the camera manually and prevent it from following the character.

Creating an in-game surveillance camera

Although using a second viewport can be useful in many situations, there will be times when you need to output the image rendered from a camera to a texture at runtime. To illustrate this point, in this recipe, we will make use of **Render Texture** to create an in-game surveillance camera that transmits its video to a monitor.

In-game surveillance cameras

Getting ready

For this recipe, we have prepared the `BasicScene` Unity package, containing a scene named `BasicScene`, and also two FBX 3D models for the monitor and camera objects. The package is in the `1362_05_codes` folder, and the 3D models are in the `1362_05_06` folder.

How to do it...

To create a picture-in-picture display, just follow these steps:

1. Import the `BasicScene` package and the `monitor` and `camera` models into your Unity Project.

2. From the **Project** view, open the **BasicScene** level. This is a basic scene featuring an animated character and some extra geometry.

3. From the **Project** view, place the **monitor** and **camera** objects into the scene by dragging them into the **Hierarchy** panel. Their **Transform** settings should be (shown in the following screenshot): **monitor: Position: X:** 0; **Y:** 0.09; **Z:** 4. **Rotation: X:** 0; **Y:** 180; **Z:** 0. **camera: Position: X:** -3; **Y:** 0.06; **Z:** 4. **Rotation: X:** 0; **Y:** 90; **Z:** 0:

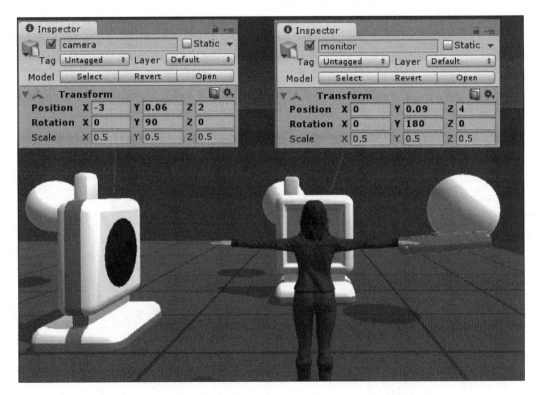

4. Create, from the **Project** view, a new **Render Texture**, and rename it `screen`. Then, from the **Inspector** view, change its **Size** to 512 x 512.

5. Add a new **Camera** to the scene through the **Create** drop-down menu on top of the **Hierarchy** view (**Create | Camera**). Then, from the **Inspector** view, name it `Surveillance` and make it a child of the **camera** GameObject. Then, change its **Transform** settings to the following: **Position: X:** 0; **Y:** 2; **Z:** 0, and **Rotation: X:** 0; **Y:** 0; **Z:** 0.

6. Select the `Surveillance` camera you have created, and, from the **Inspector** view, change its **Clipping Planes | Near** to 0.6. Also, populate the **Target Texture** slot with the **Render Texture** screen and disable the camera's **Audio Listener** component, as shown in the following screenshot:

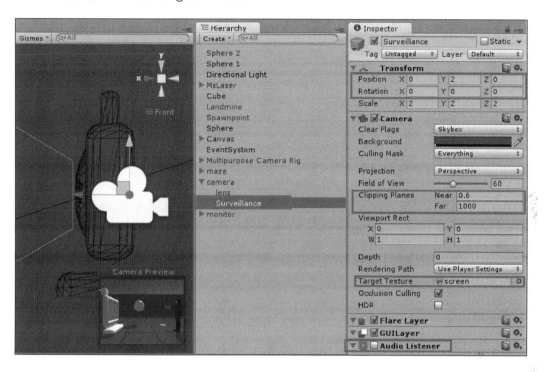

7. From the **Hierarchy** view, expand the **monitor** object and select its **screen** child. Then, from the **Inspector**, find its material (named **Desert**), and, from the **Shader** drop-down menu, change itto **Unlit/Texture**. Finally, set the **screen** texture as its base texture, as shown in the following screenshot:

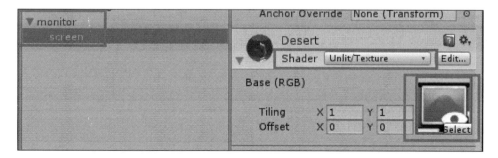

8. Now it's time to add some post-processing to the texture. From the main menu, import the **Effects** package (**Assets | Import Package | Effects**).

9. From the **Hierarchy** view, select the `Surveillance` camera. Then, from the main menu, add the **Grayscale** image effect component (**Component | Image Effects | Color Adjustments | Grayscale**). Also, add the **Noise And Grain** image effect (**Component | Image Effects | Noise | Noise and Grain (Filmic)**). Finally, from the **Inspector** view, set the **Intensity Multiplier** of the **Noise And Grain** to 4.

10. Play your scene. You should be able to see your actions in real time on the monitor's screen, as shown here:

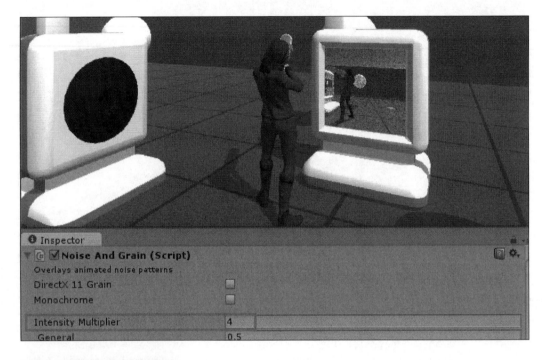

How it works...

We achieved the final result by using the surveillance camera as source for the **Render Texture** applied to the **screen**. The camera was made a child of the camera's 3D model for easier relocation. Also, its **Near Clipping** plane was readjusted in order to avoid displaying parts of the camera's 3D model geometry, and its **Audio Source** component was disabled so that it wouldn't clash with the main camera's component.

In addition to setting up the surveillance camera, two **Image Effects** were added to it: **Noise And Grain** and **Greyscale**. Together, these effects should make **Render Texture** look more like a cheap monitor's screen.

Finally, our **screen** render texture was applied to the screen's 3D object's material (which had its shader changed to **Unlit/texture** so it could be seen in low/no light conditions, like a real monitor).

6

Lights and Effects

In this chapter, we will cover:

- ▸ Using lights and cookie textures to simulate a cloudy day
- ▸ Adding a custom Reflection map to a scene
- ▸ Creating a laser aim with Projector and Line Renderer
- ▸ Reflecting surrounding objects with Reflection Probes
- ▸ Setting up an environment with Procedural Skybox and Directional Light
- ▸ Lighting a simple scene with Lightmaps and Light Probes

Introduction

Whether you're willing to make a better-looking game, or add interesting features, lights and effects can boost your project and help you deliver a higher quality product. In this chapter, we will look at the creative ways of using lights and effects, and also take a look at some of Unity's new features, such as **Procedural Skyboxes**, **Reflection Probes**, **Light Probes**, and custom **Reflection Sources**.

Lighting is certainly an area that has received a lot of attention from Unity, which now features real-time **Global Illumination** technology provided by **Enlighten**. This new technology provides better and more realistic results for both real-time and baked lighting. For more information on Unity's Global Illumination system, check out its documentation at `http://docs.unity3d.com/Manual/GIIntro.html`.

The big picture

There are many ways of creating light sources in Unity. Here's a quick overview of the most common methods.

Lights

Lights are placed into the scene as game objects, featuring a **Light** component. They can function in **Realtime, Baked**, or **Mixed** modes. Among the other properties, they can have their **Range, Color, Intensity**, and **Shadow Type** set by the user. There are four types of lights:

  ▶ **Directional Light**: This is normally used to simulate the sunlight

  ▶ **Spot Light**: This works like a cone-shaped spot light

  ▶ **Point Light**: This is a bulb lamp-like, omnidirectional light

  ▶ **Area Light**: This baked-only light type is emitted in all directions from a rectangle-shaped entity, allowing for a smooth, realistic shading

For an overview of the light types, check Unity's documentation at `http://docs.unity3d.com/Manual/Lighting.html`.

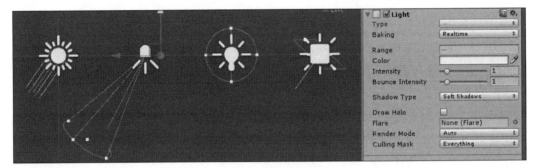

Different types of lights

Environment Lighting

Unity's **Environment Lighting** is often achieved through the combination of a **Skybox** material and sunlight defined by the scene's **Directional Light**. Such a combination creates an ambient light that is integrated into the scene's environment, and which can be set as **Realtime** or **Baked into Lightmaps**.

Emissive materials

When applied to static objects, materials featuring the **Emission** colors or maps will cast light over surfaces nearby, in both real-time and baked modes, as shown in the following screenshot:

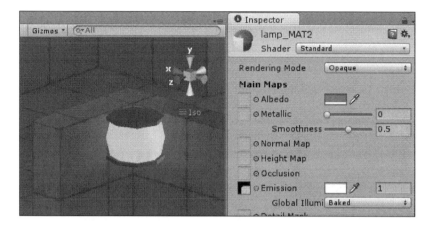

Projector

As its name suggests, a **Projector** can be used to simulate projected lights and shadows, basically by projecting a material and its texture map onto the other objects.

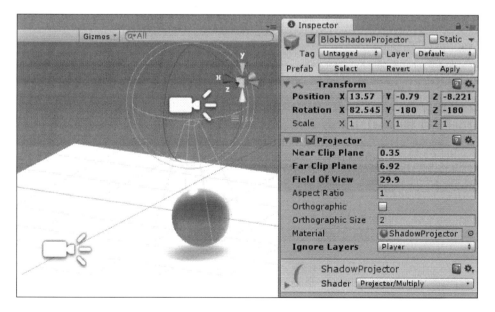

Lightmaps and Light Probes

Lightmaps are basically texture maps generated from the scene's lighting information and applied to the scene's static objects in order to avoid the use of processing-intensive real-time lighting.

Light Probes are a way of sampling the scene's illumination at specific points in order to have it applied onto dynamic objects without the use of real-time lighting.

The Lighting window

The **Lighting** window, which can be found through navigating to the **Window | Lighting** menu, is the hub for setting and adjusting the scene's illumination features, such as Lightmaps, Global Illumination, Fog, and much more. It's strongly recommended that you take a look at Unity's documentation on the subject, which can be found at `http://docs.unity3d.com/Manual/GlobalIllumination.html`.

Using lights and cookie textures to simulate a cloudy day

As it can be seen in many first-person shooters and survival horror games, lights and shadows can add a great deal of realism to a scene, helping immensely to create the right atmosphere for the game. In this recipe, we will create a cloudy outdoor environment using cookie textures. Cookie textures work as masks for lights. It functions by adjusting the intensity of the light projection to the cookie texture's alpha channel. This allows for a silhouette effect (just think of the bat-signal) or, as in this particular case, subtle variations that give a filtered quality to the lighting.

Getting ready

If you don't have access to an image editor, or prefer to skip the texture map elaboration in order to focus on the implementation, please use the image file called `cloudCookie.tga`, which is provided inside the `1362_06_01` folder.

How to do it...

To simulate a cloudy outdoor environment, follow these steps:

1. In your image editor, create a new 512 x 512 pixel image.

2. Using black as the foreground color and white as the background color, apply the Clouds filter (in Photoshop, this is done by navigating to the **Filter** | **Render** | **Clouds** menu).

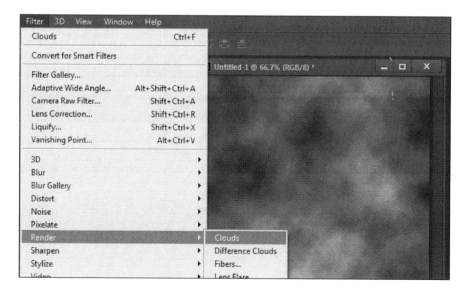

Learning about the Alpha channel is useful, but you could get the same result without it. Skip steps 3 to 7, save your image as `cloudCookie.png` and, when changing texture type in step 9, leave Alpha from Greyscale checked.

3. Select your entire image and copy it.

4. Open the **Channels** window (in Photoshop, this can be done by navigating to the **Window | Channels** menu).

5. There should be three channels: **Red**, **Green**, and **Blue**. Create a new channel. This will be the **Alpha** channel.

6. In the **Channels** window, select the **Alpha 1** channel and paste your image into it.

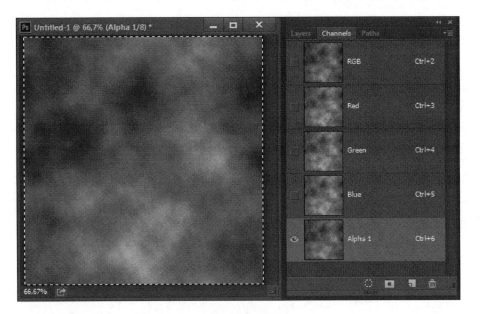

7. Save your image file as `cloudCookie.PSD` or `TGA`.

8. Import your image file to Unity and select it in the **Project** view.

9. From the **Inspector** view, change its **Texture Type** to **Cookie** and its **Light Type** to **Directional**. Then, click on **Apply**, as shown:

10. We will need a surface to actually see the lighting effect. You can either add a plane to your scene (via navigating to the **GameObject | 3D Object | Plane** menu), or create a **Terrain** (menu option **GameObject | 3D Object | Terrain**) and edit it, if you so you wish.

11. Let's add a light to our scene. Since we want to simulate sunlight, the best option is to create a **Directional Light**. You can do this through the drop-down menu named **Create | Light | Directional Light** in the **Hierarchy** view.

12. Using the **Transform** component of the **Inspector** view, reset the light's **Position** to **X:** 0, **Y:** 0, **Z:** 0 and its **Rotation** to **X:** 90; **Y:** 0; **Z:** 0.

13. In the **Cookie** field, select the **cloudCookie** texture that you imported earlier. Change the **Cookie Size** field to 80, or a value that you feel is more appropriate for the scene's dimension. Please leave **Shadow Type** as **No Shadows**.

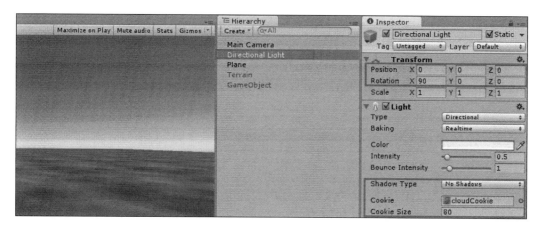

14. Now, we need a script to translate our light and, consequently, the **Cookie** projection. Using the **Create** drop-down menu in the **Project** view, create a new C# Script named MovingShadows.cs.

15. Open your script and replace everything with the following code:

```
using UnityEngine;
using System.Collections;

public class MovingShadows : MonoBehaviour{
  public float windSpeedX;
  public float windSpeedZ;
  private float lightCookieSize;
  private Vector3 initPos;

  void Start(){
    initPos = transform.position;
    lightCookieSize = GetComponent<Light>().cookieSize;
  }

  void Update(){
    Vector3 pos = transform.position;
    float xPos= Mathf.Abs (pos.x);
    float zPos= Mathf.Abs (pos.z);
    float xLimit = Mathf.Abs(initPos.x) + lightCookieSize;
    float zLimit = Mathf.Abs(initPos.z) + lightCookieSize;

    if (xPos >= xLimit)
      pos.x = initPos.x;

    if (zPos >= zLimit)
      pos.z = initPos.z;

    transform.position = pos;
    float windX = Time.deltaTime * windSpeedX;
    float windZ = Time.deltaTime * windSpeedZ;
    transform.Translate(windX, 0, windZ, Space.World);
  }
}
```

16. Save your script and apply it to the **Directional Light**.

17. Select the **Directional Light**. In the **Inspector** view, change the parameters **Wind Speed X** and **Wind Speed Z** to 20 (you can change these values as you wish, as shown).

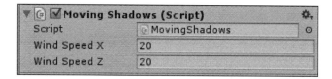

18. Play your scene. The shadows will be moving.

How it works...

With our script, we are telling the **Directional Light** to move across the X and Z axis, causing the **Light Cookie** texture to be displaced as well. Also, we reset the light object to its original position whenever it traveled a distance that was either equal to or greater than the **Light Cookie Size**. The light position must be reset to prevent it from traveling too far, causing problems in real-time render and lighting. The **Light Cookie Size** parameter is used to ensure a smooth transition.

The reason we are not enabling shadows is because the light angle for the X axis must be 90 degrees (or there will be a noticeable gap when the light resets to the original position). If you want dynamic shadows in your scene, please add a second **Directional Light**.

There's more...

In this recipe, we have applied a cookie texture to a **Directional Light**. But what if we were using the **Spot** or **Point Lights**?

Creating Spot Light cookies

Unity documentation has an excellent tutorial on how to make the **Spot Light** cookies. This is great to simulate shadows coming from projectors, windows, and so on. You can check it out at http://docs.unity3d.com/Manual/HOWTO-LightCookie.html.

Creating Point Light Cookies

If you want to use a cookie texture with a **Point Light**, you'll need to change the **Light Type** in the **Texture Importer** section of the **Inspector**.

Adding a custom Reflection map to a scene

Whereas Unity **Legacy Shaders** use individual **Reflection Cubemaps** per material, the new **Standard Shader** gets its reflection from the scene's **Reflection Source**, as configured in the **Scene** section of the **Lighting** window. The level of reflectiveness for each material is now given by its **Metallic** value or **Specular** value (for materials using Specular setup). This new method can be a *real* time saver, allowing you to quickly assign the same reflection map to every object in the scene. Also, as you can imagine, it helps keep the overall look of the scene coherent and cohesive. In this recipe, we will learn how to take advantage of the **Reflection Source** feature.

Getting ready

For this recipe, we will prepare a **Reflection Cubemap**, which is basically the environment to be projected as a reflection onto the material. It can be made from either six or, as shown in this recipe, a single image file.

To help us with this recipe, it's been provided a Unity package, containing a prefab made of a 3D object and a basic Material (using a TIFF as Diffuse map), and also a JPG file to be used as the reflection map. All these files are inside the `1362_06_02` folder.

How to do it...

To add Reflectiveness and Specularity to a material, follow these steps:

1. Import `batteryPrefab.unitypackage` to a new project. Then, select `battery_prefab` object from the **Assets** folder, in the **Project** view.

2. From the **Inspector** view, expand the **Material** component and observe the asset preview window. Thanks to the **Specular** map, the material already features a reflective look. However, it looks as if it is reflecting the scene's default **Skybox**, as shown:

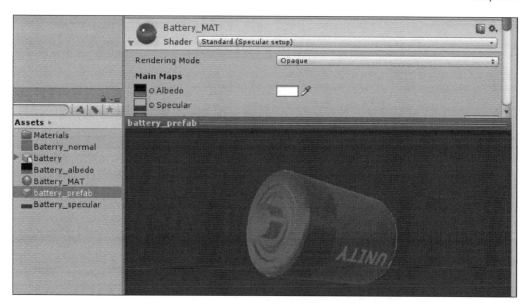

3. Import the `CustomReflection.jpg` image file. From the **Inspector** view, change its **Texture Type** to **Cubemap**, its **Mapping** to **Latitude - Longitude Layout (Cylindrical)**, and check the boxes for **Glossy Reflection** and **Fixup Edge Seams**. Finally, change its **Filter Mode** to **Trilinear** and click on the **Apply** button, shown as follows:

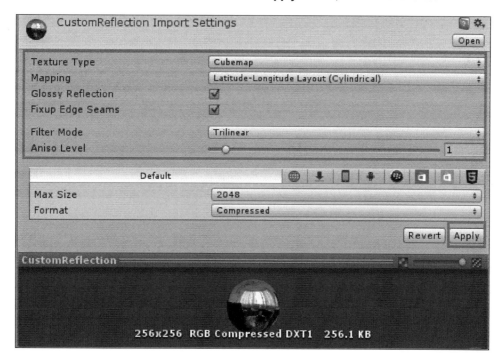

4. Let's replace the Scene's Skybox with our newly created **Cubemap**, as the **Reflection map** for our scene. In order to do this, open the **Lighting** window by navigating to the **Window | Lighting** menu. Select the **Scene** section and use the drop-down menu to change the **Reflection Source** to **Custom**. Finally, assign the newly created CustomReflection texture as the **Cubemap**, shown as follows:

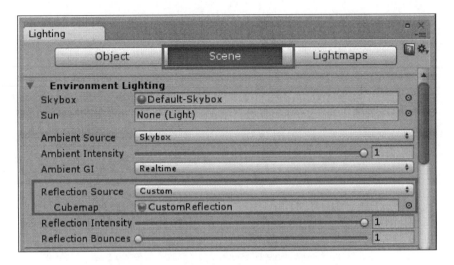

5. Check out for the new reflections on the battery_prefab object.

How it works...

While it is the material's specular map that allows for a reflective look, including the intensity and smoothness of the reflection, the refection itself (that is, the image you see on the reflection) is given by the **Cubemap** that we have created from the image file.

Reflection Cubemaps can be achieved in many ways and have different mapping properties.

Mapping coordinates

The **Cylindrical** mapping that we applied was well-suited for the photograph that we used. However, depending on how the reflection image is generated, a **Cubic** or **Spheremap**-based mapping can be more appropriate. Also, note that the **Fixup Edge Seams** option will try to make the image seamless.

Sharp reflections

You might have noticed that the reflection is somewhat blurry compared to the original image; this is because we have ticked the **Glossy Reflections** box. To get a sharper-looking reflection, deselect this option; in which case, you can also leave the **Filter Mode** option as default (Bilinear).

Maximum size

At 512 x 512 pixels, our reflection map will probably run fine on the lower-end machines. However, if the quality of the reflection map is not so important in your game's context, and the original image dimensions are big (say, 4096 x 4096), you might want to change the texture's **Max Size** at the **Import Settings** to a lower number.

Creating a laser aim with Projector and Line Renderer

Although using GUI elements, such as a cross-hair, is a valid way to allow players to aim, replacing (or combining) it with a projected laser dot might be a more interesting approach. In this recipe, we will use the **Projector** and **Line** components to implement this concept.

To help us with this recipe, it's been provided with a Unity package containing a sample scene featuring a character holding a laser pointer, and also a texture map named `LineTexture`. All files are inside the `1362_06_03` folder. Also, we'll make use of the **Effects** assets package provided by Unity (which you should have installed when installing Unity).

How to do it...

To create a laser dot aim with a Projector, follow these steps:

1. Import `BasicScene.unitypackage` to a new project. Then, open the scene named **BasicScene**. This is a basic scene, featuring a player character whose aim is controlled via mouse.

2. Import the **Effects** package by navigating to the **Assets | Import Package | Effects** menu. If you want to import only the necessary files within the package, deselect everything in the **Importing package** window by clicking on the **None** button, and then check the **Projectors** folder only. Then, click on **Import**, as shown:

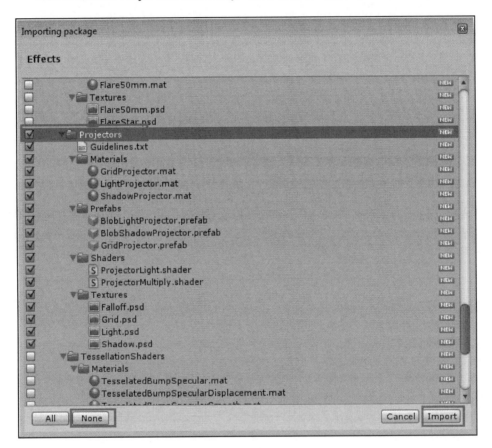

3. From the **Inspector** view, locate the `ProjectorLight` shader (inside the **Assets | Standard Assets | Effects | Projectors | Shaders** folder). Duplicate the file and name the new copy as `ProjectorLaser`.

4. Open `ProjectorLaser`. From the first line of the code, change
Shader `"Projector/Light"` to Shader `"Projector/Laser"`. Then, locate
the line of code – `Blend DstColor One` and change it to `Blend One One`. Save
and close the file.

> The reason for editing the shader for the laser was to make
> it stronger by changing its blend type to **Additive**. Shader
> programming is a complex subject, which is beyond the scope
> of this book. However, if you want to learn more about it, check
> out Unity's documentation on the subject, which is available at
> `http://docs.unity3d.com/Manual/SL-Reference.`
> `html`, and also the book called *Unity Shaders and Effects*
> *Cookbook*, published by Packt.

5. Now that we have fixed the shader, we need a material. From the **Project** view, use
the **Create** drop-down menu to create a new **Material**. Name it `LaserMaterial`.
Then, select it from the **Project** view and, from the **Inspector** view, change its **Shader**
to **Projector/Laser**.

6. From the **Project** view, locate the **Falloff** texture. Open it in your image editor and,
except for the first and last columns column of pixels that should be black, paint
everything white. Save the file and go back to Unity.

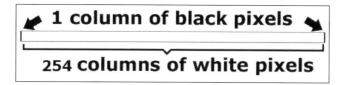

7. Change the **LaserMaterial**'s **Main Color** to red (RGB: `255, 0, 0`). Then, from the
texture slots, select the **Light** texture as **Cookie** and the **Falloff** texture as **Falloff**.

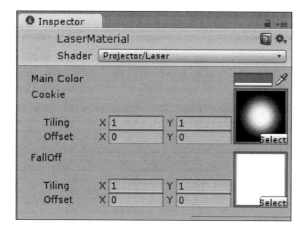

8. From the **Hierarchy** view, find and select the **pointerPrefab** object (**MsLaser** | **mixamorig:Hips** | **mixamorig:Spine** | **mixamorig:Spine1** | **mixamorig:Spine2** | **mixamorig:RightShoulder** | **mixamorig:RightArm** | **mixamorig:RightForeArm** | **mixamorig:RightHand** | **pointerPrefab**). Then, from the **Create** drop-down menu, select **Create Empty Child**. Rename the new child of **pointerPrefab** as **LaserProjector**.

9. Select the **LaserProjector** object. Then, from the **Inspector** view, click the **Add Component** button and navigate to **Effects | Projector**. Then, from the **Projector** component, set the **Orthographic** option as true and set **Orthographic Size** as 0.1. Finally, select **LaserMaterial** from the **Material** slot.

10. Test the scene. You will be able to see the laser aim dot, as shown:

11. Now, let's create a material for the **Line Renderer** component that we are about to add. From the **Project** view, use the **Create** drop-down menu to add a new **Material**. Name it as **Line_Mat**.

12. From the **Inspector** view, change the shader of the **Line_Mat** to **Particles/Additive**. Then, set its **Tint Color** to red (RGB: 255;0;0).

13. Import the LineTexture image file. Then, set it as the **Particle Texture** for the **Line_Mat**, as shown:

14. Use the **Create** drop-down menu from **Project** view to add a C# script named
    LaserAim. Then, open it in your editor.

15. Replace everything with the following code:

```
using UnityEngine;
using System.Collections;
public class LaserAim : MonoBehaviour {

  public float lineWidth = 0.2f;
  public Color regularColor = new Color (0.15f, 0, 0, 1);
  public Color firingColor = new Color (0.31f, 0, 0, 1);
  public Material lineMat;
  private Vector3 lineEnd;
  private Projector proj;
  private LineRenderer line;

  void Start () {
    line = gameObject.AddComponent<LineRenderer>();
    line.material = lineMat;
    line.material.SetColor("_TintColor", regularColor);
    line.SetVertexCount(2);
    line.SetWidth(lineWidth, lineWidth);
    proj = GetComponent<Projector> ();
  }

  void Update () {
    RaycastHit hit;
    Vector3 fwd = transform.TransformDirection(Vector3.forward);

    if (Physics.Raycast (transform.position, fwd, out hit))
    {
      lineEnd =  hit.point;
      float margin = 0.5f;
      proj.farClipPlane = hit.distance + margin;

    } else {
      lineEnd = transform.position + fwd * 10f;
    }
    line.SetPosition(0, transform.position);
```

```
            line.SetPosition(1, lineEnd);

        if(Input.GetButton("Fire1")){
            float lerpSpeed = Mathf.Sin (Time.time * 10f);
            lerpSpeed = Mathf.Abs(lerpSpeed);
            Color lerpColor = Color.Lerp(regularColor,
    firingColor, lerpSpeed);
            line.material.SetColor("_TintColor", lerpColor);

        }
        if(Input.GetButtonUp("Fire1")){
            line.material.SetColor("_TintColor", regularColor);
        }
    }
}
```

16. Save your script and attach it to the **LaserProjector** game object.

17. Select the **LaserProjector** GameObject. From the **Inspector** view, find the **Laser Aim** component and fill the **Line Material** slot with the Line_Mat material, as shown:

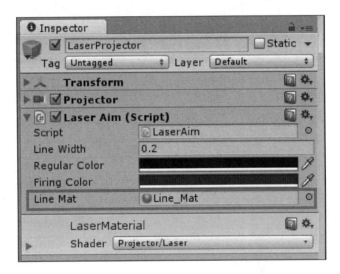

18. Play the scene. The laser aim is ready, and looks as shown:

In this recipe, the width of the laser beam and its aim dot have been exaggerated. Should you need a more realistic thickness for your beam, change the **Line Width** field of the **Laser Aim** component to 0.05, and the **Orthographic Size** of the **Projector** component to 0.025. Also, remember to make the beam more opaque by setting the **Regular Color** of the **Laser Aim** component brighter.

How it works...

The laser aim effect was achieved by combining two different effects: a **Projector** and **Line Renderer**.

A **Projector**, which can be used to simulate light, shadows, and more, is a component that projects a material (and its texture) onto other game objects. By attaching a projector to the **Laser Pointer** object, we have ensured that it will face the right direction at all times. To get the right, vibrant look, we have edited the projector material's **Shader**, making it brighter. Also, we have scripted a way to prevent projections from going through objects, by setting its **Far Clip Plane** on approximately the same level of the first object that is receiving the projection. The line of code that is responsible for this action is—proj.farClipPlane = hit. distance + margin;.

Regarding the **Line Renderer**, we have opted to create it dynamically, via code, instead of manually adding the component to the game object. The code is also responsible for setting up its appearance, updating the line vertices position, and changing its color whenever the fire button is pressed, giving it a glowing/pulsing look.

For more details on how the script works, don't forget to check out the commented code, available within the 1362_06_03 | End folder.

Reflecting surrounding objects with Reflection Probes

If you want your scene's environment to be reflected by game objects, featuring reflective materials (such as the ones with high Metallic or Specular levels), then you can achieve such effect using **Reflection Probes**. They allow for real-time, baked, or even custom reflections through the use of Cubemaps.

Real-time reflections can be expensive in terms of processing; in which case, you should favor baked reflections, unless it's really necessary to display dynamic objects being reflected (mirror-like objects, for instance). Still, there are some ways real-time reflections can be optimized. In this recipe, we will test three different configurations for reflection probes:

- ▶ Real-time reflections (constantly updated)
- ▶ Real-time reflections (updated on-demand) via script
- ▶ Baked reflections (from the Editor)

Getting ready

For this recipe, we have prepared a basic scene, featuring three sets of reflective objects: one is constantly moving, one is static, and one moves whenever it is interacted with. The Probes.unitypackage package that is containing the scene can be found inside the 1362_06_04 folder.

How to do it...

To reflect the surrounding objects using the Reflection probes, follow these steps:

1. Import Probes.unitypackage to a new project. Then, open the scene named **Probes**. This is a basic scene featuring three sets of reflective objects.

2. Play the scene. Observe that one of the systems is dynamic, one is static, and one rotates randomly, whenever a key is pressed.

3. Stop the scene.

4. First, let's create a constantly updated real-time reflection probe. From the **Create** drop-down button of the **Hierarchy** view, add a **Reflection Probe** to the scene (**Create | Light | Reflection Probe**). Name it as `RealtimeProbe` and make it a child of the **System 1 Realtime | MainSphere** game object. Then, from the **Inspector** view, the **Transform** component, change its **Position** to **X**: 0; **Y**: 0; **Z**: 0, as shown:

5. Now, go to the **Reflection Probe** component. Set **Type** as **Realtime**; **Refresh Mode** as **Every Frame** and **Time Slicing** as **No time slicing**, shown as follows:

6. Play the scene. The reflections will be now be updated in real time. Stop the scene.

7. Observe that the only object displaying the real-time reflections is **System 1 Realtime | MainSphere**. The reason for this is the **Size** of the Reflection Probe. From the **Reflection Probe** component, change its **Size** to **X**: 25; **Y**: 10; **Z**: 25. Note that the small red spheres are now affected as well. However, it is important to notice that all objects display the same reflection. Since our reflection probe's origin is placed at the same location as the **MainSphere**, all reflective objects will display reflections from that point of view.

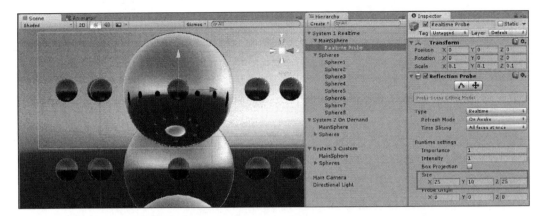

8. If you want to eliminate the reflection from the reflective objects within the reflection probe, such as the small red spheres, select the objects and, from the **Mesh Renderer** component, set **Reflection Probes** as **Off**, as shown in the following screenshot:

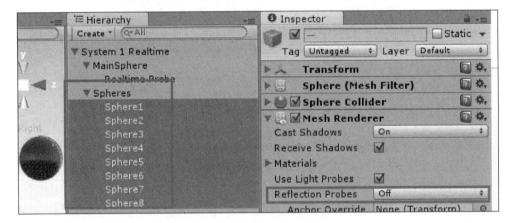

9. Add a new **Reflection Probe** to the scene. This time, name it OnDemandProbe and make it a child of the **System 2 On Demand | MainSphere** game object. Then, from the **Inspector** view, **Transform** component, change its **Position** to **X**: 0; **Y**: 0; **Z**: 0.

10. Now, go to the **Reflection Probe** component. Set **Type** as **Realtime**, **Refresh Mode** as **Via scripting**, and **Time Slicing** as **Individual faces**, as shown in the following screenshot:

11. Using the **Create** drop-down menu in the **Project** view, create a new C# Script named UpdateProbe.

12. Open your script and replace everything with the following code:

```
using UnityEngine;
using System.Collections;

public class UpdateProbe : MonoBehaviour {
  private ReflectionProbe probe;

  void Awake () {
    probe = GetComponent<ReflectionProbe> ();
    probe.RenderProbe();
  }

  public void RefreshProbe(){
    probe.RenderProbe();
  }
}
```

13. Save your script and attach it to the **OnDemandProbe**.

14. Now, find the script named RandomRotation, which is attached to the **System 2 On Demand | Spheres** object, and open it in the code editor.

15. Right before the `Update()` function, add the following lines:

```
private GameObject probe;
private UpdateProbe up;
void Awake(){
  probe = GameObject.Find("OnDemandProbe");
  up = probe.GetComponent<UpdateProbe>();
}
```

16. Now, locate the line of code called `transform.eulerAngles = newRotation;` and, immediately after it, add the following line:

```
up.RefreshProbe();
```

17. Save the script and test your scene. Observe how the **Reflection Probe** is updated whenever a key is pressed.

18. Stop the scene. Add a third **Reflection Probe** to the scene. Name it as `CustomProbe` and make it a child of the **System 3 On Custom | MainSphere** game object. Then, from the **Inspector** view, the **Transform** component, change its **Position** to **X**: 0; **Y**: 0; **Z**: 0.

19. Go to the **Reflection Probe** component. Set **Type** as **Custom** and click on the **Bake** button, as shown:

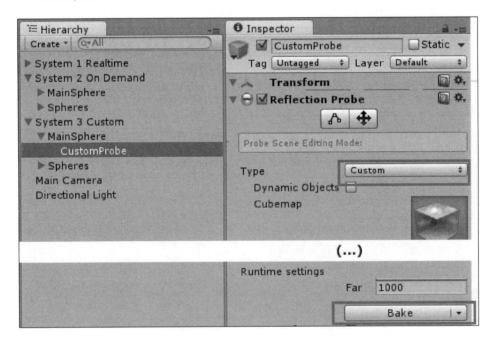

20. A **Save File** dialog window will show up. Save the file as
    `CustomProbe-reflectionHDR.exr`.

21. Observe that the reflection map does not include the reflection of red spheres on
    it. To change this, you have two options: set the **System 3 On Custom | Spheres**
    GameObject (and all its children) as **Reflection Probe Static** or, from the **Reflection
    Probe** component of the **CustomProbe** GameObject, check the **Dynamic Objects**
    option, as shown, and bake the map again (by clicking on the **Bake** button).

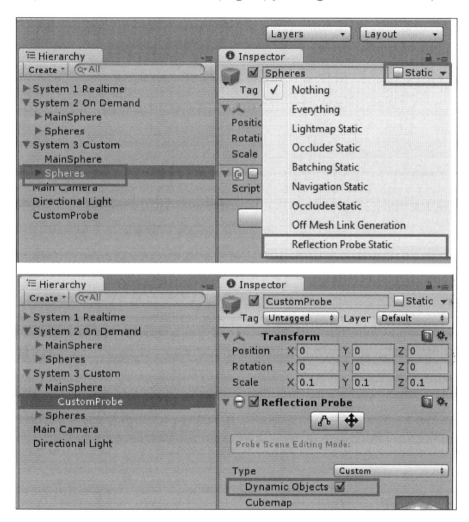

22. If you want your reflection **Cubemap** to be dynamically baked while you edit your scene, you can set the **Reflection Probe Type** to **Baked**, open the **Lighting** window (the **Assets | Lighting** menu), access the **Scene** section, and check the **Continuous Baking** option as shown. Please note that this mode won't include dynamic objects in the reflection, so be sure to set **System 3 Custom | Spheres** and **System 3 Custom | MainSphere** as **Reflection Probe Static**.

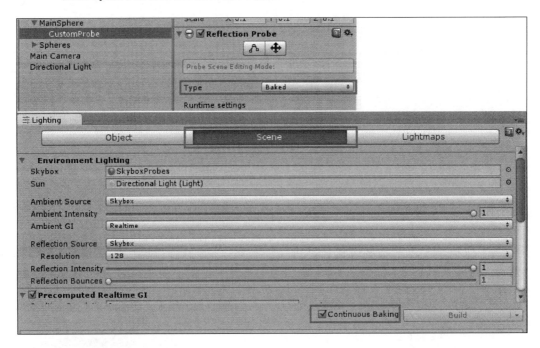

How it works...

The **Reflection Probes** element act like omnidirectional cameras that render **Cubemaps** and apply them onto the objects within their constraints. When creating **Reflection Probes**, it's important to be aware of how the different types work:

▶ **Real-time Reflection Probes**: Cubemaps are updated at runtime. The real-time Reflection Probes have three different **Refresh Modes**: **On Awake** (Cubemap is baked once, right before the scene starts); **Every frame** (Cubemap is constantly updated); **Via scripting** (Cubemap is updated whenever the **RenderProbe** function is used).

Since Cubemaps feature six sides, the **Reflection Probes** features **Time Slicing**, so each side can be updated independently. There are three different types of Time Slicing: **All Faces at Once** (renders all faces at once and calculates mipmaps over 6 frames. Updates the probe in 9 frames); **Individual Faces** (each face is rendered over a number of frames. It updates the probe in 14 frames. The results can be a bit inaccurate, but it is the least expensive solution in terms of frame-rate impact); **No Time Slicing** (The **Probe** is rendered and mipmaps are calculated in one frame. It provides high accuracy, but it also the most expensive in terms of frame-rate).

▸ **Baked:** Cubemaps are baked during editing the screen. Cubemaps can be either manually or automatically updated, depending whether the **Continuous Baking** option is checked (it can be found at the **Scene** section of the **Lighting** window).

▸ **Custom:** The Custom Reflection Probes can be either manually baked from the scene (and even include Dynamic objects), or created from a premade Cubemap.

There's more...

There are a number of additional settings that can be tweaked, such as **Importance**, **Intensity**, **Box Projection**, **Resolution**, **HDR**, and so on. For a complete view on each of these settings, we strongly recommend that you read Unity's documentation on the subject, which is available at `http://docs.unity3d.com/Manual/class-ReflectionProbe.html`.

Setting up an environment with Procedural Skybox and Directional Light

Besides the traditional 6 Sided and Cubemap, Unity now features a third type of skybox: the **Procedural Skybox**. Easy to create and setup, the **Procedural Skybox** can be used in conjunction with a **Directional Light** to provide **Environment Lighting** to your scene. In this recipe, we will learn about different parameters of the **Procedural Skybox**.

Getting ready

For this recipe, you will need to import Unity's Standard Assets Effects package, which you should have installed when installing Unity.

How to do it...

To set up an **Environment Lighting** using the **Procedural Skybox** and **Directional Light**, follow these steps:

1. Create a new scene inside a Unity project. Observe that a new scene already includes two objects: the **Main Camera** and a **Directional Light**.

2. Add some cubes to your scene, including one at **Position X**: 0; **Y**: 0; **Z**: 0 scaled to **X**: 20; **Y**: 1; **Z**: 20, which is to be used as the ground, as shown:

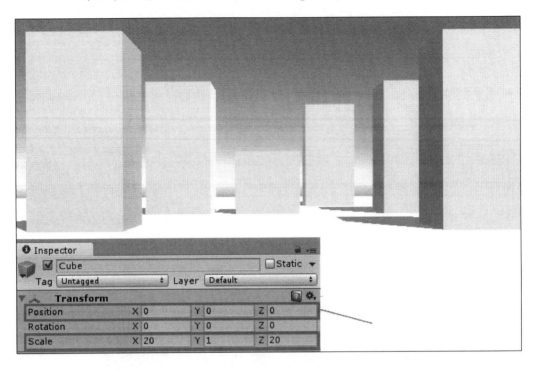

3. Using the **Create** drop-down menu from the **Project** view, create a new Material and name it MySkybox. From the **Inspector** view, use the appropriate drop-down menu to change the **Shader** of **MySkybox** from **Standard** to **Skybox/Procedural**.

4. Open the **Lighting** window (menu **Window** | **Lighting**), access the **Scene** section. At the **Environment Lighting** subsection, populate the **Skybox** slot with the **MySkybox** material, and the **Sun** slot with the **Directional Light** from the **Scene**.

5. From the **Project** view, select **MySkybox**. Then, from the **Inspector** view, set **Sun size** as 0.05 and **Atmosphere Thickness** as 1.4. Experiment by changing the **Sky Tint** color to RGB: 148; 128; 128, and the **Ground** color to a value that resembles the scene cube floor's color (such as RGB: 202; 202; 202). If you feel the scene is too bright, try bringing the **Exposure** level down to 0.85, shown as follows:

6. Select the **Directional Light** and change its **Rotation** to **X**: 5; **Y**: 170; **Z**: 0.
   Note that the scene should resemble a dawning environment, something like the following scene:

7. Let's make things even more interesting. Using the **Create** drop-down menu in the **Project** view, create a new C# Script named RotateLight. Open your script and replace everything with the following code:

```
using UnityEngine;
using System.Collections;
public class RotateLight : MonoBehaviour {
  public float speed = -1.0f;
  void Update () {
    transform.Rotate(Vector3.right * speed * Time.deltaTime);
  }
}
```

8. Save it and add it as a component to the **Directional Light**.

9. Import the **Effects** Assets package into your project (via the **Assets | Import Package | Effects** menu).

10. Select the **Directional Light**. Then, from **Inspector** view, **Light** component, populate the **Flare** slot with the Sun flare.

11. From the **Scene** section of the **Lighting** window, find the **Other Settings** subsection. Then, set **Flare Fade Speed** as 3 and **Flare Strength** as 0.5, shown as follows:

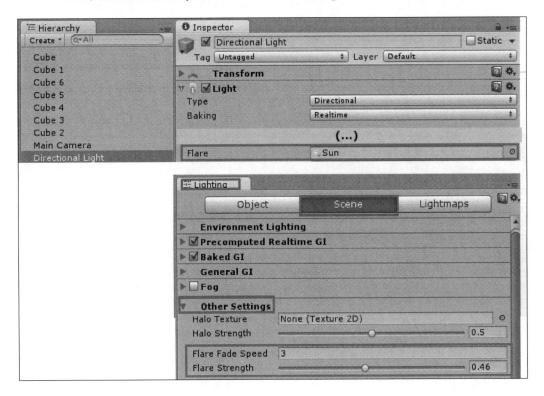

12. Play the scene. You will see the sun rising and the Skybox colors changing accordingly.

How it works...

Ultimately, the appearance of Unity's native Procedural Skyboxes depends on the five parameters that make them up:

  ▶ **Sun size**: The size of the bright yellow sun that is drawn onto the skybox is located according to the **Directional Light**'s **Rotation** on the *X* and *Y* axes.

- ▶ **Atmosphere Thickness**: This simulates how dense the atmosphere is for this skybox. Lower values (less than `1.0`) are good for simulating the outer space settings. Moderate values (around `1.0`) are suitable for the earth-based environments. Values that are slightly above `1.0` can be useful when simulating air pollution and other dramatic settings. Exaggerated values (like more than `2.0`) can help to illustrate extreme conditions or even alien settings.

- ▶ **Sky Tint**: It is the color that is used to tint the skybox. It is useful for fine-tuning or creating stylized environments.

- ▶ **Ground**: This is the color of the ground. It can really affect the **Global Illumination** of the scene. So, choose a value that is close to the level's terrain and/or geometry (or a neutral one).

- ▶ **Exposure**: This determines the amount of light that gets in the skybox. The higher levels simulate overexposure, while the lower values simulate underexposure.

It is important to notice that the **Skybox** appearance will respond to the scene's **Directional Light**, playing the role of the **Sun**. In this case, rotating the light around its *X* axis can create dawn and sunset scenarios, whereas rotating it around its *Y* axis will change the position of the sun, changing the cardinal points of the scene.

Also, regarding the **Environment Lighting**, note that although we have used the **Skybox** as the **Ambient Source**, we could have chosen a **Gradient** or a single **Color** instead—in which case, the scene's illumination wouldn't be attached to the Skybox appearance.

Finally, also regarding the **Environment Lighting**, please note that we have set the **Ambient GI** to **Realtime**. The reason for this was to allow the real-time changes in the GI, promoted by the rotating **Directional Light**. In case we didn't need these changes at runtime, we could have chosen the **Baked** alternative.

Lighting a simple scene with Lightmaps and Light Probes

Lightmaps are a great alternative to real-time lighting, as they can provide the desired look to an environment without being processor-intensive. There is one downside, though—since there is no way of baking Lightmaps onto the dynamic objects, the lighting of the important elements of the game (such as player characters themselves) can look artificial, failing to match the intensity of the surrounding area. The solution? **Light Probes**.

Light Probes work by sampling the light intensity over the location that they are placed at. Dynamic objects, once **Light Probe**-enabled, will be lit according to the interpolation of the nearest probes around them.

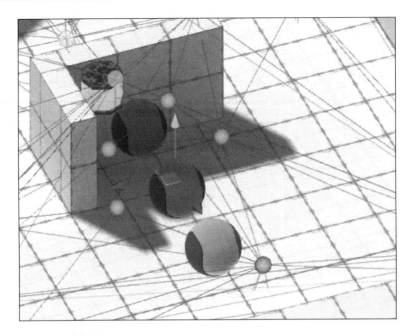

Getting ready

For this recipe, we have prepared a basic scene, including a simple game environment and an instance of Unity's Rollerball sample asset, which will be used as the player character. The geometry for the scene was created using **ProBuilder 2.0**, an extension developed by ProCore, and was sold at Unity's Asset Store and at ProCore's website (http://www.protoolsforunity3d.com). ProBuilder is a fantastic level design tool that speeds up the design process considerably for both simple and complex level design.

The LightProbes.unitypackage package, containing the scene and all necessary files, can be found inside the 1362_06_06 folder.

How to do it...

To reflect the surrounding objects using the **Reflection Probes**, follow these steps:

1. Import `LightProbes.unitypackage` to a new project. Then, open the scene named **LightProbes**. The scene features a basic environment and a playable Rollerball game sequence.

2. First, let's set up the light from our scene. From the **Hierarchy** view, select the **Directional Light**. Then, from the **Inspector** view, set **Baking** as **Baked**. Also, at the top of the **Inspector**, to the right of the object's name, check the **Static** box, shown as follows:

3. Now, let's set up the **Global Illumination** for the scene. Open the **Lighting** window (via the menu **Window | Lighting**) and select the **Scene** section. Then, from the **Environment Lighting** subsection, set `SkyboxProbes` (available from the **Assets**) as **Skybox**, and the scene's **Directional Light** as **Sun**. Finally, change the **Ambient GI** option from **Realtime** to **Baked**, as shown in the following screenshot:

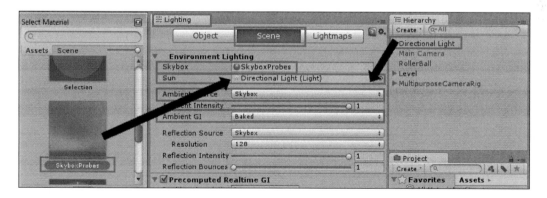

4. **Lightmaps** can be applied onto static objects only. From the **Hierarchy** view, expand the **Level** game object to reveal the list of the children objects. Then, select every child and set them as **Static**, as shown:

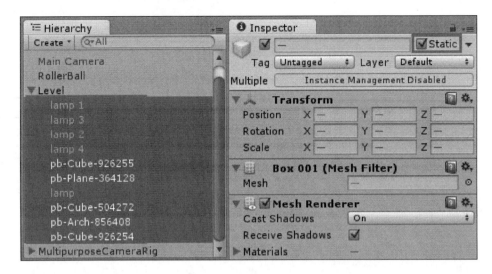

5. Imported 3D meshes must feature **Lightmap UV Coordinates**. From the **Project** view, find and select the `lamp` mesh. Then, from the **Inspector** view, within the **Model** section of the **Import Settings**, check the **Generate Lightmap UVs** option, and click on the **Apply** button to confirm changes, shown as follows:

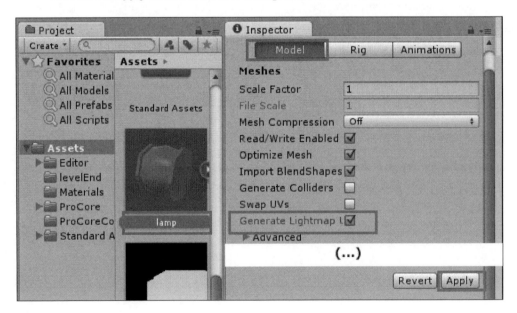

6. Scroll down the **Import Settings** view and expand the lamp's **Material** component. Then, populate the **Emission** field with the texture named `lamp_EMI`, available from the **Assets** folder. Finally, change **the Global Illumination** option to **Baked**. This will make the lamp object emit a green light that will be baked into the **Lightmap**.

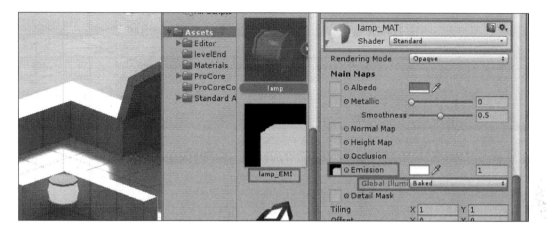

7. Open the **Lighting** window. By default, the **Continuous Baking** option will be checked. Uncheck it, as shown, so that we can bake the **Lightmaps** on demand.

8. Click on the **Build** button and wait for the Lightmaps to be generated.

9. From the **Hierarchy** view, select the **RollerBall**. Then, from the **Inspector** view, find the **Mesh Renderer** component and check the **Use Light Probes** option, as shown:

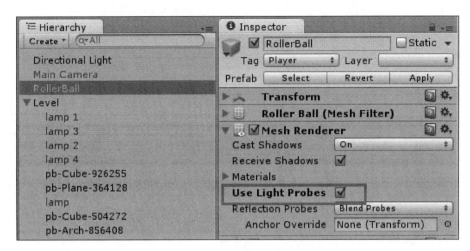

10. Now, we need to create the **Light Probes** for the scene. From the **Hierarchy** view, click on the **Create** drop-down menu and add a **Light Probe Group** to the scene (**Create | Light | Light Probe Group**).

11. To facilitate the manipulation of the probes, type `Probe` into the search field of the **Hierarchy** view. This will isolate the newly created **Light Probe Group**, making it the only editable object on the scene.

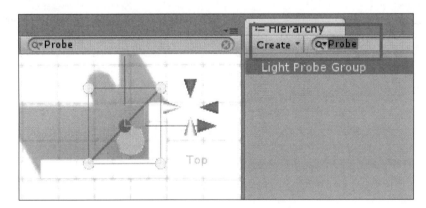

12. Change your viewport layout to **4 Split** by navigating to **Window | Layouts | 4 Split**. Then, set viewports as **Top**, **Front**, **Right**, and **Persp**. Optionally, change **Top**, **Front** and **Right** views to the **Wireframe** mode. Finally, make sure that they are set to orthographic view, as shown in the following screenshot. This will make it easier for you to position the **Light Probes**.

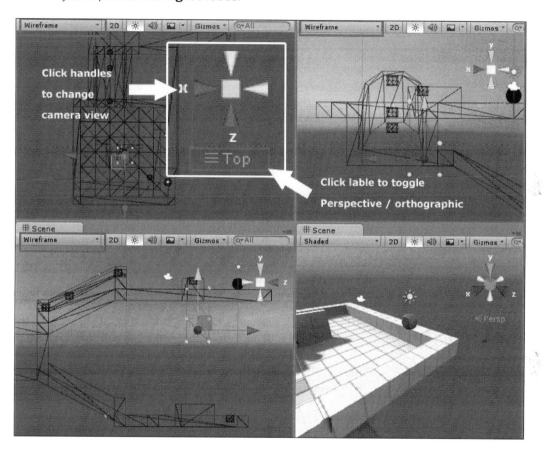

13. Position the initial **Light Probes** at the corners of the top room of the level. To move the Probes around, simply click and drag them, as shown:

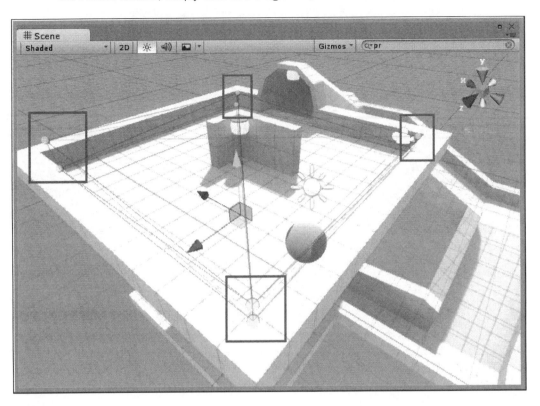

14. Select the four probes to the left side of the tunnel's entrance. Then, duplicate them by clicking on the appropriate button on the **Inspector** view or, alternatively, use the *Ctrl/Cmd + D* keys. Finally, drag the new probes slightly to the right, to a point that they are no longer over the shadow that is projected by the wall, shown as follows:

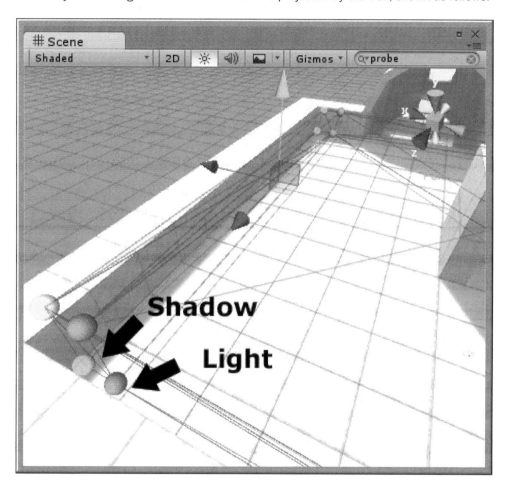

15. Repeat the last step, this time duplicating the probes next to the tunnel's entrance and bringing them inward towards the group. To delete the selected probes, either use the respective button on the **Light Probe Group** component, or use the *Ctrl/Cmd + Backspace* keys.

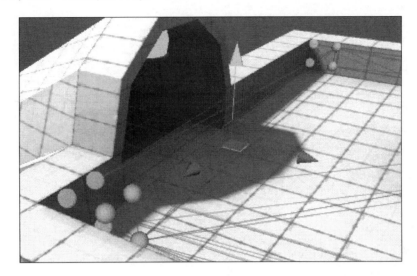

16. Duplicate and reposition the four probes that are nearest to the tunnel, repeating the operation five times and conforming each duplicate set to the shadow, projected by the tunnel.

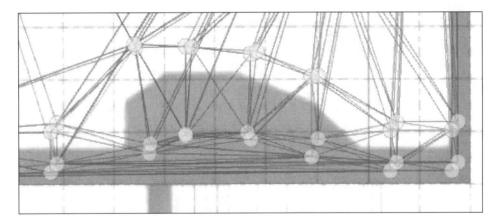

17. Use the **Add Probe** button to place the three probes over well-lit areas of the scene.

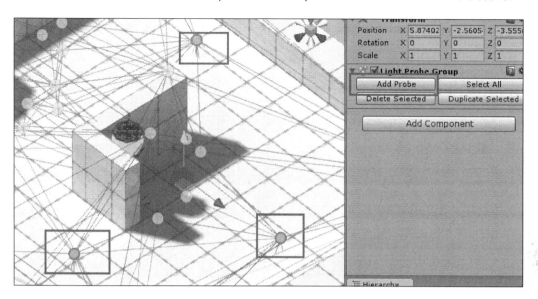

18. Now, add **Light Probes** within the shadow that is projected by the L-shaped wall.

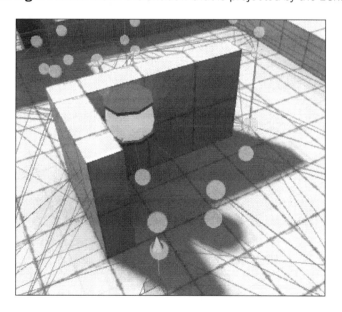

19. Since the Rollerball is able to jump, place the higher probes even higher, so that they will sample the lighting above the shadowed areas of the scene.

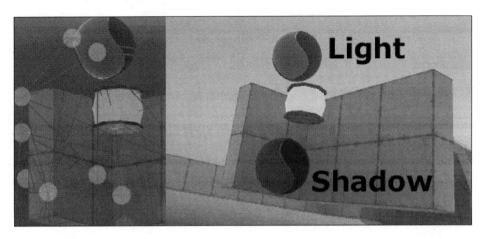

20. Placing too many **Light Probes** on a scene might be memory intensive. Try optimizing the **Light Probes Group** by removing the probes from the regions that the player won't have access to. Also, avoid overcrowding the regions of continuous lighting conditions by removing the probes that are too close to others in the same lighting condition.

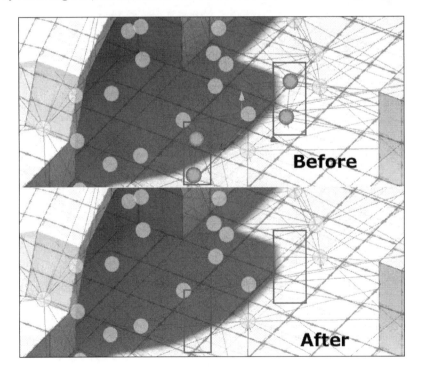

21. To check out which Light Probes are influencing the **Rollerball** at any place, move the **Rollerball** GameObject around the scene. A polyhedron will indicate which probes are being interpolated at that position, as shown:

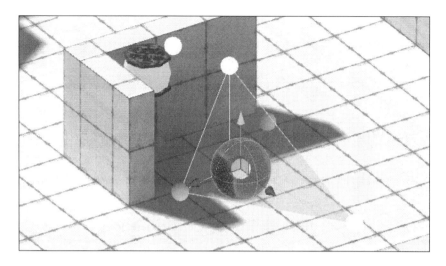

22. From the bottom of the **Lighting** window, click on the **Build** button and wait for the Lightmaps to be baked.

23. Test the scene. The Rollerball will be lit according to the Light Probes.

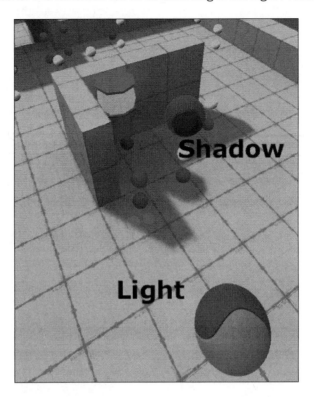

24. Keep adding probes until the level is completely covered.

How it works...

Lighmaps are basically texture maps including scene lights/shadows, global illumination, indirect illumination, and objects featuring the **Emissive** materials. They can be generated automatically or on demand by Unity's lighting engine. However, there are some points that you should pay attention to, such as:

 ▸ Set all the non-moving objects and lights to be baked as **Static**

 ▸ Set the game lights as **Baked**

 ▸ Set the scene's **Ambient GI** as **Baked**

 ▸ Set the **Global Illumination** option of the emissive materials as **Baked**

 ▸ **Generate Light UV**s for all 3D meshes (specially the imported ones)

 ▸ Either **Build** the Lightmaps manually from the **Lighting** window, or set the **Continuous Baking** option checked

Light Probes work by sampling the scene's illumination at the point that they're placed at. A dynamic object that has **Use Light Probes** enabled has its lighting determined by the interpolation between the lighting values of the four Light Probes defining a volume around it (or, in case there are no probes suited to define a volume around the dynamic object, a triangulation between the nearest probes is used).

It is important to notice that even if you are working on a level that is flat, you shouldn't place all your probes on the same level, as **Light Probe Groups** will form a volume in order to the interpolation to be calculated correctly. This and more information on the subject can be found in the Unity's documentation at `http://docs.unity3d.com/Manual/LightProbes.html`.

There's more...

In case you can spare some processing power, you can exchange the use of Light probes for a **Mixed** light. Just delete the **Light Probe Group** from your scene, select the **Directional Light** and, from the **Light** component, change **Baking** to **Mixed**. Then, set **Shadow Type** as **Soft Shadows** and **Strength** as `0.5`, as shown in the following screen. Finally, click on the **Build** button and wait for the Lightmaps to be baked. The real-time light/shadows will be cast into/from the dynamic objects, such as **Rollerball**.

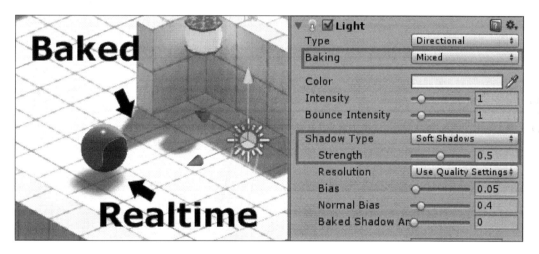

Conclusion

This chapter aimed to present you with some of the Unity's new features in lighting, and occasionally teaches you a few tricks with lights and effects. By now, you should be familiar with some of the concepts introduced by Unity 5, comfortable with a variety of techniques, and, hopefully, willing to explore some of the functionalities discussed throughout the recipes deeper.

As always, Unity's documentation on the subject is excellent, so we encourage you to go back to the recipes and follow the provided URLs.

7
Controlling 3D Animations

In this chapter, we will cover:

- ▸ Configuring a character's Avatar and idle animation
- ▸ Moving your character with root motion and Blend Trees
- ▸ Mixing animations with Layers and Masks
- ▸ Organizing States into Sub-State Machines
- ▸ Transforming the Character Controller via script
- ▸ Adding rigid props to animated characters
- ▸ Using Animation Events to throw an object
- ▸ Applying Ragdoll physics to a character
- ▸ Rotating the character's torso to aim a weapon

Introduction

The **Mecanim** animation system has revolutionized how characters are animated and controlled within Unity. In this chapter, we will learn how to take advantage of its flexibility, power, and friendly and highly visual interface.

The big picture

Controlling a playable character with the Mecanim System might look like a complex task, but it is actually very straightforward.

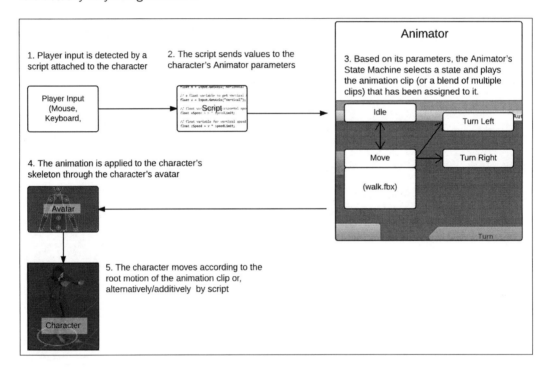

Hopefully, by the end of the chapter, you will have gained at least a basic understanding of the Mecanim system. For a more complete overview of the subject, consider taking a look at Jamie Dean's *Unity Character Animation* with Mecanim, also published by Packt Publishing.

An additional note—all the recipes will make use of **Mixamo** motion packs. Mixamo is a complete solution for character production, rigging, and animation. In fact, the character in use was designed with Mixamo's character creation software called **Fuse**, and rigged with the Mixamo **Auto-rigger**. You can find out more about Mixamo and their products at Unity's Asset Store (https://www.assetstore.unity3d.com/en/#!/publisher/150) or their website at https://www.mixamo.com/.

Please note that although Mixamo offers Mecanim-ready characters and animation clips, we will use, for the recipes in this chapter, unprepared animation clips. The reason is to make you more confident when dealing with assets obtained by other methods and sources.

Configuring a character's Avatar and idle animation

A feature that makes Mecanim so flexible and powerful is the ability of quickly reassigning animation clips from one character to another. This is made possible through the use of **Avatars**, which are basically a layer between your character's original rig and the Unity's **Animator** system.

In this recipe, we will learn how to configure an Avatar skeleton on a rigged character.

Getting ready

For this recipe, you will need the `MsLaser@T-Pose.fbx` and `Swat@rifle_aiming_idle.fbx` files, which are contained inside the `1362_07_code/character_and_clips/` folder.

How to do it...

To configure an Avatar skeleton, follow these steps:

1. Import the `MsLaser@T-Pose.fbx` and `Swat@rifle_aiming_idle.fbx` files to your project.

2. Select from the **Project** view, the `MsLaser@T-Pose` model.

3. In the **Inspector** view, under **MsLaser@T-Pose Import Settings**, activate the **Rig** section. Change **Animation Type** to **Humanoid**. Then, leave **Avatar Definition** as **Create From this Model**. Finally, click on the **Configure...** button.

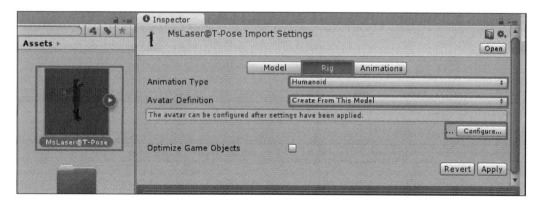

4. **Inspector** view will show the newly created Avatar. Observe how Unity correctly mapped the bones of our character into its structure, assigning, for instance, the **mixamoRig:LeftForeArm** bone as the Avatar's **Lower Arm**. We could, of course, reassign bones if needed. For now, just click on the **Done** button to close the view.

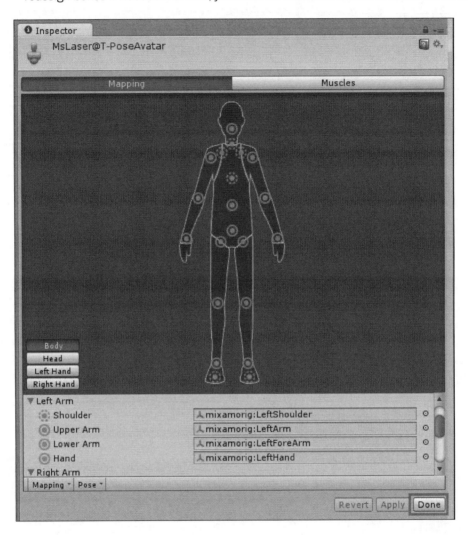

5. Now that we have our Avatar ready, let's configure our animation for the **Idle** state. From the **Project** view, select the **Swat@rifle_aiming_idle** file.

6. Activate the **Rig** section, change **Animation Type** to **Humanoid** and **Avatar Definition** to **Create From This Model**. Confirm by clicking on **Apply**.

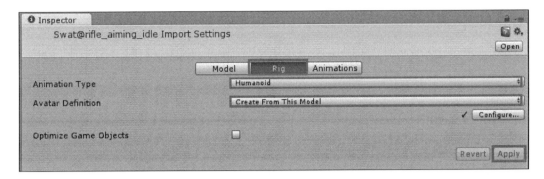

7. Activate the **Animations** section (to the right of the **Rig**). Select the **rifle_aiming_idle** clip (from the **Clips** list). The **Preview area** (at the bottom of the Inspector) will display the message as **No model is available for preview. Please drag a model into this Preview area**. Drag **MsLaser@T-Pose** to the **Preview** area to correct this.

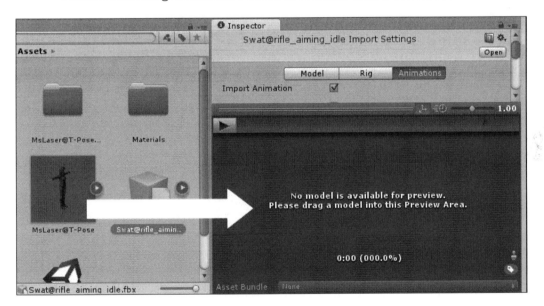

8. With **rifle_aiming_idle** selected from the **Clips** list, check the **Loop Time** and **Loop Pose** options. Also, click on the **Clamp Range** button to adjust the timeline to the actual time of the animation clip. Then, under **Root Transform Rotation**, check **Bake Into Pose**, and select **Baked Upon | Original**. Under **Root Transform Position (Y)**, check **Bake Into Pose**, and select **Baked upon (at Start) | Original**. Under **Root Transform Position (XZ)**, leave **Bake Into Pose** unchecked, and select **Baked Upon (at Start) | Center of Mass**. Finally, click on **Apply** to confirm the changes.

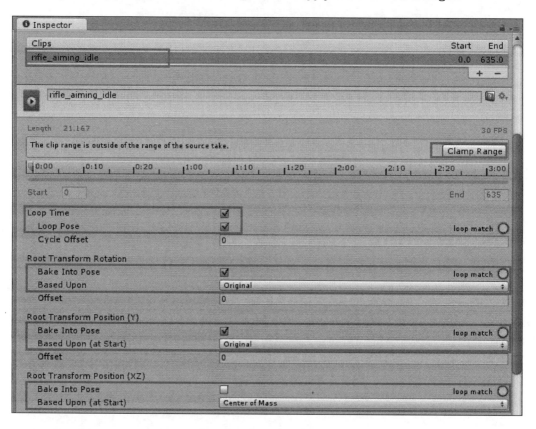

9. In order to access animation clips and play them, we need to create a controller. Do this by clicking on the **Create** button from the **Project** view, and then selecting the **Animator Controller** option. Name it as `MainCharacter`.

10. Double-click on the **Animator Controller** to open the **Animator** view.

11. From the **Animator** view, right-click on the grid to open a context menu. Then, select the **Create State | Empty** option. A new box named **New State** will appear. It will be in orange, indicating that it is the default state.

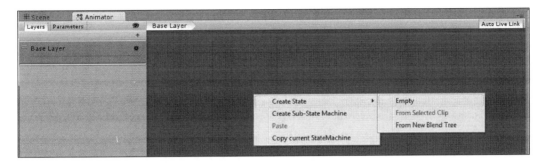

12. Select **New State** and, in the **Inspector** view, change its name to Idle. Also, in the **Motion** field, choose **rifle_aiming_idle** by either selecting it from the list or dragging it from the **Project** view.

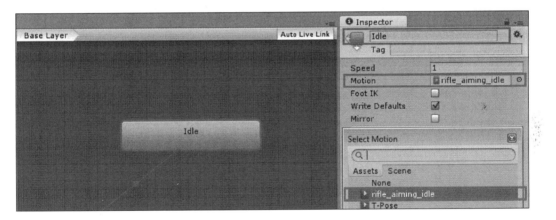

13. Drag the MsLaser@T-Pose model from the **Project** view into the **Hierarchy** view and place it on the scene.

14. Select **MsLaser@T-Pose** from the **Hierarchy** view and observe its **Animator** component in the **Inspector** view. Then, assign the newly created **MainCharacter controller** to its **Controller** field.

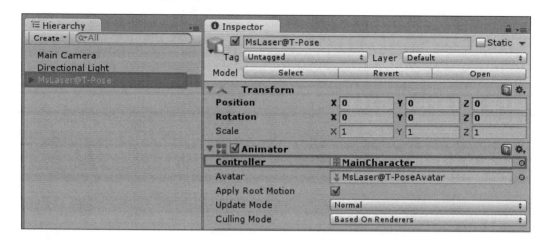

15. Play your scene to see the character correctly animated.

How it works...

Preparing our character for animation took many steps. First, we created its **Avatar**, based on the character model's original bone structure. Then, we set up the **animation clip** (which, as the character mesh, is stored in a `.fbx` file), using its own Avatar. After this, we adjusted the animation clip, clamping its size and making it a loop. We also baked its **Root Transform Rotation** to obey the original file's orientation. Finally, an **Animator Controller** was created, and the edited animation clip was made into its default **Animation state**.

The concept of the Avatar is what makes Mecanim so flexible. Once you have a **Controller**, you can apply it to other humanoid characters, as long as they have an Avatar body mask. If you want to try it yourself, import `mascot.fbx`, which is also available inside the `charater_and_clips` folder, apply steps 3 and 4 into this character, place it on the scene, and apply **MainCharacter** as its **Controller** in the **Animator** component. Then, play the scene to see the mascot playing the **rifle_aiming_idle** animation clip.

There's more...

To read more information about the Animator Controller, check out Unity's documentation at `http://docs.unity3d.com/Manual/class-AnimatorController.html`.

Moving your character with root motion and Blend Trees

The Mecanim animation system is capable of applying Root Motion to characters. In other words, it *actually* moves the character according to the animation clip, as opposed to arbitrarily translating the character model while playing an in-place animation cycle. This makes most of the Mixamo animation clips perfect for use with Mecanim.

Another feature of the animation system is **Blend Trees**, which can blend animation clips smoothly and easily. In this recipe, we will take advantage of these features to make our character walk/run forward and backwards, and also strafe right and left at different speeds.

Getting ready

For this recipe, we have prepared a Unity package named `Character_02`, containing a character and featuring a basic Animator Controller. The package can be found inside the `1362_07_02` folder, along with the `.fbx` files for the necessary animation clips.

How to do it...

To apply the Root Motion to your character using **Blend Trees**, follow these steps:

1. Import `Character_02.unityPackage` into a new project. Also, import `Swat@rifle_run`, `Swat@run_backwards`, `Swat@strafe`, `Swat@strafe_2`, `Swat@strafe_left`, `Swat@strafe_right`, `Swat@walking`, and `Swat@walking_backwards` `.fbx` files.

2. We need to configure our animation clips. From the **Project view**, select **Swat@rifle_run**.

3. Activate the **Rig** section. Change **Animation Type** to **Humanoid** and **Avatar Definition** to **Create From this Model**. Confirm by clicking on **Apply**.

4. Now, activate the **Animations** section (to the right of **Rig**). Select the **rifle_run** clip (from the **Clips** list). The **Preview area** (at the bottom of the **Inspector** view) will display the message as **No model is available for preview. Please drag a model into this Preview area**. Drag **MsLaser@T-Pose** onto the **Preview** area to correct this.

5. With **rifle_run** selected from the **Clips** list, select the **rifle_run** clip (from the **Clips** list) and check the **Loop Time** and **Loop Pose** options. Also, click on the **Clamp Range** button to adjust the timeline to the actual time of the animation clip.

6. Then, under **Root Transform Rotation**, check **Bake Into Pose**, and select **Baked Upon (at Start) | Original**. Under **Root Transform Position (Y)**, check **Bake Into Pose**, and select **Baked Upon | Original**. Under **Root Transform Position (XZ)**, leave **Bake Into Pose** unchecked, and select **Baked Upon (at Start) | Center of Mass**. Finally, click on **Apply** to confirm the changes.

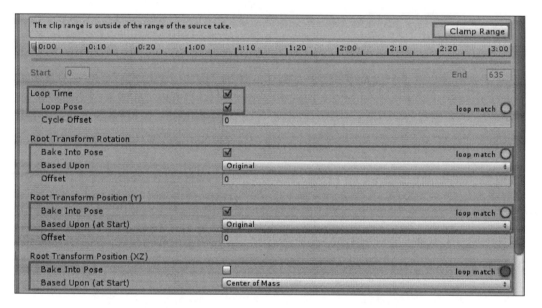

7. Repeat steps 3 to 6 for each one of the following animation clips: **Swat@run_backwards**, **Swat@strafe**, **Swat@strafe_2**, **Swat@strafe_left**, **Swat@strafe_right**, **Swat@walking**, and **Swat@walking_backwards**.

8. From the **Project view**, select the **MsLaser** prefab and drag it onto the **Hierarchy** view, placing it on the scene.

9. From the **Hierarchy** view, select the **MsLaser** GameObject and attach a **Character Controller** component to it (**menu Component | Physics | Character Controller**). Then, set its **Skin Width** as 0.0001, and its **Center** as **X: 0**, **Y: 0.9**, **Z: 0**; also change its **Radius** to **0.34** and its **Height** to **1.79**.

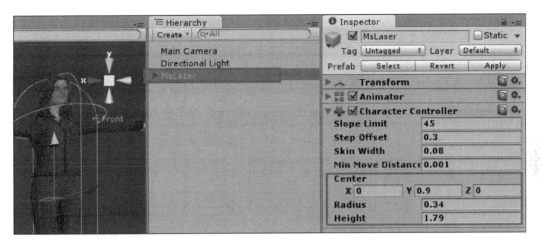

10. In the **Project view**, open the **MainCharacter** controller.

11. In the top-left corner of the **Animator** view, activate the **Parameters** section and use the **+** sign to create three new **Parameters (Float)** named xSpeed, zSpeed, and Speed.

12. We do have an **Idle** state for our character, but we need the new ones. Right-click on the gridded area and, from the context menu, navigate to **Create State | From New Blend Tree**. Change its name, from the **Inspector** view, to Move.

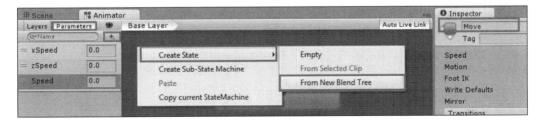

13. Double-click on the **Move** state. You will see the empty blend tree that you have created. Select it and, in the **Inspector** view, rename it to Move. Then, change its **Blend Type** to **2D Freeform Directional**, also setting **xSpeed** and **zSpeed** in the **Parameters** tab. Finally, using the **+** sign from the bottom of the **Motion** list, add nine new **Motion Fields**.

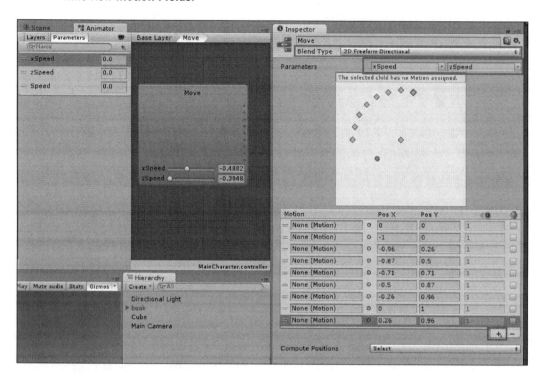

14. Now, populate the **Motion** list with the following motion clips and respective **Pos X** and **Pos Y** values: **run_backwards**, 0, -1; **walking_backwards**, 0,-0.5; **rifle_aiming_idle**, 0, 0; **walking**, 0, 0.5; **rifle_run**, 0, 1; **strafe**, -1, 0; **strafe_left**, -0.5, 0; **strafe_right**, 0.5, 0; **strafe_2**, 1, 0. You can populate the **Motion** list by selecting it from the list or, if there are more than one clip with the same name, you can drag it from the **Project view** onto the slot (by expanding the appropriate model icon).

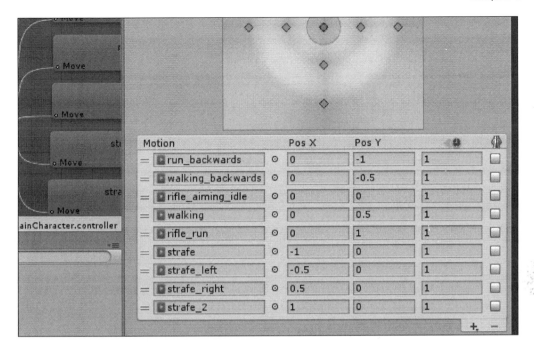

Motion		Pos X	Pos Y		
= run_backwards	⊙	0	-1	1	☐
= walking_backwards	⊙	0	-0.5	1	☐
= rifle_aiming_idle	⊙	0	0	1	☐
= walking	⊙	0	0.5	1	☐
= rifle_run	⊙	0	1	1	☐
= strafe	⊙	-1	0	1	☐
= strafe_left	⊙	-0.5	0	1	☐
= strafe_right	⊙	0.5	0	1	☐
= strafe_2	⊙	1	0	1	☐

15. Double-click on the gridded area to go from the **Move** blend tree back to the **Base Layer**.

16. Since we have the `rifle_aiming_idle` Motion clip within our **Move** blend tree, we can get rid of the original **Idle** state. Right-click on the **Idle** state box and, from the menu, select **Delete**. The **Move** blend state will become the new default state, turning orange.

17. Now, we must create the script that will actually transform the player's input into those variables that are created to control the animation.

18. From the **Project view**, create a new **C# Script** and name it as `BasicController`.

19. Open your script and replace everything with the following code:

```csharp
using UnityEngine;
using System.Collections;

public class BasicController: MonoBehaviour {
  private Animator anim;
  private CharacterController controller;
  public float transitionTime = .25f;
  private float speedLimit = 1.0f;
  public bool moveDiagonally = true;
  public bool mouseRotate = true;
  public bool keyboardRotate = false;

  void Start () {
    controller = GetComponent<CharacterController>();
    anim = GetComponent<Animator>();
  }

  void Update () {
    if(controller.isGrounded){
      if (Input.GetKey (KeyCode.RightShift) ||Input.GetKey
(KeyCode.LeftShift))
        speedLimit = 0.5f;
      else
        speedLimit = 1.0f;

      float h = Input.GetAxis("Horizontal");
      float v = Input.GetAxis("Vertical");
      float xSpeed = h * speedLimit;
      float zSpeed = v * speedLimit;
      float speed = Mathf.Sqrt(h*h+v*v);

      if(v!=0 && !moveDiagonally)
```

```
        xSpeed = 0;

    if(v!=0 && keyboardRotate)
        this.transform.Rotate(Vector3.up * h, Space.World);

    if(mouseRotate)
        this.transform.Rotate(Vector3.up * (Input.GetAxis("Mouse
X")) * Mathf.Sign(v), Space.World);

    anim.SetFloat("zSpeed", zSpeed, transitionTime, Time.
deltaTime);
    anim.SetFloat("xSpeed", xSpeed, transitionTime, Time.
deltaTime);
    anim.SetFloat("Speed", speed, transitionTime, Time.
deltaTime);
    }
  }
}
```

20. Save your script and attach it to the **MsLaser** GameObject in the **Hierarchy** view. Then, add **Plane** (menu option **GameObject | 3D Object | Plane**) and place it beneath the character.

21. Play your scene and test the game. You will be able to control your character with the arrow keys (or *WASD* keys). Keeping the *Shift* key pressed will slow it down.

How it works...

Whenever the `BasicController` script detects any directional keys in use, it sets the `Speed` variable of the **Animator** state to a value higher than 0, changing the **Animator** state from **Idle** to **Move**. The **Move** state, in its turn, blends the motion clips that it was populated with, according to the input values for `xSpeed` (obtained from **Horizontal Axis** input, typically *A* and *D* keys) and `zSpeed` (obtained from **Vertical Axis** input, typically *W* and *S* keys). Since Mecanim is capable of applying root motion to the characters, our character will actually move in the resulting direction.

For instance, if *W* and *D* keys are pressed, $xSpeed$ and $zSpeed$ values will rise to 1.0. From the **Inspector** view, it is possible to see that such combination will result in a blend between the motion clips called **rifle_run** and **strafe_2**, making the character run diagonally (front + right).

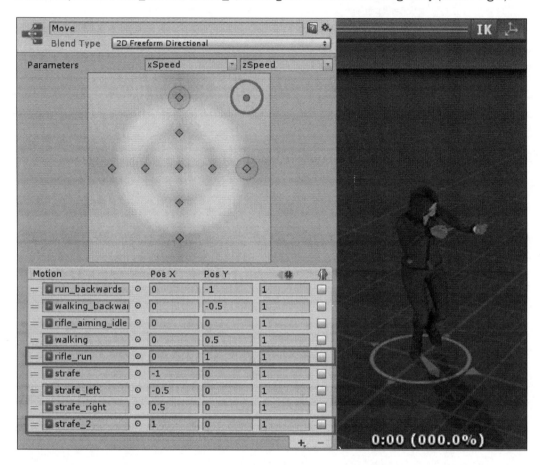

Our **BasicController** includes three checkboxes for more options: **Move Diagonally**—set as **true**, by default, which allows for blends between forward/backward and left/right clips; **Mouse Rotate**—set as **true**, by default, which allows for rotating the character with the mouse, changing their direction while moving; **Keyboard Rotate**—set as **false**, by default, which allows for rotating the character through simultaneous use of left/right and forward/backwards directional keys.

There's more...

Our blend tree used the **2D Freeform Directional Blend Type**. However, if we had only four animation clips (forward, backwards, left, and right), **2D Simple Directional** would have been a better option. Learn more on the following links:

▶ Learn more about Blend Trees and 2D blending from Unity's Documentation at: `http://docs.unity3d.com/Manual/BlendTree-2DBlending.html`.

▶ Also, if you want to learn more about Mecanim Animation System, there are some links that you might want to check out, such as Unity's documentation at: `http://docs.unity3d.com/Manual/AnimationOverview.html`.

▶ Mecanim Example Scenes are available at Unity Asset Store at: `https://www.assetstore.unity3d.com/en/#!/content/5328`.

▶ Mecanim Video Tutorial are available at: `http://www.video.unity3d.com/video/7362044/unity-40-mecanim-animation`.

Mixing animations with Layers and Masks

Mixing animations is a great way of adding complexity to your animated characters without requiring a vast number of animated clips. Using **Layers** and **Masks**, we can combine different animations by playing specific clips for the specific body parts of the character. In this recipe, we will apply this technique to our animated character, triggering animation clips for firing a rifle, and throwing a grenade with the character's upper body. We will do this while keeping the lower body moving or idle, according to the player's input.

Getting ready

For this recipe, we have prepared a Unity Package named `Mixing`, containing a basic scene that features an animated character. The package can be found inside the `1362_07_03` folder, along with the animation clips called `Swat@firing_rifle.fbx` and `Swat@toss_grenade.fbx`.

How to do it...

To mix animations using layers and masks, follow these steps:

1. Create a new project and import the `Mixing` Unity Package. Then, from the **Project view**, open the **mecanimPlayground** level.

2. Import the `Swat@firing_rifle.fbx` and `Swat@toss_grenade.fbx` files to the project.

3. We need to configure the animation clips. From the **Project view**, select the **Swat@firing_rifle** animation clip.

4. Activate the **Rig** section. Change **Animation Type** to **Humanoid**, and **Avatar Definition** to **Create From this Model**. Confirm this by clicking on **Apply**.

5. Now, activate the **Animations** section. Select the **firing_rifle** clip (from the **Clips** list), click on the **Clamp Range** button to adjust the timeline, and check the **Loop Time** and **Loop Pose** options. Under **Root Transform Rotation**, check **Bake Into Pose**, and select **Baked Upon | Original**. Under **Root Transform Position (Y)**, check **Bake Into Pose**, and select **Baked Upon (at Start) | Original**. Under **Root Transform Position (XZ)**, leave **Bake Into Pose** unchecked. Click on **Apply** to confirm the changes.

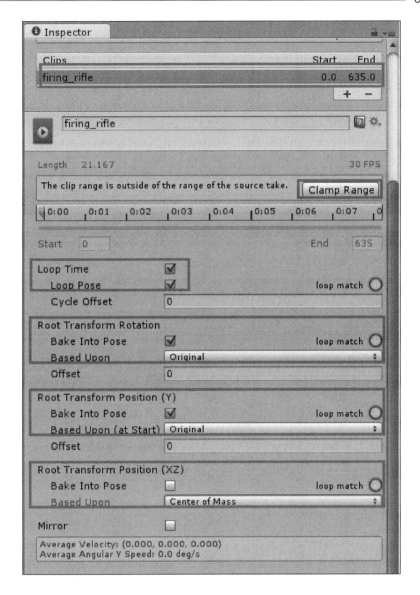

6. Select the **Swat@toss_grenade** animation clip. Activate the **Rig** section. Then, change **Animation Type** to **Humanoid**, and **Avatar Definition** to **Create From this Model**. Confirm it by clicking on **Apply**.

7. Now, activate the **Animations** section. Select the **toss_grenade** clip (from the **Clips** list), click on the button **Clamp Range** to adjust the timeline, and leave the **Loop Time** and **Loop Pose** options unchecked. Under **Root Transform Rotation**, check **Bake Into Pose**, and select **Baked Upon (at Start) | Original**. Under **Root Transform Position (Y)**, check **Bake Into Pose**, and select **Baked Upon (at Start) | Original)**. Under **Root Transform Position (XZ)**, leave **Bake Into Pose** unchecked. Click on **Apply** to confirm the changes.

8. Let's create a Mask. From the **Project** view, click on the **Create** button and add an **Avatar Mask** to the project. Name it as **BodyMask**.

9. Select the **BodyMask** tab and, in the **Inspector** view, expand the **Humanoid** section to unselect the character's legs, base, and **IK** spots, turning their outline red.

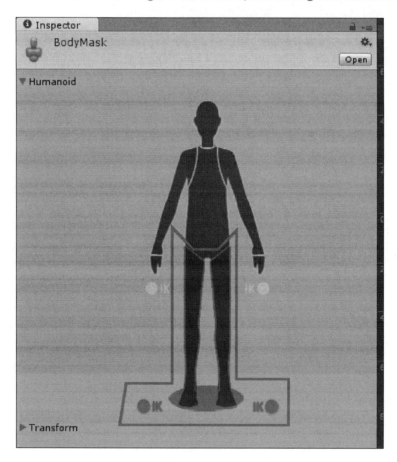

10. From the **Hierarchy** view, select the **MsLaser** character. Then, from the **Animator** component in the **Inspector** view, double-click on the **MainCharacter** controller to open it.

11. In the **Animator** view, create a new layer by clicking on the **+** sign at the top-left **Layers** tab, above the **Base Layer**.

12. Name the new layer as **UpperBody** and click on the gear icon for the settings. Then, change its **Weight** to 1, and select the **BodyMask** in the **Mask** slot. Also, change Blending to **Additive**.

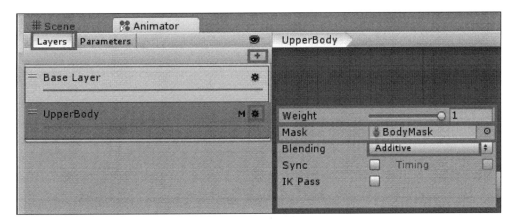

13. Now, in the **Animator** view, with the **UpperBody** layer selected, create three new empty states (by right-clicking on the gridded area and navigating to, from the menu, **Create State | Empty**). Name the default (orange) state **null**, and the other two as **Fire** and **Grenade**.

14. Now, access the **Parameters** tab and add two new parameters of the Boolean type: Fire and Grenade.

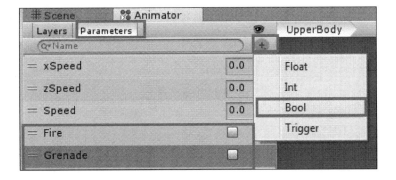

15. Select the **Fire** state and, in the **Inspector** view, add the **firing_rifle** animation clip to the **Motion** field.

16. Now, select the **Grenade** state and, in the **Inspector** view, add the **toss_grenade** animation clip to the **Motion** field.

17. Right-click on the **null** state box and, from the menu, select **Make Transition**. Then, drag the white arrow onto the **Fire** box.

18. Select the arrow (it will turn blue). From the **Inspector** view, uncheck the **Has Exit Time** option. Then, access the **Conditions** list, click on the **+** sign to add a new condition, and set it as **Fire** and **true**.

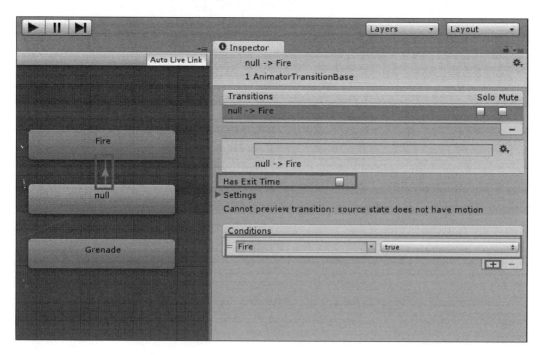

19. Now, make a transition from **null** to **Grenade**. Select the arrow (it will turn blue). From the **Inspector** view, uncheck the **Has Exit Time** option. Then, access the **Conditions** list, click on the **+** sign to add a new condition, and set it as **Grenade** and **true**.

20. Now, create transitions from **Fire** to **null**, and from **Grenade** to **null**. Then, select the arrow that goes from **Fire** to **null** and, in the **Conditions** box, select the **Fire** and **false** options. Leave the **Has Exit Time** option checked.

21. Finally, select the arrow that goes from **Grenade** to **null**. In the Conditions box, select the options Grenade, false. Leave the **Has Exit Time** option checked.

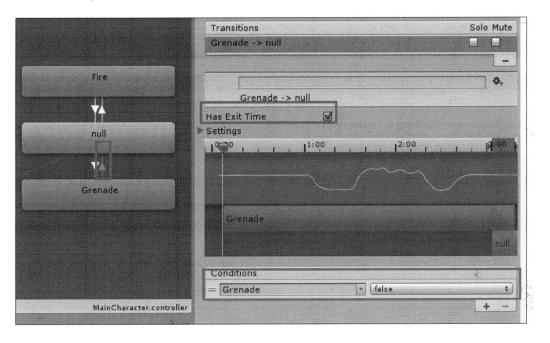

22. From the **Hierarchy** view, select the **MsLaser** character. Locate, in the **Inspector** view, the **Basic Controller** component and open its script.

23. Immediately before the end of the Update() function, add the following code:

```
if(Input.GetKeyDown(KeyCode.F)){
  anim.SetBool("Grenade", true);
} else {
  anim.SetBool("Grenade", false);
}
if(Input.GetButtonDown("Fire1")){
  anim.SetBool("Fire", true);
```

```
    }
    if(Input.GetButtonUp("Fire1")){
      anim.SetBool("Fire", false);
    }
```

24. Save the script and play your scene. You will be able to trigger the **firing_rifle** and **toss_grenade** animations by clicking on the **fire** button and pressing the *F* key. Observe how the character's legs still respond to the **Move** animation state.

How it works...

Once the Avatar mask is created, it can be used as a way of filtering the body parts that would actually play the animation states of a particular layer. In our case, we have constrained our **fire_rifle** and **toss_grenade** animation clips to the upper body of our character, leaving the lower body free to play the movement-related animation clips, such as walking, running, and strafing.

There's more...

You might have noticed that the **UpperBody** layer has a parameter named **Blending**, which we have set to **Additive**. This means that animation states in this layer will be added to the ones from the lower layers. If changed to **Override**, the animation from this would override animation states from the lower layers when played. In our case, **Additive** helped in keeping the aim stable when firing while running.

For more information on **Animation Layers** and **Avatar Body Masks**, check out Unity's documentation at `http://docs.unity3d.com/Manual/AnimationLayers.html` and `http://www.docs.unity3d.com/Manual/class-AvatarBodyMask.html`.

Organizing States into Sub-state Machines

Whenever the Animator area gets too cluttered, you can always think of organizing your Animation States into Sub-State Machines. In this recipe, we will use this technique to organize animation states for turning the character. Also, since the provided animation clips do not include Root Motion, we will use the opportunity to illustrate how to overcome the lack of Root Motion via script, using it to turn the character 45 degrees to the left and right.

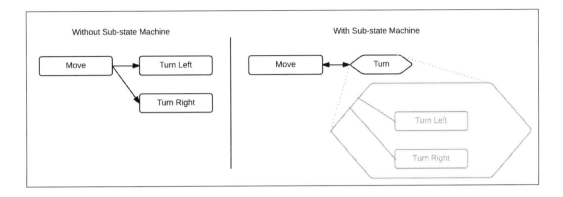

Getting ready

For this recipe, we have prepared a Unity Package named `Turning`, containing a basic scene that features an animated character. The package can be found inside the `1362_07_04` folder, along with animation clips called `Swat@turn_right_45_degrees.fbx` and `Swat@turn_left.fbx`.

How to do it...

To apply Root Motion via script, please follow these steps:

1. Create a new project and import the `Turning` Unity Package. Then, from the **Project** view, open the **mecanimPlayground** level.

2. Import the `Swat@turn_right_45_degrees.fbx` and `Swat@turn_left.fbx` files in the project.

3. We need to configure our animation clips. Select the **Swat@turn_left** file from the **Project** view.

4. Activate the **Rig** section. Change **Animation Type** to **Humanoid**, and **Avatar Definition** to **Create From this Model**. Confirm by clicking on **Apply**.

5. Now, activate the **Animations** section. Select the **turn_left** clip (from the **Clips** list), click on the **Clamp Range** button to adjust the timeline, and check the **Loop Time** option. Under **Root Transform Rotation**, check **Bake Into Pose**, and navigate to **Baked Upon (at Start) | Original**. Under **Root Transform Position (Y)**, check **Bake Into Pose**, and select **Baked Upon (at Start) | Original**. Under **Root Transform Position (XZ)**, leave **Bake Into Pose** unchecked. Click on **Apply** to confirm the changes.

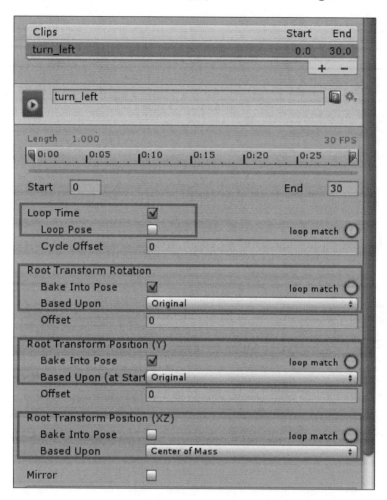

6. Repeat steps 4 and 5 for **Swat@turning_right_45_degrees**.

7. From the **Hierarchy** view, select the **MsLaser** character. Then, from the **Animator** component in the **Inspector** view, open the **MainCharacter** controller.

8. From the top-left corner of the **Animator** view, activate the **Parameters** section and use the **+** sign to create the two new **Parameters (Boolean)** named `TurnLeft` and `TurnRight`.

9. Right-click on the gridded area. From the context menu, select **Create Sub-State Machine**. From the **Inspector** view, rename it `Turn`.

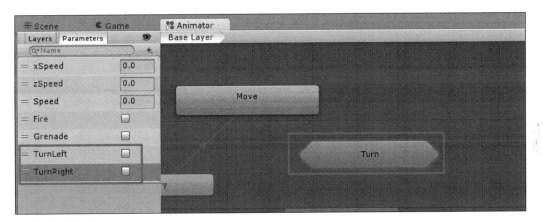

10. Double-click on the **Turn** sub-state machine. Right-click on the gridded area, select **Create State | Empty**, and add a new state. Rename it to `Turn Left`. Then, add another state named `Turn Right`.

11. From the **Inspector** view, populate `Turn Left` with the **turn_left** motion clip. Then, populate `Turn Right` with **turning_right_45_degrees**.

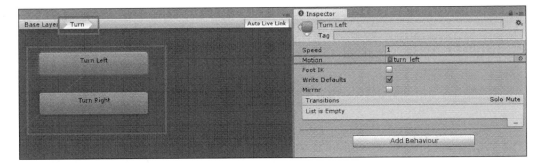

12. Get out of the **Turn** sub-state machine back into the **Base Layer**. By right-clicking on each state and selecting the option **Make Transition**, create transitions between **Move** and **Turn Left**, and **Move** and **Turn Right**.

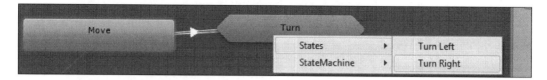

13. Enter the **Turn** sub-state machine. Then, create transitions from **Turn Left** and **Turn Right** into the **Move** state.

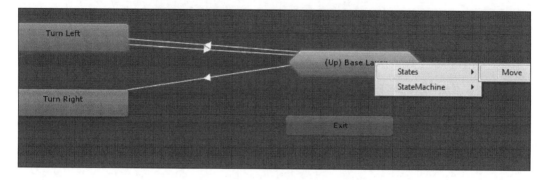

14. Select the arrow that goes form **Turn Right** to **(Up) Base Layer**. It will turn blue. From the **Inspector** view, uncheck the **Has Exit Time** option. Then, access the **Conditions** list, click the **+** sign to add a new condition, and set it as **TurnRight** and **false**.

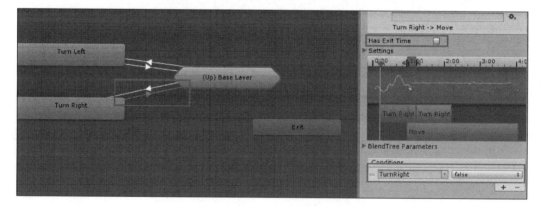

15. Select the arrow that goes from **(Up) Base Layer** to **Turn Right**. From the **Inspector** view, uncheck the **Has Exit Time** option. Then, access the **Conditions** list, click the **+** sign to add a new condition, and set it as **TurnRight** and **true**.

16. Repeat steps 14 and 15 with the arrows that go between **(Up) Base Layer** and **Turn Left**, using **TurnLeft** as a condition, this time.

17. From the **Hierarchy** view, select the **MsLaser** character. Then, from the **Inspector** view, open the script from the **BasicController** component.

18. Immediately after the `if(controller.isGrounded){` line, add:

```
if(Input.GetKey(KeyCode.Q)){
  anim.SetBool("TurnLeft", true);
  transform.Rotate(Vector3.up * (Time.deltaTime * -45.0f),
Space.World);
} else {
  anim.SetBool("TurnLeft", false);
}
if(Input.GetKey(KeyCode.E)){
  anim.SetBool("TurnRight", true);
  transform.Rotate(Vector3.up * (Time.deltaTime * 45.0f), Space.
World);
} else {
  anim.SetBool("TurnRight", false);
}
```

19. Save your script. Then, select the **MsLaser** character and, from the **Inspector** view, access the **Basic Controller** component. Leave the **Move Diagonally** and **Mouse Rotate** options unchecked. Also, leave the **Keyboard Rotate** option checked. Finally, play the scene. You will be able to turn left and right by using the *Q* and *E* keys, respectively.

How it works...

As it should be clear from the recipe, the sub-state machines work in a similar way to groups or folders, allowing you to encapsulate a series of state machines into a single entity for easier reference. States from the sub-state machines can be transitioned from external states, in our case, the **Move** state, or even from different sub-state machines.

Regarding the character's rotation, we have overcome the lack of root motion by using the `transform.Rotate(Vector3.up * (Time.deltaTime * -45.0f), Space.World);` command to make the character actually turn around when the *Q* and *E* keys are being held down. This command was used in conjunction with `animator.SetBool("TurnLeft", true);`, which triggers the right animation clip.

Transforming the Character Controller via script

Applying **Root Motion** to your character might be a very practical and accurate way to animate it. However, every now and then, you might need to manually control one or two aspects of the character movement. Perhaps you only have an in-place animation to work with, or maybe you want the character's movement to be affected by other variables. In these cases, you will need to override the root motion via script.

To illustrate this issue, this recipe makes use of an animation clip for jumping, which originally moves the character only in the Y-axis. In order to make her move forward or backwards while jumping, we will learn how to access the character's velocity to inform the jump's direction via the script.

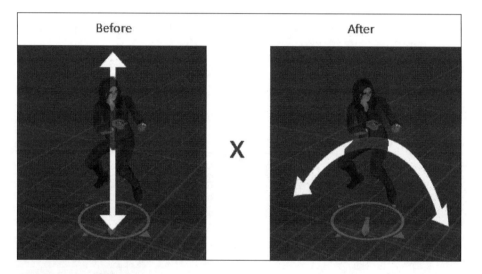

Getting ready

For this recipe, we have prepared a Unity Package named Jumping, containing a basic scene that features an animated character. The package can be found inside the 1362_07_05 folder, along with the animation clip called Swat@rifle_jump.

How to do it...

To apply the Root Motion via script, please follow these steps:

1. Create a new project and import the Jumping Unity Package. Then, from the **Project** view, open the **mecanimPlayground** level.

2. Import the `Swat@rifle_jump.fbx` file to the project.

3. We need to configure our animation clip. From the **Project** view, select the **Swat@rifle_jump** file.

4. Activate the **Rig** section. Change **Animation Type** to **Humanoid**, and **Avatar Definition** to **Create From this Model**. Confirm this by clicking on **Apply**.

5. Now, activate the **Animations** section. Select the **rifle_jump** clip (from the **Clips** list), click on the **Clamp Range** button to adjust the timeline, and check the **Loop Time** and **Loop Pose** options. Under **Root Transform Rotation**, check **Bake Into Pose**, and select **Baked Upon (at Start) | Original**. Under **Root Transform Position (Y)**, leave **Bake into Pose** unchecked, and select **Baked Upon (at Start) | Original**. Under **Root Transform Position (XZ)**, leave **Bake Into Pose** unchecked. Click on **Apply** to confirm the changes.

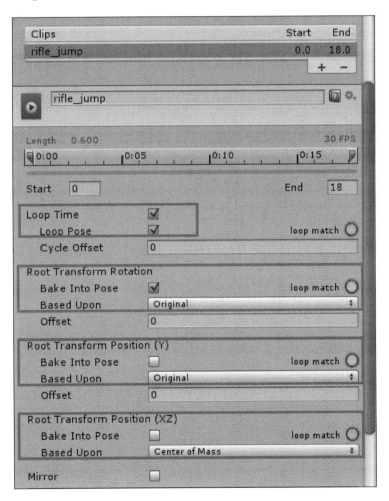

6. From the **Hierarchy** view, select the **MsLaser** character. Then, from the **Animator** component in the **Inspector** view, open the **MainCharacter** controller.

7. From the top-left corner of the **Animator** view, activate the **Parameters** section, and use the **+** sign to create a new **Parameters (Boolean)** named Jump.

8. Right-click on the gridded area and, from the context menu, select **Create State | Empty**. Change its name, from the **Inspector** view, to Jump.

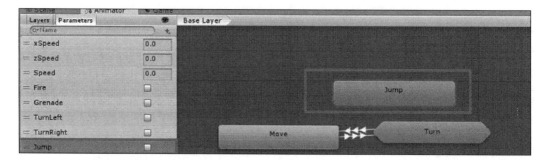

9. Select the **Jump** state. Then, from the **Inspector** view, populate it with the **rifle_jump** Motion clip.

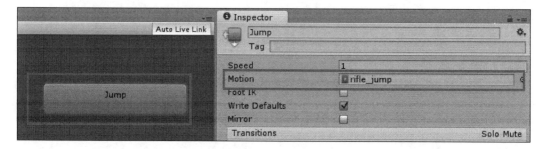

10. Find and right-click on the **Any State**. Then, selecting the **Make Transition** option, create a transition from **Any State** to **Jump**. Select the transition, uncheck **Has Exit Time**, and use the **Jump** variable as a condition (**true**).

11. Now, create a transition from **Jump** to **Move**.

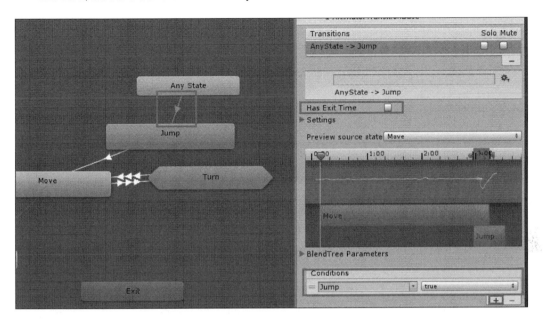

12. Configure the transitions between **Jump** and **Move**, leaving **Has Exit Time** checked, and use the **Jump** variable as a condition (**false**).

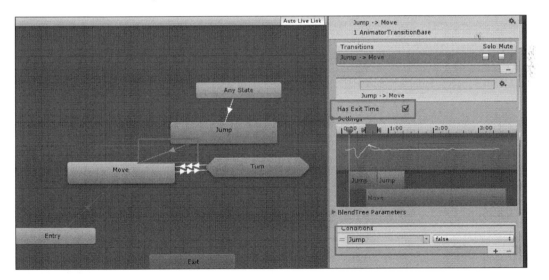

13. From the **Hierarchy** view, select the **MsLaser** character. Then, from the **Inspector** view, open the script from the **BasicController** component.

14. Right before the `Start()` function, add the following code:

```
public float jumpHeight = 3f;
private float verticalSpeed = 0f;
private float xVelocity = 0f;
private float zVelocity = 0f;
```

15. Inside the `Update()` function, find the line containing the following code:

```
if(controller.isGrounded){
```

And add the following lines immediatly after it:

```
if (Input.GetKey (KeyCode.Space)) {
  anim.SetBool ("Jump", true);
  verticalSpeed = jumpHeight;
}
```

16. Finally, add a new function, following immediately before the final } of the code:

```
void OnAnimatorMove(){
  Vector3 deltaPosition = anim.deltaPosition;
  if (controller.isGrounded) {
    xVelocity = controller.velocity.x;
    zVelocity = controller.velocity.z;
  } else {
    deltaPosition.x = xVelocity * Time.deltaTime;
    deltaPosition.z = zVelocity * Time.deltaTime;
    anim.SetBool ("Jump", false);
  }
  deltaPosition.y = verticalSpeed * Time.deltaTime;
  controller.Move (deltaPosition);
  verticalSpeed += Physics.gravity.y * Time.deltaTime;
  if ((controller.collisionFlags & CollisionFlags.Below)
!= 0) {
    verticalSpeed = 0;
  }
}
```

17. Save your script and play the scene. You will be able to jump around using the *Space* key. Observe how the character's velocity affects the direction of the jump.

How it works...

Observe that once this function is added to the script, the **Apply Root Motion** field, in the **Animator** component, changes from a checked box to **Handled by Script**. The reason is that in order to override the animation clip's original movement, we have placed, inside Unity's `OnAnimatorMove()` function, a series of commands to move our character controller while jumping. The line of code: `controller.Move (deltaPosition);` basically replaces the jump's direction from the original animation with the `deltaPosition` 3D Vector, which is made of the character's velocity at the instant before the jump (*x* and *z*-axis) and the calculation between the `jumpHeight` variable and gravity force overtime (*y*-axis).

Adding rigid props to animated characters

In case you haven't included a sufficient number of props to your character when modeling and animating it, you might want to give her the chance of collecting new ones at runtime. In this recipe, we will learn how to instantiate a GameObject and assign it to a character, respecting the animation hierarchy.

Getting ready

For this recipe, we have prepared a Unity Package named `Props`, containing a basic scene that features an animated character and a prefab named **badge**. The package can be found inside the `1362_07_06` folder.

How to do it...

To add a rigid prop at runtime to an animated character, follow these steps:

1. Create a new project and import the `Props` Unity Package. Then, from the **Project** view, open the **mecanimPlayground** level.

2. From the **Project** view, add the **badge** prop to the scene by dragging it onto the **Hierarchy** view. Then, make it a child of the **mixamorig:Spine2** transform (use the **Hierarchy** tree to navigate to **MsLaser | mixamorig:Hips | mixamorig:Spine | mixamorig:Spine1 | mixamorig:Spine2**). Then, make the **badge** object visible above the character's chest by changing its **Transform Position** to **X**: -0.08, **Y**: 0, **Z**: 0.15; and **Rotation** to **X**: 0.29, **Y**: 0.14, **Z**:-13.29.

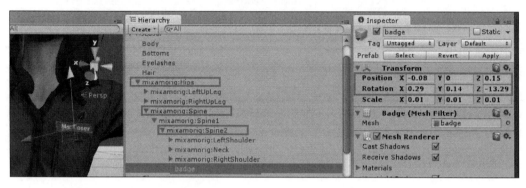

3. Make a note of the **Position** and **Rotation** values, and delete the **badge** object from the scene.

4. Add a new **Cube** to the scene (drop-down **Create | 3D Object | Cube**), rename it as **PropTrigger**, and change its Position to **X**: 0, **Y**: 0.5, **Z**: 2.

5. From the **Inspector** view's **Box Collider** component, check the **Is Trigger** option.

6. From the **Project** view, create a new **C# Script** named AddProp.cs.

7. Open the script and add the following code:

```
using UnityEngine;
using System.Collections;

public class AddProp : MonoBehaviour {
  public GameObject prop;
  public Transform targetBone;
  public Vector3 positionOffset;
  public Vector3 rotationOffset;
  public bool  destroyTrigger = true;

  void  OnTriggerEnter ( Collider collision  ){

   if (targetBone.IsChildOf(collision.transform)){
     bool  checkProp = false;
     foreach(Transform child in targetBone){
       if (child.name == prop.name)
         checkProp = true;
     }

     if(!checkProp){
```

```
        GameObject newprop;
        newprop = Instantiate(prop, targetBone.position,
targetBone.rotation) as GameObject;
        newprop.name = prop.name;
        newprop.transform.parent = targetBone;
        newprop.transform.localPosition += positionOffset;
        newprop.transform.localEulerAngles +=
rotationOffset;
        if(destroyTrigger)
          Destroy(gameObject);
      }
    }
  }
}
```

8. Save and close the script.

9. Attach the **AddProp.cs** script to the **PropTrigger** GameObject.

10. Select the **PropTrigger** textbox and check out its **Add Prop** component. First, populate the **Prop** field with the **badge** prefab. Then, populate **Target Bone** with the **mixamorig:Spine2** transform. Finally, assign the **Position** and **Rotation** values that we have previously made a note of to the **Position Offset** and **Rotation Offset** fields, respectively (**Position Offset**: **X**: -0.08, **Y**: 0, **Z**: 0.15; **Rotation Offset**: **X**: 0.29, **Y**: 0.14, **Z**:-13.29).

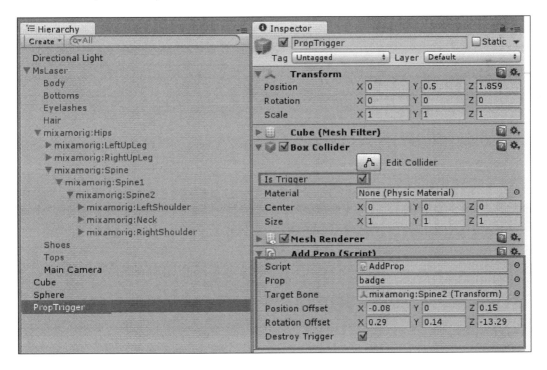

11. Play the scene. Using the 'WASD' keyboard control scheme, direct the character to the **PropTrigger** textbox. Colliding with it will add a badge to the character.

How it works...

Once it's been triggered by the character, the script attached to **PropTrigger** instantiates the assigned prefab, making it a child of the bones that they have been "placed into". The **Position Offset** and **Rotation Offset** can be used to fine-tune the exact position of the prop (relative to its parent transform). As the props become parented by the bones of the animated character, they will follow and respect its hierarchy and animation. Note that the script checks for the preexisting props of the same name before actually instantiating a new one.

There's more...

You can make a similar script to remove the props. In this case, the `OnTriggerEnter` function will contain only the following code:

```
if (targetBone.IsChildOf(collision.transform)){
    foreach(Transform child in targetBone){
        if (child.name == prop.name)
            Destroy (child.gameObject);
    }
}
```

Using Animation Events to throw an object

Now that your animated character is ready, you might want to coordinate some of her actions with her animation states. In this recipe, we will exemplify this by making the character throw an object whenever the appropriate animation clip reaches the right time. To do so, we will make use of **Animation Events**, which basically trigger a function from the animation clip's timeline. This feature, recently introduced to the **Mecanim** system, should feel familiar to those experienced with the **Add Event** feature of the classic **Animation** panel.

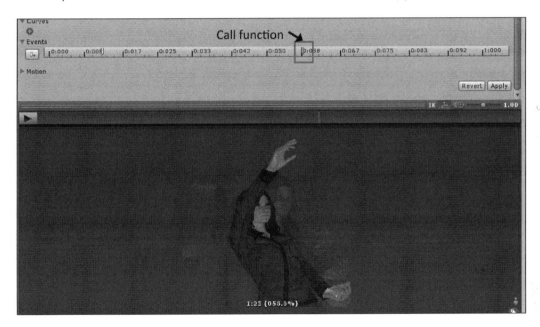

Getting ready

For this recipe, we have prepared a Unity Package named Throwing, containing a basic scene that features an animated character and a prefab named **EasterEgg**. The package can be found inside the 1362_07_07 folder.

How to do it...

To make an animated character throw an Easter egg (!), follow these steps:

1. Create a new project and import the Throwing Unity Package. Then, from the **Project** view, open the **mecanimPlayground** level.

2. Play the level and press *F* on your keyboard. The character will move as if she is throwing something with her right hand.

3. From the **Project** view, create a new **C# Script** named `ThrowObject.cs`.

4. Open the script and add the following code:

```csharp
using UnityEngine;
using System.Collections;

public class ThrowObject : MonoBehaviour {
    public GameObject prop;
    private GameObject proj;
    public Vector3 posOffset;
    public Vector3 force;
    public Transform hand;
    public float compensationYAngle = 0f;

    public void Prepare () {

        proj = Instantiate(prop, hand.position, hand.rotation) as
GameObject;
        if(proj.GetComponent<Rigidbody>())
            Destroy(proj.GetComponent<Rigidbody>());
        proj.GetComponent<SphereCollider>().enabled = false;
        proj.name = "projectile";
        proj.transform.parent = hand;
        proj.transform.localPosition = posOffset;
        proj.transform.localEulerAngles = Vector3.zero;
    }

    public void Throw () {

        Vector3 dir = transform.rotation.eulerAngles;
        dir.y += compensationYAngle;
        proj.transform.rotation = Quaternion.Euler(dir);
        proj.transform.parent = null;
        proj.GetComponent<SphereCollider>().enabled = true;
        Rigidbody rig = proj.AddComponent<Rigidbody>();
        Collider projCollider = proj.GetComponent<Collider> ();
        Collider col = GetComponent<Collider> ();
        Physics.IgnoreCollision(projCollider, col);
        rig.AddRelativeForce(force);
    }
}
```

5. Save and close the script.

6. Attach the **ThrowObject.cs** script to the character's GameObject named **MsLaser**.

7. Select the **MsLaser** object. From the **Inspector** view, check out its **Throw Object** component. Then, populate the **Prop** field with a prefab named **EasterEgg**. Populate **Hand** with **mixamorig:RightHand**. Also, change **Pos Offset** to **X**: 0; **Y**: 0.07; **Z**: 0.04. Finally, change **Force** to **X**: 0; **Y**: 200; **Z**: 500.

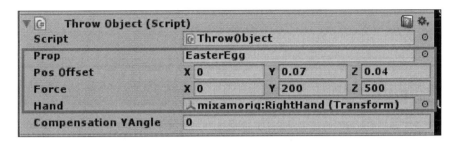

8. From the **Project** view, select the **Swat@toss_grenade** file. Then, from the **Inspector** view, access the **Animation** section and scroll down to the **Events** section.

9. Expand the **Events** section. Drag the playhead to approximately **0:17 (017.9%)** of the animation timeline. Then, click on the button with the *marker* + icon to add an **Animation Event**. From the **Edit Animation Event** window, set **Function** as Prepare. Close the window.

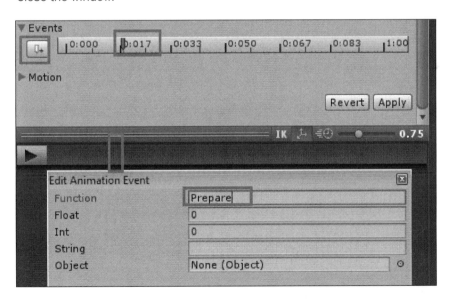

10. Add a new animation event at approximately **1:24 (057.1%)** of the animation timeline. This time, from the **Edit Animation Event** window, set **Function** as Throw. Close the window.

11. Click on the **Apply** button to save the changes.

12. Play your scene. Your character will now be able to throw an Easter egg when you press the *F* key.

How it works...

Once the **toss_grenade** animation reaches the moments that we have set our **Events** to, the `Prepare()` and `throw()` functions are called. The former instantiates a prefab, now named **projectile**, into the character's hand (**Projectile Offset** values are used to fine-tune its position), also making it respect the character's hierarchy. Also, it disables the prefab's collider and destroys its `Rigidbody` component, provided it has one. The latter function enables the projectile's collider, and adds a `Rigidbody` component to it, making it independent from the character's hand. Finally, it adds a relative force to the projectile's `Rigidbody` component, so it will behave as if thrown by the character. The **Compensation YAngle** can be used to adjust the direction of the grenade, if necessary.

Applying Ragdoll physics to a character

Action games often make use of **Ragdoll physics** to simulate the character's body reaction to being unconsciously under the effect of a hit or explosion. In this recipe, we will learn how to set up and activate Ragdoll physics to our character whenever she steps in a landmine object. We will also use the opportunity to reset the character's position and animations a number of seconds after that event has occurred.

Getting ready

For this recipe, we have prepared a Unity Package named `Ragdoll`, containing a basic scene that features an animated character and two prefabs, already placed into the scene, named **Landmine** and **Spawnpoint**. The package can be found inside the `1362_07_08` folder.

How to do it...

To apply Ragdoll physics to your character, follow these steps:

1. Create a new project and import the `Ragdoll` Unity Package. Then, from the **Project** view, open the **mecanimPlayground** level.

2. You will see the animated MsLaser character and two discs: **Landmine** and **Spawnpoint**.

3. First, let's set up our **Ragdoll**. Access the **GameObject | 3D Object | Ragdoll...** menu and the **Ragdoll wizard** will pop-up.

4. Assign the transforms as follows:

- ❏ **Pelvis**: mixamorig:Hips
- ❏ **Left Hips**: mixamorig:LeftUpLeg
- ❏ **Left Knee**: mixamorig:LeftLeg
- ❏ **Left Foot**: mixamorig:LeftFoot
- ❏ **Right Hips**: mixamorig:RightUpLeg
- ❏ **Right Knee**: mixamorig:RightLeg
- ❏ **Right Foot**: mixamorig:RightFoot
- ❏ **Left Arm**: mixamorig:LeftArm
- ❏ **Left Elbow**: mixamorig:LeftForeArm
- ❏ **Right Arm**: mixamorig:RightArm
- ❏ **Right Elbow**: mixamorig:RightForeArm
- ❏ **Middle Spine**: mixamorig:Spine1
- ❏ **Head**: mixamorig:Head
- ❏ **Total Mass**: 20
- ❏ **Strength**: 50

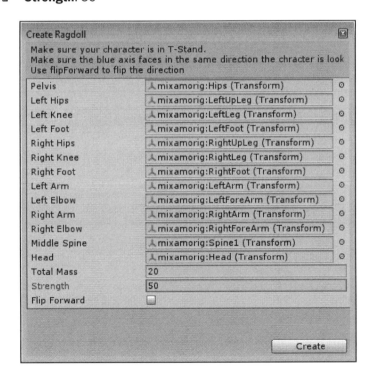

5. From the **Project** view, create a new **C# Script** named `RagdollCharacter.cs`.

6. Open the script and add the following code:

```csharp
using UnityEngine;
using System.Collections;

public class RagdollCharacter : MonoBehaviour {

  void Start () {
     DeactivateRagdoll();
  }

    public void ActivateRagdoll(){
    gameObject.GetComponent<CharacterController> ().enabled
= false;
    gameObject.GetComponent<BasicController> ().enabled =
false;
    gameObject.GetComponent<Animator> ().enabled = false;
    foreach (Rigidbody bone in
GetComponentsInChildren<Rigidbody>()) {
        bone.isKinematic = false;
        bone.detectCollisions = true;
    }
    foreach (Collider col in
GetComponentsInChildren<Collider>()) {
        col.enabled = true;
    }
    StartCoroutine (Restore ());

    }
  public void DeactivateRagdoll(){

    gameObject.GetComponent<BasicController>().enabled =
true;
    gameObject.GetComponent<Animator>().enabled = true;
    transform.position = GameObject.Find("Spawnpoint").transform.
position;
    transform.rotation = GameObject.Find("Spawnpoint").transform.
rotation;
    foreach(Rigidbody bone in
GetComponentsInChildren<Rigidbody>()){
        bone.isKinematic = true;
          bone.detectCollisions = false;
      }
```

```
    foreach (CharacterJoint joint in
GetComponentsInChildren<CharacterJoint>()) {
        joint.enableProjection = true;
    }
    foreach(Collider col in
GetComponentsInChildren<Collider>()){
        col.enabled = false;
    }
  gameObject.GetComponent<CharacterController>().enabled
 = true;


    }

  IEnumerator Restore(){
    yield return new WaitForSeconds(5);
    DeactivateRagdoll();
  }
}
```

7. Save and close the script.

8. Attach the **RagdollCharacter.cs** script to the **MsLaser** GameObject. Then, select the **MsLaser** character and, from the top of the **Inspector** view, change its tag to **Player**.

9. From the **Project** view, create a new **C# Script** named Landmine.cs.

10. Open the script and add the following code:

```
using UnityEngine;
using System.Collections;

public class Landmine : MonoBehaviour {
  public float range = 2f;
  public float force = 2f;
  public float up = 4f;
  private bool active = true;

  void  OnTriggerEnter ( Collider collision  ){
    if(collision.gameObject.tag == "Player" && active){
      active = false;
      StartCoroutine(Reactivate());
      collision.gameObject.GetComponent<RagdollCharacter>().
ActivateRagdoll();
      Vector3 explosionPos = transform.position;
          Collider[] colliders =
Physics.OverlapSphere(explosionPos, range);
          foreach (Collider hit in colliders) {
```

```
        if (hit.GetComponent<Rigidbody>())
                hit.GetComponent<Rigidbody>().
AddExplosionForce(force, explosionPos, range, up);
            }
        }
    }
    IEnumerator Reactivate(){
        yield return new WaitForSeconds(2);
        active = true;
    }
}
```

11. Save and close the script.

12. Attach the script to the **Landmine** GameObject.

13. Play the scene. Using the *WASD* keyboard control scheme, direct the character to the **Landmine** GameObject. Colliding with it will activate the character's Ragdoll physics and apply an explosion force to it. As a result, the character will be thrown away to a considerable distance and will no longer be in the control of its body movements, akin to a ragdoll.

How it works...

Unity's **Ragdoll Wizard** assigns, to selected transforms, the components `Collider`, `Rigidbody`, and `Character Joint`. In conjunction, those components make Ragdoll physics possible. However, those components must be disabled whenever we want our character to be animated and controlled by the player. In our case, we switch those components on and off using the `RagdollCharacter` script and its two functions: `ActivateRagdoll()` and `DeactivateRagdoll()`, the latter includes instructions to re-spawn our character in the appropriate place.

For the testing purposes, we have also created the `Landmine` script, which calls `RagdollCharacter` script's function named `ActivateRagdoll()`. It also applies an explosion force to our ragdoll character, throwing it outside the explosion site.

There's more...

Instead of resetting the character's transform settings, you could have destroyed its GameObject and instantiated a new one over the respawn point using **Tags**. For more information on this subject, check Unity's documentation at `http://docs.unity3d.com/ScriptReference/GameObject.FindGameObjectsWithTag.html`.

Rotating the character's torso to aim a weapon

When playing a third-person character, you might want her to aim her weapon at some target that is not directly in front of her, without making her change her direction. In these cases, you will need to apply what is called a *procedural animation*, which does not rely on premade animation clips, but rather on the processing of other data, such as player input, to animate the character. In this recipe, we will use this technique to rotate the character's spine by moving the mouse, allowing for adjustments in the character's aim. We will also use this opportunity to cast a ray from the character's weapon and display a crosshair over the nearest object on target. Please note that this approach will work with the cameras standing behind the third-person controlled characters.

Getting ready

For this recipe, we have prepared a Unity Package named `AimPointer`, containing a basic scene that features a character armed with a laser pointer. The package, which also includes the `crossAim` sprite that is to be used as a crosshair for aiming, can be found inside the `1362_07_09` folder.

How to do it...

1. Create a new project and import the `AimPointer` Unity Package. Then, from the **Project** view, open the **mecanimPlayground** level. You will see an animated character named **MsLaser** holding the **pointerPrefab** object.

2. From the **Project** view, create a new **C# Script** named `MouseAim.cs`.

3. Open the script and add the following code:

```
using UnityEngine;
using System.Collections;

public class MouseAim : MonoBehaviour {

    public Transform spine;
    private float xAxis = 0f;
    private float yAxis = 0f;
    public Vector2 xLimit = new Vector2(-30f,30f);
    public Vector2 yLimit= new Vector2(-30f,30f);
```

```
public Transform weapon;
public GameObject crosshair;
private Vector2 aimLoc;

public void LateUpdate(){

    yAxis += Input.GetAxis ("Mouse X");
    yAxis = Mathf.Clamp (yAxis, yLimit.x, yLimit.y);
    xAxis -= Input.GetAxis ("Mouse Y");
    xAxis = Mathf.Clamp (xAxis, xLimit.x, xLimit.y);
    Vector3 corr = new Vector3(xAxis,yAxis, spine.
localEulerAngles.z);
    spine.localEulerAngles = corr;
    RaycastHit hit;
    Vector3 fwd = weapon.TransformDirection(Vector3.forward);
    if (Physics.Raycast (weapon.position, fwd, out hit)) {
      print (hit.transform.gameObject.name);
      aimLoc =  Camera.main.WorldToScreenPoint(hit.point);
      crosshair.SetActive(true);
      crosshair.transform.position = aimLoc;
    } else {
     crosshair.SetActive(false);
    }
    Debug.DrawRay (weapon.position, fwd, Color.red);
  }
}
```

4. Save and close the script.

5. From the **Hierarchy** view, create a new **UI | Image** GameObject. Then, from the **Inspector** view, change its name to crosshair. Also, in **Rect Transform**, set its **Width** and **Height** to 16 and populate **Source Image** field with the **crossAim** sprite.

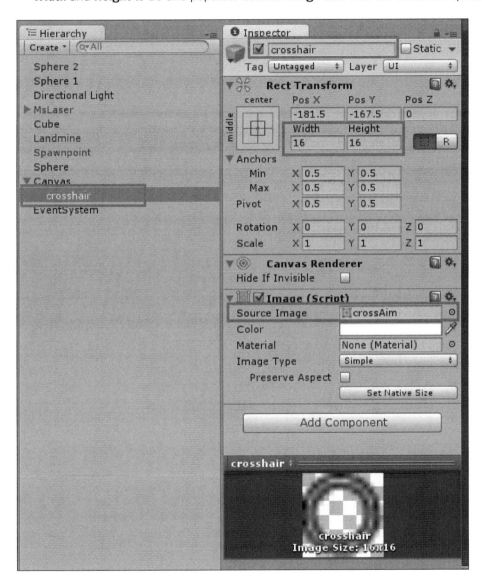

6. Attach the **MouseAim.cs** script to the **MsLaser** GameObject.

7. Select the **MsLaser** GameObject and from the **Inspector** view's **Mouse Aim** component, populate the **Spine** field with **mixamorig:Spine**; the **Weapon** field with **pointerPrefab**; and the **Crosshair** field with the **crosshair** UI GameObject.

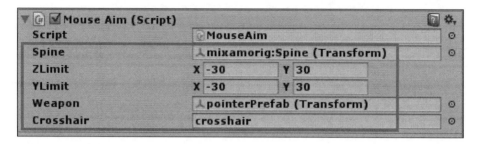

8. Play the scene. You will now be able to rotate the character's torso by moving the mouse. Even better, the crosshair GUI texture will be displayed at the top of the object that is being aimed at by the pointer.

How it works...

You might have noticed that all the code for rotating the character's spine is inside the `LateUpdate` function, as opposed to the more common `Update` function. The reason for this is to make sure that all the transform manipulation will be executed after the original animation clip is played, overriding it.

Regarding the spine rotation, our script adds the horizontal and vertical speed of the mouse to the `xAxis` and `yAxis` float variables. These variables are then constrained within the specified limits, avoiding distortions to the character's model. Finally, the `spine` object transform rotation for *x* and *y* axes are set to `xAxis` and `yAxis` respectively. The *z*-axis is preserved from the original animation clip.

Additionally, our script uses a `Raycast` command to detect if there is any object's collider within the weapon's aim, in which case a crosshair will be drawn on the screen.

There's more...

Since this recipe's script was tailored for cameras standing behind the third-person controlled characters, we have included a more generic solution to the problem—in fact, a similar approach to the one presented in *Unity 4.x Cookbook, Packt Publishing*. An alternate script named `MouseAimLokkAt`, which can be found inside the `1362_07_09` folder, starts by converting our bi-dimensional mouse cursor screen's coordinates to the three-dimensional world space coordinates (stored in a `point` variable). Then, it rotates the character's torso towards the *point* location, using the `LookAt()` command to do so. Additionally, it makes sure that the spine does not extrapolate `minY` and `maxY` angles, otherwise causing distortions to the character model. Also, we have included a `Compensation YAngle` variable that makes it possible for us to fine-tune the character's alignment with the mouse cursor. Another addition is the option to freeze the X-axis rotation, in case you just want the character to rotate the torso laterally, but not look up or down. Again, this script uses a `Raycast` command to detect objects in front of the weapon's aim, drawing a crosshair on the screen when they are present.

8

Positions, Movement and Navigation for Character GameObjects

In this chapter, we will cover:

- ▶ Player control of a 2D GameObject (and limiting the movement within a rectangle)
- ▶ Player control of a 3D GameObject (and limiting the movement within a rectangle)
- ▶ Choosing destinations – find the nearest (or a random) spawn point
- ▶ Choosing destinations – respawn to the most recently passed checkpoint
- ▶ NPC NavMeshAgent to seek or flee destination while avoiding obstacles
- ▶ NPC NavMeshAgent to follow waypoints in sequence
- ▶ Controlling the object group movement through flocking

Introduction

Many GameObjects in games move! Movement can be controlled by the player, by the (simulated) laws of physics in the environment, or by the **Non-Player Character** (**NPC**) logic; for example, objects that follow a path of waypoints, or seek (move towards) or flee (away) from the current position of a character. Unity provides several controllers, for first and third-person characters, and for vehicles such as cars and airplanes. GameObject movement can also be controlled through the state machines of the Unity Mecanim animation system.

However, there maybe times when you wish to tweak the Player character controllers from Unity, or write your own. You might wish to write directional logic—simple or sophisticated **Artificial Intelligence** (**AI**) to control the game's NPC and enemy characters. Such AI might involve your computer program making objects orient and move towards or away from characters or other game objects.

This chapter presents a range of such directional recipes, from which many games can benefit in terms of a richer and more exciting user experience.

Unity provides sophisticated classes and components including the Vector3 class and rigid body physics for modeling realistic movements, forces, and collisions in games. We make use of these game engine features to implement some sophisticated NPC and enemy character movements in the recipes of this chapter.

The big picture

For 3D games (and to some extent, 2D games as well), a fundamental class of object is the Vector3 class—objects that store and manipulate (x,y,z) values representing locations in 3D space. If we draw an imaginary arrow from the origin (0,0,0) to a point on space, then the direction and length of this arrow (vector) can represent a velocity or force (that is, a certain amount of magnitude in a certain direction).

If we ignore all the character controller components, colliders, and the physics system in Unity, we can write code that teleports objects directly to a particular (x, y, z) location in our scene. And sometimes this is just what we want to do; for example, we may wish to spawn an object at a location. However, in most cases, if we want objects to move in more physically realistic ways, then we either apply a force to the object, or change its velocity component. Or if it has a Character Controller component, then we can send it a Move() message. With the introduction of Unity NavMeshAgents (and associated Navigation Meshes), we can now set a destination for an object with a NavMeshAgent, and then the built-in pathfinding logic will do the work of moving our NPC object on a path towards the given (x, y, z) destination location.

As well as deciding which technique will be used to move an object, our game must also do the work of deciding how to choose the destination locations, or the direction and magnitude of changes to movement. This can involve logic to tell an NPC or enemy object the destination of the Player's character (to be moved towards, and then perhaps attacked when close enough). Or perhaps shy NPC objects will be given the direction to the Player's character, so that they can flee in the opposite direction, until they are a safe distance away.

Other core concepts in the NPC object movement and creation (instantiation) include:

- ▶ Spawn points

  - ❑ Specific locations in the scene where objects are to be created, or moved to

▸ Waypoints

- ❏ The sequence of locations to define a path for NPCs or perhaps, the Player's character to follow

▸ Checkpoints

- ❏ Locations (or colliders) that, once passed through, change what happens in the game (for example, extra time, or if a Player's character gets killed, they respawn to the last crossed checkpoint, and so on)

Player control of a 2D GameObject (and limiting the movement within a rectangle)

While the rest of the recipes in this chapter are demonstrated in 3D projects, basic character movement in 2D, and also limiting the movement to a bounding rectangle, are core skills for many 2D games, and so this first recipe illustrates how to achieve these features for a 2D game.

Since in *Chapter 3*, *Inventory GUI*, we already have a basic 2D game, we'll adapt this game to restrict the movement to a bounding rectangle.

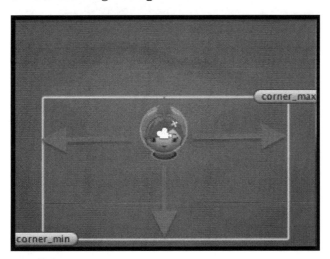

Getting ready

This recipe builds on a simple 2D game called *Creating the Simple2DGame_SpaceGirl* mini-game from *Chapter 3*, *Inventory GUI*. Start with a copy of this game, or use the provided completed recipe project as the basis for this recipe.

How to do it...

To create a 2D sprite controlled by the user with the movement that is limited within a rectangle, follow these steps:

1. Create a new empty GameObject named **corner_max**, and position it somewhere above and to the right of the GameObject called **Player-girl1**. With this GameObject selected in the **Hierarchy** view, choose the large yellow oblong icon, highlighted in the **Inspector** panel.

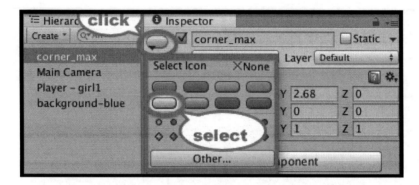

2. Duplicate the **corner_max** GameObject by naming the clone as **corner_min**, and position this clone somewhere below and to the left of the **player-spaceGirl1** GameObject. The coordinates of these two GameObjects will determine the maximum and minimum bounds of movement, permitted for the player's character.

3. Modify the C# Script called `PlayerMove` to declare some new variables at the beginning of the class:

```
public Transform corner_max;
public Transform corner_min;
private float x_min;
private float y_min;
private float x_max;
private float y_max;
```

4. Modify the C# Script called `PlayerMove` so that the `Awake()` method now gets a reference to the SpriteRenderer, and uses this object to help setup the maximum and minimum X and Y movement limits:

```
void Awake() {
    rigidBody2D = GetComponent<Rigidbody2D>();
    x_max = corner_max.position.x;
    x_min = corner_min.position.x;
    y_max = corner_max.position.y;
```

```
    y_min = corner_min.position.y;
}
```

5. Modify the C# Script called `PlayerMove` to declare a new method called `KeepWithinMinMaxRectangle()`:

```
private void KeepWithinMinMaxRectangle(){
    float x = transform.position.x;
    float y = transform.position.y;
    float z = transform.position.z;
    float clampedX = Mathf.Clamp(x, x_min, x_max);
    float clampedY = Mathf.Clamp(y, y_min, y_max);
    transform.position = new Vector3(clampedX, clampedY, z);
}
```

6. Modify the C# Script called `PlayerMove` so that, after having done everything else in the `FixedUpdate()` method, a call will finally be made to the `KeepWithinMinMaxRectangle()` method:

```
void FixedUpdate(){
    float xMove = Input.GetAxis("Horizontal");
    float yMove = Input.GetAxis("Vertical");

    float xSpeed = xMove * speed;
    float ySpeed = yMove * speed;

    Vector2 newVelocity = new Vector2(xSpeed, ySpeed);

    rigidBody2D.velocity = newVelocity;

    // restrict player movement
    KeepWithinMinMaxRectangle();
}
```

7. With the **player-SpaceGirl1** GameObject in the **Hierarchy** view, drag the **corner_max** and **corner_min** GameObjects over the public variables called `corner_max` and `corner_min` in the **Inspector**.

8. Before running the scene in the **Scene** panel, try repositioning the **corner_max** and **corner_min** GameObjects. When you run the scene, the positions of these two GameObjects (max and min, and X and Y) will be used as the limits of movement for the Player's **player-SpaceGirl1** character.

9. While all this works fine, let's make the rectangular bounds of the movement visually explicit in the **Scene** panel by having a yellow "gizmo" rectangle drawn. Add the following method to the C# script class called `PlayerMove`:

```
void OnDrawGizmos(){
    Vector3 top_right = Vector3.zero;
```

```
Vector3 bottom_right = Vector3.zero;
Vector3 bottom_left = Vector3.zero;
Vector3 top_left = Vector3.zero;

if(corner_max && corner_min){
  top_right = corner_max.position;
  bottom_left = corner_min.position;

  bottom_right = top_right;
  bottom_right.y = bottom_left.y;

  top_left = top_right;
  top_left.x = bottom_left.x;
}

//Set the following gizmo colors to YELLOW
Gizmos.color = Color.yellow;

//Draw 4 lines making a rectangle
Gizmos.DrawLine(top_right, bottom_right);
Gizmos.DrawLine(bottom_right, bottom_left);
Gizmos.DrawLine(bottom_left, top_left);
Gizmos.DrawLine(top_left, top_right);
}
```

How it works...

You added the empty GameObjects called **corner_max** and **corner_min** to the scene. The X- and Y- coordinates of these GameObjects will be used to determine the bounds of movement that we will permit for the character called **player-SpaceGirl1**. Since these are the empty GameObjects, they will not be seen by the player when in the play-mode. However, we can see and move them in the **Scene** panel, and having added the yellow oblong icons, we can see their positions and names very easily.

Upon `Awake()` the `PlayerMoveWithLimits` object, inside the **player-SpaceGirl1** GameObject, records the maximum and minimum X- and Y- values of the GameObjects called **corner_max** and **corner_min**. Each time the physics system is called via the `FixedUpdate()` method, the velocity of the **player-SpaceGirl1** character is set according to the horizontal and vertical keyboard/joystick inputs. However, the final action of the `FixedUpdate()` method is to call the `KeepWithinMinMaxRectangle()` method, which uses the `Math.Clamp(...)` function to move the character back inside the X- and Y- limits. This happens so that the player's character is not permitted to move outside the area defined by the **corner_max** and **corner_min** GameObjects.

The `OnDrawGizmos()` method tests that the references to the **corner_max** and **corner_min** GameObjects are not null, and then sets the positions of the four Vector3 objects, representing the four corners defined by the rectangle with **corner_max** and **corner_min** at the opposite corners. It then sets the Gizmo color to yellow, and draws lines, connecting the four corners in the **Scene** panel.

See also

Refer to the next recipe for more information about limiting player controlled character movements.

Player control of a 3D GameObject (and limiting the movement within a rectangle)

Many of the 3D recipes in this chapter are built on this basic project, which constructs a scene with a textured terrain, a **Main Camera**, and a red cube that can be moved around by the user with the four directional arrow keys. The bounds of movement of the cube are constrained using the same technique as in the previous 2D recipe.

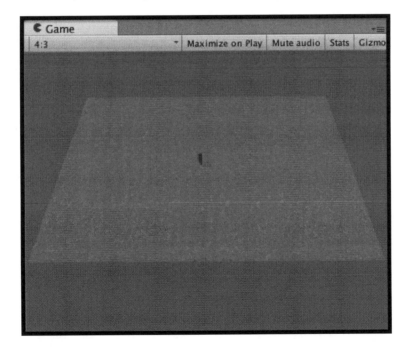

How to do it...

To create a basic 3D cube controlled game, follow these steps:

1. Create a new, empty 3D project.

2. Once the project has been created, import the single Terrain Texture named `SandAlbedo` (it was named `GoodDirt` in Unity 4). Choose menu: **Assets | Import Package | Environments**, deselect everything, and then locate and tick the asset: `Assets/Environment/TerrainAssets/SurfaceTextures/SandAlbedo.psd`.

> You could have just added the Environment Asset Package when creating the project—but this would have imported 100s of files, and we only needed this one. Starting a project in Unity, then selectively importing just what we need is the best approach to take, if you want to keep the project's Asset folders to small sizes.

3. Create a terrain positioned at (-15, 0, -10) and sized 30 by 20.

> The transform position for the terrains relates to their corner and not their center.
>
> Since the Transform position of the terrains relates to the corner of the object, we center such objects at (0,0,0) by setting the X-coordinate equal to (-1*width/2), and the Z-coordinate equal to (-1*length/2). In other words, we slide the object by half its width and half its height to ensure that its center is just where we want it.
>
> In this case, the width is 30 and the length is 20, hence we get -15 for X (-1 * 30/2), and -10 for Z (-1 * 20/2).

4. Texture paint this terrain with your texture called `SandAlbedo`.

5. Create a directional light (it should face downwards to the terrain with the default settings—but if it doesn't for some reason, then rotate it so that the terrain is well lit).

6. Make the following changes to the Main Camera:
   - position = (0, 20, -15)
   - rotation = (60, 0, 0)

7. Change the **Aspect Ratio** of the **Game Panel** from **Free Aspect** to **4:3**. You will now see the whole of the **Terrain** in the **Game Panel**.

8. Create a new empty GameObject named **corner_max**, and position it at (14, 0, 9). With this GameObject selected in the **Hierarchy,** choose the large, yellow oblong icon, highlighted in the **Inspector** panel.

9. Duplicate the **corner_max** GameObject, naming the clone as **corner_min**, and position this clone at (-14, 0, -9). The coordinates of these two GameObjects will determine the maximum and minimum bounds of the movement permitted for the player's character.

10. Create a new **Cube** GameObject named **Cube-player** at a position called (0, 0.5, 0), and size it as (1,1,1).

11. Add to the **Cube-player** GameObject, apply a component called **Physics | RigidBody**, and uncheck the **RigidBody** property **Use Gravity**.

12. Create a red **Material** named **m_red**, and apply this **Material** to **Cube-player**.

13. Add the following C# script class called `PlayerControl` to the **Cube-player**:

```csharp
using UnityEngine;
using System.Collections;

public class PlayerControl : MonoBehaviour {
  public Transform corner_max;
  public Transform corner_min;

  public float speed = 40;
  private Rigidbody rigidBody;

  private float x_min;
  private float x_max;
  private float z_min;
  private float z_max;

  void Awake (){
    rigidBody = GetComponent<Rigidbody>();
    x_max = corner_max.position.x;
    x_min = corner_min.position.x;
    z_max = corner_max.position.z;
    z_min = corner_min.position.z;
  }

  void FixedUpdate() {
    KeyboardMovement();
    KeepWithinMinMaxRectangle();
  }

  private void KeyboardMovement (){
```

```
        float xMove = Input.GetAxis("Horizontal") * speed * Time.
deltaTime;
        float zMove = Input.GetAxis("Vertical") * speed * Time.
deltaTime;

    float xSpeed = xMove * speed;
    float zSpeed = zMove * speed;

    Vector3 newVelocity = new Vector3(xSpeed, 0, zSpeed);

    rigidBody.velocity = newVelocity;

    // restrict player movement
    KeepWithinMinMaxRectangle ();
  }

  private void KeepWithinMinMaxRectangle (){
    float x = transform.position.x;
    float y = transform.position.y;
    float z = transform.position.z;
    float clampedX = Mathf.Clamp(x, x_min, x_max);
    float clampedZ = Mathf.Clamp(z, z_min, z_max);
    transform.position = new Vector3(clampedX, y, clampedZ);
  }

  void OnDrawGizmos (){
    Vector3 top_right = Vector3.zero;
    Vector3 bottom_right = Vector3.zero;
    Vector3 bottom_left = Vector3.zero;
    Vector3 top_left = Vector3.zero;

    if(corner_max && corner_min){
      top_right = corner_max.position;
      bottom_left = corner_min.position;

      bottom_right = top_right;
      bottom_right.z = bottom_left.z;

      top_left = bottom_left;
      top_left.z = top_right.z;
    }

    //Set the following gizmo colors to YELLOW
```

```
        Gizmos.color = Color.yellow;

        //Draw 4 lines making a rectangle
        Gizmos.DrawLine(top_right, bottom_right);
        Gizmos.DrawLine(bottom_right, bottom_left);
        Gizmos.DrawLine(bottom_left, top_left);
        Gizmos.DrawLine(top_left, top_right);
    }
}
```

14. With the **Cube-player** GameObject selected in the **Hierarchy,** drag the GameObjects called **corner_max** and **corner_min** over the public variables called `corner_max` and `corner_min` in the **Inspector** panel.

15. When you run the scene, the positions of the **corner_max** and **corner_min** GameObjects will define the bounds of movement for the Player's **Cube-player** character.

How it works...

The scene contains a positioned terrain so that its center is `(0,0,0)`. The red cube is controlled by the user's arrow keys through the `PlayerControl` script.

Just as with the previous 2D recipe, a reference to the (3D) RigidBody component is stored when the `Awake()` method executes, and the maximum and minimum X- and Z- values are retrieved from the two corner GameObjects, and is stored in the `x_min`, `x_max`, `z_min`, and `z_max` variables. Note that for this basic 3D game, we won't allow any Y-movement, although such movement (and bounding limits by adding a third 'max-height' corner GameObject) can be easily added by extending the code in this recipe.

The `KeyboardMovement()` method reads the horizontal and vertical input values (which the Unity default settings read from the four directional arrow keys). Based on these left-right and up-down values, the velocity of the cube is updated. The amount it will move depends on the speed variable.

The `KeepWithinMinMaxRectangle()` method uses the `Math.Clamp(…)` function to move the character back inside the X and Z limits, so that the player's character is not permitted to move outside the area defined by the **corner_max** and **corner_min** GameObjects.

The `OnDrawGizmos()` method tests that the references to the **corner_max** and **corner_min** GameObjects are not null, and then sets the positions of the four Vector3 objects, representing the four corners defined by the rectangle with the **corner_max** and **corner_min** GameObjects at the opposite corners. It then sets the Gizmo color to **yellow**, and draws lines connecting the four corners in the **Scene** panel.

Choosing destinations – find the nearest (or a random) spawn point

Many games make use of spawn points and waypoints. This recipe demonstrates two very common examples of spawning—the choosing of either a random spawn point, or the nearest one to an object of interest (such as the Player's character), and then the instantiation of an object at that chosen point.

Getting ready

This recipe builds upon the previous recipe. So, make a copy of this project, open it, and then follow the next steps.

How to do it...

To find a random spawn point, follow these steps:

1. Create a **Sphere** sized as (1,1,1) at (2,2,2) position, and apply the m_red Material.

2. Create a new Prefab named Prefab-ball, and drag your **Sphere** into it (and then delete the **Sphere** from the **Hierarchy** panel).

3. Create a new capsule object named Capsule-spawnPoint at (3, 0.5, 3), give it the tag as Respawn (this is one of the default tags that Unity provides).

> For testing, we'll leave these Respawn points visible. For the final game, we'll then uncheck the Mesh Rendered of each Respawn GameObject, so that they are not visible to the Player.

4. Make several copies of your **Capsule-spawnPoint** by moving them to different locations on the terrain.

5. Add an instance of the following C# script class called SpawnBall to the **Cube-the player** GameObject:

```
using UnityEngine;
using System.Collections;

public class SpawnBall : MonoBehaviour {
  public GameObject prefabBall;
  private SpawnPointManager spawnPointManager;
  private float destroyAfterDelay = 1;
```

```
    private float testFireKeyDelay = 0;

    void Start (){
      spawnPointManager = GetComponent<SpawnPointManager> ();
      StartCoroutine("CheckFireKeyAfterShortDelay");
    }

    IEnumerator CheckFireKeyAfterShortDelay () {
      while(true){
        yield return new WaitForSeconds(testFireKeyDelay);
        // having waited, now we check every frame
        testFireKeyDelay = 0;
        CheckFireKey();
      }
    }

    private void CheckFireKey() {
      if(Input.GetButton("Fire1")){
        CreateSphere();
        // wait half-second before alling next spawn
        testFireKeyDelay = 0.5f;
      }
    }

    private void CreateSphere(){
      GameObject spawnPoint = spawnPointManager.RandomSpawnPoint ();
      GameObject newBall = (GameObject)Instantiate (prefabBall,
spawnPoint.transform.position, Quaternion.identity);
      Destroy(newBall, destroyAfterDelay);
    }
}
```

6. Add an instance of the following C# script class called `SpawnPointManager` to the `Cube-player` GameObject:

```
using UnityEngine;
using System.Collections;

public class SpawnPointManager : MonoBehaviour {
  private GameObject[] spawnPoints;

  void Start() {
    spawnPoints = GameObject.FindGameObjectsWithTag("Respawn");
```

```
        }

        public GameObject RandomSpawnPoint (){
            int r = Random.Range(0, spawnPoints.Length);
            return spawnPoints[r];
        }
    }
```

7. Ensure that **Cube-player** is selected in the **Inspector** for the SpawnBall scripted component. Then, drag **Prefab-ball** over the public variable projectile called **Prefab Ball**.

8. Now, run your game. When you click on the mouse (fire) button, a sphere will be instantiated randomly to one of the capsule locations.

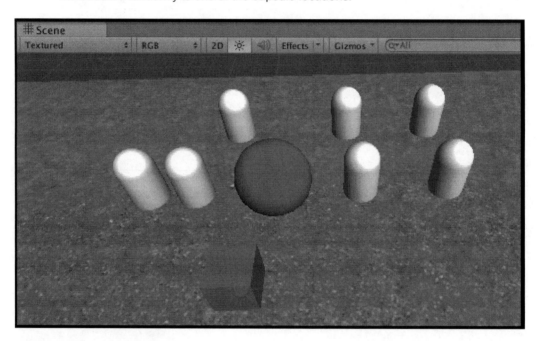

How it works...

The **Capsule-spawnPoint** objects represent candidate locations, where we might wish to create an instance of our ball Prefab. When our SpawnPointManager object, inside the **Cube-player** GameObject, receives the Start() message, the **respawns** GameObject array is set to the array, which is returned from the call to FindGameObjectsWithTag("Respawn"). This creates an array of all the objects in the scene with the tag called Respawn — that is, all our **Capsule-spawnPoint** objects.

When our `SpawnBall` object GameObject **Cube-player** receives the `Start()` message, it sets the `spawnPointManager` variable to be a reference to its sibling `SpawnPointManager` script component. Next, we start the **coroutine** method called `CheckFireKeyAfterShortDelay()`.

The `CheckFireKeyAfterShortDelay()` method uses a typical Unity coroutine technique that goes into an infinite loop using a delay controlled by the value of the `testFireKeyDelay` variable. The delay is to make Unity wait before calling `CheckFireKey()` to test if the user wants a new sphere to be spawned.

> Coroutines are an advanced technique, where execution inside the method can be paused, and resumed from the same point. The `Yield` command temporarily halts the execution of code in the method, allowing Unity to go off and execute code in the other GameObjects and undertake physics and rendering work and more. They are perfect for situations where, at regular intervals, we wish to check whether something has happened (such as testing for the Fire key, or whether a response message has been received from an Internet request and so on).
>
> Learn more about the Unity coroutines at `http://docs.unity3d.com/Manual/Coroutines.html`.

The `SpawnBall` method `CheckFireKey()` tests whether, at that instant, the user is pressing the **Fire** button. If the **Fire** button is pressed, then the `CreateSphere()` method is called. Also, the `testFireKeyDelay` variable is set to 0.5. This ensures that we won't test the **Fire** button again for half a second.

The `SpawnBall` method `CreateSphere()` assigns variable `spawnPoint` to the GameObject returned by a call to the `RandomSpawnpoint(...)` method of our `spawnPointManager`. Then it creates a new instance of `prefab_Ball` (via the public variable) at the same position as the `spawnPoint` GameObject.

There's more...

There are some details that you don't want to miss.

Choosing the nearest spawn point

Rather than just choosing a random spawn point, let's search through array spawnpoints, and choose the closest one to our player.

To find the nearest spawn point, we need to do the following:

1. Add the following method to the C# script class called `SpawnPointManager`:

    ```
    public GameObject NearestSpawnpoint (Vector3 source){
      GameObject nearestSpawnPoint = spawnPoints[0];
    ```

```
    Vector3 spawnPointPos = spawnPoints[0].transform.position;
    float shortestDistance = Vector3.Distance(source,
spawnPointPos);

    for (int i = 1; i < spawnPoints.Length; i++){
      spawnPointPos = spawnPoints[i].transform.position;
      float newDist = Vector3.Distance(source, spawnPointPos);
      if (newDist < shortestDistance){
        shortestDistance = newDist;
        nearestSpawnPoint = spawnPoints[i];
      }
    }

    return nearestSpawnPoint;
  }
```

2. We now need to change the first line in the C# class called `SpawnBall` so that the `spawnPoint` variable is set by a call to our new method called `NearestSpawnpoint(...)`:

```
private void CreateSphere(){
   GameObject spawnPoint = spawnPointManager.
NearestSpawnpoint(transform.position);

   GameObject newBall = (GameObject)Instantiate(prefabBall,
spawnPoint.transform.position, Quaternion.identity);
   Destroy(newBall, lifeDuration);
 }
```

In the `NearestSpawnpoint(...)` method, we set `nearestSpawnpoint` to the first (array index 0) GameObject in the array as our default. We then loop through the rest of the array (array index 1 up to `spawnPoints.Length`). For each GameObject in the array, we test to see if its distance is less than the shortest distance so far, and if it is, then we update the shortest distance, and also set `nearestSpawnpoint` to the current element. When the array has been searched, we return the GameObject that the `nearestSpawnpoint` variable refers to.

Avoiding errors due to an empty array

Let's make our code a little more robust, so that it can cope with the issue of an empty `spawnPoints` array—that is, when there are no objects tagged **Respawn** in the scene.

To cope with the no objects tagged **Respawn** we need to do the following:

1. Improve our `Start()` method in the C# script class called `SpawnPointManager`, so that an ERROR is logged if the array of objects tagged **Respawn** is empty:

```
public GameObject NearestSpawnpoint (Vector3 source){
void Start() {
  spawnPoints = GameObject.FindGameObjectsWithTag("Respawn");

  // logError if array empty
  if(spawnPoints.Length < 1) Debug.LogError ("SpawnPointManagaer -
cannot find any objects tagged 'Respawn'!");
}
```

2. Improve the `RandomSpawnPoint()` and `NearestSpawnpoint()` methods in the C# script class called `SpawnPointManager`, so that they still return a GameObject even if the array is empty:

```
public GameObject RandomSpawnPoint (){
  // return current GameObject if array empty
  if(spawnPoints.Length < 1) return null;

// the rest as before ...
```

3. Improve the `CreateSphere()` method in the C# class called `SpawnBall`, so that we only attempt to instantiate a new GameObject if the `RandomSpawnPoint()` and `NearestSpawnpoint()` methods have returned a non-null object reference:

```
private void CreateSphere(){
  GameObject spawnPoint = spawnPointManager.RandomSpawnPoint ();

  if(spawnPoint){
    GameObject newBall = (GameObject)Instantiate (prefabBall,
spawnPoint.transform.position, Quaternion.identity);
    Destroy(newBall, destroyAfterDelay);
  }
}
```

See also

▶ The same techniques and code can be used for selecting spawn points or waypoints. Refer to the *NPC NavMeshAgent control to follow waypoints in sequence* recipe in this chapter for more information about waypoints.

Choosing destinations – respawn to the most recently passed checkpoint

A **checkpoint** usually represents a certain distance through the game (or perhaps a **track**) in which an agent (user or NPC) has succeeded reaching. Reaching (or passing) checkpoints often results in bonus awards, such as *extra time*, *points*, *ammo*, and so on. Also, if a player has multiple lives, then often a player will be respawned only back as far as the most recently passed checkpoint, rather than right to the beginning of the level.

This recipe demonstrates a simple approach to the checkpoints, whereby once the player's character has passed a checkpoint, if they die they are moved back only to the most recently passed checkpoint.

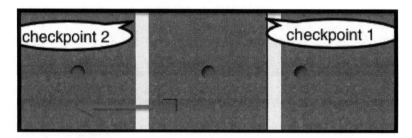

Getting ready

This recipe builds upon the player-controlled 3D cube Unity project that you created at the beginning of this chapter. So, make a copy of this project, open it, and then follow the steps for this recipe.

How to do it...

To have the respawn position upon losing a life change depending on the checkpoints passed, follow these steps:

1. Move the **Cube-player** GameObject to the (12, 0.5, 0) position.

2. Select **Cube-player** in the **Inspector** panel and add a **Character Controller** component by clicking on **Add Component | Physics | Character Controller** (this is to enable the OnTriggerEnter collision messages to be received).

3. Create a cube named **Cube-checkpoint-1** at (5, 0, 0), scaled to (1, 1, 20).

4. With **Cube-checkpoint-1** selected, check the **Is Trigger** property of its **Box Collider** component in the **Inspector** panel.

5. Create a **CheckPoint** tag, and assign this tag to **Cube-checkpoint-1**.

6. Duplicate **Cube-checkpoint-1** by naming the **Cube-checkpoint-2** clone and positioning it at (-5, 0, 0).

7. Create a sphere named **Sphere-Death** at (7, 0.5, 0). Assign the **m_red** material to this sphere to make it red.

8. With **Sphere-Death** selected, check the **Is Trigger** property of its **Sphere Collider** component in the **Inspector** panel.

9. Create a **Death** tag, and assign this tag to **Sphere-Death**.

10. Duplicate **Sphere-Death**, and position this clone at (0, 0.5, 0).

11. Duplicate **Sphere-Death** a second time, and position this second clone at (-10, 0.5, 0).

12. Add an instance of the following C# script class called `CheckPoints` to the **Cube-player** GameObject:

```csharp
using UnityEngine;
using System.Collections;

public class CheckPoints : MonoBehaviour {
  private Vector3 respawnPosition;

  void Start (){
    respawnPosition = transform.position;
  }

  void OnTriggerEnter (Collider hit){
    if(hit.CompareTag("CheckPoint")){
      respawnPosition = transform.position;
    }

    if(hit.CompareTag("Death")){
      transform.position = respawnPosition;
    }
  }
}
```

13. Run the scene. If the cube runs into a red sphere *before* crossing a checkpoint, it will be respawned back to its starting position. Once the red cube has passed a checkpoint, if a red sphere is hit, then the cube will be moved back to the location of the most recent checkpoint that it passed through.

How it works...

The C# script class called `CheckPoints` has one variable called `respawnPosition`, which is a Vector3 that refers to the position the player's cube is to be moved to (respawned) if it collides with a **Death** tagged object. The default setting for this is the position of the player's cube when the scene begins—so in the `Start()` method, we set it to the player's position.

Each time an object tagged called **CheckPoint** is collided with, the value of `respawnPosition` is updated to the current position of the player's red cube at this point in time (that is, where it is when it touches the stretched cube tagged called **CheckPoint**). So that the next time the object tagged **Death** is hit, the cube will be respawned back to where it last touched the object tagged called **CheckPoint**.

NPC NavMeshAgent to seek or flee destination while avoiding obstacles

The introduction of Unity's NavMeshAgent has greatly simplified the coding for NPC and enemy agent behaviors. In this recipe, we'll add some wall (scaled cubes) obstacles, and generate a NavMesh, so that Unity knows not to try to walk through the walls. We then add a NavMeshAgent component to our NPC GameObject, and tell it to head to a stated destination location by intelligently planning and following a path, while avoiding the wall obstacles.

In the next screenshot, we can see in the **Scene** panel the squares that represent potential points on the path. We can also see lines showing the current temporary direction and destination around the current obstacle.

When the **Navigation** panel is visible, then the **Scene** panel displays the blue-shaded *walkable* areas, and unshaded, non-walkable areas at the edge of the terrain and around each of the two *wall* objects.

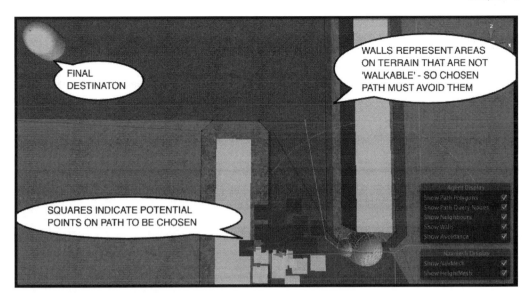

Getting ready

This recipe builds upon the player-controlled 3D cube Unity project that you created at the beginning of this chapter. So, make a copy of this project, open it, and then follow the steps for this recipe.

How to do it...

To make an object seek or flee from a position, follow these steps:

1. Delete the **Cube-player** GameObject, since we are going to be creating an NPC computer controlled agent.

2. Create a sphere named **Sphere-arrow** that is positioned at (2, 0.5, 2). Scale it as (1,1,1).

3. Create a second sphere named **Sphere-small**. Scale it as (0.5, 0.5, 0.5).

4. Child **Sphere-small** to **Sphere-arrow** and position it at (0, 0, 0.5).

Childing refers to making one GameObject, in the **Hierarchy** panel, a child of another GameObject. This is done by dragging the object that is to be childed over the object to be the parent. Once completed, the parent-child relationship is indicated visually by all children being right-indented and positioned immediately below their parent in the **Hierarchy** panel. If a parent object is transformed (moved/scaled/rotated), then all its children will also be transformed accordingly.

5. In the **Inspector** panel, add a new NavMeshAgent to **Sphere-arrow**; choose **Add Component | Navigation | Nav Mesh Agent**.

6. Set the **Stopping Distance** property of **NavMeshAgent** component to 2.

7. Add the following C# script class called `ArrowNPCMovement` to GameObject **Sphere-arrow**:

```
using UnityEngine;
using System.Collections;

public class ArrowNPCMovement : MonoBehaviour {
  public GameObject targetGO;
  private NavMeshAgent navMeshAgent;

  void Start (){
    navMeshAgent = GetComponent<NavMeshAgent>();
    HeadForDestintation();
  }

  private void HeadForDestintation (){
    Vector3 destinaton = targetGO.transform.position;
    navMeshAgent.SetDestination (destinaton);
  }
}
```

8. Ensure that **Sphere-arrow** is selected in the **Inspector** panel for the `ArrowNPCMovement` scripted component. Drag **Capsule-destination** over the variable **Projectile** called **Target GO**.

9. Create a 3D cube named **Cube-wall** at (-6, 0, 0), and scale it to (1, 2, 10).

10. Create another 3D cube named **Cube-wall** at (-2, 0, 6), and scale it to (1, 2, 7).

11. Display the **Navigation** panel by choosing **Window | Navigation**.

A great place to *dock* the **Navigation** panel is next to the **Inspector** panel since you will never be using the **Inspect** and **Navigation** panels at the same time.

12. In the **Hierarchy** tab, select both of the **Cube-wall** objects (we select the objects that are *not* supposed to be a part of the **walkable** parts of our scene), and then in the **Navigation** panel, check the **Navigation Static** checkbox. Then, click on the **Bake** button at the bottom of the **Navigation** panel. When the **Navigation** panel is displayed, you'll see a blue *tint* on the parts of the **Scene** that are walkable. Candidate areas for a **NavMeshAgent** are supposed to be considered as parts of a path to a destination.

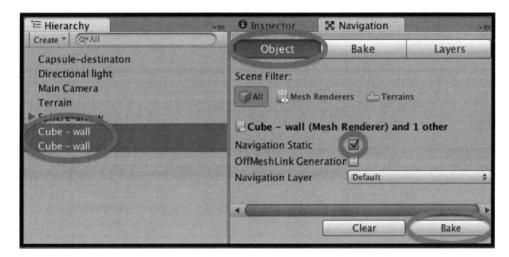

13. Now run your game. You will see the **Sphere-arrow** GameObject automatically move towards the **Capsule-destination** GameObject, following a path that avoids the two wall objects.

How it works...

The **NavMeshAgent** component that we added to GameObject **Sphere-arrow** does most of the work for us. **NavMeshAgents** need 2 things: a destination location to head towards, and a **NavMesh** component of the terrain with walkable/non-walkable areas, so that it can plan a path, avoiding obstacles. We created two obstacles (the **Cube-wall** objects), and these were selected when we created **NavMesh** for this scene in the **Navigation** panel.

The location for our NPC object to travel towards is the position of the **Capsule-destination** GameObject at (-12, 0, 8); but of course, we could just move this object in the **Scene** panel at **Design-time**, and its new position would be the destination when we run the game.

The C# script class called `ArrowNPCMovement` has two variables: one is a reference to the destination GameObject, and the second is a reference to the NavMeshAgent component of the GameObject in which our instance of the `ArrowNPCMovement` class is also a component. When the scene starts, via the `Start()` method, the **NavMeshAgent** sibling component is found, and the `HeadForDestination()` method is called, which sets the destination of the NavMeshAgent to the position of the destination GameObject.

Once the NavMeshAgent has a target to head towards, it will plan a path there and will keep moving until it arrives (or gets within the **Stopping Distance** if that parameter has been set to a distance greater than zero).

 Ensure that the object with the NavMeshAgent component is selected in the **Hierarchy** panel at runtime to be able to see this navigation data in the **Scene** panel.

There's more...

There are some details that you don't want to miss.

Constantly updating the NavMeshAgent destination to Player's character current location

Rather than a destination that is fixed when the scene starts, let's allow the **Capsule-destination** object to be moved by the player while the scene is running. In every frame, we'll get our NPC arrow to reset the NavMeshAgent's destination to wherever the **Capsule-destination** has been moved to.

To allow the user movement of the destination object and frame-by-frame updating of NavMeshAgent destination, we need to do the following:

1. Add an instance of the C# script class called `PlayerControl` as a component of **Capsule-destination**.

2. Update the C# script class called `ArrowNPCMovement` so that we call the `HeadForDestintation()` method every frame, that is, from `Update()`, rather than just once in `Start()`:

```
void Start (){
    navMeshAgent = GetComponent<NavMeshAgent>();
}

void Update (){
    HeadForDestintation();
}
```

Now, when you run the game, you can use the arrow keys to move the destination location, and the NavMeshAgent will update its paths in each frame, based on the updated position of the **Capsule-destination** GameObject.

Constantly update NavMeshAgent destination to flee away from Player's character current location

Rather than seeking towards the player's current position, let's make our NPC agent always attempt to flee away from the player's location. For example, an enemy with very low-health points might run away, and so gain time to regain its health before fighting again.

To instruct our NavMeshAgent to flee away from the player's location, we need to replace the C# script class called `ArrowNPCMovement` with the following:

```
using UnityEngine;
using System.Collections;

public class ArrowNPCMovement : MonoBehaviour {
  public GameObject targetGO;
  private NavMeshAgent navMeshAgent;
  private float runAwayMultiplier = 2;
  private float runAwayDistance;

  void Start(){
    navMeshAgent = GetComponent<NavMeshAgent>();
    runAwayDistance = navMeshAgent.stoppingDistance *
runAwayMultiplier;
  }

  void Update () {
    Vector3 enemyPosition = targetGO.transform.position;
```

```
    float distanceFromEnemy = Vector3.Distance(transform.position,
enemyPosition);
    if (distanceFromEnemy < runAwayDistance)
      FleeFromTarget (enemyPosition);
  }

  private void FleeFromTarget(Vector3 enemyPosition){
    Vector3 fleeToPosition = Vector3.Normalize(transform.position -
enemyPosition) * runAwayDistance;
    HeadForDestintation(fleeToPosition);
  }

  private void HeadForDestintation (Vector3 destinationPosition){
    navMeshAgent.SetDestination (destinationPosition);
  }
}
```

The `Start()` method caches a reference to the NavMeshAgent component, and also calculates the `runAwayDistance` variable to be twice the NavMeshAgent's stopping distance (although this can be changed by changing the value of the `runAwayMultiplier` variable accordingly). When the distance to the enemy is less than the value of this variable, then we'll instruct the computer-controlled object to flee in the opposite direction.

The `Update()` method calculates whether the distance to the enemy is within the `runAwayDistance`, and if so, it calls the `FleeFromTarget (...)` method that passes the location of the enemy as a parameter.

The `FleeFromTarget (...)` method calculates a point that is the `runAwayDistance` Unity units away from the Player's cube, in a direction that is directly away from the computer-controlled object. This is achieved by subtracting the enemy position vector from the current transform's position. Finally, the `HeadForDestintation (...)` method is called, passing the flee-to position, which results in the NavMeshAgent being told to set the location as its new destination.

The Unity units are arbitrary, since they are just numbers in a computer. However, in most cases, it simplifies things to think of distances in terms of meters (1 Unity unit = 1 meter), and mass in terms of kilograms (1 Unity unit = 1 kilogram). Of course, if your game is based on a microscopic world, or a pan-galatic space travel and more, then you need to decide what each Unity unit corresponds to for your game context. For more discussion of units in Unity, check out the `http://forum.unity3d.com/threads/best-units-of-measurement-in-unity.284133/#post-1875487` link.

As the following screenshot illustrates, the NavMeshAgent plans a path to the position to flee towards:

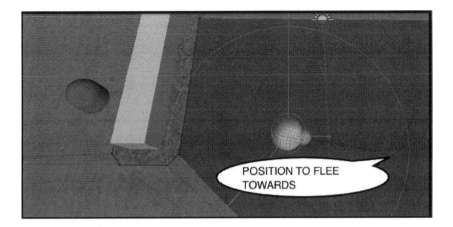

POSITION TO FLEE
TOWARDS

Create a mini point-and-click game

Another way to choose the destination for our **Sphere-arrow** GameObject is by the user clicking on an object on the screen, and then the **Sphere-arrow** GameObject moving to the location of the clicked object.

To allow the user to select the destination objects with point-and-click, we need to do the following:

1. Remove the ArrowNPCMovement component from the **Sphere-arrow** GameObject.

2. Create some target objects, such as a black cube, a blue sphere, and a green cylinder. Note that, to be a target, each object needs to have a collider component in order to receive the OnMouseOver event messages (when creating primitives objects from the Unity menu **Create | 3D Object**, the colliders are automatically created).

3. Add an instance of the following C# script class called ClickMeToSetDestination to each of the GameObjects that you wish to be a clickable target:

```
using UnityEngine;
using System.Collections;

public class ClickMeToSetDestination : MonoBehaviour {
  private NavMeshAgent playerNavMeshAgent;
  private MeshRenderer meshRenderer;
  private bool mouseOver = false;

  private Color unselectedColor;

  void Start (){
```

```
        meshRenderer = GetComponent<MeshRenderer>();
        unselectedColor = meshRenderer.sharedMaterial.color;

        GameObject playerGO = GameObject.FindGameObjectWithTag("Play
    er");
        playerNavMeshAgent = playerGO.GetComponent<NavMeshAgent>();
    }

    void Update (){
        if (Input.GetButtonDown("Fire1") && mouseOver)
            playerNavMeshAgent.SetDestination(transform.position);
    }

    void OnMouseOver (){
        mouseOver = true;
        meshRenderer.sharedMaterial.color = Color.yellow;
    }

    void OnMouseExit (){
        mouseOver = false;
        meshRenderer.sharedMaterial.color = unselectedColor;
    }
}
```

Now, while running the game, when your mouse is over one of the three objects, that object will be highlighted yellow. If you click on the mouse button when the object is highlighted, the **Sphere-arrow** GameObject will make its way up to (but stopping just before) the clicked object.

NPC NavMeshAgent to follow the waypoints in a sequence

Waypoints are often used as a guide to make autonomously moving NPCs and enemies follow a path in a general way (but be able to respond with other directional behaviors, such as flee or seek, if friends/predators/prey are sensed nearby). The waypoints are arranged in a sequence, so that when the character reaches, or gets close to a waypoint, it will then select the next waypoint in the sequence as the target location to move towards. This recipe demonstrates an arrow object moving towards a waypoint, and then, when it gets close enough, it will choose the next waypoint in the sequence as the new target destination. When the last waypoint has been reached, it again starts heading towards the first waypoint.

Since Unity's NavMeshAgent has simplified coding NPC behavior, our work in this recipe becomes basically finding the position of the next waypoint, and then telling the NavMeshAgent that this waypoint is its new destination.

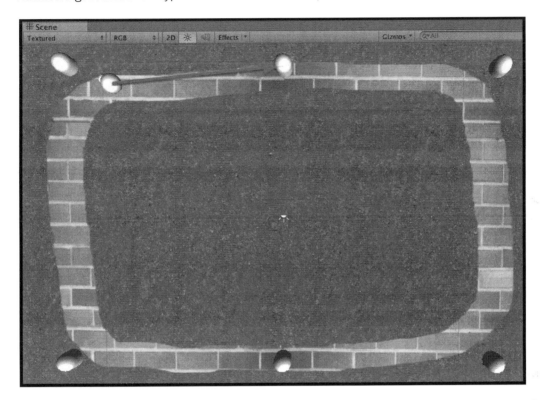

Getting ready

This recipe builds upon the player-controlled 3D cube Unity project that you created at the beginning of this chapter. So, make a copy of this project, open it, and then follow the steps for this recipe.

For this recipe, we have prepared the yellow brick texture image that you need in a folder named `Textures` in the `1362_08_06` folder.

How to do it...

To instruct an object to follow a sequence of waypoints, follow these steps:

1. Delete the **Cube-player** GameObject, since we are going to be creating an NPC computer controlled agent.

2. Create a sphere named **Sphere-arrow**, position at (2, 0.5, 2), and scale it as (1,1,1).

3. Create a second sphere named **Sphere-small**, and scale it as (0.5, 0.5, 0.5).

4. Child **Sphere-small** to **Sphere-arrow**, and then position it at (0, 0, 0.5).

5. In the **Inspector,** add a new NavMeshAgent to **Sphere-arrow**, and then choose **Add Component | Navigation | NavMeshAgent**.

6. Set the **Stopping Distance** property of the **NavMeshAgent** component to 2.

7. Display the **Navigation** panel by choosing **Window | Navigation**.

8. Click on the **Bake** button at the bottom of the **Navigation** panel. When the **Navigation** panel is displayed, you'll see a blue *tint* on the parts of the **Scene** panel that are walkable, which will be all parts of the terrain, except near the edges.

9. Add an instance of the following C# script class called `ArrowNPCMovement` to the **Sphere-arrow** GameObject:

```csharp
using UnityEngine;
using System.Collections;

public class ArrowNPCMovement : MonoBehaviour {
  private GameObject targetGO = null;
  private WaypointManager waypointManager;
  private NavMeshAgent navMeshAgent;

  void Start (){
    navMeshAgent = GetComponent<NavMeshAgent>();
    waypointManager = GetComponent<WaypointManager>();
    HeadForNextWayPoint();
  }

  void Update (){
    float closeToDestinaton = navMeshAgent.stoppingDistance * 2;
    if (navMeshAgent.remainingDistance < closeToDestinaton){
      HeadForNextWayPoint ();
    }
  }

  private void HeadForNextWayPoint (){
    targetGO = waypointManager.NextWaypoint (targetGO);
    navMeshAgent.SetDestination (targetGO.transform.position);
  }
}
```

10. Create a new capsule object named **Capsule-waypoint-0** at (-12, 0, 8), and give it the **waypoint** tag.

11. Copy **Capsule-waypoint -0,** name the copy as **Capsule-waypoint -3,** and position this copy at (8, 0, -8).

 We are going to add some intermediate waypoints numbered 1 and 2 later on. This is why our second waypoint here is numbered 3, in case you were wondering.

12. Add the following C# script class called `WaypointManager` to the **Sphere-arrow** GameObject:

```
using UnityEngine;

public class WaypointManager : MonoBehaviour {
  public GameObject wayPoint0;
  public GameObject wayPoint3;

  public GameObject NextWaypoint(GameObject current){
    if(current == wayPoint0)
      return wayPoint3;
    else
      return wayPoint0;
  }
}
```

13. Ensure that **Sphere-arrow** is selected in the **Inspector** for the `WaypointManager` scripted component. Drag **Capsule-waypoint-0** and **Capsule-waypoint-3** over the public variable projectile called **Way Point 0** and **Way Point 3,** respectively.

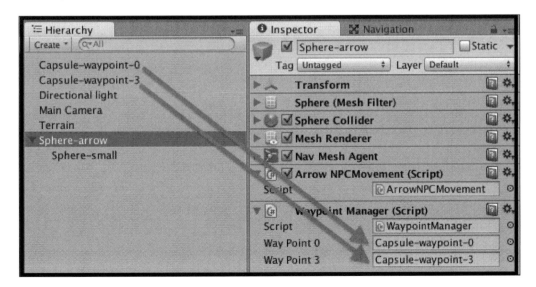

14. Display the Navigation panel by choosing **Window | Navigation**.

15. Click on the **Bake** button at the bottom of the **Navigation** panel. When the **Navigation** panel is displayed, you'll see a blue *tint* on the parts of the **Scene** that are *walkable*, which will be all the parts of the terrain, except near the edges.

16. Now, run your game. The arrow object will first move towards one of the waypoint capsules, then when it gets close to it, it will slow down, turn around, head towards the other waypoint capsule, and keep doing that continuously.

How it works...

The **NavMeshAgent** component that we added to the **Sphere-arrow** GameObject does most of the work for us. **NavMeshAgents** need two things: a destination location to head towards, and a NavMesh, so that it can plan a path, avoiding obstacles.

We created two possible waypoints to be the location for our NPC to move towards: **Capsule-waypoint-0** and **Capsule-waypoint-3**.

The C# script class called `WaypointManager` has one job — to return a reference to the next waypoint that our NPC should head towards. There are two variables: `wayPoint0` and `wayPoint3` that reference to the two waypoint GameObjects in our scene. The `NextWaypoint(...)` method takes a single parameter named `current`, which is a reference to the current waypoint that the object was moving towards (or null). This method's task is to return a reference to the **next** waypoint that the NPC should travel towards. The logic for this method is simple—if `current` refers to `waypoint0`, then we'll return `waypoint3`, otherwise we'll return `waypoint0`. Note that if we pass this `null` method, then we'll get `waypoint0` back (so, it is our default first waypoint).

The C# script class called `ArrowNPCMovement` has three variables: one is a reference to the destination GameObject named `targetGO`. The second is a reference to the `NavMeshAgent` component of the GameObject in which our instance of the class called `ArrowNPCMovement` is also a component. The third variable called `WaypointManager` is a reference to the sibling scripted component, an instance of our `WaypointManager` script class.

When the scene starts, via the `Start()` method, the **NavMeshAgent** and `WaypointManager` sibling components are found, and the `HeadForDestination()` method is called.

The `HeadForDestination()` method first sets the variable called `targetGO` to refer to the GameObject that is returned by a call to `NextWaypoint(...)` of the scripted component called `WaypointManager` (that is, `targetGO` is set to refer to either **Capsule-waypoint-0** or **Capsule-waypoint-3**). Next, it instructs the `NavMeshAgent` to make its destination the position of the `targetGO` GameObject.

Each frame method called `Update()` is called. A test is made to see if the distance from the NPC arrow object is close to the destination waypoint. If the distance is smaller than twice the *stopping distance*, set in our `NavMeshAgent`, then a call is made to `WaypointManager.NextWaypoint(...)` to update our target destination to be the next waypoint in the sequence.

There's more...

There are some details that you don't want to miss.

More efficient to avoid using NavMeshes for waypoints

NavMeshes are far superior to waypoints, since a location in a general area (not a specific point) can be used, and the path finding the algorithm will automatically find the shortest route. For a succinct recipe (such as the above), we can simplify the implementation of waypoints using NavMeshes for calculating movements for us. However, for optimized, real-world games the most common way to move from one waypoint to the next is via linear interpolation, or by implementing Craig Reynold's Seek algorithm (for details follow the link listed in the Conclusion section, at the end of this chapter).

Working with arrays of waypoints

Having a separate C# script class called `WaypointManager` to simply swap between **Capsule-waypoint-0** and **Capsule-waypoint-3** may have seemed to be a heavy duty and over-engineering task, but this was actually a very good move. An object of the script class called `WaypointManager` has the job of returning the *next* waypoint. It is now very straightforward to add a more sophisticated approach of having an array of waypoints, without us having to change any code in the script class called `ArrowNPCMovement`. We can choose a random waypoint to be the next destination (see the *Choosing destinations – find nearest (or a random) spawnpoint* recipe). Or, we can have an array of waypoints, and choose the next one in the sequence.

To improve our game to work with an array of waypoints in the sequence to be followed, we need to do the following:

1. Copy **Capsule-waypoint-0**, name the copy as **Capsule-waypoint-1**, and position this copy at (0, 0, 8).

2. Make four more copies (named **Capsule-waypoint-1, 2, 4, 5**), and position them as follows:

   - **Capsule-waypoint-1**: Position = (-2, 0, 8)
   - **Capsule-waypoint-2**: Position = (8, 0, 8)
   - **Capsule-waypoint-4**: Position = (-2, 0, -8)
   - **Capsule-waypoint-5**: Position = (-12, 0, -8)

3. Replace the C# script class called `WaypointManager` with the following code:

```
using UnityEngine;
using System.Collections;
using System;

public class WaypointManager : MonoBehaviour {
  public GameObject[] waypoints;

  public GameObject NextWaypoint (GameObject current)
  {
    if ( waypoints.Length < 1)
      Debug.LogError ("WaypointManager:: ERROR - no waypoints have
been added to array!");

    int currentIndex = Array.IndexOf(waypoints, current);
    int nextIndex = ((currentIndex + 1) % waypoints.Length);
    return waypoints[nextIndex];
  }
}
```

4. Ensure that **Sphere-arrow** is selected. In the **Inspector** panel for the `WaypointManager` scripted component set the size of the `Waypoints` array to 6. Now, drag in all the six capsule waypoint objects called as `Capsule-waypoint-0/1/2/3/4/5`.

5. Run the game. Now, the **Sphere-arrow** GameObject will first move towards the waypoint 0 (top left, and then follow the sequence around the terrain).

6. Finally, you can make it look as if the Sphere is following a yellow brick road. Import the provided yellow brick texture, add this to your terrain, and paint the texture an oval-shaped path between the waypoints. You may also uncheck the Mesh Rendered component for each waypoint capsule, so that the user does not see any of the way points, but just the arrow object following the yellow brick path

In the `NextWaypoint (...)` method, first we check in case the array is empty, in which case an error is logged. Next, the array index for the current waypoint GameObject is found (if present in the array). Finally, the array index for the next waypoint is calculated using a modulus operator to support a cyclic sequence, returning to the beginning of the array after the last element has been visited.

Increased flexibility with a WayPoint class

Rather than forcing a GameObject to follow a single rigid sequence of locations, we can make things more flexible by defining a `WayPoint` class, whereby each waypoint GameObject has an array of possible destinations, and each of these has its own array and so on. In this way a **di-graph (directed graph)** can be implemented, of which a linear sequence is just one possible instance.

To improve our game to work with a di-graph of waypoints, do the following:

1. Remove the scripted `WayPointManager` component from the **Sphere-arrow** GameObject.

2. Replace the C# script class called `ArrowNPCMovement` with the following code:

```
using UnityEngine;
using System.Collections;

public class ArrowNPCMovement : MonoBehaviour {
  public Waypoint waypoint;
  private bool firstWayPoint = true;
  private NavMeshAgent navMeshAgent;

  void Start (){
    navMeshAgent = GetComponent<NavMeshAgent>();
    HeadForNextWayPoint();
  }

  void Update () {
    float closeToDestinaton = navMeshAgent.stoppingDistance * 2;
    if (navMeshAgent.remainingDistance < closeToDestinaton){
      HeadForNextWayPoint ();
    }
  }

  private void HeadForNextWayPoint (){
    if(firstWayPoint)
      firstWayPoint = false;
    else
      waypoint = waypoint.GetNextWaypoint();

    Vector3 target = waypoint.transform.position;
    navMeshAgent.SetDestination (target);
  }
}
```

3. Create a new C# script class called `WayPoint` with the following code:

```
using UnityEngine;
using System.Collections;

public class Waypoint: MonoBehaviour {
```

```
public Waypoint[] waypoints;

public Waypoint GetNextWaypoint () {
  return waypoints[ Random.Range(0, waypoints.Length) ];
}
}
```

4. Select all the six GameObjects called **Capsule-waypoint -0/1/2/3/4/5,** and add to them a scripted instance of C# class called `WayPoint`.

5. Select the **Sphere-arrow** GameObject and add to it a scripted instance of C# class called `WayPoint`.

6. Ensure that the **Sphere-arrow** GameObject is selected: in the **Inspector** panel for the `ArrowNPCMovement` scripted component drag **Capsule-waypoint-0** into the **Waypoint** public variable slot.

7. Now, we need to link **Capsule-waypoint-0** to **Capsule-waypoint-1**, **Capsule-waypoint-1** to **Capsule-waypoint -2**, and so on. Select **Capsule-waypoint-0**, set its `Waypoints` array size to 1, and drag in **Capsule-waypoint-1**. Next, select **Capsule-waypoint-1**, set its **Waypoints** array size to 1, and drag in **Capsule-waypoint-2**. Do the following until you finally link **Capsule-waypoint-5** back to **Capsule-waypoint-0**.

You now have a much more flexible game architecture, allowing GameObjects to randomly select one of several different paths at each waypoint reached. In this final recipe variation, we have implemented a waypoint sequence, since each waypoint has an array of just one linked waypoint. However, if you change the array size to 2 or more, you will then be creating a graph of linked waypoints, adding random variations in the sequence of waypoints that a computer controlled character follows for any given run of your game.

Controlling the object group movement through flocking

A realistic, natural-looking, flocking behavior (for example birds or antelopes or bats) can be created through creating collections of objects with the following four simple rules:

- **Separation**: Avoiding getting too close to neighbors
- **Avoid Obstacle**: Turning away from an obstacle immediately ahead
- **Alignment**: Moving in the general direction the flock is heading
- **Cohesion**: Moving towards the location in the middle of the flock

Each member of the flock acts independently, but needs to know about the current heading and location of the members of its flock. This recipe shows you how to create a scene with two flocks of cubes: one flock of green cubes and, one flock of yellow cubes. To keep things simple, we'll not worry about separation in our recipe.

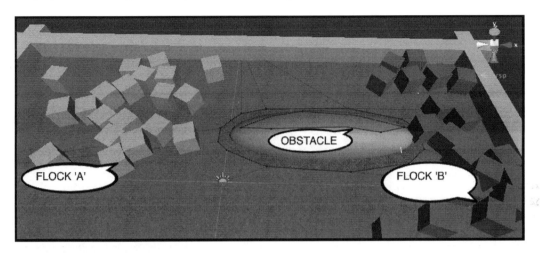

Getting ready

This recipe builds upon the player-controlled cube Unity project that you created in the first recipe. So, make a copy of this project, open it, and then follow the steps for this recipe.

How to do it...

To make a group of objects flock together, please follow these steps:

1. Create a Material in the **Project** panel, and name it as m_green with the Main Color tinted green.

2. Create a Material in the **Project** panel, and name it as m_yellow with Main Color tinted yellow.

3. Create a 3D Cube GameObject named Cube-drone at (0,0,0). Drag the m_yellow Material into this object.

4. Add a **Navigation | NavMeshAgent** component to Cube-drone. Set the **Stopping Distance** property of the **NavMeshAgent** component to 2.

5. Add a **Physics RigidBody** component to Cube-drone with the following properties:

   - **Mass** is 1
   - **Drag** is 0

- ❑ **Angular Drag** is 0.05
- ❑ **Use Gravity** and **Is Kinematic** are both unchecked
- ❑ Under **Constrains Freeze Position** for the **Y**-axis is checked

6. You will see the following Inspector values for your cube's rigid body component:

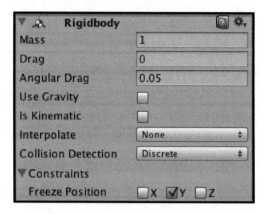

7. Create the following C# script class called `Drone`, and add an instance as a component to the `Cube-drone` GameObject:

```
using UnityEngine;
using System.Collections;

public class Drone : MonoBehaviour {
  private NavMeshAgent navMeshAgent;

  void Start() {
    navMeshAgent = GetComponent<NavMeshAgent>();
  }

  public void SetTargetPosition(Vector3 swarmCenterAverage,
Vector3 swarmMovementAverage) {
    Vector3 destination = swarmCenterAverage +
swarmMovementAverage;
    navMeshAgent.SetDestination(destination);
  }
}
```

8. Create a new empty Prefab named `dronePrefabYellow`, and from the **Hierarchy** panel, drag your `Cube-boid` GameObject into this Prefab.

9. Now, drag the `m_green` Material into the `Cube-boid` GameObject.

10. Create a new empty Prefab named `dronePrefabGreen`, and from the **Hierarchy** panel, drag your `Cube-drone` GameObject into this Prefab.

11. Delete the `Cube-drone` GameObject from the **Scene** panel.

12. Add the following C# script `Swarm` class to the **Main Camera**:

```csharp
using UnityEngine;
using System.Collections;
using System.Collections.Generic;

public class Swarm : MonoBehaviour {
  public int droneCount = 20;
  public GameObject dronePrefab;

  private List<Drone> drones = new List<Drone>();

  void Awake() {
    for (int i = 0; i < droneCount; i++)
      AddDrone();
  }

  void FixedUpdate() {
    Vector3 swarmCenter = SwarmCenterAverage();
    Vector3 swarmMovement = SwarmMovementAverage();

    foreach(Drone drone in drones)
      drone.SetTargetPosition(swarmCenter, swarmMovement);
  }

  private void AddDrone() {
    GameObject newDroneGO =
(GameObject)Instantiate(dronePrefab);
    Drone newDrone = newDroneGO.GetComponent<Drone>();
    drones.Add(newDrone);
  }

  private Vector3 SwarmCenterAverage() {
    // cohesion (swarm center point)
    Vector3 locationTotal = Vector3.zero;

    foreach(Drone drone in drones)
      locationTotal += drone.transform.position;

    return (locationTotal / drones.Count);
```

```
      }

      private Vector3 SwarmMovementAverage() {
        // alignment (swarm direction average)
        Vector3 velocityTotal = Vector3.zero;

        foreach(Drone drone in drones)
          velocityTotal += drone.rigidbody.velocity;

        return (velocityTotal / drones.Count);
      }
    }
```

13. With **Main Camera** selected in the **Hierarchy** panel, drag `prefab_boid_yellow`, from the **Project** panel, over the public variable of **Drone** Prefab.

14. With **Main Camera** selected in the **Hierarchy** panel, add a second instance of the script class called `Swarm` to this GameObject, and then drag `prefab_boid_green`, from the **Project** panel, over the public variable of **Drone** Prefab.

15. Create a new Cube named `wall-left` with the following properties:

    ❑ Position = (-15, 0.5, 0)

    ❑ Scale = (1, 1, 20)

16. Duplicate the `wall-left` object by naming the new object as `wall-right`, and change the position of `wall-right` to (15, 0.5, 0).

17. Create a new Cube named as `wall-top` with the following properties:

    ❑ Position = (0, 0.5, 10)

    ❑ Scale = (31, 1, 1)

18. Duplicate the `wall-top` object by naming the new object as `wall-bottom`, and change the position of `wall-bottom` to (0, 0.5, -10).

19. Create a new Sphere named as `Sphere-obstacle` with the following properties:

    ❑ Position = (5, 0, 3)

    ❑ Scale = (10, 3, 3)

20. In the **Hierarchy** panel, select the `Sphere-obstacle` GameObject. Then in the **Navigation** panel, check the **Navigation Static** checkbox. Then, click on the **Bake** button at the bottom of the **Navigation** panel.

21. Finally, make the player's red cube larger by setting its scale to (3,3,3).

How it works...

The `Swarm` class contains three variables:

- ▸ `droneCount`: It is an integer referencing the number of the `Swarm` class members created
- ▸ `dronePrefab`: It references to the Prefab to be cloned to create swarm members
- ▸ `Drone`: A list of objects that reference `drones`, a list of all the scripted `Drone` components inside all the `Swarm` objects that have been created

Upon creation, as the scene starts, the `Swarm` script class `Awake()` method loops to create `droneCount` swarm members by repeatedly calling the `AddDrone()` method. This method instantiates a new `GameObject` from the prefab, and then sets the `newDrone` variable to be a reference to the Drone-scripted object, inside the new `Swarm` class member. In each frame, the `FixedUpdate()` method loops through the list of `Drone` objects by calling their `SetTargetPosition(...)` method, and passing in the `Swarm` center location and the average of all the swarm member velocities.

The rest of this `Swarm` class is made up of two methods: one (`SwarmCenterAverage`) returns a Vector3 object, representing the average position of all the `Drone` objects, and the other (`SwarmMovementAverage`) returns a `Vector3` object, representing the average velocity (movement force) of all the `Drone` objects as described in the following list.

- ▸ `SwarmMovementAverage()`:
  - ❑ What is the general direction that the swarm is moving in?
  - ❑ This is known as **alignment**—a swarm member attempting to move in the same direction as the swarm average

- ▸ `SwarmCenterAverage()`:
  - ❑ What is the center position of the swarm?
  - ❑ This is known as **cohesion**—a swarm member attempting to move towards the center of the swarm

The core work is undertaken by the `Drone` class. Each drone's `Start(...)` method finds and caches a reference to its NavMeshAgent component.

Each drone's `UpdateVelocity(...)` method takes as input two Vector3 arguments: `swarmCenterAverage` and `swarmMovementAverage`. This method then calculates the desired new velocity for this Drone (by simply adding the two vectors), and then uses the result (a Vector3 location) to update the NavMeshAgent's target location.

There's more...

There are some details that you don't want to miss.

Learn more about flocking Artificial Intelligence

Most of the flocking models in modern computing owe much to the work of Craig Reynolds in the 1980s. Learn more about Craig and his boids program at `http://en.wikipedia.org/wiki/Craig_Reynolds_(computer_graphics)`.

Conclusion

In this chapter, we have introduced recipes demonstrating a range of player and computer controlled characters, vehicles, and objects. Player character controllers are fundamental to the usability experience of every game, while the NPC objects and characters add rich interactions to many games:

- Learn more about Unity NavMeshes from this Unity tutorial, which is available at `http://unity3d.com/learn/tutorials/modules/beginner/live-training-archive/navmeshes`
- Learn more about the Unity 2D character controllers at `http://unity3d.com/learn/tutorials/modules/beginner/2d/2d-controllers`
- Learn lots about the computer-controlled moving GameObjects from the classic paper entitled *Steering Behaviors For Autonomous Characters* by Craig W. Reynolds, presented at the GDC-99 (Game Developer's Conference) at `http://www.red3d.com/cwr/steer/gdc99/`
- Learn about the Unity 3D character component and control at:
  - `http://docs.unity3d.com/Manual/class-CharacterController.html`
  - `http://unity3d.com/learn/tutorials/projects/survival-shooter/player-character`

Every game needs textures—here are some of the sources of free textures suitable for many games:

- CG Textures are available at `http://www.cgtextures.com/`
- Naldz Graphics blog are available at `http://naldzgraphics.net/textures/`

9
Playing and Manipulating Sounds

In this chapter, we will cover:

- ▶ Matching the audio pitch to the animation speed
- ▶ Simulating acoustic environments with Reverb Zones
- ▶ Preventing an Audio Clip from restarting if it is already playing
- ▶ Waiting for audio to finish playing before auto-destructing an object
- ▶ Adding volume control with Audio Mixers
- ▶ Making a dynamic soundtrack with Snapshots
- ▶ Balancing in-game audio with Ducking

Introduction

Sound is a very important part of the gaming experience. In fact, we can't stress enough how crucial it is to the player's immersion in a virtual environment. Just think of the engine running in your favorite racing game, the distant urban buzz in a simulator game, or the creeping noises in horror games. Think of how these sounds transport you *into* the game.

The big picture

Before getting on with the recipes, let's step back and have a quick review on how sound works on Unity 5.

Audio files can be embedded into GameObjects through the **Audio Source** component. Unity supports **3D sounds**, which means that the location and distance between the audio sources and **Audio Listener** matter in the way the sound is perceived in terms of loudness and the left/right balance. This is unless the audio source is specified as **2D sound** (which is usually the case for the background soundtrack music).

Although all sound is sent to the scene's **Audio Listener** (a component that is usually attached to the **Main Camera**, and that shouldn't be attached simultaneously on more than one object), Unity 5 brings a new player to the audio scene: the **Audio Mixer**. The Audio mixer radically changes the way in which sound elements can be experienced and worked with. It allows developers to mix and arrange audio pretty much in the same way that musicians and producers do in their **Digital Audio Workstations** (**D.A.W**), such as **GarageBand** or **ProTools**. It allows you to route audio source clips into specific channels that can have their volumes individually adjusted and processed by customized effects and filters. You can work with multiple Audio Mixers, send a mixer's output to a parent mixer, and save mix preferences as **Snapshots**. Also, you can access mixer parameters from scripting. The following figure represents the main Unity 5 audio mixing concepts and their relationships:

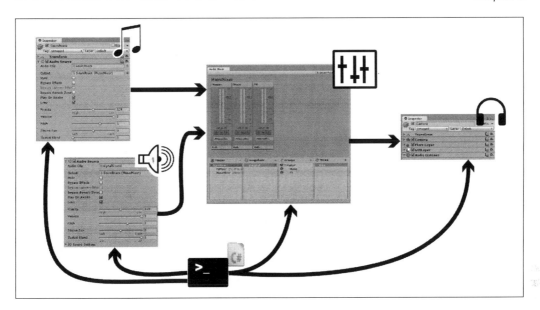

Taking advantage of the new Audio Mixer feature in many example projects, this chapter is filled with recipes that will hopefully help you implement a better and more efficient sound design for your projects, augmenting the player's sense of immersion, transporting him or her into the game environment, and even improving the gameplay.

Matching the audio pitch to the animation speed

Many artifacts sound higher in pitch when accelerated and lower when slowed down. Car engines, fan coolers, Vinyl—a record player... the list goes on. If you want to simulate this kind of sound effect in an animated object that can have its speed changed dynamically, follow this recipe.

Getting ready

For this recipe, you'll need an animated 3D object and an audio clip. Please use the files `animatedRocket.fbx` and `engineSound.wav`, available in the `1362_09_01` folder of the code bundle.

How to do it...

To change the pitch of an audio clip according to the speed of an animated object, please follow these steps:

1. Import the `animatedRocket.fbx` file into your **Project**.

2. Select the `animatedRocket` file in the **Project** view. Then, from the **Inspector** view, check its **Import Settings**. Select **Animations**, then select the clip **Take 001**, and make sure to check the **Loop Time** option. Click on the **Apply** button, shown as follows, to save the changes:

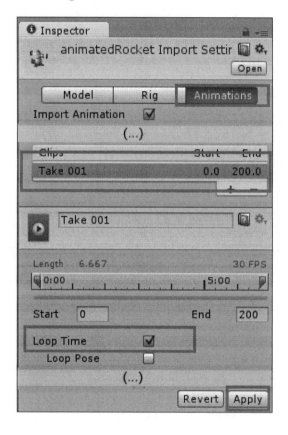

 The reason why we didn't need to check **Loop Pose** option is because our animation already loops in a seamless fashion. If it didn't, we could have checked that option to automatically create a seamless transition from the last to the first frame of the animation.

3. Add the **animatedRocket** GameObject to the scene by dragging it from the **Project** view into the **Hierarchy** view.

4. Import the `engineSound.wav` audio clip.

5. Select the **animatedRocket** GameObject. Then, drag **engineSound** from the **Project** view into the **Inspector** view, adding it as an **Audio Source** for that object.

6. In the **Audio Source** component of **animatedRocket**, check the box for the **Loop** option, as shown in the following screenshot:

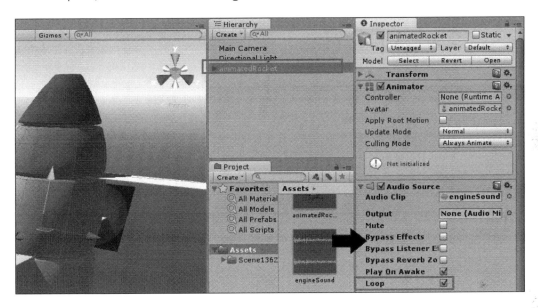

7. We need to create a **Controller** for our object. In the **Project** view, click **Create** and select **Animator Controller**. Name it as `rocket1Controller`.

8. Double-click on **rocketController** object to open the **Animator** window, as shown. Then, right-click on the gridded area and select the **Create State | Empty** option, from the contextual menu:

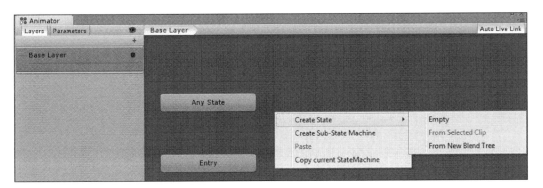

9. Name the new state `spin` and set **Take 001** as its motion in the **Motion** field:

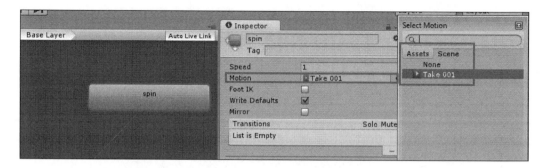

10. From the **Hierarchy** view, select **animatedRocket**. Then, in the **Animator** component (in the **Inspector** view), set **rocketController** as its **Controller** and make sure that the **Apply Root Motion** option is unchecked as shown:

11. In the **Project** view, create a new **C# Script** and rename it to `ChangePitch`.

12. Open the script in your editor and replace everything with the following code:

```csharp
using UnityEngine;

public class ChangePitch : MonoBehaviour{
  public float accel = 0.05f;
  public float minSpeed = 0.0f;
  public float maxSpeed = 2.0f;
  public float animationSoundRatio = 1.0f;
  private float speed = 0.0f;
  private Animator animator;
  private AudioSource audioSource;

  void Start(){
    animator = GetComponent<Animator>();
    audioSource = GetComponent<AudioSource>();
    speed = animator.speed;
```

```
        AccelRocket (0f);
    }

    void Update(){
      if (Input.GetKey (KeyCode.Alpha1))
        AccelRocket(accel);

      if (Input.GetKey (KeyCode.Alpha2))
        AccelRocket(-accel);
    }

    public void AccelRocket(float accel){
      speed += accel;
      speed = Mathf.Clamp(speed,minSpeed,maxSpeed);
      animator.speed = speed = Mathf.Clamp (speed, 0, maxSpeed);
      float soundPitch = animator.speed * animationSoundRatio;
      audioSource.pitch = soundPitch;
    }
  }
```

13. Save your script and add it as a component to **animatedRocket** GameObject.

14. Play the scene and change the animation speed by pressing key *1* (accelerate) and *2* (decelerate) on your alphanumeric keyboard. The audio pitch will change accordingly.

How it works...

At the `Start()` method, besides storing the **Animator** and **AudioSource** components in variables, we'll get the initial `speed` from the **Animator**, and we'll call the `AccelRocket()` function by passing `0` as an argument, only for that function to calculate the resulting pitch for the **Audio Source**. During `Update()` function, the lines of the `if(Input.GetKey (KeyCode.Alpha1))` and `if(Input.GetKey (KeyCode.Alpha2))` code detect whenever the *1* or *2* keys are being pressed on the alphanumeric keyboard to call the `AccelRocket()` function, passing a `accel` float variable as an argument. The `AccelRocket()` function, in its turn, increments `speed` with the received argument (the `accel` float variable). However, it uses the `Mathf.Clamp()` command to limit the new speed value between the minimum and maximum speed as set by the user. Then, it changes the **Animator** speed and **Audio Source** pitch according to the new `speed` absolute value. The value is clamped a second time to avoid negative numbers. Should you reverse the animation, check out a solution in the completed project included with the code files. Also, please note that setting the animation speed and therefore, the sound pitch to `0` will cause the sound to stop, making it clear that stopping the object's animation also prevents the engine sound from playing.

There's more...

Here is some information on how to fine-tune and customize this recipe.

Changing the Animation/Sound Ratio

If you want the audio clip pitch to be more or less affected by the animation speed, change the value of the **Animation/Sound Ratio** parameter.

Accessing the function from other scripts

The `AccelRocket()` function was made public so that it can be accessed from other scripts. As an example, we have included the `ExtChangePitch.cs` script in `1362_09_01` folder. Try attaching this script to the **Main Camera** object and use it to control the speed by clicking on the left and right mouse buttons.

Simulating acoustic environments with Reverb Zones

Once you have created your level's geometry and the scene is looking just the way you want it to, you might want your sound effects to correspond to that look. Sound behaves differently depending upon the environment in which it is projected, so it can be a good idea to make it reverberate accordingly. In this recipe, we will address this acoustic effect by using **Reverb Zones**.

Getting ready

For this recipe, we have prepared the `ReverbZone.unitypackage` file, containing a basic level named `reverbScene` and the `Signal` prefab. The package is in the `1362_09_02` folder in the code bundle.

How to do it...

Follow these steps to simulate the sonic landscape of a tunnel:

1. Import the `ReverbZone` package into your Unity Project.

2. In the **Project** view, open the **reverbScene** level, inside the `ReverbZones` folder. This is a basic scene, featuring a controllable character and a tunnel.

3. Now, drag the **Signal** prefab from the **Project** view into **Hierarchy**, as shown in the following screenshot. This will add a sound-emitting object to the scene. Place it in the center of the tunnel.

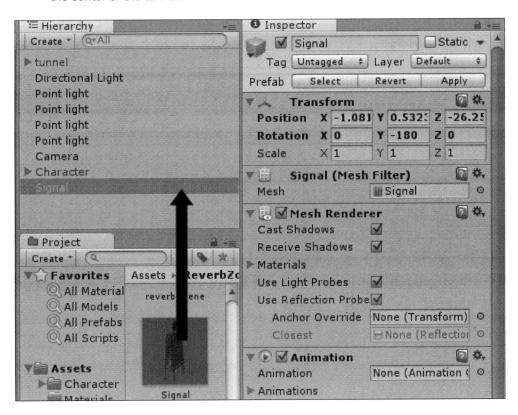

4. Make five copies of the **Signal** GameObject and distribute them across the tunnel (leaving a copy just outside each entrance):

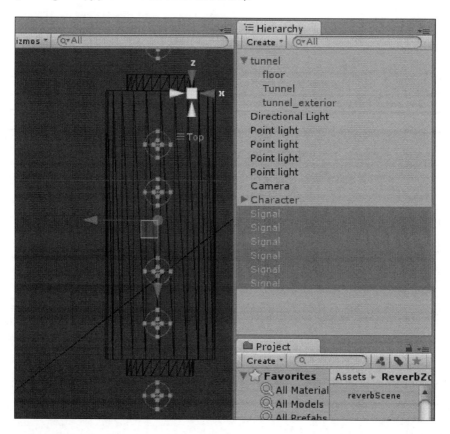

5. In in the **Hierarchy** view, navigate to **Create | Audio | Audio Reverb Zone** to add a **Reverb Zone** to the scene. Then, place it in the center of the tunnel.

6. Select the **Reverb Zone** GameObject. In the **Inspector** view, change the **Reverb Zone** component parameters to these values: **Min Distance**: 6; **Max Distance**: 18; and **Preset**: StoneCorridor as shown in the following screenshot:

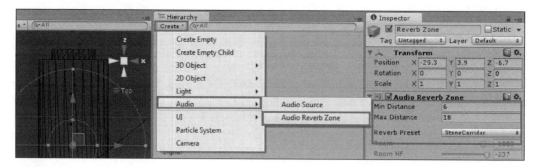

7. Play the scene and walk through the tunnel using the *W A S D* keys (and pressing *Shift* to run). You will hear the audio reverberate when inside the **Reverb Zone** area.

How it works...

Once positioned, the **Audio Reverb Zone** applies an audio filter to all audio sources within its radius.

There's more...

Here are more options for you to try.

Attaching the Audio Reverb Zone component to Audio Sources

Instead of creating an **Audio Reverb Zone** GameObject, you can attach it to the sound emitting object (in our case, **Signal**) as a component through the **Component | Audio | Audio Reverb Zone** menu. In this case, the **Reverb Zone** will be individually set up around the object.

Making your own Reverb settings

Unity comes with several **Reverb Presets**. We have used **StoneCorridor**, but your scene can ask for something less intense (such as **Room**) or more radical (such as **Psychotic**). If these presets still won't be able to recreate the effect that you have in mind, change it to **User** and edit its parameters as you wish.

Preventing an Audio Clip from restarting if it is already playing

In a game, there may be several different events that cause a sound to start playing. If the sound is already playing, then in almost all cases, we won't wish to restart the sound. This recipe includes a test, so that an **Audio Source** component is only sent a `Play()` message if it is currently not playing.

Getting ready

Try this with any audio clip that is one second or longer in duration. We have included the `engineSound` audio clip inside the `1362_09_03` folder.

How to do it...

To prevent an **Audio Clip** from restarting, follow these steps:

1. Create an **Empty** GameObject and rename it to **AudioObject**. Then, add an **Audio Source** component to this object (in the **Component | Audio | Audio Source** menu).

2. Import the `engineSound` audio clip and drag it from the **Project** view to populate the **Audio Clip** parameter of the **Audio Source** component of **AudioObject**:

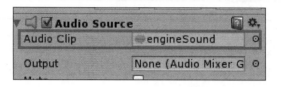

3. Create a UI button named **PlaySoundButton** on the screen and attach the following script to this button:

```csharp
using UnityEngine;
using System.Collections;
using UnityEngine.UI;
public class AvoidEarlySoundRestart : MonoBehaviour {
  public AudioSource audioSource;
  public Text message;

  void Update(){
    string statusMessage = "Play sound";
    if(audioSource.isPlaying)
      statusMessage = "(sound playing)";
    message.text = statusMessage;
  }

  // button click handler
  public void PlaySoundIfNotPlaying(){
    if( !audioSource.isPlaying)
      audioSource.Play();
  }
}
```

4. With **PlaySoundButton** selected in the **Hierarchy** panel, drag **AudioObject** into the **Inspector** view for the public **Audio Source** variable, and drag the **Text** child of **PlaySoundButton** for the public **ButtonText**:

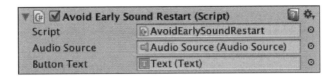

5. With **PlaySoundButton** selected in the **Hierarchy** panel, create a new on-click event handler, dragging the **PlaySoundButton** into the **Object** slot, and selecting the **PlaySoundIfNotPlaying()** function.

How it works...

The **Audio Source** components have a public readable property **isPlaying**, which is a Boolean true/false flag, indicating if the sound is currently playing. The text of the button is set to display Play Sound when the sound is not playing, and (sound playing) when it is. When the button is clicked, the PlaySoundIfNotPlaying() method is called. This method uses an if statement, ensuring that a Play() message is only sent to the Audio Source component if its **isPlaying** is false.

See also

▸ The *Waiting for the audio to finish before auto-destructing an object* recipe in this chapter.

Waiting for audio to finish playing before auto-destructing an object

An event may occur (such as an object pickup or the killing of an enemy) that we wish to notify to the player by playing an audio clip, and an associated visual object (such as an explosion particle system, or a temporary object in the location of the event). However, as soon as the clip has finished playing, we will wish for the visual object to be removed from the scene. This recipe provides a simple way to link the ending of a playing audio clip with the automatic destruction of its containing object.

Getting ready

Try this with any audio clip that is a second or more in duration. We have included the engineSound audio clip inside the 1362_09_04 folder.

How to do it...

To wait for audio to finish playing before destroying a GameObject, follow these steps:

1. Create an **Empty** GameObject and rename it to **AudioObject**. Then, add an **Audio Source** component to this object (in the **Component | Audio | Audio Source** menu).

2. Import the `engineSound` audio clip and drag it from the **Project** view to populate the **Audio Clip** parameter of the **Audio Source** component of **AudioObject**, and deselect the component's **Play On Awake** checkbox:

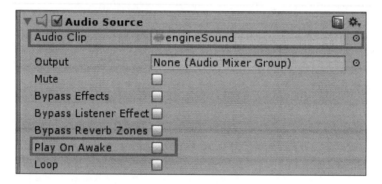

3. Add the following script class to **AudioObject**:

```
using UnityEngine;
using System.Collections;

public class AudioDestructBehaviour : MonoBehaviour {
  private AudioSource audioSource;

  void Start(){
    audioSource = GetComponent<AudioSource>();
  }

  private void Update(){
    if( !audioSource.isPlaying )
      Destroy(gameObject);
  }
}
```

4. In **Inspector** view, disable (un-check) the `AudioDestructBehaviour` scripted component of **AudioObject** (when needed, it will be re-enabled via C# code):

5. Create a new C# file named **ButtonActions**, containing the following code:

```
using UnityEngine;
using System.Collections;

public class ButtonActions : MonoBehaviour{
  public AudioSource audioSource;
  public AudioDestructBehaviour audioDestructScriptedObject;

  public void PlaySound(){
    if( !audioSource.isPlaying )
      audioSource.Play();
  }

  public void DestroyAfterSoundStops(){
    audioDestructScriptedObject.enabled = true;
  }
}
```

6. Create a UI button named **PlaySoundButton** on the screen with a button `Play Sound` text, and attach the **ButtonActions** script to this button.

7. With **PlaySoundButton** selected in the **Hierarchy**, create a new on-click event handler, dragging **PlaySoundButton** into the **Object** slot, and selecting the **PlaySound()** function.

8. With the **PlaySoundButton** selected in the **Hierarchy** panel, drag **AudioObject** into the **Inspector** view for the public **Audio Source** variable **AudioObject**. Also, drag **AudioObject** into the **Inspector** view for the public **Script** variable **AudioDestructScriptedObject**, shown as follows:

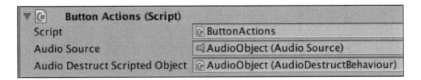

9. Create a second UI button named **DestoryWhenSoundFinishedButton** on screen, with the button text `Destroy When Sound Finished`, and attach the **ButtonActions** script to this button.

10. With **DestoryWhenSoundFinishedButton** selected in the **Hierarchy** panel, create a new on-click event handler, dragging **PlaySoundButton** into the **GO** slot, and then selecting the **DestroyAfterSoundStops()** function.

11. Just as you did with the other button, now the **DestoryWhenSoundFinishedButton** selected in the **Hierarchy** panel, drag **AudioObject** into the **Inspector** view for the public **Script** variable **MyAudioDestructObect**.

How it works...

The GameObject named **AudioObject** contains an Audio Source component, which stores and manages the playing of the audio clip. **AudioObject** also contains a scripted component, which is an instance of the **AudioDestructBehaviour** class. This script is initially disabled. When enabled, every frame this object (via its `Update()` method) tests whether the audio source is not playing (`!audio.isPlaying`). As soon as the audio is found to be not playing, the GameObject is destroyed.

There are two UI buttons created. Button **PlaySoundButton** calls the `PlaySound()` method. This method will start playing the audio clip, if it is not already playing.

The second button called **DestoryWhenSoundFinishedButton** calls the `DestoryAfterSoundStops()` method. This method enables the scripted component **AudioDestructBehaviour** in GameObject **AudioObject**—so that that GameObject will be destroyed, once the sound has finished playing.

See also

> ▶ The *Preventing an Audio Clip from restarting if it is already playing* recipe in this chapter

Adding volume control with Audio Mixers

Sound volume adjustment can be a very important feature, especially if your game is a standalone. After all, it can be very frustrating to access the operational system volume control. In this recipe, we will use the new **Audio Mixer** feature to create independent volume controls for Music and Sound FX.

Getting ready

For this recipe, we have provided a Unity package named `Volume.unitypackage`, containing an initial scene featuring soundtrack music and sound effects. The file is available inside the `1362_09_05` folder.

How to do it...

To add volume control sliders to your scene, follow these steps:

1. Import `Volume.unitypackage` into your project.

2. Open the **Volume** scene (available in the **Assets | Volume** folder). Play the scene and walk towards the semitransparent green wall in the tunnel, using the *W A S D* keys (while pressing the *Shift* key to run). You will be able to listen to:

   ❑ A looping soundtrack music

   ❑ Bells ringing

   ❑ A robotic speech whenever the character collides with the wall

3. From the **Project** view, use the **Create** drop-down menu to add **Audio Mixer** to the project. Name it **MainMixer**. Double-click on it to open the **Audio Mixer** window.

4. From the **Groups** view, highlight **Master** and click the **+** sign to add a child to the **Master** group. Name it **Music**. Then, highlight **Master** again and add a new child group named **FX**, as shown in the following screenshot:

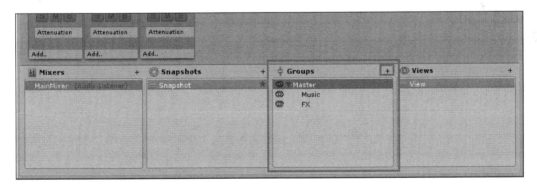

5. From the **Mixers** view, highlight **MainMixer** and click the **+** sign to add a new **Mixer** to the project. Name it **MusicMixer**. Then, drag it into the **MainMixer** and select the **Music** group as its **Output**. Repeat the operation to add a mixer named **FxMixer** to the project by selecting the **FX** group as its output:

6. Now, select **MusicMixer**. Select its **Master** group and add a child named **Soundtrack**. Then, select **FxMixer** and add two children to its **Master** group: one named **Speech**, and another named **Bells**, as shown:

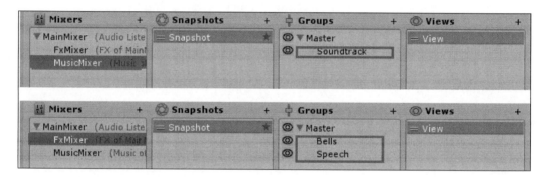

7. From the **Hierarchy** view, select the **DialogueTrigger** object. Then, in the **Inspector** view, change its **Output** track to **FxMixer | Speech** in the **Audio Source** component:

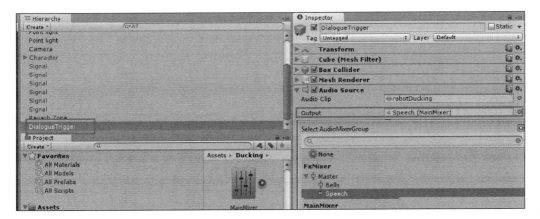

8. Now, select the **Soundtrack** GameObject. From the **Inspector** view, find the **Audio Source** component and change its **Output** track to **MusicMixer | Soundtrack**:

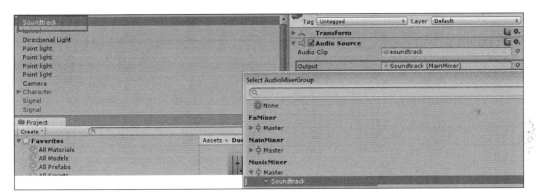

9. Finally, from the **Assets** folder in the **Project** view, select the **Signal** prefab . From the **Inspector** view, access its **Audio Source** component and change its **Output** to **FxMixer | Bells**:

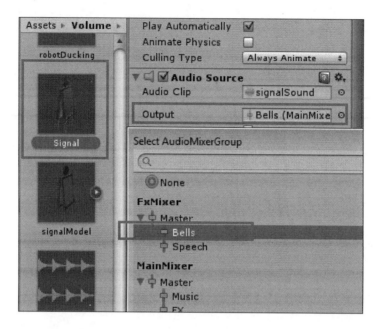

10. From the **Audio Mixer** window, choose **MainMixer** and select its **Master** track. Then, from the **Inspector** view, right-click on **Volume** in the **Attenuation** component. From the context menu, select **Expose 'Volume (of Master) to script** as shown in the following screenshot. Repeat the operation for the **Music and FX** tracks:

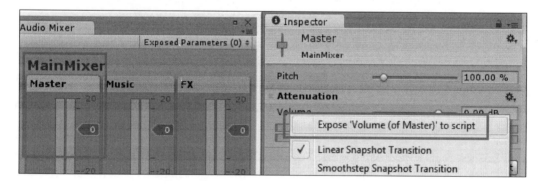

11. From the top of the **Audio Mixer** with the **MainMixer** selected, access the **Exposed Parameters** drop-down menu. Then, right-click on **MyExposedParam** and rename it to OverallVolume. Then, rename **MyExposedParam1** as MusicVolume and **MyExposedParam2** as FxVolume.

12. From the **Project** view, create a new **C# Script** and rename it to VolumeControl.

13. Open the script in your editor and replace everything with the following code:

```
using UnityEngine;

using UnityEngine.Audio;
using System.Collections;

public class VolumeControl : MonoBehaviour{
  public AudioMixer myMixer;
  private GameObject panel;
  private bool isPaused = false;

  void Start(){
    panel = GameObject.Find("Panel");
    panel.SetActive(false);
  }

  void Update() {
    if (Input.GetKeyUp (KeyCode.Escape)) {
      panel.SetActive(!panel.activeInHierarchy);

      if(isPaused)
        Time.timeScale = 1.0f;
      else
        Time.timeScale = 0.0f;

      isPaused = !isPaused;
    }
  }

  public void ChangeMusicVol(float vol){
    myMixer.SetFloat ("MusicVolume", Mathf.Log10(vol) *
20f);
  }
```

```
public void ChangeFxVol(float vol){
    myMixer.SetFloat ("FxVolume", Mathf.Log10(vol) * 20f);
}

public void ChangeOverallVol(float vol){
    myMixer.SetFloat ("OverallVolume", Mathf.Log10(vol) * 20f);
}
}
```

14. From the **Hierarchy** view, use the **Create** dropdown menu to add a **Panel** to the scene (**Create | UI | Panel**). Note that it will automatically add a **Canvas** to the scene.

15. From the **Hierarchy** view, use the **Create** dropdown menu to add a **Slider** to the scene (**Create | UI | Slider**). Make it a child of the **Panel** object.

16. Rename the slider as **OverallSlider**. Duplicate it and rename the new copy to **MusicSlider**. Then, in the **Inspector** view, **Rect Transform** component, change its **Pos Y** parameter to -40.

17. Duplicate **MusicSlider** and rename the new copy to **FxSlider**. Then, change its **Pos Y** parameter to -70:

18. Select the **Canvas** GameObject and add the **VolumeControl** script to it. Then, populate the **MyMixer** field of **Volume Control** with **MainMixer**:

19. Select the **OverallSlider** component. From the **Inspector** view at the **Slider** component, change **Min Value** to 0.000025 (or **2.5e-05**). Then, below the **On Value Changed** list, click the **+** sign to add an action. From **Hierarchy** panel, drag **Canvas** into the **Object** slot and using the drop-down menu, choose **VolumeControl | ChangeOverallVol** option, as shown in the following screenshot, For testing purposes, change the appropriate selector from **Runtime Only** to **Editor and Runtime**.

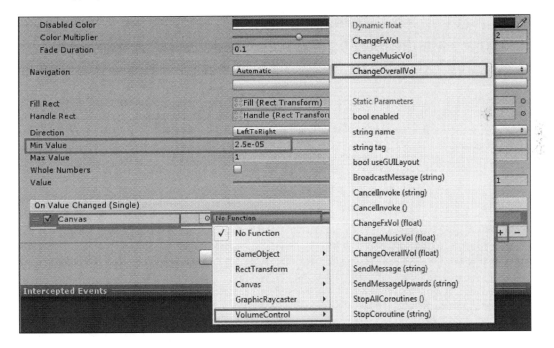

20. Repeat the previous step with **MusicSlider** and **FxSlider**, but this time, choose **ChangeMusicVol** and **ChangeFxVol** options respectively from the drop-down menu.

21. Play the scene. You will be able to access the sliders when pressing *Escape* on your keyboard and adjust volume settings from there.

How it works...

The new **Audio Mixer** feature works in a similar fashion to Digital Audio Workstations, such as Logic and Sonar. Through **Audio Mixers**, you can organize and manage audio elements by routing them into specific groups that can have individual audio tracks to be tweaked around, allowing for adjustments in volume level and sound effects.

By organizing and routing our audio clips into two groups (**Music** and **FX**), we established the **MainMixer** as a unified controller for volume. Then, we have used the **Audio Mixer** to expose the volume levels for each track of the **MainMixer**, making them accessible to our script.

Also, we have set up a basic GUI featuring three sliders that, when in use, will pass their float values (between 0.000025 and 1) as arguments to three specific functions in our script: ChangeMusicVol, ChangeFxVol, and ChangeOverallVol. These functions, on their turn, use the SetFloat command to effectively change the volume levels at runtime. However, before passing on the new volume levels, the script converts linear values (between 0.000025 and 1) to the decibel levels that are used by the **Audio Mixer**. This conversion is calculated through the *log(x) * 20* mathematical function.

 For a full explanation on issues regarding the conversion of linear values to decibel levels and vice-versa, check out Aaron Brown's excellent article at http://www.playdotsound.com/portfolio-item/decibel-db-to-float-value-calculator-making-sense-of-linear-values-in-audio-tools/.

It's worth mentioning that the VolumeControl script also includes code to enable and disable the **GUI** and the **EventSystem**, depending upon if the player hits the Escape key to activate/deactivate the volume control sliders.

A very important note—do not change the volume of any **MainMixer**'s tracks; leave them at 0 dB. The reason is that our VolumeControl script sets their maximum volume level. For general adjustments, use the secondary Mixers **MusicMixer** and **FxMixer**.

There's more...

Here is some extra information on Audio Mixers.

Playing with Audio Production

There are many creative uses for exposed parameters. We can, for instance, add effects such as **Distortion**, **Flange**, and **Chorus** to audio channels, allowing users to operate virtual sound tables/mixing boards.

▸ The *Making a dynamic soundtrack with Snapshots* recipe in this chapter

▸ The *Balancing the in-game audio with Ducking* in this chapter

Making a dynamic soundtrack with Snapshots

Dynamic soundtracks are the ones that change according to what is happening to the player in the game, musically reflecting that place or moment of the character's adventure. In this recipe, we will implement a soundtrack that changes twice; the first time when entering a tunnel, and the second time when coming out of its end. To achieve this, we will use the new **Snapshot** feature of the **Audio Mixer**.

Snapshots are a way of saving the state of your **Audio Mixer**, keeping your preferences for volume levels, audio effects, and more. We can access these states through script, creating transitions between mixes, and by bringing up the desired sonic ambience for each moment of the player's journey.

Getting ready

For this recipe, we have prepared a basic game level, contained inside the Unity package named `DynamicSoundtrack`, and two soundtrack audio clips in `.ogg` format: `Theme01_Percussion` and `Theme01_Synths`. All these files can be found in the `1362_09_06` folder.

How to do it...

To make a dynamic soundtrack, follow these steps:

1. Import the `DynamicSoundtrack` package and both `.ogg` files to your Unity Project.

2. Open the level named **Dynamic**.

3. From the **Project** view, use the **Create** drop-down menu to add **Audio Mixer** to the project. Name it **MusicMixer**. Double-click on it to open the **Audio Mixer** window.

4. From the **Groups** view, highlight **Master** and click the **+** sign to add a child to the **Master** group. Name it as **Music**. Then, add two child groups to **Music**: **Percussion** and **Synths**:

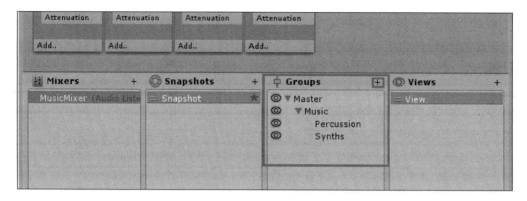

5. From the **Hierarchy** view, create a new **Empty** GameObject. Name it **Music**. Then, add two **Empty Child** GameObjects to it. Name them as **Percussion** and **Synth**.

6. From the **Project** view, drag the **Audio Clip** named **Theme01_Percussion** into the **Percussion** GameObject in **Hierarchy**. Select **Percussion** and in the **Inspector** view, access the **Audio Source** component. Change its **Output** to **Percussion (MusicMixer)**, make sure the **Play On Awake** option is checked, check the **Loop** option, and make sure its **Spatial Blend** is set to **2D**, as shown in the following screenshot:

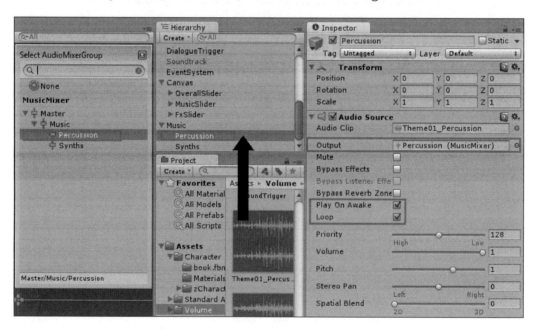

7. Now, drag the **Theme01_Synths** audio file into the **Synths** GameObject. From the **Inspector** view, change its **Output** to **Synths (MusicMixer)**, make sure the **Play On Awake** option is checked, check the **Loop** option, and make sure its **Spatial Blend** is set to **2D**, as shown:

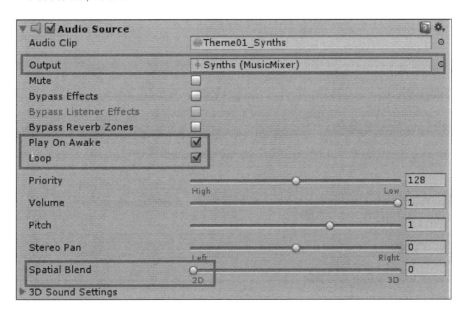

8. Open the **Audio Mixer** and play the scene. We will now use the mixer to set the soundtrack for the start of the scene. With the scene playing, click on the **Edit in Play Mode** button, as shown in the screenshot, at the top of the **Audio Mixer**. Then, drop the volume on the **Synths** track down to **-30 dB**:

9. Now, select the **Percussion** track. Right-click on **Attenuation** and add the **High-pass** effect before it:

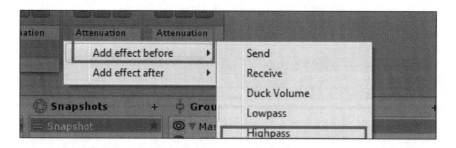

10. From the **Inspector** view, change the **Cutoff frequency** of the **High-pass** effect to **544.00 Hz**:

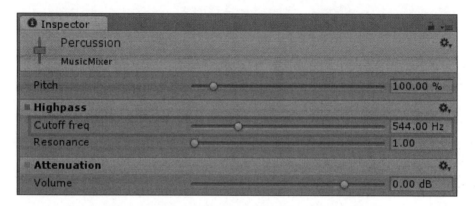

11. Every change, so far, has been assigned to the current **Snapshot**. From the **Snaphots** view, right-click on the current **Snapshot** and rename it to **Start**. Then, right-click on **Start** and select the **Duplicate** option. Rename the new snapshot as **Tunnel**, as shown:

12. Select the **Tunnel** snapshot. Then, from the **Inspector** view, change the **Cutoff frequency** of the **Highpass** effect to **10.00 Hz**:

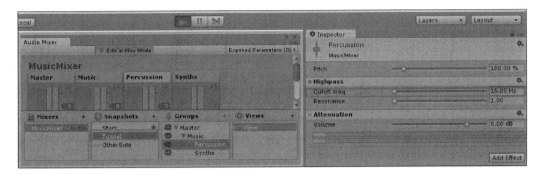

13. Switch between the **Tunnel** and **Start** snapshots. You'll be able to hear the difference.

14. Duplicate the **Tunnel** snapshot, rename it as **OtherSide**, and select it.

15. Raise the volume of the **Synths** track up to **0 dB**:

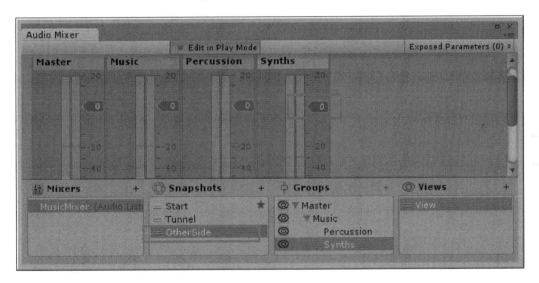

16. Now that we have our three **Snapshots**, it's time to create triggers to make transitions among them. From the **Hierarchy** view, use the **Create** drop-down menu to add a **Cube** to the scene (**Create | 3D Object | Cube**).

17. Select the new **Cube** and rename it `SnapshotTriggerTunnel`. Then, from the **Inspector** view, access the **Box Collider** component and check the **Is Trigger** option, as shown in the following screenshot. Also, uncheck its **Mesh Renderer** component. Finally, adjust its size and position to the scene tunnel's interior:

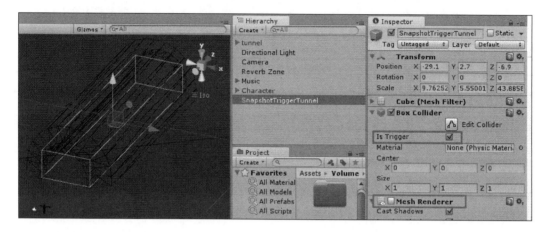

18. Make two copies of `SnapshotTriggerTunnel` and rename them to `SnapshotTriggerStart` and `SnapshotTriggerOtherSide`. Then, adjust their size and position, so that they occupy the areas before the tunnel's entrance (where the character is) and after its other end, as shown in the following screenshot:

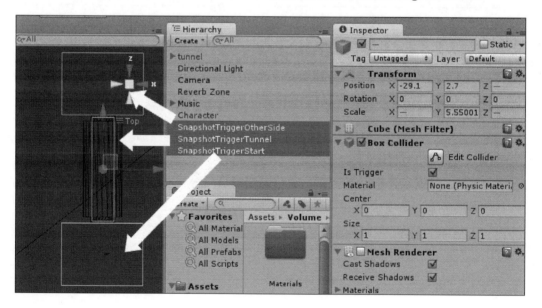

19. In the **Project** view, create a new **C# Script** file and rename it to `SnapshotTrigger`.

20. Open the script in your editor and replace everything with the following code:

```
using UnityEngine;
using UnityEngine.Audio;
using System.Collections;

public class SnapshotTrigger : MonoBehaviour{
  public AudioMixerSnapshot snapshot;
  public float crossfade;

  private void OnTriggerEnter(Collider other){
    snapshot.TransitionTo (crossfade);
  }
}
```

21. Save your script and attach it to `SnapshotTriggerTunnel`, `SnapshotTriggerStart`, and `SnapshotTriggerOtherSide` objects.

22. Select `SnapshotTriggerTunnel`. Then, from the **Inspector** view, access the **Snapshot Trigger** component, setting **Snapshot** as **Tunnel**, and **Crossfade** as 2, as shown in the following screenshot:

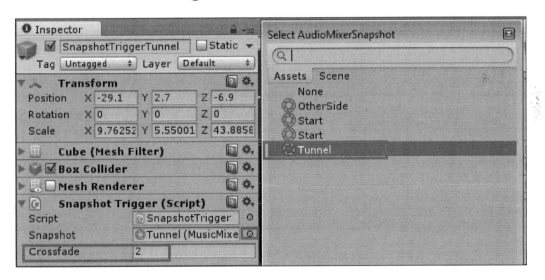

23. Make changes to `SnapshotTriggerStart` and `SnapshotTriggerOtherSide` by setting their **Snapshots** to **Start** and **OtherSide** respectively.

24. Test the scene. The background music will change as the character moves from its starting point, through the tunnel, and into the other side.

How it works...

The **Snapshot** feature allows you to save **Audio Mixer** states (including all volume levels, every filter setting, and so on) so that you can change those mixing preferences at runtime, making the audio design more suitable for specific locations or gameplay settings. For this recipe, we have created three **Snapshots** for different moments in the player's journey: before entering the tunnel, inside the tunnel, and outside the tunnel. We have used the **Highpass** filter to make the initial Snapshot less intense. We have also turned the **Synths** track volume up to emphasize the open environment outside the tunnel. Hopefully, changes in the audio mix will collaborate with setting the right mood for the game.

To activate our snapshots, we have placed **trigger colliders**, featuring our **Snapshot Trigger** component in which we set the desired Snapshot and the time in seconds, that it takes to make the transition (a crossfade) between the previous Snapshot and the next. In fact, the function in our script is really this straightforward—the line of `snapshot.TransitionTo (crossfade)` code simply starts a transition lasting `crossfade` seconds to the desired `Snapshot`.

There's more...

Here is some information on how to fine-tune and customize this recipe.

Reducing the need for multiple audio clips

You might have noticed how different the `Theme01_Percussion` audio clip sounds when the **Cutoff frequency** of the **High-pass** filter is set as `10.00 Hz`. The reason for this is that the high-pass filter, as its name suggests, cuts off lower frequencies of the audio signal. In this case, it attenuated the bass drum down to inaudible levels while keeping the shakers audible. The opposite effect can be achieved through the **Lowpass** filter. A major benefit is the opportunity of virtually having two separate tracks into the same audio clip.

Dealing with audio file formats and compression rates

To avoid loss of audio quality, you should import your sound clips using the appropriate file format, depending upon your target platform. If you are not sure which format to use, please check out Unity's documentation on the subject at `http://docs.unity3d.com/Manual/AudioFiles.html`.

Applying Snapshots to background noise

Although we have applied Snapshots to our music soundtrack, background noise can also benefit immensely. If your character travels across places that are significantly different, transitioning from open spaces to indoor environments, you should consider applying snapshots to your environment audio mix. Be careful, however, to create separate Audio Mixers for Music and Environment—unless you don't mind having musical and ambient sound tied to the same Snapshot.

Getting creative with effects

In this recipe, we have mentioned the High-pass and Low-pass filters. However, there are many effects that can make audio clips sound radically different. Experiment! Try applying effects such as Distortion, Flange, and Chorus. In fact, we encourage you to try every effect, playing with their settings. The creative use of these effects can bring out different expressions to a single audio clip.

See also

> ▶ The *Adding volume control with Audio Mixers* recipe in this chapter
>
> ▶ The *Balancing soundtrack volume with Ducking* recipe in this chapter

Balancing in-game audio with Ducking

As much as the background music can be important in establishing the right atmosphere, there will be times when other audio clips should be emphasized, and the music volume turned down for the duration of that clip. This effect is known as **Ducking**. Maybe you will need it for dramatic effect (simulating hearing loss after an explosion took place), or maybe you want to make sure that the player listens to a specific bit of information. In this recipe, we will learn how to emphasize a piece of dialog by ducking the audio whenever a specific sound message is played. For that effect, we will use the new **Audio Mixer** to send information between tracks.

Getting ready

For this recipe, we have provided the `soundtrack.mp3` audio clip and a Unity package named `Ducking.unitypackage`, containing an initial scene. All these files are available inside the `1362_09_07` folder.

How to do it...

To apply Audio Ducking to your soundtrack, follow these steps:

1. Import `Ducking.unitypackage` and `soundtrack.mp3` into your project.

2. Open the **Ducking** scene (available in the **Assets | Ducking** folder). Play the scene and walk towards the semitransparent green wall in the tunnel, using the *W A S D* keys (by pressing *Shift* to run). You will hear the **robotDucking** audio clip play as the character collides with the wall.

3. From the **Create** drop-down at the top of the **Hierarchy** view, choose **Create Empty** to add a new GameObject to the scene. Name it **Soundtrack**.

4. Drag the **soundtrack** audio clip you have imported into the **Soundtrack** GameObject. Then, select the **Soundtrack** object and from the **Inspector** view, **Audio Source** component, check the **Loop** option. Make sure the **Play On Awake** option is checked and **Spatial Blend** set to **2D**, as shown in the following in the following screenshot:

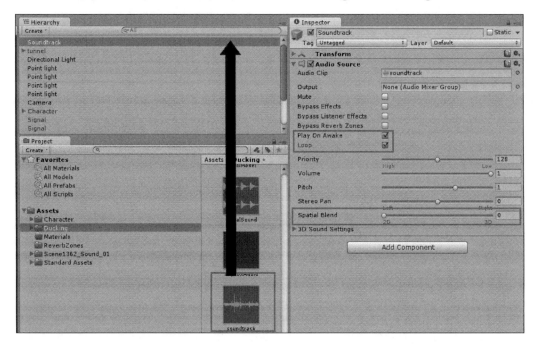

5. Test the scene again. The soundtrack music should be playing.

6. From the **Project** view, use the **Create** drop-down menu to add an **Audio Mixer** to the project. Name it **MainMixer**. Double-click on it to open the **Audio Mixer** window.

7. From the **Groups** view, highlight **Master** and click the **+** sign to add a child to the **Master** group. Name it **Music**. Then, highlight **Master** again and add a new child group named **FX**, as shown in the following screenshot. Finally, add a third child to the **Master** group, named **Input**:

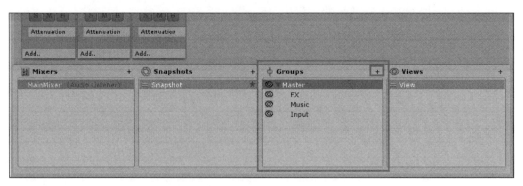

8. From the **Mixers** view, highlight **MainMixer** and click the **+** sign to add a new **Mixer** to the project. Name it **MusicMixer**. Then, drag it into the **MainMixer** and select the group **Music** as its **Output**. Repeat the operation to add a mixer named **FxMixer** to the project, selecting the **FX** group as the output:

9. Now, select **MusicMixer**. Select its **Master** group and add a child named **Soundtrack**. Then, select **FxMixer** and add a child named **Bells**, as shown:

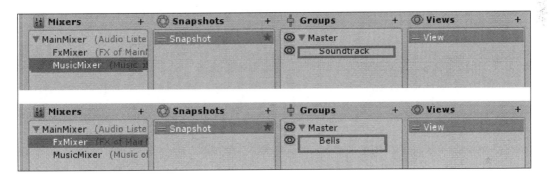

10. From the **Hierarchy** view, select the **DialogueTrigger** object. Then, in the **Inspector** view, **Audio Source** component, Change its **Output** track to **MainMixer | Input**:

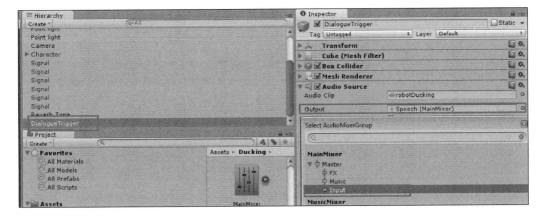

11. Now, select the **Soundtrack** GameObject and in the **Inspector** view, in the **Audio Source** component, change its **Output** track to **MusicMixer | Soundtrack**:

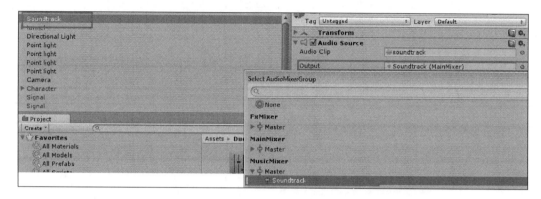

12. Finally, from the **Assets** folder in the **Project** view, select the **Signal** prefab. From the **Inspector** view, access its the **Audio Source** component and change its **Output** to **FxMixer | Bells**:

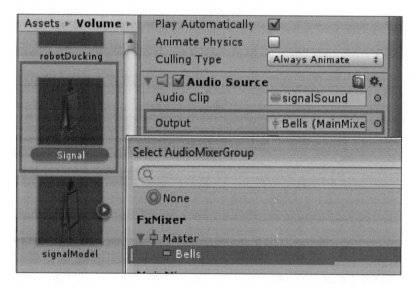

13. Open the **Audio Mixer** window. Choose **MainMixer**, select the **Music** track controller, right-click on **Attenuation**, and using the context menu, add the **Duck Volume** effect before **Attenuation**:

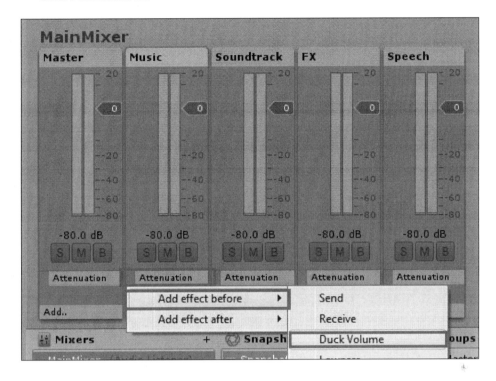

14. Now, select the **Input** track, right-click on **Attenuation**, and using the context menu, add **Send** after **Attenuation**:

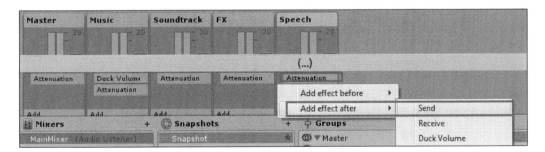

15. With **Input** track still selected, go to the **Inspector** view and change the **Receive** setting in **Send** to **Music\Duck Volume** and its **Send** level to 0.00 db, as shown:

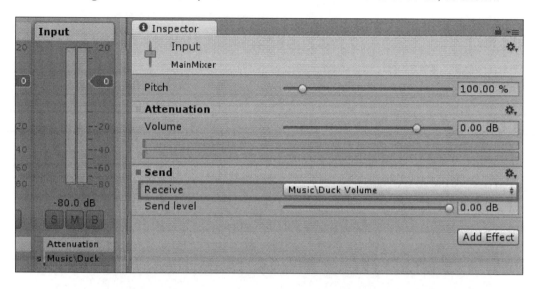

16. Select the **Music** track. From the **Inspector** view, change the settings on the **Duck Volume** as follows: **Threshold**: -40.00 db; **Ratio**: 300.00 %; **Attack Time**: 100.00 ms; **Release Time**: 2000.00 ms, as shown in the following screenshot:

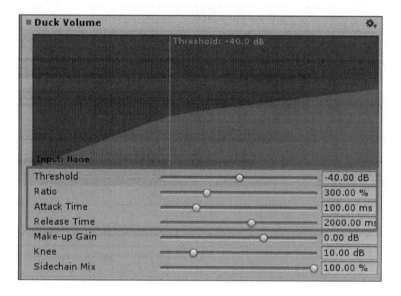

17. Test the scene again. Entering the trigger object will cause the soundtrack volume to drop considerably, recovering the original volume in 2 seconds.

How it works...

In this recipe, we have created, in addition to Music and Sound FX, a group named **Input**, to which we have routed the audio clip that triggers the **Duck Volume** effect attached to our music track. The **Duck Volume** effect changes the track's volume whenever it receives an input that is louder than indicated in its **Threshold** setting. In our case, we have sent the **Input** track as input, and adjusted the settings so the volume will be reduced as soon as 0.1 seconds after the input had been received, turning back to its original value of 2 seconds after the input has ceased. The amount of volume reduction was determined by our **Ratio** of **300.00** %. Playing around with the setting values will give you a better idea on how each parameter affects the final result. Also, make sure to visualize the graphic as the trigger sound is played. You will be able to see how the **Input** sound passes the threshold, triggering the effect.

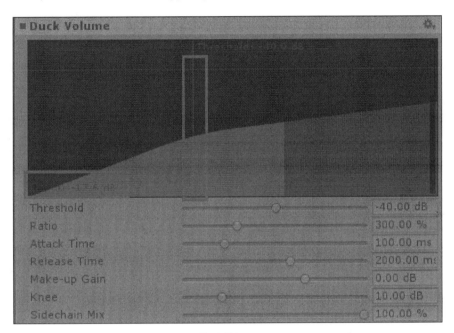

Duck Volume

Also, please note that we have organized our tracks so that the other sound clips (other than speech) will not affect the volume of the music—but every music clip will be affected by audio clips sent to the input track.

See also

▸ The *Adding volume control with Audio Mixers* recipe in this chapter

▸ The *Making a dynamic soundtrack with Snapshots* recipe in this chapter

10

Working with External Resource Files and Devices

In this chapter, we will cover:

- ▸ Loading external resource files – using Unity Default Resources
- ▸ Loading external resource files – by downloading files from the Internet
- ▸ Loading external resource files – by manually storing files in the Unity Resources folder
- ▸ Saving and loading player data – using static properties
- ▸ Saving and loading player data – using PlayerPrefs
- ▸ Saving screenshots from the game
- ▸ Setting up a leaderboard using PHP/MySQL
- ▸ Loading game data from a text file map
- ▸ Managing Unity project code using Git version control and GitHub hosting
- ▸ Publishing for multiple devices via Unity Cloud

Introduction

For some projects, it works fine to use the **Inspector** window to manually assign imported assets to the component slots, and then build and play the game with no further changes. However, there are also many times when external data of some kind can add flexibility and features to a game. For example, it might add updateable or user-editable content; it can allow memory of user preferences and achievements between scenes, and even game-playing sessions. Using code to read local or Internet file contents at runtime can help file organization and separation of tasks between game programmers and the content designers. Having an arsenal of different assets and long-term game memory techniques means providing a wide range of opportunities to deliver a rich experience to players and developers alike.

The big picture

Before getting on with the recipes, let's step back and have a quick review of the role of the asset files and the Unity game building and running process. The most straightforward way to work with assets is to import them into a Unity project, use the **Inspector** window to assign the assets to the components in the **Inspector**, and then build and play the game.

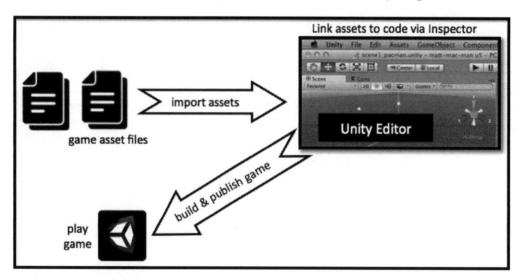

Standalone executables offer another possible workflow, which is the adding of files into the `Resources` folder of the game after it has been built. This will support game media asset developers being able to provide the final version of assets after development and building has been completed.

However, another option is to use the WWW class to dynamically read assets from the web at runtime; or perhaps, for communication with a high score or multiplayer server, and sending and receiving information and files.

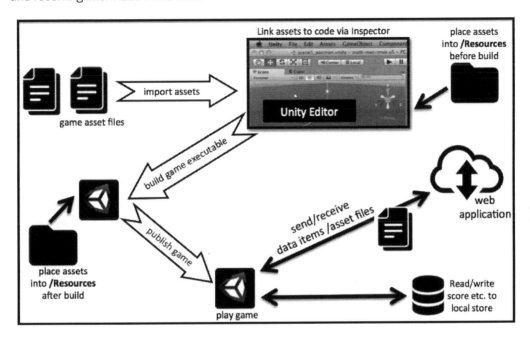

When loading/saving data either locally or via the web interface, it is important to keep in mind the data types that can be used. When writing C# code, our variables can be of any type permitted by the language, but when communicated by the web interface, or to a local storage using Unity's PlayerPrefs class, we are restricted in the types of data that we can work with. Unity's WWW class permits three file types (text files, binary audio clips, and binary image textures), but, for example, for 2D UIs we sometimes need Sprite images and not Textures, so that we have provided in this chapter a C# method to create a Sprite from a Texture. When using the PlayerPrefs class, we are limited to saving and loading integers, floats, and strings. Similarly, when communicating with a web server using the URL encoded data, we are restricted to whatever we can place into strings (we include a PHP web-based high score recipe, where the user scores can be loaded and saved via such a method).

Finally, managing Unity project source code with an online **Distributed Version Control System** (**DVCS**) like Git and GitHub opens up new workflows for the continuous integration of code updates to the working builds. Unity Cloud will *pull* the updated source code projects from your online repository, and then build the game for designated versions of Unity and the deployment devices. Developers will get e-mails to confirm the build success, or to list the reasons for any build failure. The final two recipes in this chapter show you how to manage your code with Git and GitHub, and use Unity Cloud to build projects for multiple devices.

Acknowledgement: Thanks to the following for publishing *Creative Commons (BY 3.0)* licensed icons: **Elegant Themes**, **Picol**, **Freepik**, **Yannick**, **Google**, www.flaticon.com.

Loading external resource files – using Unity Default Resources

In this recipe, we will load an external image file, and display it on the screen, using the **Unity Default Resources** file (a library created at the time the game was compiled).

This method is perhaps the simplest way to store and read the external resource files. However, it is only appropriate when the contents of the resource files will not change after compilation, since the contents of these files are combined and compiled into the resources.assets file.

The resources.assets file can be found in the Data folder for a compiled game.

Getting ready

In the 1362_10_01 folder, we have provided an image file, a text file, and an audio file in the .ogg format for this recipe:

- externalTexture.jpg
- cities.txt
- soundtrack.ogg

How to do it...

To load the external resources by Unity Default Resources, do the following:

1. Create a new 3D Unity project.
2. In the **Project** window, create a new folder and rename it `Resources`.
3. Import the `externalTexture.jpg` file and place it in the `Resources` folder.
4. Create a 3D cube.
5. Add the following C# Script to your cube:

    ```csharp
    using UnityEngine;
    using System.Collections;

    public class ReadDefaultResources : MonoBehaviour {
      public string fileName = "externalTexture";
      private Texture2D externalImage;

      void Start () {
        externalImage = (Texture2D)Resources.Load(fileName);
        Renderer myRenderer = GetComponent<Renderer>();
        myRenderer.material.SetTexture("_MainTex", externalImage);
      }
    }
    ```

6. Play the scene. The texture will be loaded and displayed on the screen.
7. If you have another image file, put a copy into the `Resources` folder. Then, in the **Inspector** window, change the public file name to the name of your image file and play the scene again. The new image will now be displayed.

How it works...

The `Resources.Load(fileName)` statement makes Unity look inside its compiled project data file called `resources.assets` for the contents of a file named `externalTexture`. The contents are returned as a texture image, which is stored into the `externalImage` variable. The last statement in the `Start()` method sets the texture of the GameObject the script has been attached to our `externalImage` variable.

> Note: The filename string passed to `Resources.Load()` does *not* include the file extension (such as `.jpg` or `.txt`).

There's more...

There are some details that you don't want to miss.

Loading text files with this method

You can load the external text files using the same approach. The private variable needs to be a string (to store the text file contents). The `Start()` method uses a temporary `TextAsset` object to receive the text file contents, and the text property of this object contains the string contents that are to be stored in the private variable `textFileContents`:

```
public class ReadDefaultResourcesText : MonoBehaviour {
  public string fileName = "textFileName";
  private string textFileContents;

  void Start () {
    TextAsset textAsset = (TextAsset)Resources.Load(fileName);
    textFileContents = textAsset.text;
    Debug.Log(textFileContents);
  }
}
```

Finally, this string is displayed on the console.

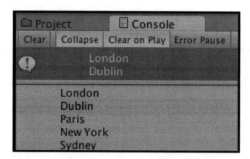

Loading and playing audio files with this method

You can load external audio files using the same approach. The private variable needs to be an `AudioClip`:

```
using UnityEngine;
using System.Collections;

[RequireComponent (typeof (AudioSource))]
public class ReadDefaultResourcesAudio : MonoBehaviour {
  public string fileName = "soundtrack";
  private AudioClip audioFile;
```

```
void  Start (){
  AudioSource audioSource = GetComponent<AudioSource>();
  audioSource.clip = (AudioClip)Resources.Load(fileName);
  if(!audioSource.isPlaying && audioSource.clip.isReadyToPlay)
    audioSource.Play();
  }
}
```

See also

Refer to the following recipes in this chapter for more information:

▶ *Loading external resource files – by manually storing files in Unity Resources folder*

▶ *Loading external resource files – by downloading files from the Internet*

Loading external resource files – by downloading files from the Internet

One way to store and read a text file data is to store the text files on the Web. In this recipe, the contents of a text file for a given URL are downloaded, read, and then displayed.

Getting ready

For this recipe, you need to have access to the files on a web server. If you run a local web server such as **Apache**, or have your own web hosting, then you can use the files in the `1362_10_01` folder and the corresponding URL.

Otherwise, you may find the following URLs useful; since they are the web locations of an image file (a Packt Publishing logo) and a text file (an ASCII-art badger picture):

▶ `www.packtpub.com/sites/default/files/packt_logo.png`

▶ `www.ascii-art.de/ascii/ab/badger.txt`

How to do it...

To load external resources by downloading them from the Internet, do the following:

1. In a 2D project, create a new `RawImage` UI GameObject.

2. Add the following C# script class as a component of your image object:

   ```
   using UnityEngine;
   using UnityEngine.UI;
   using System.Collections;
   ```

```
public class ReadImageFromWeb : MonoBehaviour {
   public string url = "http://www.packtpub.com/sites/default/
files/packt_logo.png";

   IEnumerator Start() {
     WWW www = new WWW(url);
     yield return www;
     Texture2D texture = www.texture;
     GetComponent<RawImage>().texture = texture;
   }
}
```

3. Play the scene. Once downloaded, the contents of the image file will be displayed:

How it works...

Note the need to use the `UnityEngine.UI` package for this recipe.

When the game starts, our `Start()` method starts the **coroutine** method called `LoadWWW()`. A coroutine is a method that can keep on running in the background without halting or slowing down the other parts of the game and the frame rate. The `yield` statement indicates that once a value can be returned for `imageFile`, the remainder of the method can be executed—that is, until the file has finished downloading, no attempt should be made to extract the texture property of the `WWW` object variable.

Once the image data has been loaded, execution will progress past the `yield` statement. Finally, the `texture` property of the `RawImage` GameObject, to which the script is attached, is changed to the image data that is downloaded from the Web (inside the `texture` variable of the `www` object).

There's more...

There are some details that you don't want to miss.

Converting from Texture to Sprite

While in the recipe we used a UI **RawImage**, and so could use the downloaded **Texture** directly, there may be times when we wish to work with a **Sprite** rather than a **Texture**. Use this method to create a **Sprite** object from a **Texture**:

```
private Sprite TextureToSprite(Texture2D texture){
  Rect rect = new Rect(0, 0, texture.width, texture.height);
  Vector2 pivot = new Vector2(0.5f, 0.5f);
  Sprite sprite = Sprite.Create(texture, rect, pivot);
  return sprite;
}
```

Downloading a text file from the Web

Use this technique to download a text file:

```
using UnityEngine;
using System.Collections;
using UnityEngine.UI;

public class ReadTextFromWeb : MonoBehaviour {
  public string url = "http://www.ascii-art.de/ascii/ab/badger.txt";

  IEnumerator Start(){
    Text textUI = GetComponent<Text>();
    textUI.text = "(loading file ...)";

    WWW www = new WWW(url);
    yield return www;
    string textFileContents = www.text;
    Debug.Log(textFileContents);

    textUI.text = textFileContents;
  }
}
```

The WWW class and the resource contents

The WWW class defines several different properties and methods to allow the downloaded media resource file data to be extracted into appropriate variables for use in the game. The most useful of these include:

▸   .text: A read-only property, returning the web data as string

▸   .texture: A read-only property, returning the web data as a Texture2D image

▸   .GetAudioClip(): A method that returns the web data as an AudioClip

> For more information about the Unity WWW class visit http://docs.unity3d.com/ScriptReference/WWW.html.

See also

Refer to the following recipes in this chapter for more information:

▸   *Loading external resource files – by Unity Default Resources*

▸   *Loading external resource files – by manually storing files in the Unity Resources folder*

Loading external resource files – by manually storing files in the Unity Resources folder

At times, the contents of the external resource files may need to be changed after the game compilation. Hosting the resource files on the web may not be an option. There is a method of manually storing and reading files from the Resources folder of the compiled game, which allows for those files to be changed after the game compilation.

> This technique only works when you compile to a Windows or Mac stand alone executable—it will not work for Web Player builds, for example.

Getting ready

The 1362_10_01 folder provides the texture image that you can use for this recipe:

▸   externalTexture.jpg

How to do it...

To load external resources by manually storing the files in the `Resources` folder, do the following:

1. In a 2D project, create a new Image UI GameObject.

2. Add the following C# script class as a component of your Image object:

```csharp
using UnityEngine;
using System.Collections;

using UnityEngine.UI;
using System.IO;

public class ReadManualResourceImageFile : MonoBehaviour {
  private string fileName = "externalTexture.jpg";
  private string url;
  private Texture2D externalImage;

  IEnumerator Start () {
    url = "file:" + Application.dataPath;
    url = Path.Combine(url, "Resources");
    url = Path.Combine(url, fileName);

    WWW www = new WWW (url);
    yield return www;

    Texture2D texture = www.texture;
    GetComponent<Image>().sprite = TextureToSprite(texture);
  }

  private Sprite TextureToSprite(Texture2D texture){
    Rect rect = new Rect(0, 0, texture.width, texture.height);
    Vector2 pivot = new Vector2(0.5f, 0.5f);
    Sprite sprite = Sprite.Create(texture, rect, pivot);
    return sprite;
  }
}
```

3. Build your (Windows or Mac) standalone executable.

4. Copy the `externalTexture.jpg` image to your standalone's `Resources` folder.

You will need to place the files in the `Resources` folder manually after every compilation.

When you create a Windows or Linux standalone executable, there is also a _Data folder, created with the executable application file. The `Resources` folder can be found inside this `Data` folder.

A Mac standalone application executable looks like a single file, but it is actually a MacOS `package` folder. Right-click on the executable file and select **Show Package Contents**. You will then find the standalone's `Resources` folder inside the `Contents` folder.

5. Run your standalone game application and the image will be displayed:

How it works...

Note the need to use the `System.IO` and `UnityEngine.UI` packages for this recipe.

When the executable runs, the `WWW` object spots that the URL starts with the word file, and so Unity attempts to find the external resource file in its `Resources` folder, and then load its contents.

There's more...

There are some details that you don't want to miss.

Avoiding cross-platform problems with Path.Combine() rather than "/" or "\"

The filepath folder separator character is different for Windows and Mac file systems (backslash (\) for Windows, forward slash (/) for the Mac). However, Unity knows which kind of standalone you are compiling your project into, therefore the `Path.Combine()` method will insert the appropriate separator slash character form the file URL that is required.

Refer to the following recipes in this chapter for more information:

- ▶ *Loading external resource files – by Unity Default Resources*
- ▶ *Loading external resource files – by downloading files from the Internet*

Saving and loading player data – using static properties

Keeping track of the player's progress and user settings during a game is vital to give your game a greater feel of depth and content. In this recipe, we will learn how to make our game remember the player's score between the different levels (scenes).

Getting ready

We have included a complete project in a Unity package named game_HigherOrLower in the 1362_10_04 folder. In order to follow this recipe, we will import this package as the starting point.

How to do it...

To save and load player data, follow these steps:

1. Create a new 2D project and import the game_HigherOrLower package.
2. Add each of the scenes to the build in the sequence (scene0_mainMenu, then scene1_gamePlaying, and so on).
3. Make yourself familiar with the game by playing it a few times and examining the contents of the scenes. The game starts on the scene0_mainMenu scene, inside the Scenes folder.
4. Let's create a class to store the number of correct and incorrect guesses made by the user. Create a new C# script called Player with the following code:

```csharp
using UnityEngine;

public class Player : MonoBehaviour {
  public static int scoreCorrect = 0;
  public static int scoreIncorrect = 0;
}
```

5. In the lower-left corner of the `scene0_mainMenu` scene, create a UI Text GameObject named **Text – score**, containing the placeholder text **Score: 99 / 99**.

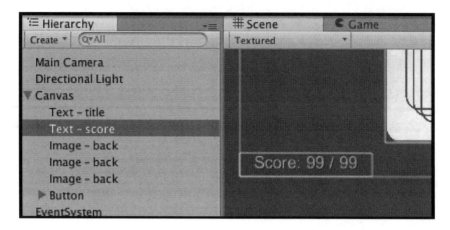

6. Next, attach the following C# script to UI GameObject **Text – score**:

```
using UnityEngine;
using System.Collections;

using UnityEngine.UI;

public class UpdateScoreText : MonoBehaviour {
  void Start(){
    Text scoreText = GetComponent<Text>();
    int totalAttempts = Player.scoreCorrect + Player.
scoreIncorrect;
    string scoreMessage = "Score = ";
    scoreMessage += Player.scoreCorrect + " / " + totalAttempts;

    scoreText.text = scoreMessage;
  }
}
```

7. In the `scene2_gameWon` scene, attach the following C# script to the Main Camera:

```
using UnityEngine;

public class IncrementCorrectScore : MonoBehaviour {
  void Start () {
    Player.scoreCorrect++;
  }
}
```

8. In the `scene3_gameLost` scene, attach the following C# script to the Main Camera:

```
using UnityEngine;

public class IncrementIncorrectScore : MonoBehaviour {
  void Start () {
    Player.scoreIncorrect++;
  }
}
```

9. Save your scripts and play the game. As you progress from level (scene) to level, you will find that the score and player's name are remembered, until you quit the application.

How it works...

The `Player` class uses static (class) properties `scoreCorrect` and `scoreIncorrect` to store the current total number of correct and incorrect guesses. Since these are public static properties, any object from any scene can access (set or get) these values, since the static properties are remembered from scene to scene. This class also provides the public static method called `ZeroTotals()` that resets both the values to zero.

When the `scene0_mainMenu` scene is loaded, all the GameObjects with scripts will have their `Start()` methods executed. The UI Text GameObject called **Text – score** has an instance of the `UpdateScoreText` class as s script component, so that the scripts `Start()` method will be executed, which retrieves the correct and incorrect totals from the `Player` class, creates the `scoreMessage` string about the current score, and updates the text property so that the user sees the current score.

When the game is running and the user guesses correctly (higher), then the `scene2_gameWon` scene is loaded. So the `Start()` method, of the `IncrementCorrectScore` script component, of the Main Camera in this scene is executed, which adds 1 to the `scoreCorrect` variable of the `Player` class.

When the game is running and the user guesses wrongly (lower), then scene `scene3_gameLost` is loaded. So the `Start()` method, of the `IncrementIncorrectScore` script component, of the Main Camera in this scene is executed, which adds 1 to the `scoreIncorrect` variable of the `Player` class.

The next time the user visits the main menu scene, the new values of the correct and incorrect totals will be read from the `Player` class, and the UI Text on the screen will inform the user of their updated total score for the game.

There's more...

There are some details that you don't want to miss.

Hiding the score before the first attempt completed

Showing a score of zero out of zero isn't very professional. Let's add some logic so that the score is only displayed (a non-empty string) if the total number of attempts is greater than zero:

```
void Start(){
  Text scoreText = GetComponent<Text>();
  int totalAttempts = Player.scoreCorrect + Player.scoreIncorrect;

  // default is empty string
  string scoreMessage = "";
  if( totalAttempts > 0){
    scoreMessage = "Score = ";
    scoreMessage += Player.scoreCorrect + " / " + totalAttempts;
  }

  scoreText.text = scoreMessage;
}
```

See also

Refer to the following recipe in this chapter for more information:

> ▸ *Saving and loading player data – using PlayerPrefs*

Saving and loading player data – using PlayerPrefs

While the previous recipe illustrates how the static properties allow a game to remember values between different scenes, these values are forgotten once the game application has quit. Unity provides the `PlayerPrefs` feature to allow a game to store and retrieve data, between the different game playing sessions.

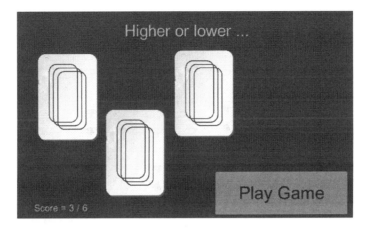

Getting ready

This recipe builds upon the previous recipe. In case you haven't completed the previous recipe, we have included a `Unity` package named `game_scoreStaticVariables` in the the `1362_10_05` folder. In order to follow this recipe using this package, you must do the following:

1. Create a new 2D project and import the `game_HigherOrLower` package.

2. Add each of the scenes to the build in the sequence (`scene0_mainMenu`, then `scene1_gamePlaying`, and so on).

How to do it...

To save and load the player data using `PlayerPrefs`, follow these steps:

1. Delete the C# script called `Player`.

2. Edit the C# script called `UpdateScoreText` by replacing the `Start()` method with the following:

```
void Start(){
  Text scoreText = GetComponent<Text>();

  int scoreCorrect = PlayerPrefs.GetInt("scoreCorrect");
  int scoreIncorrect = PlayerPrefs.GetInt("scoreIncorrect");

  int totalAttempts = scoreCorrect + scoreIncorrect;
  string scoreMessage = "Score = ";
  scoreMessage += scoreCorrect + " / " + totalAttempts;

  scoreText.text = scoreMessage;
}
```

3. Now, edit the C# script called `IncrementCorrectScore` by replacing the `Start()` method with the following code:

```
void Start () {
   int newScoreCorrect = 1 + PlayerPrefs.GetInt ("scoreCorrect");
   PlayerPrefs.SetInt ("scoreCorrect", newScoreCorrect);
}
```

4. Now, edit the C# script called `IncrementIncorrectScore` by replacing the `Start()` method with the following code:

```
void Start () {
   int newScoreIncorrect = 1 + PlayerPrefs.
GetInt ("scoreIncorrect");
   PlayerPrefs.SetInt ("scoreIncorrect", newScoreIncorrect);
}
```

5. Save your scripts and play the game. Quit from Unity and then restart the application. You will find that the player's name, level, and score are now kept between the game sessions.

How it works...

We had no need for the `Player` class, since this recipe uses the built-in runtime class called `PlayerPrefs`, provided by Unity.

Unity's `PlayerPrefs` runtime class is capable of storing and accessing information (the string, int, and float variables) in the user's machine. Values are stored in a `plist` file (Mac) or the registry (Windows), in a similar way to web browser cookies, and therefore, remembered between game application sessions.

Values for the total correct and incorrect scores are stored by the `Start()` methods in the `IncrementCorrectScore` and `IncrementIncorrectScore` classes. These methods use the `PlayerPrefs.GetInt ("<variableName>")` method to retrieve the old total, add 1 to it, and then store the incremented total using the `PlayerPrefs.SetInt ("<variableName>")` method.

These correct and incorrect totals are then read each time the `scene0_mainMenu` scene is loaded, and the score totals displayed via the UI Text object on the screen.

 For more information on `PlayerPrefs`, see Unity's online documentation at `http://docs.unity3d.com/ScriptReference/PlayerPrefs.html`.

See also

Refer to the following recipe in this chapter for more information:

▶ *Saving and loading player data – using static properties*

Saving screenshots from the game

In this recipe, we will learn how to take in-game snapshots, and save them in an external file. Better yet, we will make it possible to choose between three different methods.

 This technique only works when you compile to a Windows or Mac standalone executable—it will not work for Web Player builds, for example.

Getting ready

In order to follow this recipe, please import the `screenshots` package, which is available in the `1362_10_06` folder, to your project. The package includes a basic terrain, and a camera that can be rotated via mouse.

How to do it...

To save the screenshots from your game, follow these steps:

1. Import the `screenshots` package and open the `screenshotLevel` scene.

2. Add the following C# Script to the Main Camera:

```
using UnityEngine;
using System.Collections;
using System;
using System.IO;

public class TakeScreenshot : MonoBehaviour {
  public string prefix = "Screenshot";
  public enum method{captureScreenshotPng, ReadPixelsPng,
ReadPixelsJpg};
  public method captMethod = method.captureScreenshotPng;
  public int captureScreenshotScale = 1;
  [Range(0, 100)]
  public int jpgQuality = 75;
  private Texture2D texture;
  private int sw;
```

```
      private int sh;
      private Rect sRect;
      string date;

      void Start(){
        sw = Screen.width;
        sh = Screen.height;
        sRect = new Rect(0,0,sw,sh);
      }

      void  Update (){
        if (Input.GetKeyDown (KeyCode.P)){
          TakeShot();
        }
      }

      private void TakeShot(){
        date = System.DateTime.Now.ToString("_d-MMM-yyyy-HH-mm-ss-f");

        if (captMethod == method.captureScreenshotPng){
          Application.CaptureScreenshot(prefix + date + ".png",
captureScreenshotScale);
        } else {
          StartCoroutine(ReadPixels());
        }
      }

      IEnumerator  ReadPixels (){
        yield return new WaitForEndOfFrame();

        byte[] bytes;
        texture = new Texture2D (sw,sh,TextureFormat.RGB24,false);
        texture.ReadPixels(sRect,0,0);
        texture.Apply();

        if (captMethod == method.ReadPixelsJpg){
          bytes = texture.EncodeToJPG(jpgQuality);
          WriteBytesToFile(bytes, ".jpg");
        } else if (captMethod == method.ReadPixelsPng){
          bytes = texture.EncodeToPNG();
          WriteBytesToFile(bytes, ".png");
        }
      }
```

```
    private void WriteBytesToFile(byte[] bytes, string format){
       Destroy (texture);
       File.WriteAllBytes(Application.dataPath + "/../"+prefix + date
+ format, bytes);
    }
}
```

3. Save your script and attach it to the Main Camera GameObject, by dragging it from the **Project** view to the Main Camera GameObject, in the **Hierarchy** view.

4. Access the **Take Screenshot** component. Set **Capt Method** as **Capture Screenshot Png**. Change **Capture Screenshot Scale** to **2**.

 If you want your image file's name to start with something different than Screenshot, then change it in the **Prefix** field.

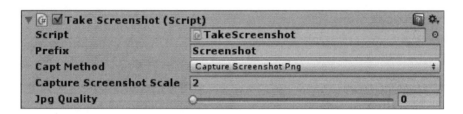

5. Play the scene. A new screenshot with twice the original size will be saved in your project folder every time you press *P*.

How it works...

The Start() method creates a Rect object with the screen width and height. Each frame the Update() methods tests whether the *P* key has been pressed.

Once the script has detected that the *P* key was pressed, the screen is captured and stored as an image file into the same folder where the executable is. In case the **Capture Screenshot Png** option is selected, the script will call a built-in Unity function called CaptureScreenshot(), which is capable of scaling up the original screen size (in our case, based on the Scale variable of our script). If not, the image will be captured by the ReadPixels function, encoded to PNG or JPG and finally, written via the WriteAllBytes function.

In all cases the file created will have the appropriate ".png" or ".jpg" file extension, to match its image file format.

There's more...

We have included the options using the `ReadPixel` function as a demonstration of how to save your images to a disk without using Unity's `CaptureScreenshot()` function. One advantage of this method is that it can be adapted to capture and save only a portion of the screen. The `captureScreenshotScale` variable from our script will not affect screenshots created with the ReadPixel function though.

Setting up a leaderboard using PHP/MySQL

Games are more fun when there is a leaderboard of high scores that the players have achieved. Even single player games can communicate to a shared web-based leaderboard. This recipe includes both, the client side (Unity) code, as well as the web-server side (PHP) scripts to set and get the player scores from a MySQL database.

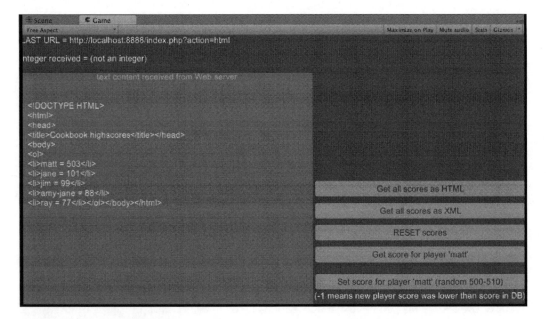

Getting ready

This recipe assumes that you either have your own web hosting, or are running a local web server and a database server, such as XAMPP or MAMP. Your web server needs to support PHP, and you also need to be able to create the MySQL databases.

All the SQL, PHP, and C# scripts for this recipe can be found in the `1362_10_07` folder.

Since the scene contains several UI elements and the code of the recipe is the communication with the PHP scripts and SQL database, in 1362_10_07 folder, we have provided a Unity package called PHPMySQLeaderboard, containing a scene with everything set up for the Unity project.

 If you are hosting your leaderboard on a public website, you will change the names of the database, database user and password for reasons of security. You should also implement some form of secret game code, as described in the *There's more...* section.

How to do it...

To set up a leaderboard using PHP and MySQL, do the following:

1. On your server, create a new MySQL database named cookbook_highscores.

2. On your server, create a new database user (username=cookbook, password=cookbook) with full rights to the database that you just created.

3. On your server, execute the following SQL to create the database table called score_list:

```
CREATE TABLE `score_list` (
  `id` int(11) NOT NULL AUTO_INCREMENT,
  `player` varchar(25) NOT NULL,
  `score` int(11) NOT NULL,
  PRIMARY KEY (`id`)
) ENGINE=InnoDB  DEFAULT CHARSET=latin1 AUTO_INCREMENT=1;
```

4. Copy the provided PHP script files to your web server:

    1. index.php

    2. scoreFunctions.php

    3. htmlMenu.php

5. Create a new 2D Unity project and extract the Unity package called PHPMySQLeaderboard.

6. Run the provided scene, and click on the buttons to make Unity communicate with the PHP scripts that have access to the high score database.

How it works...

The player's scores are stored in a MySQL database. Access to the database is facilitated through the PHP scripts provided. In our example, all the PHP scripts were placed in the web server root folder for a local Apache webserver. So, the scripts are accessed via `http://localhost:8888/`. However, since URL is a public string variable, this can be set before running to the location of your server and site code.

All the access is through the PHP file called `index.php`. There are five actions implemented, and each is indicated by adding the action name at the end of the URL (this is the GET HTTP method, which is sometimes used for web forms. Take a look at the address bar of your browser next time you search Google for example). The actions and their parameters (if any) are as follows:

- ▶ `action = html`: This action asks for HTML text listing all player scores to be returned. This action takes no parameters. It returns: HTML text.

- ▶ `action = xml`: This action asks for XML text listing all player scores to be returned. This action takes no parameters. It returns: XML text.

- ▶ `action = reset`: This action asks for a set of default player name and score values to replace the current contents of the database table. This action takes no argument. It returns: the string `reset`.

- ▶ `action = get`: This action asks for the integer score of the named player that is to be found. It takes parameters in the form `player = matt`. It returns: the score integer.

- ▶ `action = set`: This action asks for the provide score of the named player to be stored in the database (but only if this new score is greater than the currently stored score). It takes parameters in the form `player = matt, score = 101`. It returns: the score integer (if the database update was successful), otherwise a negative value (to indicate that no update took place).

There are five buttons in the Unity scene (corresponding to the five actions) which set up the corresponding action and the parameters to be added to the URL, for the next call to the web server, via the `LoadWWW()` method. The `OnClick` actions have been set up for each button to call the corresponding methods of the `WebLeaderBoard` C# script of the Main Camera.

There are also three UI Text objects. The first displays the most recent URL string sent to the server. The second displays the integer value that was extracted from the response message that was received from the server (or a message as "not an integer" if some other data was received). The third UI Text object is inside a panel, and has been made large enough to display a full, multi-line, text string, received from the server (which is stored inside the `textFileContents` variable).

The three UI Text objects have been assigned to the public variables of the `WebLeaderBoard` C# script for the Main Camera. When the scene first starts, the `Start()` method calls the `UpdateUI()` method to update the three text UI elements. When any of the buttons are clicked, the corresponding method of the `WebLeaderBoard` method is called, which builds the URL string with parameters, and then calls the `LoadWWW()` method. This method sends the request to the URL, and waits (by virtue of being a coroutine) until a response is received. It then stores the content, received in the `textFileContents` variable, and calls the `UpdateUI()` method.

There's more...

The following sections will fine-tune and customize this recipe for you:

Extracting the full leaderboard data as XML for display within Unity

The XML text that can be retrieved from the PHP web server provides a useful method for allowing a Unity game to retrieve the full set of the leaderboard data from the database. Then, the leaderboard can be displayed to the user in the Unity game (perhaps, in some nice 3D fashion, or through a game-consistent GUI).

Using the secret game codes to secure your leaderboard scripts

The Unity and PHP code that is presented illustrates a simple, unsecured web-based leaderboard. To prevent players hacking into the board with false scores, it is usual to encode some form of secret game code (or key) into the communications. Only update requests that include the correct code will actually cause a change to the database.

The Unity code will combine the secret key (in this example, the string called `harrypotter`) with something related to the communication—for example, the same MySQL/PHP leader board may have different database records for different games that are identified with a game ID:

```
// Unity Csharp code
string key = "harrypotter"
string gameId = 21;
string gameCode = Utility.Md5Sum(key + gameId);
```

The server-side PHP code will receive both the encrypted game code, and also the piece of game data that is used to create that encrypted code (in this example, the game ID and MD5 hashing function, which is available in both, Unity and in PHP). The secret key (`harrypotter`) is used with the game ID to create an encrypted code that can be compared with the code received from the Unity game (or whatever user agent or browser is attempting to communicate with the leaderboard server scripts). The database actions will only be executed if the game code created on the server matches that send along with the request for a database action.

```
// PHP - security code
$key = "harrypotter"
$game_id =  $_GET['game_id'];
```

```
$provided_game_code =  $_GET['game_code'];
$server_game_code = md5($key.$game_id);

if( $server_game_code == $provided_game_code ) {
  // codes match - do processing here
}
```

See also

Refer to the following recipe for more Information:

▸ *Preventing your game from running on unknown servers* in *Chapter 11, Improving Games With Extra Features and Optimization*

Loading game data from a text file map

Rather than, for every level of a game, having to create and place every GameObject on the screen by hand, a better approach can be to create the text files of rows, and columns of characters, where each character corresponds to the type of GameObject that is to be created in the corresponding location. In this recipe, we'll use a text file and set of prefab sprites to display a graphical version of a text-data file for a screen from the classic game called **NetHack**.

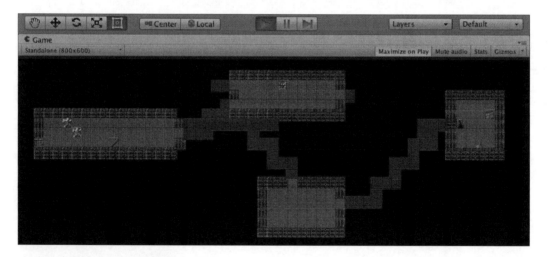

Getting ready

In the `1362_10_08` folder, we have provided the following two files for this recipe:

▸ `level1.txt` (a text file, representing a level)

▸ `absurd128.png` (a 128 x 128 sprite sheet for Nethack).

The level data came from the Nethack Wikipedia page, and the sprite sheet came from SourceForge:

- `http://en.wikipedia.org/wiki/NetHack`
- `http://sourceforge.net/projects/noegnud/files/tilesets_` `nethack-3.4.1/absurd%20128x128/`

Note that we also included a Unity package with all the prefabs set up, since this can be a laborious task.

How to do it...

To load game data from a text file map, do the following:

1. Import the text file called `level1.txt`, and the image file called `absurd128.png`.

2. Select `absurd128.png` in the Inspector, and set **Texture Type** to **Sprite (2D/uGUI)**, and **Sprite Mode** to **Multiple**.

3. Edit this sprite in the **Sprite Editor**, choosing **Type** as **Grid** and **Pixel Size** as `128` x `128`, and apply these settings.

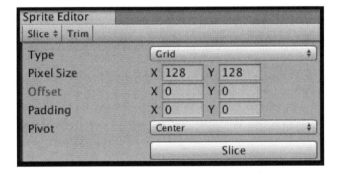

4. In the **Project** panel, click on the right-facing white triangle to *explode* the icon, to show all the sprites in this sprite sheet individually.

5. Drag the Sprite called `absurd128_175` onto the scene.

6. Create a new **Prefab** named `corpse_175` in the **Project** panel, and drag onto this blank prefab Sprite `absurd128_175` from the scene. Now, delete the sprite instance from the scene. You have now created a prefab containing the Sprite `175`.

7. Repeat this process for the following sprites (that is, create prefabs for each one):

    1. `floor_848`
    2. `corridor_849`
    3. `horiz_1034`
    4. `vert_1025`
    5. `door_844`
    6. `potion_675`

    ❑ `chest_586`
    ❑ `alter_583`
    ❑ `stairs_up_994`
    ❑ `stairs_down_993`
    ❑ `wizard_287`

8. Select the **Main Camera** in the Inspector, and ensure that it is set to an **Orthographic** camera, sized **20**, with **Clear Flags** as **Solid Color** and **Background** as **Black**.

9. Attach the following C# code to the Main Camera as the script class called `LoadMapFromTextfile`:

```csharp
using UnityEngine;
using System.Collections;

using System.Collections.Generic;

public class LoadMapFromTextfile : MonoBehaviour
{
  public TextAsset levelDataTextFile;

  public GameObject floor_848;
  public GameObject corridor_849;
  public GameObject horiz_1034;
  public GameObject vert_1025;
  public GameObject corpse_175;
  public GameObject door_844;
  public GameObject potion_675;
  public GameObject chest_586;
  public GameObject alter_583;
  public GameObject stairs_up_994;
```

```
   public GameObject stairs_down_993;
   public GameObject wizard_287;

   public Dictionary<char, GameObject> dictionary = new
Dictionary<char, GameObject>();

   void Awake(){
     char newlineChar = '\n';

     dictionary['.'] = floor_848;
     dictionary['#'] = corridor_849;
     dictionary['('] = chest_586;
     dictionary['!'] = potion_675;
     dictionary['_'] = alter_583;
     dictionary['>'] = stairs_down_993;
     dictionary['<'] = stairs_up_994;
     dictionary['-'] = horiz_1034;
     dictionary['|'] = vert_1025;
     dictionary['+'] = door_844;
     dictionary['%'] = corpse_175;
     dictionary['@'] = wizard_287;

     string[] stringArray = levelDataTextFile.text.
Split(newlineChar);
     BuildMaze( stringArray );
   }

   private void BuildMaze(string[] stringArray){
     int numRows = stringArray.Length;

     float yOffset = (numRows / 2);

     for(int row=0; row < numRows; row++){
       string currentRowString = stringArray[row];
       float y = -1 * (row - yOffset);
       CreateRow(currentRowString, y);
     }
   }

   private void CreateRow(string currentRowString, float y) {
     int numChars = currentRowString.Length;
     float xOffset = (numChars/2);

     for(int charPos = 0; charPos < numChars; charPos++){
       float x = (charPos - xOffset);
       char prefabCharacter = currentRowString[charPos];
```

```
        if (dictionary.ContainsKey(prefabCharacter)){
          CreatePrefabInstance( dictionary[prefabCharacter], x, y);
        }
      }
    }
  }

    private void CreatePrefabInstance(GameObject objectPrefab, float
  x, float y){
      float z = 0;
      Vector3 position = new Vector3(x, y, z);
      Quaternion noRotation = Quaternion.identity;
      Instantiate (objectPrefab, position, noRotation);
    }
  }
```

10. With the **Main Camera** selected, drag the appropriate prefabs onto the prefabs slots in the **Inspector**, for the `LoadMapFromTextfile` Script component.

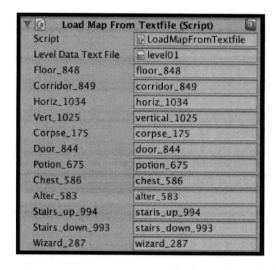

11. When you run the scene, you will see that a sprite-based Nethack map will appear, using your prefabs.

How it works...

The Sprite sheet was automatically sliced up into hundreds of 128 x 128 pixel Sprite squares. We created the prefab objects from some of these sprites, so that the copies can be created at runtime when needed.

The text file called `level1.txt` contains the lines of text characters. Each non-space character represents where a sprite prefab should be instantiated (`column = X, row = Y`). A C# dictionary variable named `dictionary` is declared and initialized in the `Start()` method to associate specific prefab GameObjects with some particular characters in the text file.

The `Awake()` method splits the string into an array using the newline character as a separator. So now, we have `stringArray` with an entry for each row of the text data. The `BuildMase(...)` method is called with the `stringArray`.

The `BuildMaze(...)` method interrogates the array to find its length (the number of rows of data for this level), and sets `yOffSet` to half this value. This is done to allow the placing of the prefabs half above `Y = 0` and half below, so `(0,0,0)` is the center of the level map. A `for`-loop is used to read each row's string from the array. It passes it to the `CreateRow(...)` method along with the Y-value corresponding to the current row.

The `CreateRow(...)` method extracts the length of the string, and sets `xOffSet` to half this value. This is done to allow the placing of the prefabs half to the left of `X = 0` and half to the right, so `(0,0,0)` is the center of the level map. A `for`-loop is used to read each character from the current row's string, and (if there is an entry in our dictionary for that character) then the `CreatePrefabIInstance (...)` method is called, passing the prefab reference in the dictionary for that character, and the *x* and *y* value.

The `CreatePrefabInstance(...)` method instantiates the given prefab at a position of (*x*, *y*, *z*) where *z* is always zero, and there is no rotation (`Quarternion.identity`).

Managing Unity project code using Git version control and GitHub hosting

Distributed Version Control Systems (**DVCS**) are becoming a bread-and-butter everyday tool for software developers. An issue with Unity projects can be the many binary files in each project. There are also many files in a local system's Unity project directory that are not needed for archiving/sharing, such as OS specific thumbnail files, trash files, and so on. Finally, some Unity project folders themselves do not need to be archived, such as Temp and Library.

While Unity provides its own "Asset Server", many small game developers chose not to pay for this extra feature. Also, Git and Mercurial (the most common DVCSs) are free, and work with any set of documents that are to be maintained (programs in any programming language, text-files, and so on). So, it makes sense to learn how to work with a third-party, industry standard DVCS for the Unity projects. In fact, the documents for this very book were all archived and version-controlled using a private GitHub repository!

In this recipe, we will set up a Unity project for GIT DVCS through a combination of Unity Application settings and use of the GitHub GUI-client application.

 We created a real project this way—a pacman-style game, which you can explore and download/pull from the public GitHub's URL, available at `https://github.com/dr-matt-smith/matt-mac-man`.

Getting ready

This recipe can be used with any Unity project. In the `1362_10_09` folder, we have provided a Unity package of our `matt-mac-man` game, if you wish to use that one - in which case create a new 2D project in Unity, and import this package.

Since this recipe illustrates hosting code on GitHub, you'll need to create a (free) GitHub account at `github.com` if you do not already have one.

Before starting this recipe you need to have installed Git and the GitHub client application.

Learn how, and download the client from the following links:

- `http://git-scm.com/book/en/Getting-Started-Installing-Git`
- `http://git-scm.com/downloads/guis`

How to do it...

To load the external resources by Unity Default Resources, do the following:

1. In the root directory of your Unity project, add the following code into a file named `.gitignore` (ensure that the filename starts with the *dot*):

```
# =============== #
# Unity generated #
# =============== #
Temp/
Library/

# ==================================== #
# Visual Studio / MonoDevelop generated #
# ==================================== #
ExportedObj/
obj/
*.svd
*.userprefs
/*.csproj
```

```
*.pidb
*.suo
/*.sln
*.user
*.unityproj
*.booproj

# =========== #
# OS generated #
# =========== #
.DS_Store
.DS_Store?
._*
.Spotlight-V100
.Trashes
ehthumbs.db
Thumbs.db
```

 This special file (.gitignore) tells the version control system which files do *not* need to be archived. For example, we don't need to record the Windows or Mac image thumbnail files (DS_STORE or Thumbs.db).

2. Open **Editor Settings** in the **Inspector** by navigating to **Edit | Project Settings | Editor**.

3. In the **Editor Settings**, set the **Version Control Mode** to **Visible Meta Files**.

4. In the **Editor Settings**, set the **Asset Serialization Mode** to **Force Text**.

5. Save your project so that these new settings are stored. Then, close the Unity application.

6. Log on to your GitHub account.

7. On your GitHub home page, click on the green **New** button to start creating a new repository.

8. Give your new repository a name (we chose **matt-mac-man**) and check the **Initialize this repository with a README** option.

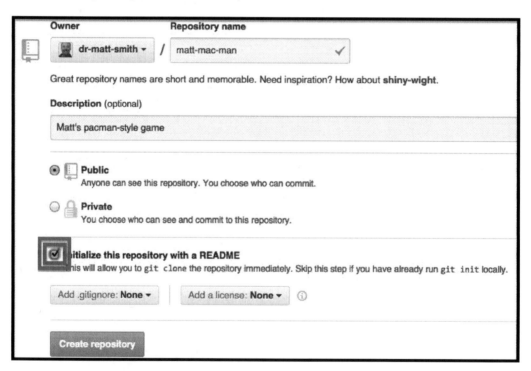

9. Startup your GitHub client application on your computer, and get a list of the repositories to clone to the local computer by navigating to **File | Clone Repository ...** From the list provided, select your new repository (for us, it was matt-mac-man) and click on the **Clone** button to this repository.

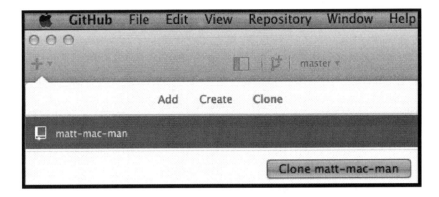

10. You'll be asked where to store this repository on your local computer (we simply chose our **Desktop**). You will now see a folder with the repository name on your computer's disk, containing a hidden .git folder, and a single file named README.md.

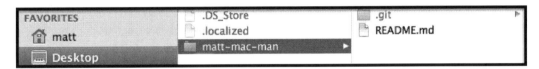

11. Now, copy to this local repository folder the following files and folders from your Unity project:

    1. .gitignore

    2. /Assets

    3. /Library

    4. /ProjectSettings

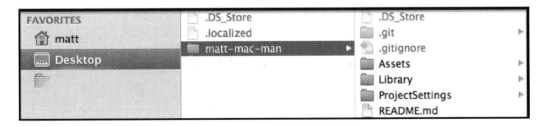

12. In your GitHub client application, you will now see lots of **Uncommitted Changes**. Type in a short comment for your first commit (we typed our standard—v0.1 - first commit), and click on the **Commit & Sync** to push the contents of this Unity project folder up to your GitHub account repository.

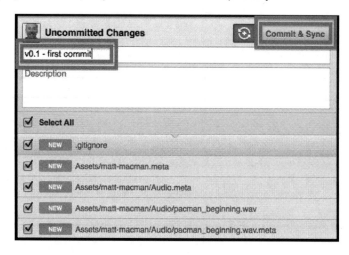

13. Now, if you visit your GitHub project page, you will see that all these Unity project files are available for download for people's computers either as a ZIP archive, or to be cloned using a Git client.

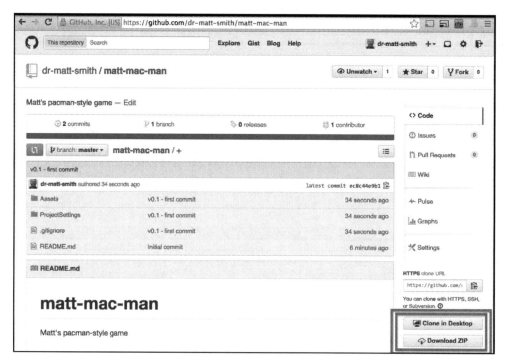

How it works...

The special file called `.gitngnore` lists all the files and directories that are *not* to be archived.

Changing the Unity **Editor Settings** for **Version Control Mode** to **Meta Files** ensures that Unity stores the required housekeeping data for each asset in its associated meta file. Selecting **Visible** rather than **Hidden** simply avoids any confusion as to whether GIT will record the meta files or not—GIT will record them whether visible or not. So, by making them visible, it is obvious to the developers working with the files that they will be included.

Changing the Unity **Editor Settings** for **Asset Serialization Mode** to **Force Text** attempts to solve some of the difficulties of managing changes with the large binary files. Unity projects tend to have quite a few binary files, such as the `.unity` scene files, prefabs, and so on. There seems to be some debate about the best setting that should be used; we have found that **Force Text** works fine and so, we will use this at present. You'll see two commits on GitHub, since the very first was when we created the new repository, and the second was our first commit of the repository using the GitHub client, when we added all of our code into the local repository and pushed (committed) it to the remote server.

There's more...

There are some details that you don't want to miss.

Learn more about Distributed Version Control Systems (DVCS)

The following video link is a short introduction to DVCS:

▶ `http://youtu.be/1BbK9o5fQD4`

Note that the Fogcreek Kiln "harmony" feature now allows seamless work between GIT and Mercurial with the same Kiln repository:

▶ `http://blog.fogcreek.com/kiln-harmony-internals-the-basics/`

Using Bitbucket and SourceTree

If you prefer to use Bitbucket and SourceTree with your Unity projects, you can find a good tutorial at the following URL:

▶ `http://yeticrabgames.blogspot.ie/2014/02/using-git-with-unity-without-using.html`

Using the command line rather than Git-client application

While for many, using a GUI client, such as the GitHub application, is a gentler introduction to using DVCS, at some point, you'll want to learn more and get to grips with working in the command line.

Since both Git and Mercurial are open source, there are lots of great, free online resources available. The following are some good sources to get started on:

- ▶ Learn all about Git, download free GUI clients, and even get free online access to The Pro Git book (by Scott Chacon), available through Creative Commons license at the following URL:

  ❏ `http://git-scm.com/book`

- ▶ You will find an online interactive Git command line to practice in:

  ❏ `https://try.github.io/levels/1/challenges/1`

- ▶ The main Mercurial website, including free online access to the *Mercurial: The Definitive Guide* (by Bryan O'Sullivan) book is available through the Open Publication License at:

  ❏ `http://mercurial.selenic.com/`

- ▶ SourceTree is a free Mercurial and Git GUI client, available at:

  ❏ `http://www.sourcetreeapp.com/`

See also

Refer to the following recipe for more information:

- ▶ *Publishing for multiple devices via Unity Cloud*

Publishing for multiple devices via Unity Cloud

One reason for the Git recipe in this chapter is to allow you to prepare your projects for one of the most exciting new services offered to Unity developers in recent years—Unity Cloud! Unity Cloud takes all the work out of building different versions of your project for different devices—you PUSH your updated Unity project to your online DVCS (such as GitHub). Then, Unity Cloud will see the update and PULL your new code, and build your game for the range of devices/deployment platforms that you have set up.

Getting ready

First, log on to the Unity Cloud Build website and create an account at:

▸ `http://unity3d.com/unity/cloud-build`

For this recipe, you need access to a project's source code. If you don't have your own (for example, you haven't completed the Git recipe in this chapter), then feel free to use the matt-mac-man project available at the public GitHub URL at:

▸ `https://github.com/dr-matt-smith/matt-mac-man`

 A common reason for a test project that was first built to fail is forgetting to add at least one scene to the build settings for the project.

How to do it...

To load external resources by Unity Default Resources, do the following:

1. Log on to your Unity Cloud Build account.

2. On the **Projects** page, click on the **Add a New Project** button.

3. Next, you'll need to add the URL for your source code, and the **Source Control Method** (**SCM**). For our project, we entered our *matt-mac-man* URL, and **GIT** for the SCM.

4. Next, you need to enter some settings. Unity Cloud Build will choose your source code project name as the default application name (most times, this is fine). You need to enter a **Bundle ID**—commonly, the reverse of your website URL is used here to ensure that the **App Name** plus **Bundle ID** is unique. So, we entered `com.mattsmithdev`. Unless testing branches of the code, the default master branch is fine, and likewise, unless testing subfolders, the default (no subfolder) is fine. Unless you are using the latest "beta" versions, the **Unity Version** option should be left to the default **Always Use Latest Version**. Finally, check the build options that you wish to have created. Note that you'll need to have set up the Apple codes if building for iOS; but you will be able to build for Unity Web Player and Android immediately.

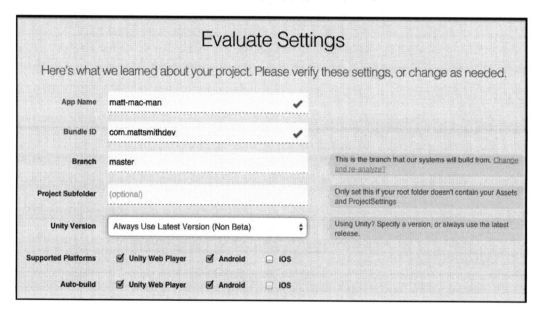

5. Next are the app "credentials". Unless you have Android credentials, you can choose the default "development" credentials. But this means that users will be warned when installing the application.

6. Unity Cloud will then start to build your application—this will take a few minutes (depending on the load on their server).

7. When built, you'll get an e-mail (for each deployment target—so, we got one for Web Player, and one for Android). If the build fails, you'll still get an e-mail, and you can look up the logs for the reasons why the build failed.

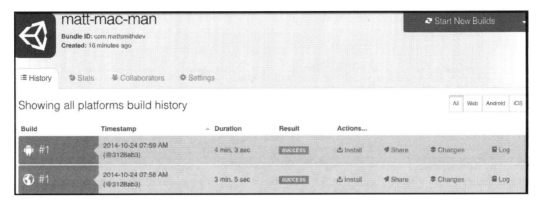

8. You can then play web player version immediately:

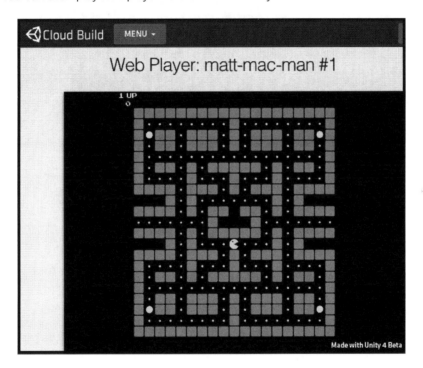

9. To test with Android or iOS, you download it onto the device (from the Unity Cloud web server) and play the game:

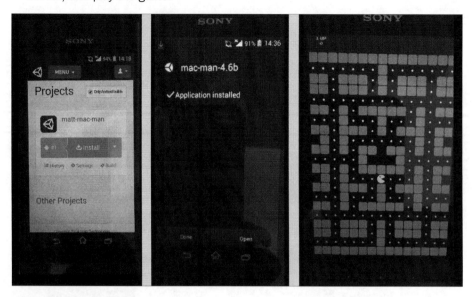

How it works...

Unity Cloud pulls your project source code from the DVCS system (such as GitHub). It then compiles your code using the settings chosen for Unity version and deployment platforms (we chose Web Player and Android in this recipe). If the build is successful, Unity Cloud makes the build applications available to download and run.

There's more...

There are some details that you don't want to miss.

Learn more about Unity Cloud

Learn more in the Support section of the Unity Cloud website (after logging-in), and the Unity main website Cloud Build information page at:

▶ https://build.cloud.unity3d.com/support/

▶ http://unity3d.com/unity/cloud-build

See also

▶ For more information refer the *Managing Unity project code using Git version control and GitHub hosting* recipe

11

Improving Games with Extra Features and Optimization

In this chapter, we will cover the following topics:

- ▶ Pausing the game
- ▶ Implementing slow motion
- ▶ Preventing your game from running on unknown servers
- ▶ State-driven behavior Do-It-Yourself states
- ▶ State-driven behavior using the State Design pattern
- ▶ Reducing the number of objects by destroying objects at a death time
- ▶ Reducing the number of enabled objects by disabling objects whenever possible
- ▶ Reducing the number of active objects by making objects inactive whenever possible
- ▶ Improving efficiency with delegates and events and avoiding SendMessage!
- ▶ Executing methods regularly but independent of frame rate with coroutines
- ▶ Spreading long computations over several frames with coroutines
- ▶ Evaluating performance by measuring max and min frame rates (FPS)
- ▶ Identifying performance bottlenecks with the Unity performance Profiler
- ▶ Identifying performance bottlenecks with Do-It-Yourself performance profiling
- ▶ Cache GameObject and component references to avoid expensive lookups
- ▶ Improving performance with LOD groups
- ▶ Improving performance through reduced draw calls by designing for draw call batching

Introduction

The first three recipes in this chapter provide some ideas for adding some extra features to your game (pausing, slow motion, and securing online games). The next two recipes then present ways to manage complexity in your games through managing states and their transitions.

The rest of the recipes in this chapter provide examples of how to investigate and improve the efficiency and performance of your game. Each of these optimization recipes begins by stating an optimization principle that it embodies.

The big picture

Before getting on with the recipes, let's step back and think about the different parts of Unity games and how their construction and runtime behavior can impact on game performance.

Games are made up of several different kinds of components:

- Audio assets
- 2D and 3D graphical assets
- Text and other file assets
- Scripts

When a game is running, there are many competing processing requirements for your CPU and GPU, including:

- Audio processing
- Script processing
- 2D physics processing
- 3D physics processing
- Graphical rendering
- GPU processing

One way to reduce the complexity of graphical computations and to improve frame rates is to use simpler models whenever possible—this is the reduction of the **Level Of Detail** (**LOD**). The general strategy is to identify situations where a simpler model will not degrade the user's experience. Typically, situations include where a model is only taking up a small part of the screen (so less detail in the model will not change what the user sees), when objects are moving very fast across the screen (so the user is unlikely to have time to notice less detail), or where we are sure the users' visual focus is elsewhere (for example, in a car racing game, the user is not looking at the quality of the trees but on the road ahead). We provide a LOD recipe, *Improving performance with LOD groups*, in this chapter.

Unity's draw call batching may actually be *more efficient* than you or your team's 3D modelers are at reducing the triangle/vertex geometry. So, it may be that by manually simplifying a 3D model, you have removed Unity's opportunity to apply its highly effective vertex reduction algorithms; then, the geometric complexity may be larger for a small model than for a larger model, and so a smaller model may lead to a lower game performance! One recipe presents advice collected from several sources and the location of tools to assist in different strategies to try to reduce draw calls and improve graphical performance.

We will present several recipes allowing you to analyze actual processing times and frame rates, so that you can collect data to confirm whether your design decisions are having the desired efficiency improvements.

"You have a limited CPU budget and you have to live with it"

Joachim Ante, Unite-07

At the end of the day, the best *balance* of heuristic strategies for your particular game project can only be discovered by an investment of time and hard work, and some form of profiling investigation. Certain strategies (such as caching to reduce component reflection lookups) should perhaps be standard practice in all projects, while other strategies may require *tweaking* for each unique game and level, to find which approaches work effectively to improve efficiency, frame rates, and, most importantly, the user experience when playing the game.

"Premature Optimization is the root of all evil"

Donald Knuth, "Structured Programming With Go To Statements". Computing Surveys, Vol 6, No 4, December 1974

Perhaps, the core strategy to take away from this chapter is that there are many parts of a game that are candidates for possible optimization, and you should drive the actual optimizations you finally implement for a particular game based on the evidence you gain by profiling its performance.

Pausing the game

As compelling as your next game will be, you should always let players pause it for a short break. In this recipe, we will implement a simple and effective pause screen including controls for changing the display's quality settings.

Getting ready

For this recipe, we have prepared a package named `BallGame` containing a playable scene. The package is in the `1362_11_01` folder.

How to do it...

To pause your game upon pressing the *Esc* key, follow these steps:

1. Import the `BallGame` package into your project and, from the **Project** view, open the level named `BallGame_01`.

2. In the **Inspector**, create a new tag **Ball**, apply this tag to prefab `ball` in `Prefabs` folder, and save the scene.

3. From the **Hierarchy** view, use the **Create** drop-down menu to add a **Panel** to the UI (**Create | UI | Panel**). Note that it will automatically add it to the current **Canvas** in the scene. Rename the panel `QualityPanel`.

4. Now use the **Create** drop-down menu to add a **Slider** to the UI (**Create | UI | Slider**). Rename it `QualitySlider`.

5. Finally, use the **Create** drop-down menu to add a **Text** to the UI (**Create | UI | Text**). Rename it `QualityLabel`. Also, from the **Inspector** view, **Rect Transform**, change its **Pos Y** to **-25**.

6. Add the following C# script **PauseGame** to **First Person Controller**:

```
using UnityEngine;
using UnityEngine.UI;
using System.Collections;

public class PauseGame : MonoBehaviour {
  public GameObject qPanel;
  public GameObject qSlider;
  public GameObject qLabel;
  public bool expensiveQualitySettings = true;
  private bool isPaused = false;

  void Start () {
    Cursor.visible = isPaused;
    Slider slider = qSlider.GetComponent<Slider> ();
    slider.maxValue = QualitySettings.names.Length;
    slider.value = QualitySettings.GetQualityLevel ();
    qPanel.SetActive(false);
  }

  void Update () {
    if (Input.GetKeyDown (KeyCode.Escape)) {
      isPaused = !isPaused;
      SetPause ();
    }
  }
```

```
  private void SetPause(){
    float timeScale = !isPaused ? 1f : 0f;
    Time.timeScale = timeScale;
    Cursor.visible = isPaused;
    GetComponent<MouseLook> ().enabled = !isPaused;
    qPanel.SetActive (isPaused);
  }

  public void SetQuality(float qs){
    int qsi = Mathf.RoundToInt (qs);
    QualitySettings.SetQualityLevel (qsi);
    Text label = qLabel.GetComponent<Text> ();
    label.text = QualitySettings.names [qsi];
  }
}
```

7. From the **Hierarchy** view, select the **First Person Controller**. Then, from the
   Inspector, access the **Pause Game** component and populate the **QPanel**,
   QSlider, and **QLabel** fields with the game objects **QualityPanel**, **QualitySlider**,
   and **QualityLabel** respectively, as shown in the following screenshot:

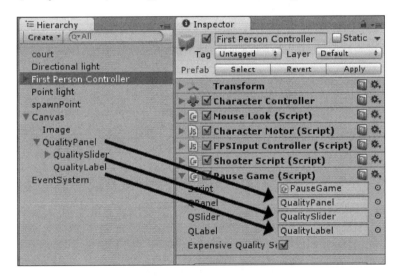

8. From the **Hierarchy** view, select **QualitySlider**. Then, from the **Inspector** view, **Slider**
   component, find the list named **On Value Changed (Single)**, and click on the **+** sign
   to add a command.

9. Drag the **First Person Controller** from the **Hierarchy** view into the game object field of the new command. Then, use the function selector to find the **SetQuality** function under **Dynamic float** (**No Function | PauseGame | Dynamic float | SetQuality**), as shown in the following screenshot:

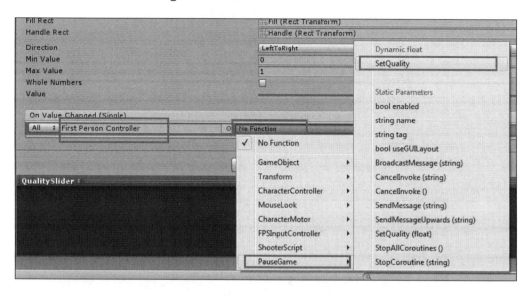

10. When you play the scene, you should be able to pause/resume the game by pressing the *Esc* key, also activating a slider that controls the game's quality settings.

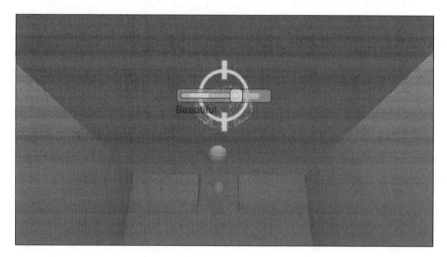

How it works...

Pausing the game is actually an easy, straightforward task in Unity: all we need to do is set the game's **Time Scale** to 0 (and set it back to 1 to resume). In our code, we have included such a command within the SetPause() function, which is called whenever the player presses the *Esc* key, also toggling the isPaused variable. To make things more functional, we have included a **GUI panel** featuring a *QualitySettings* slider that is activated whenever the game is paused.

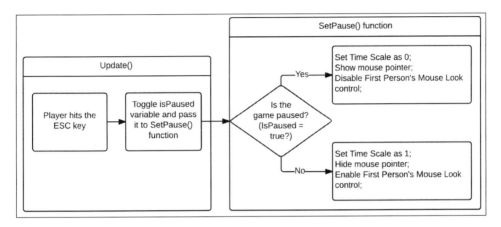

Regarding the behavior for the QualitySettings slider and text, their parameters are adjusted at the start based on the game's variety of quality settings, their names, and its current state. Then, changes in the slider's value redefine the quality settings, also updating the label text accordingly.

There's more...

You can always add more functionality to the *pause* screen by displaying sound volume controls, save/load buttons, and so on.

Learning more about QualitySettings

Our code for changing quality settings is a slight modification of the example given by Unity's documentation. If you want to learn more about the subject, check out http://docs.unity3d.com/ScriptReference/QualitySettings.html.

See also

Refer to the *Implementing slow motion* recipe in this chapter for more information.

Implementing slow motion

Since Remedy Entertainment's *Max Payne*, slow motion, or bullet time, became a popular feature in games. For example, Criterion's *Burnout* series has successfully explored the slow motion effect in the racing genre. In this recipe, we will implement a slow motion effect triggered by the pressing of the mouse's right button.

Getting ready

For this recipe, we will use the same package as the previous recipe, `BallGame` in the `1362_11_02` folder.

How to do it...

To implement slow motion, follow these steps:

1. Import the `BallGame` package into your project and, from the **Project** view, open the level named `BallGame_01`.

2. In the **Inspector**, create a new tag **Ball**, apply this tag to prefab `ball` in the `Prefabs` folder, and save the scene.

3. Add the following C# script **BulletTime** to **First Person Controller**:

```csharp
using UnityEngine;
using UnityEngine.UI;
using System.Collections;

public class BulletTime : MonoBehaviour
{
    public float sloSpeed = 0.1f;
    public float totalTime = 10f;
    public float recoveryRate = 0.5f;
    public Slider EnergyBar;
    private float elapsed = 0f;
    private bool isSlow = false;

    void Update ()
    {

        if (Input.GetButtonDown ("Fire2")
&& elapsed < totalTime)
            SetSpeed (sloSpeed);

        if (Input.GetButtonUp ("Fire2"))
            SetSpeed (1f);
```

```
        if (isSlow) {
            elapsed += Time.deltaTime / sloSpeed;
            if (elapsed >= totalTime) {
                SetSpeed (1f);
            }

        } else {
            elapsed -= Time.deltaTime * recoveryRate;
            elapsed = Mathf.Clamp (elapsed, 0, totalTime);
        }
        float remainingTime =
(totalTime - elapsed) / totalTime;
        EnergyBar.value = remainingTime;
    }

    private void SetSpeed (float speed)
    {
        Time.timeScale = speed;
        Time.fixedDeltaTime = 0.02f * speed;
        isSlow = !(speed >= 1.0f);
    }
}
```

4. From the **Hierarchy** view, use the **Create** drop-down menu to add a **Slider** to the UI (**Create | UI | Slider**). Please note that it will be created as a child of the preexisting **Canvas** object. Rename it `EnergySlider`.

5. Select **EnergySlider** and, from the **Inspector** view, **Rect Transform** component, set its position as follows: **Left: 0**; **Pos Y: 0**; **Pos Z: 0**; **Right: 0**; **Height: 50**. Then, expand the **Anchors** settings and change it to: **Min X: 0**; **Y: 1**; **Max X: 0.5**; **Y: 1**; **Pivot X: 0**; **Y: 1**, as shown in the following screenshot:

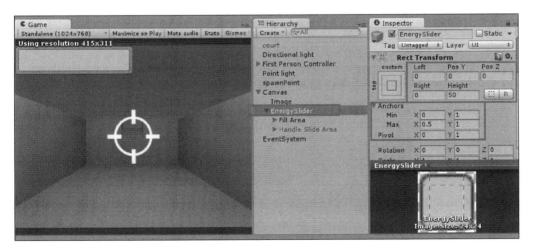

6. Also select the **Handle Slide Area** child and disable it from the **Inspector** view, as shown in the following screenshot:

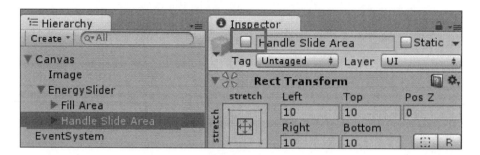

7. Finally, select the **First Person Controller** from the **Hierarchy** view, find the **Bullet Time** component, and drag the **EnergySlider** from the **Hierarchy** view into its **Energy Bar** slot, as shown in the next screenshot:

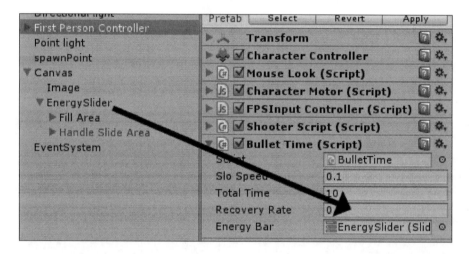

8. Play your game. You should be able to activate slow motion by holding down the right mouse button (or whatever alternative you have set for **Input** axis **Fire2**). The slider will act as a progress bar that slowly shrinks, indicating the remaining *bullet time* you have.

How it works...

Basically, all we need to do to have the slow motion effect is decrease the Time. timeScale variable. In our script, we do that by using the sloSpeed variable. Please note that we also need to adjust the Time.fixedDeltaTime variable, updating the physics simulation of our game.

In order to make the experience more challenging, we have also implemented a sort of *energy bar* to indicate how much bullet time the player has left (the initial value is given, in seconds, by the `totalTime` variable). Whenever the player is not using bullet time, he has his quota filled according to the `recoveryRate` variable.

Regarding the *GUI slider*, we have used the **Rect Transform** settings to place it on the top-left corner and set its dimensions to half of the screen's width and 50 pixels tall. Also, we have hidden the *handle slide area* to make it more similar to a traditional energy bar. Finally, instead of allowing direct interaction from the player with the slider, we have used the `BulletTime` script to change the slider's value.

There's more...

Some suggestions for you to improve your slow motion effect even further are as follows.

Customizing the slider

Don't forget that you can personalize the slider's appearance by creating your own sprites, or even by changing the slider's *fill* color based on the slider's value. Try adding the following lines of code to the end of the `Update` function:

```
GameObject fill = GameObject.Find("Fill").gameObject;
Color sliderColor =
Color.Lerp(Color.red, Color.green, remainingTime);
fill.GetComponent<Image> ().color = sliderColor;
```

Adding Motion Blur

Motion Blur is an image effect frequently identified with slow motion. Once attached to the camera, it could be enabled or disabled depending on the `speed` float value. For more information on the Motion Blur image effect, refer to `http://docs.unity3d.com/Manual/script-MotionBlur.html`.

Creating sonic ambience

Max Payne famously used a strong, heavy heartbeat sound as sonic ambience. You could also try lowering the sound effects volume to convey the character focus when in slow motion. Plus, using audio filters on the camera could be an interesting option.

See also

Refer to the recipe *Pausing the game* in this chapter for more information.

Preventing your game from running on unknown servers

After all the hard work you've had to go through to complete your web game project, it wouldn't be fair if it ended up generating traffic and income on someone else's website. In this recipe, we will create a script that prevents the main game menu from showing up unless it's hosted by an authorized server.

Getting ready

To test this recipe, you will need access to a webspace provider where you can host the game.

How to do it...

To prevent your web game from being pirated, follow these steps:

1. From the **Hierarchy** view, use the **Create** drop-down menu to create a **UI Text** GameObject (**Create | UI | Text**). Name it Text - warning. Then, from the **Text** component in the **Inspector**, change its **text** field to Getting Info. Please wait.

2. Add the following C# script to the Text - warning game object:

```
using UnityEngine;
using System.Collections;
using UnityEngine.UI;

public class BlockAccess : MonoBehaviour {
  public bool checkDomain = true;
  public bool fullURL = true;
  public string[] domainList;
  public string warning;


  private void Start(){
    Text scoreText = GetComponent<Text>();
    bool illegalCopy = true;

    if (Application.isEditor)
      illegalCopy = false;

    if (Application.isWebPlayer && checkDomain){
      for (int i = 0; i < domainList.Length; i++){
        if (Application.absoluteURL == domainList[i]){
          illegalCopy = false;
```

```
        }else if (Application.absoluteURL.Contains(domainList[i])
&& !fullURL){
            illegalCopy = false;
        }
      }
    }

    if (illegalCopy)
      scoreText.text = warning;
    else
      Application.LoadLevel(Application.loadedLevel + 1);
  }
}
```

3. From the **Inspector** view, leave the options **Check Domain** and **Full URL** checked, and increase **Size** of **Domain List** to 1 and fill out **Element 0** with the complete URL for your game. Type in the sentence `This is not a valid copy of the game` in the **Message** field, as shown in the following screenshot. You might have to change the paragraph's **Horizontal Overflow** to **Overflow**.

 Note: Remember to include the Unity 3D file name and extension in the URL, and not the HTML where it is embedded.

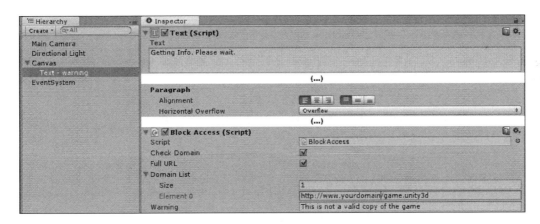

4. Save your scene as `menu`.

5. Create a new scene and change its **Main Camera** background color to black. Save this scene as `nextLevel`.

6. Let's build the game. Go to the **File | Build Settings...** menu and include the scenes **menu** and **nextLevel**, in that order, in the build list (**Scenes in Build**). Also, select **Web Player** as your platform and click on **Build**.

How it works...

As soon as the scene starts, the script compares the actual URL of the `.unity3d` file to the ones listed in the `Block Access` component. If they don't match, the next level in the build is not loaded and a message appears on the screen. If they do match, the line of code `Application.LoadLevel(Application.loadedLevel + 1)` will load the next scene from the build list.

There's more...

Here is some information on how to fine tune and customize this recipe.

Improving security by using full URLs in your domain list

Your game will be more secure if you fill out the domain list with complete URLs (such as `http://www.myDomain.com/unitygame/game.unity3d`). In fact, it's recommended that you leave the **Full URL** option selected so that your game won't be stolen and published under a URL such as `www.stolenGames.com/yourgame.html?www.myDomain.com`.

Allowing redistribution with more domains

If you want your game to run from several different domains, increase **Size** and fill out more URLs. Also, you can leave your game completely free of protection by leaving the **Check Domain** option unchecked.

State-driven behavior Do-It-Yourself states

Games as a whole, and individual objects or characters, can often be thought of (or modeled as) passing through different *states* or *modes*. Modeling states and changes of state (due to *events* or game conditions) is a very common way to manage the complexity of games and game components. In this recipe, we create a simple three-state game (game playing/game won/game lost) using a single `GameManager` class.

How to do it...

To use states to manage object behavior, follow these steps:

1. Create two UI buttons at the top middle of the screen. Name one **Button-win** and edit its text to read **Win Game**. Name the second **Button-lose** and edit its text to read **Lose Game**.

2. Create a UI text object at the top left of the screen. Name this **Text-state-messages**, and set its **Rect Transform** height property to **300** and its **Text (Script) Paragraph Vertical Overflow** property to **Overflow**.

3. Add the following C# script class `GameManager` to **Main Camera**:

```csharp
using UnityEngine;
using System.Collections;
using System;
using UnityEngine.UI;

public class GameManager : MonoBehaviour {
  public Text textStateMessages;
  public Button buttonWinGame;
  public Button buttonLoseGame;

  private enum GameStateType {
    Other,
    GamePlaying,
    GameWon,
    GameLost,
  }

  private GameStateType currentState = GameStateType.Other;
  private float timeGamePlayingStarted;
  private float timeToPressAButton = 5;

  void Start () {
    NewGameState( GameStateType.GamePlaying );
  }

  private void NewGameState(GameStateType newState) {
    // (1) state EXIT actions
    OnMyStateExit(currentState);

    // (2) change current state
    currentState = newState;

    // (3) state ENTER actions
```

```
      OnMyStateEnter(currentState);

      PostMessageDivider();
   }

   public void PostMessageDivider(){
      string newLine = "\n";
      string divider = "-------------------------------";
      textStateMessages.text += newLine + divider;
   }

   public void PostMessage(string message){
      string newLine = "\n";
      string timeTo2DecimalPlaces =
String.Format("{0:0.00}", Time.time);
      textStateMessages.text += newLine +
timeTo2DecimalPlaces + " :: " + message;
   }

   public void BUTTON_CLICK_ACTION_WIN_GAME(){
      string message = "Win Game BUTTON clicked";
      PostMessage(message);
      NewGameState( GameStateType.GameWon );
   }

   public void BUTTON_CLICK_ACTION_LOSE_GAME(){
      string message = "Lose Game BUTTON clicked";
      PostMessage(message);
      NewGameState( GameStateType.GameLost );
   }

   private void DestroyButtons(){
      Destroy (buttonWinGame.gameObject);
      Destroy (buttonLoseGame.gameObject);
   }

   //--------- OnMyStateEnter[ S ] - state specific actions
   private void OnMyStateEnter(GameStateType state){
      string enterMessage = "ENTER state: " +
state.ToString();
      PostMessage(enterMessage);

      switch (state){
      case GameStateType.GamePlaying:
```

```
      OnMyStateEnterGamePlaying();
      break;
    case GameStateType.GameWon:
      // do nothing
      break;
    case GameStateType.GameLost:
      // do nothing
      break;
    }
  }

  private void OnMyStateEnterGamePlaying(){
    // record time we enter state
    timeGamePlayingStarted = Time.time;
  }

  //--------- OnMyStateExit[ S ] - state specific actions
  private void OnMyStateExit(GameStateType state){
    string exitMessage = "EXIT state: " + state.ToString();
    PostMessage(exitMessage);

    switch (state){
    case GameStateType.GamePlaying:
      OnMyStateExitGamePlaying();
      break;
    case GameStateType.GameWon:
      // do nothing
      break;
    case GameStateType.GameLost:
      // do nothing
      break;
    case GameStateType.Other:
      // cope with game starting in state 'Other'
      // do nothing
      break;
    }
  }

  private void OnMyStateExitGamePlaying(){
// if leaving gamePlaying state then destroy the 2 buttons
    DestroyButtons();
  }

  //--------- Update[ S ] - state specific actions
```

```
void Update () {
  switch (currentState){
  case GameStateType.GamePlaying:
    UpdateStateGamePlaying();
    break;
  case GameStateType.GameWon:
    // do nothing
    break;
  case GameStateType.GameLost:
    // do nothing
    break;
  }
}

private void UpdateStateGamePlaying(){
  float timeSinceGamePlayingStarted =
Time.time - timeGamePlayingStarted;
  if(timeSinceGamePlayingStarted > timeToPressAButton){
    string message =
"User waited too long - automatically going to
Game LOST state";
    PostMessage(message);
    NewGameState(GameStateType.GameLost);
  }
}
}
```

4. In the **Hierarchy**, select the **Button-win** button, and for its **Button (Script)** component, add an `OnClick` action to call the `BUTTON_CLICK_ACTION_WIN_GAME()` method from the **GameManager** component in the **Main Camera** GameObject.

5. In the **Hierarchy**, select the **Button-lose** button, and for its **Button (Script)** component, add an `OnClick` action to call the `BUTTON_CLICK_ACTION_LOSE_GAME()` method from the **GameManager** component in the **Main Camera** GameObject.

6. In the **Hierarchy**, select the **Main Camera** GameObject. Next, drag into the **Inspector** to ensure that all three **GameManager (Script)** public variables, **Text State Messages**, **Button Win Game**, and **Button Lose Game**, have the corresponding Canvas GameObjects dragged into them (the two buttons and the UI text GameObject).

How it works...

As can be seen in the following state chart figure, this recipe models a simple game, which starts in the **GAME PLAYING** state; then, depending on the button clicked by the user, the game moves either into the **GAME WON** state or the **GAME LOST** state. Also, if the user waits too long to click on a button, the game moves into the **GAME LOST** state.

The possible states of the system are defined using the enumerated type GameStateType, and the current state of the system at any point in time is stored in the currentState variable.

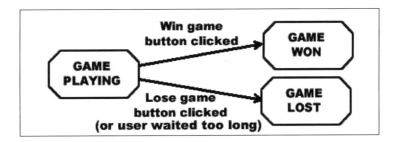

A fourth state is defined (Other) to allow us to explicitly set the desired GamePlaying state in our Start() method. When we wish the game state to be changed, we call the NewGameState(...) method, passing the new state the game is to change into. The NewGameState(...) method first calls the OnMyStateExit(...) method with the current state, since there may be actions to be performed when a particular state is exited; for example, when the GamePlaying state is exited, it destroys the two buttons. Next, the NewGameState(...) method sets the currentState variable to be assigned the new state. Next, the OnMyStateEnter(...) method is called, since there may be actions to be performed immediately when a new state is entered. Finally, a message divider is posted to the UI Text box, with a call to the PostMessageDivider() method.

When the GameManager object receives messages (for example, every frame for Update()), its behavior must be appropriate for the current state. So, we see in this method a Switch statement, which calls state-specific methods. For example, if the current state is GamePlaying, then when an Update() message is received, the UpdateStateGamePlaying() method will be called.

The BUTTON_CLICK_ACTION_WIN_GAME() and BUTTON_CLICK_ACTION_LOSE_GAME() methods are executed if their corresponding buttons have been clicked. They move the game into the corresponding **WIN** or **LOSE** state.

Logic has been written in the UpdateStateGamePlaying() method, so once the GameManager has been in the GamePlaying state for more than a certain time (defined in variable timeToPressAButton), the game will automatically change into the GameLost state.

So, for each state, we may need to write methods for state exit, state entry, and update events, and also a main method for each event with a `Switch` statement to determine which state method should be called (or not). As can be imagined, the size of our methods and the number of methods in our `GameManager` class will grow significantly as more states and a more complex game logic are needed for non-trivial games. The next recipe takes a more sophisticated approach to state-driven games, where each state has its own class.

See also

Refer to the next recipe in this chapter for more information on how to manage the complexity of states with class inheritance and the State Design Pattern.

State-driven behavior using the State Design pattern

The previous pattern illustrated not only the usefulness of modeling game states, but also how a game manager class can grow in size and become unmanageable. To manage the complexity of many states and complex behaviors of states, the State pattern has been proposed in the software development community. Design patterns are general purpose software component architectures that have been tried and tested and found to be good solutions to commonly occurring software system features. The key features of the State pattern are that each state is modeled by its own class and that all states inherit (are subclassed) from a single parent state class. The states need to know about each other in order to tell the game manager to change the current state. This is a small price to pay for the division of the complexity of the overall game behaviors into separate state classes.

[NOTE: Many thanks to the contribution from Bryan Griffiths which has helped improve this recipe.]

Getting ready

This recipe builds upon the previous recipe. So, make a copy of that project, open it, and then follow the steps for this recipe.

How to do it...

To manage an object's behavior using the state pattern architecture, perform the following steps:

1. Replace the contents of C# script class `GameManager` with the following:

```
using UnityEngine;
using System.Collections;
using UnityEngine.UI;

public class GameManager : MonoBehaviour {
  public Text textGameStateName;
  public Button buttonWinGame;
  public Button buttonLoseGame;

  public StateGamePlaying stateGamePlaying{get; set;}
  public StateGameWon stateGameWon{get; set;}
  public StateGameLost stateGameLost{get; set;}

  private GameState currentState;

  private void Awake () {
    stateGamePlaying = new StateGamePlaying(this);
    stateGameWon = new StateGameWon(this);
    stateGameLost = new StateGameLost(this);
  }

  private void Start () {
    NewGameState( stateGamePlaying );
  }

  private void Update () {
    if (currentState != null)
      currentState.StateUpdate();
  }

  public void NewGameState(GameState newState)
  {
    if( null != currentState)
      currentState.OnMyStateExit();

    currentState = newState;
    currentState.OnMyStateEntered();
  }
```

```
    public void DisplayStateEnteredMessage(string
  stateEnteredMessage){
      textGameStateName.text = stateEnteredMessage;
    }

    public void BUTTON_CLICK_ACTION_WIN_GAME(){
      if( null != currentState){
  currentState.OnButtonClick(GameState.ButtonType.ButtonWinGame);
        DestroyButtons();
      }
    }

    public void BUTTON_CLICK_ACTION_LOSE_GAME(){
      if( null != currentState){
  currentState.OnButtonClick(GameState.ButtonType.ButtonLoseGame);
        DestroyButtons();
      }
    }

    private void DestroyButtons(){
      Destroy (buttonWinGame.gameObject);
      Destroy (buttonLoseGame.gameObject);
    }
  }
```

2. Create a new C# script class called GameState:

```
using UnityEngine;
using System.Collections;

public abstract class GameState {
  public enum ButtonType {
    ButtonWinGame,
    ButtonLoseGame
  }

  protected GameManager gameManager;
  public GameState(GameManager manager) {
    gameManager = manager;
  }

  public abstract void OnMyStateEntered();
  public abstract void OnMyStateExit();
  public abstract void StateUpdate();
  public abstract void OnButtonClick(ButtonType button);
}
```

3. Create a new C# script class called `StateGamePlaying`:

```csharp
using UnityEngine;
using System.Collections;

public class StateGamePlaying : GameState {
  public StateGamePlaying(GameManager
manager):base(manager){}

  public override void OnMyStateEntered(){
    string stateEnteredMessage =
"ENTER state: StateGamePlaying";
    gameManager.DisplayStateEnteredMessage(stateEnteredMessage);
    Debug.Log(stateEnteredMessage);
  }
  public override void OnMyStateExit(){}
  public override void StateUpdate() {}


  public override void OnButtonClick(ButtonType button){
    if( ButtonType.ButtonWinGame == button )
      gameManager.NewGameState(gameManager.stateGameWon);

    if( ButtonType.ButtonLoseGame == button )
      gameManager.NewGameState(gameManager.stateGameLost);
  }
}
```

4. Create a new C# script class called `StateGameWon`:

```csharp
using UnityEngine;
using System.Collections;

public class StateGameWon : GameState {
  public StateGameWon(GameManager manager):base(manager){}

  public override void OnMyStateEntered(){
    string stateEnteredMessage =
"ENTER state: StateGameWon";
gameManager.DisplayStateEnteredMessage(stateEnteredMessage);
    Debug.Log(stateEnteredMessage);
  }
  public override void OnMyStateExit(){}
  public override void StateUpdate() {}
  public override void OnButtonClick(ButtonType button){}
}
```

5. Create a new C# script class called `StateGameLost`:

```csharp
using UnityEngine;
using System.Collections;

public class StateGameLost : GameState {
  public StateGameLost(GameManager manager):base(manager){}

  public override void OnMyStateEntered(){
    string stateEnteredMessage =
"ENTER state: StateGameLost";
gameManager.DisplayStateEnteredMessage(stateEnteredMessage);
    Debug.Log(stateEnteredMessage);
  }
  public override void OnMyStateExit(){}
  public override void StateUpdate() {}
  public override void OnButtonClick(ButtonType button){}
}
```

6. In the **Hierarchy**, select the **Button-win** button, and for its **Button (Script)** component, add an `OnClick` action to call the `BUTTON_CLICK_ACTION_WIN_GAME()` method from the **GameManager** component in the **Main Camera** GameObject.

7. In the **Hierarchy**, select the **Button-lose** button, and for its **Button (Script)** component, add an `OnClick` action to call the `BUTTON_CLICK_ACTION_LOSE_GAME()` method from the **GameManager** component in the **Main Camera** GameObject.

8. In the **Hierarchy**, select the **Main Camera** GameObject. Next, drag into the **Inspector** to ensure that all three **GameManager (Script)** public variables, **Text State Messages**, **Button Win Game**, and **Button Lose Game**, have the corresponding Canvas GameObjects dragged into them (the two buttons and the UI text GameObject).

How it works...

The scene is very straightforward for this recipe. There is the single **Main Camera** GameObject that has the `GameManager` script object component attached to it.

A C# scripted class is defined for each state that the game needs to manage—for this example, the three states `StateGamePlaying`, `StateGameWon`, and `StateGameLost`. Each of these state classes is a subclass of `GameState`. `GameState` defines properties and methods that all subclass states will possess:

▸ An enumerated type `ButtonType`, which defines the two possible button clicks that the game might generate: `ButtonWinGame` and `ButtonLoseGame`.

▸ The `gameManager` variable: so that each state object has a link to the game manager.

- ▶ The constructor method that accepts a reference to the GameManager: that automatically makes the gameManager variable refer to the passed in GameManager object.

- ▶ The four abstract methods OnMyStateEntered(), OnMyStateExit(), OnButtonClick(...), and StateUpdate(). Note that abstract methods must have their own implementation for each subclass.

When the GameManager class' Awake() method is executed, three state objects are created, one for each of the playing/win/lose classes. These state objects are stored in their corresponding variables: stateGamePlaying, stateGameWon, and stateGameLost.

The GameManager class has a variable called currentState, which is a reference to the current state object at any time while the game runs (initially, it will be null). Since it is of the GameState class (the parent of all state classes), it can refer to any of the different state objects.

After Awake(), GameManager will receive a Start() message. This method initializes the currentState to be the stateGamePlaying object.

For each frame, the GameManager will receive Update() messages. Upon receiving these messages, GameManager sends a StateUpdate() messages to the currentState object. So, for each frame, the object for the current state of the game will execute those methods. For example, when the currentState is set to game playing, for each frame, the gamePlayingObject will calls its (in this case, empty) StateUpdate() method.

The StateGamePlaying class implements statements in its OnButtonClick() method so that when the user clicks on a button, the gamePlayingObject will call the GameManager instance's NewState() method, passing it the object corresponding to the new state. So, if the user clicks on **Button-win**, the NewState() method is passed to gameManager.stateGameWon.

Reducing the number of objects by destroying objects at death a time

Optimization principal 1: Minimize the number of active and enabled objects in a scene.

One way to reduce the number of active objects is to destroy objects when they are no longer needed. As soon as an object is no longer needed, we should destroy it; this saves both memory and processing resources since Unity no longer needs to send the object such messages as Update() and FixedUpdate(), or consider object collisions or physics and so on.

However, there may be times when we wish not to destroy an object immediately, but at some known point in the future. Examples might include after a sound has finished playing (see that recipe *Waiting for audio to finish before auto-destructing object* in *Chapter 9, Playing and Manipulating Sounds*), the player only has a certain time to collect a bonus object before it disappears, or perhaps an object displaying a message to the player should disappear after a certain time.

This recipe demonstrates how objects can be told to *start dying*, and then to automatically destroy them after a given delay has passed.

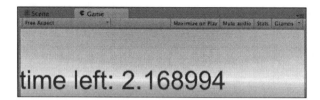

How to do it...

To destroy objects after a specified time, follow these steps:

1. Create a new 2D project.

2. Create a UI **Button** named **Click Me**, and make it stretch to fill the entire window.

3. In the **Inspector**, set the Button's **Text child** to have left-aligned and large text.

4. Add the following script class `DeathTimeExample.cs` to **Button Click Me**:

```
using UnityEngine;
using System.Collections;
using UnityEngine.UI;

public class DeathTimeExample : MonoBehaviour {
  public void BUTTON_ACTION_StartDying() {
    deathTime = Time.time + deathDelay;
  }

  public float deathDelay = 4f;
  private float deathTime = -1;

  public Text buttonText;

  void Update(){
    if(deathTime > 0){
      UpdateTimeDisplay();
      CheckDeath();
```

```
        }
    }

    private void UpdateTimeDisplay(){
        float timeLeft = deathTime - Time.time;
        string timeMessage = "time left: " + timeLeft;
        buttonText.text = timeMessage;
    }

    private void CheckDeath(){
        if(Time.time > deathTime) Destroy( gameObject );
    }
}
```

5. Drag the **Text** child of **Button Click Me** into the script's public variable **Button Text**, so this script is able to change the button text to show the countdown.

6. With **Button Click Me** selected in the **Hierarchy**, add a new **On Click()** event for this button, dragging the button itself as the target GameObject and selecting public function BUTTON_ACTION_StartDying(), as shown in the following screenshot:

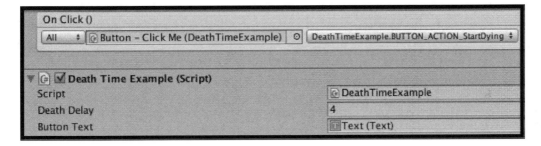

7. Now, run the scene; once the button is clicked, the button's text should show the countdown. Once the countdown gets to zero, **Button Click Me** will be destroyed (including all its children, in this case, just the GameObject **Text**).

How it works...

The float variable deathDelay stores the number of seconds the object waits before destroying itself once the decision has been made for the object to start dying. The float variable deathTime either has a value of -1 (no death time yet set) or it is a non-negative value, which is the time we wish the object to destroy itself.

When the button is clicked, the BUTTON_ACTION_StartDying() method is called. This method sets this deathTime variable to the current time plus whatever value is set in deathDelay. This new value for deathTime will be a positive number, meaning the IF-statement in the Update() method will fire from this point onward.

Every frame method `Update()` checks if `deathTime` is greater than zero (that is, a death time has been set), and, if so, it then calls, the `UpdateTimeDisplay()` and `CheckDeath()` methods.

The `UpdateTimeDisplay()` methods creates a string message stating how many seconds are left and updates the **Button Text** to show this message.

The `CheckDeath()` method tests whether the current time has passed the `deathTime`. If the death time has passed, then the parent `gameObject` is immediately destroyed.

When you run the scene, you'll see the **Button** removed from the **Hierarchy** once its death time has been reached.

See also

Refer to the following recipes in this chapter for more information:

- ▶ Reducing the number of enabled objects by disabling objects whenever possible
- ▶ Reducing the number of active objects by making objects inactive whenever possible

Reducing the number of enabled objects by disabling objects whenever possible

Optimization principal 1: Minimize the number of active and enabled objects in a scene.

Sometimes, we may not want to completely remove an object, but we can identify times when a scripted component of an object can be safely disabled. If a `MonoBehaviour` script is disabled, then Unity no longer needs to send the object messages, such as `Update()` and `FixedUpdate()`, for each frame.

For example, if a **Non-Player Character** (**NPC**) should only demonstrate some behavior when the player can see that character, then we only need to be executing the behavior logic when the NPC is visible—the rest of the time, we can safely disable the scripted component.

Unity provides the very useful events `OnBecameInvisible()` and `OnBecameVisible()`, which inform an object when it moves out of and into the visible area for one or more cameras in the scene.

This recipe illustrates the following rule of thumb: if an object has no reason to be doing actions when it cannot be seen, then we should disable that object while it cannot be seen.

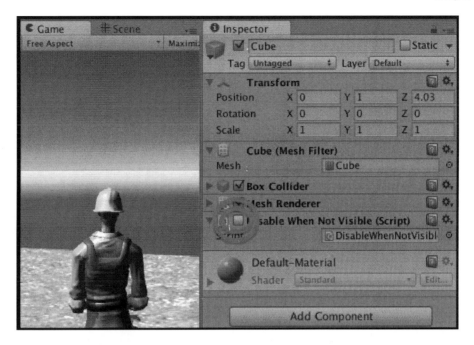

Getting ready

For this recipe, we have prepared a package named `unity4_assets_handyman_goodDirt` containing the `3rdPersonController` handyman and Terrain material `goodDirt`. The package is in the `1362_11_07` folder.

How to do it...

To disable objects to reduce computer processing workload requirements, follow these steps:

1. Create a new Unity project, importing the provided Unity package `unity4_assets_handyman_goodDirt`.

2. Create a new **Terrain** (size **20 x 20**, located at **-10, 0, -10**) and texture-paint it with **GoodDirt** (which you'll find in the **Standard Assets** folder from your import of the **Terrain Assets** package).

3. Add a **3rdPersonController** at (**0, 1, 0**).

4. Create a new **Cube** just in front of your **3rdPersonController** (so it is visible in the **Game** panel when you start running the game).

5. Add the following C# script class `DisableWhenNotVisible` to your **Cube**:

```csharp
using UnityEngine;
using System.Collections;

public class DisableWhenNotVisible : MonoBehaviour {
  private GameObject player;

  void Start(){
    player = GameObject.FindGameObjectWithTag("Player");
  }

  void OnBecameVisible() {
    enabled = true;
    print ("cube became visible again");
  }

  void OnBecameInvisible() {
    enabled = false;
    print ("cube became invisible");
  }

  void Update(){
    //do something, so we know when this script is NOT
    doing something!
    float d =
Vector3.Distance( transform.position,
player.transform.position);
    print(Time.time + ":
distance from player to cube = " + d);
  }
}
```

How it works...

When visible, the scripted `DisableWhenNotVisible` component of **Cube** recalculates and displays the distance from itself to the **3rdPersonController** object's transform, via the variable `player` in the `Update()` method for each frame. However, when this object receives the message `OnBecameInvisible()`, the object sets its `enabled` property to `false`. This results in Unity no longer sending `Update()` messages to the `GameObject`, so the distance calculation in `Update()` is no longer performed; thus, reducing the game's processing workload. Upon receiving the message `OnBecameVisible()`, the `enabled` property is set back to `true`, and the object will then receive `Update()` messages for each frame. Note that you can see the scripted component become disabled by seeing the blue *tick* in its **Inspector** checkbox disappear if you have the **Cube** selected in the **Hierarchy** when running the game.

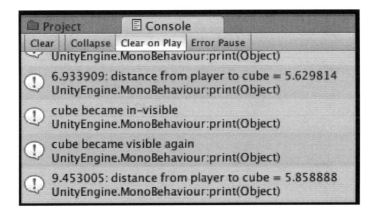

The preceding screenshot shows our **Console** text output, logging how the user must have turned away from the cube at 6.9 seconds after starting the game (and so the cube was no longer visible); then, at 9.4 seconds, the user turned so that they could see the cube again, causing it to be re-enabled.

There's more...

Some details you don't want to miss:

Note – viewable in Scene panel still counts as visible!

Note that even if the **Game** panel is not showing (rendering) an object, if the object is visible in a **Scene** panel, then it will still be considered visible. Therefore, it is recommended that you hide/close the **Scene** panel when testing this recipe, otherwise it may be that the object does only becomes non-visible when the game stops running.

Another common case – only enable after OnTrigger()

Another common situation is that we only want a scripted component to be active if the player's character is nearby (within some minimum distance). In these situations, a sphere collider (with **Is Trigger** checked) can be set up on the object to be disabled/enabled (continuing our example, this would be on our **Cube**), and the scripted component can be enabled only when the player's character enters that sphere. This can be implemented by replacing the `OnBecameInvisible()` and `OnBecameVisible()` methods with the `OnTriggerEnter()` and `OnTriggerExit()` methods as follows:

```
void OnTriggerEnter(Collider hitObjectCollider) {
  if (hitObjectCollider.CompareTag("Player")){
    print ("cube close to Player again");
    enabled = true;
```

```
    }
  }

  void OnTriggerExit(Collider hitObjectCollider) {
    if (hitObjectCollider.CompareTag("Player")){
      print ("cube away from Player");
      enabled = false;
    }
  }
}
```

The following screenshot illustrates a large sphere collider having been created around the cube, with its **Trigger** enabled:

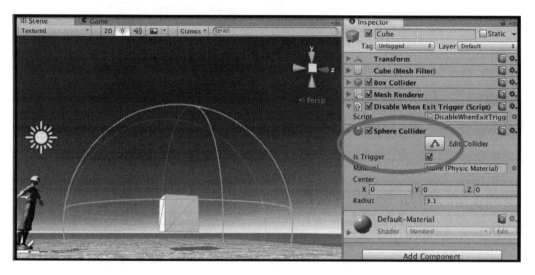

Many computer games (such as *Half Life*) use environmental design such as corridors to optimize memory usage by loading and unloading different parts of the environment. For example, when a player hits a corridor trigger, environment objects load and unload. See the following for more information about such techniques:

- http://gamearchitect.net/Articles/StreamingBestiary.html
- http://cie.acm.org/articles/level-design-optimization-guidelines-for-game-artists-using-the-epic-games/
- http://gamedev.stackexchange.com/questions/33016/how-does-3d-games-work-so-fluent-provided-that-each-meshs-size-is-so-big

See also

Refer to the following recipes in this chapter for more information:

▶ *Reducing the number of objects by destroying objects at a death time*

▶ *Reducing the number of active objects by making objects inactive whenever possible*

Reducing the number of active objects by making objects inactive whenever possible

Optimization principal 1: Minimize the number of active and enabled objects in a scene.

Sometimes, we may not want to completely remove an object, but it is possible to go one step further than disabling a scripted component by making the parent GameObject that contains the scripted component inactive. This is just like deselecting the checkbox next to the GameObject in the **Inspector**, as shown in the following screenshot:

How to do it...

To reduce computer processing *workload* requirements by making an object inactive when it becomes invisible, follow these steps:

1. Copy the previous recipe.

2. Remove the scripted component DisableWhenNotVisible from your **Cube**, and instead, add the following C# script class InactiveWhenNotVisible to **Cube**:

```
using UnityEngine;
using System.Collections;
using UnityEngine.UI;

public class InactiveWhenNotVisible : MonoBehaviour {
  // button action
  public void BUTTON_ACTION_MakeActive(){
    gameObject.SetActive(true);
    makeActiveAgainButton.SetActive(false);
  }
```

```
public GameObject makeActiveAgainButton;

private GameObject player;

void Start(){
  player = GameObject.FindGameObjectWithTag("Player");
}

void OnBecameInvisible() {
  makeActiveAgainButton.SetActive(true);
  print ("cube became invisible");
  gameObject.SetActive(false);
}

void Update(){
    float d = Vector3.Distance( transform.position, player.
transform.position);
    print(Time.time + ": distance from player to cube =
" + d);
  }
}
```

3. Create a new **Button**, containing the text `Make Cube Active Again`, and position the button so that it is at the top of the **Game** panel and stretches the entire width of the **Game** panel, as shown in the following screenshot:

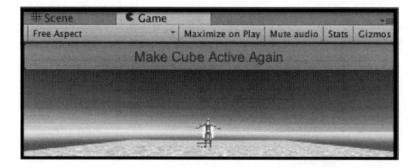

4. With the **Button** selected in the **Hierarchy**, add a new **On Click()** event for this button, dragging the **Cube** as the target GameObject and selecting public function `BUTTON_ ACTION_makeCubeActiveAgain()`.

5. Uncheck the active checkbox next to the **Button** name in the **Inspector** (in other words, manually deactivate this **Button** so that we don't see the **Button** when the scene first runs).

6. Select the **Cube** in the **Inspector** and drag the **Button** into the
   MakeActiveAgainButton variable slot of its script class
   InactiveWhenNotVisible component, as shown in the following screenshot:

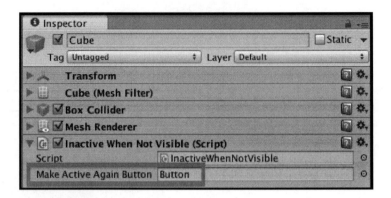

How it works...

Initially, the **Cube** is visible and the **Button** is inactive (so not visible to the user). When the
Cube receives an OnBecameInvisible event message, its OnBecameInvisible()
method will execute. This method performs two actions:

  ▸   It first enables (and therefore makes visible) the Button.

  ▸   It then makes inactive the script's parent gameObject (that is, the Cube
      GameObject).

When the **Button** is clicked, it makes the **Cube** object active again and makes the **Button**
inactive again. So, at any one time, only one of the **Cube** and **Button** objects are active, and
each makes itself inactive when the other is active.

Note that an inactive GameObject does not receive *any* messages, so it will not receive
the OnBecameVisible() message, and this may not be appropriate for every object that
is out of sight of the camera. However, when deactivating objects is appropriate, a larger
performance saving is made compared to simply disabling a single scripted Monobehaviour
component of a GameObject.

The only way to reactivate an inactive object is for another object to set the GameObject
component's active property back to true. In this recipe, it is the Button GameObject, which,
when clicked, runs the BUTTON_ACTION_makeCubeActiveAgain() method, which allows
our game to make the **Cube** active again.

Refer to the following recipes in this chapter for more information:

▸ *Reducing the number of objects by destroying objects at a death time*

▸ *Reducing the number of enabled objects by disabling objects whenever possible*

Improving efficiency with delegates and events and avoiding SendMessage!

Optimization principal 2: Minimize actions requiring Unity to perform "reflection" over objects and searching of all current scene objects.

When events can be based on visibility, distance, or collisions, we can use such events as `OnTriggerExit` and `OnBecomeInvisible`, as described in some of the previous recipes. When events can be based on time periods, we can use coroutines, as described in other recipes in this chapter. However, some events are unique to each game situation, and C# offers several methods of broadcasting user-defined event messages to scripted objects. One approach is the `SendMessage(...)` method, which, when sent to a GameObject, will check every `Monobehaviour` scripted component and execute the named method if its parameters match. However, this involves an inefficient technique known as **reflection**. C# offers another event message approach known as **delegates and events**, which we describe and implement in this recipe. Delegates and events work in a similar way to `SendMessage(...)`, but are much more efficient since Unity maintains a defined list of which objects are *listening* to the broadcast events. `SendMessage(...)` should be avoided if performance is important, since it means that Unity has to analyze each scripted object (*reflect over* the object) to see whether there is a public method corresponding to the message that has been sent; this is much slower than using delegates and events.

Delegates and events implement the **publish-subscribe design pattern (pubsub)**. This is also known as the **observer** design pattern. Objects can subscribe one of their methods to receive a particular type of event message from a particular publisher. In this recipe, we'll have a manager class that will publish new events when UI buttons are clicked. We'll create some UI objects, some of which **subscribe** to the color change events, so that each time a color change event is published, subscribed UI objects receive the event message and change their color accordingly. C# publisher objects don't have to worry about how many objects subscribe to them at any point in time (it could be none or 1,000!); this is known as **loose coupling**, since it allows different code components to be written (and maintained) independently and is a desirable feature of object-oriented code.

How to do it...

To implement delegates and events, follow these steps:

1. Create a new 2D project.

2. Add the following C# script class **ColorManager** to the **Main Camera**:

```
using UnityEngine;
using System.Collections;

public class ColorManager : MonoBehaviour {
  public void BUTTON_ACTION_make_green(){
    PublishColorEvent(Color.green);
  }

  public void BUTTON_ACTION_make_blue(){
    PublishColorEvent(Color.blue);
  }

  public void BUTTON_ACTION_make_red(){
    PublishColorEvent(Color.red);
  }

  public delegate void ColorChangeHandler(Color newColor);
  public static event ColorChangeHandler onChangeColor;

  private void PublishColorEvent(Color newColor){
    // if there is at least one listener to this delegate
    if(onChangeColor != null){
      // broadcast change color event
      onChangeColor(newColor);
    }
  }
}
```

3. Create two UI **Image** objects and two UI **Text** objects. Position one **Image** and **Text** object to the lower left of the screen and position the other to the lower right of the screen. Make the text on the lower left read **Not listening**, and make the text on the right of the screen read **I am listening**. For good measure, add a **Slider** UI object in the top right of the screen.

4. Create three UI buttons in the top left of the screen, named **Button-GREEN**, **Button-BLUE**, and **Button-RED**, with corresponding text reading `make things <color=green>GREEN</color>`, `make things <color=blue>BLUE</color>`, and `make things <color=red>RED</color>`.

5. Attach the following C# script class `ColorChangeListenerImage` to both the lower-right **Image** and also the **Slider**:

```
using UnityEngine;
using System.Collections;
using UnityEngine.UI;

public class ColorChangeListenerImage : MonoBehaviour {
  void OnEnable() {
    ColorManager.onChangeColor += ChangeColorEvent;
  }

  private void OnDisable(){
    ColorManager.onChangeColor -= ChangeColorEvent;
  }

  void ChangeColorEvent(Color newColor){
    GetComponent<Image>().color = newColor;
  }
}
```

6. Attach the following C# script class `ColorChangeListenerText` to the **I am listening Text** UI object:

```
using UnityEngine;
using System.Collections;
using UnityEngine.UI;

public class ColorChangeListenerText : MonoBehaviour {
  void OnEnable() {
    ColorManager.onChangeColor += ChangeColorEvent;
  }

  private void OnDisable(){
    ColorManager.onChangeColor -= ChangeColorEvent;
  }

  void ChangeColorEvent(Color newColor){
    GetComponent<Text>().color = newColor;
  }
}
```

7. With button-**GREEN** selected in the **Hierarchy**, add a new **On Click()** event for this button, dragging the **Main Camera** as the target GameObject and selecting public function `BUTTON_ACTION_make_green()`. Do the same for the **BLUE** and **RED** buttons with functions `BUTTON_ACTION_make_blue()` and `BUTTON_ACTION_make_red()` respectively.

8. Run the game. When you click a change color button, the three UI objects on the right of the screen show all changes to the corresponding color, while the two UI objects at the bottom left of the screen remain in the default **White** color.

How it works...

First, let's consider what we want to happen—we want the right-hand **Image**, **Slider**, and **Text** objects to change their color when they receive an event message `OnChangeColor()` with a new color argument.

This is achieved by each object having an instance of the appropriate `ColorChangeListener` class that subscribes their `OnChangeColor()` method to listen for color change events published from the `ColorManager` class. Since both the **Image** and **Slider** objects have an image component whose color will change, they have scripted components of our C# class `ColorChangeListenerImage`, while the **Text** object needs a different class since it is the color of the text component whose color is to be changed (so we add an instance of C# scripted component `ColorChangeListenerText` to the **Text** UI object). So, as we can see, different objects may respond to receiving the same event messages in ways appropriate to each different object.

Since our scripted objects may be disabled and enabled at different times, each time a scripted `ColorChangeListener` object is enabled (such as when its GameObject parent is instantiated), its `OnChangeColor()` method is added (`+=`) to the list of those subscribed to listen for color change events, likewise each time `ColorChangeListenerImage/Text` objects are disabled, those methods are removed (`-=`) from the list of event subscribers.

When a `ColorChangeListenerImage/Text` object receives a color change message, its subscribed `OnChangeColor()` method is executed and the color of the appropriate component is changed to the received `Color` value (green/red/blue).

The `ColorManager` class has a public class (static) variable `changeColorEvent`, which defines an *event* to which Unity maintains a dynamic list of all the subscribed object methods. It is to this event that `ColorChangeListenerImage/Text` objects register or deregister their methods.

The `ColorManager` class displays three buttons to the user to change all listening objects to a specific color: green, red, and blue. When a button is clicked, the `changeColorEvent` is told to publish a new event, passing a corresponding `Color` argument to all subscribed object methods.

The `ColorManager` class declares a *Delegate* named `ColorChangeHandler`. Delegates define the return type (in this case, `void`) and argument *signature* of methods that can be delegated (subscribed) to an event. In this case, methods must have the argument signature of a single parameter of type `Color`. Our `OnChangeColor()` method in classes `ColorChangeListenerImage/Text` match this argument signature and so are permitted to subscribe to the `changeColorEvent` in the `ColorManager` class.

[Note: An easy to understand video about Unity delegates and events can be found at `http://www.youtube.com/watch?v=N2zdwKIsXJs`.]

See also

Refer to the *Cache GameObject and component references to avoid expensive lookups* recipe in this chapter for more information.

Executing methods regularly but independent of frame rate with coroutines

Optimization principal 3: Call methods as few times as possible.

While it is very simple to put logic into `Update()` and have it regularly executed for each frame, we can improve game performance by executing logic as rarely as possible. So, if we can get away with only checking for a situation every 5 seconds, then great performance savings can be made to move that logic out of `Update()`.

A **coroutine** is a function that can suspend its execution until a `yield` action has completed. One kind of yield action simply waits for a given number of seconds. In this recipe, we use coroutines and yield to show how a method can be only executed every 5 seconds; this could be useful for NPCs to decide whether they should randomly *wake up* or perhaps choose a new location to start moving toward.

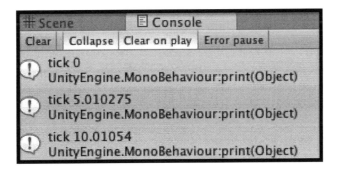

How to do it...

To implement methods at regular intervals independent of the frame rate, follow these steps:

1. Add the following C# script class `TimedMethod` to the **Main Camera**:

```csharp
using UnityEngine;
using System.Collections;

public class TimedMethod : MonoBehaviour {
  private void Start() {
    StartCoroutine(Tick());
  }

  private IEnumerator Tick() {
    float delaySeconds = 5.0F;
    while (true) {
      print("tick " + Time.time);
      yield return new WaitForSeconds(delaySeconds);
    }
  }
}
```

How it works...

When the `Start()` message is received, the `Tick()` method is started as a coroutine. The `Tick()` method sets the delay between executions (variable `delaySeconds`) to 5 seconds. An infinite loop is then started, where the method does its actions (in this case, just printing out the time); finally, a `yield` instruction is executed, which causes the method to suspend execution for the given delay of 5 seconds. After the yield instruction has completed, the loop will continue executing once again and so on. What is important to understand when working with coroutines is that the method will *resume executing* from the same state it yielded.

You may have noticed that *there are no* `Update()` *or* `FixedUpdate()` *methods at all*. So, although our game has logic being regularly executed, in this example, there is no logic that has to be executed every frame—fantastic!

There's more...

Some details you don't want to miss:

Have different actions happening at different intervals

Coroutines can be used to have different kinds of logic being executed at different regular intervals. So, logic that needs frame-by-frame execution goes into `Update()`, and logic that works fine once or twice a second might go into a coroutine with a 0.5-second delay; logic that can get away with less occasional updating can go into another coroutine with a 2- or 5-second delay, and so on. Effective and noticeable performance improvements can be found by carefully analyzing (and testing) different game logic to identify the *least frequent execution* that is still acceptable.

See also

Refer to the next recipe for more information.

Spreading long computations over several frames with coroutines

Optimization principal 3: Call methods as few times as possible.

Coroutines allow us to write asynchronous code—we can ask a method to go off and calculate something, but the rest of the game can keep on running without having to wait for that calculation to end. Or, we can call a coroutine method for each frame from `Update()` and organize the method to complete part of a complex calculation each time it is called.

Note that coroutines are not *threads*, but they are very handy in that each can progress each frame further. It also allows us to write code that does not have to wait for certain methods to complete before another can begin.

When games start requiring complex computations, such as for artificial intelligence reasoning, it may not be possible to maintain acceptable game performance when trying to complete all calculations in a single frame—this is where coroutines can be an excellent solution.

This recipe illustrates how a complex calculation can be structured into several pieces, each to be completed one frame at a time.

 Note: An excellent description of coroutines (and other Unity topics) can be found on Ray Pendergraph's wikidot website http://raypendergraph.wikidot.com/unity-developer-s-notes#toc6.

How to do it...

To spread computations over several frames, follow these steps:

1. Add the following script class SegmentedCalculation to the **Main Camera**:

```
using UnityEngine;
using System.Collections;

public class SegmentedCalculation : MonoBehaviour {
  private const int ARRAY_SIZE = 50;
  private const int SEGMENT_SIZE = 10;
  private int[] randomNumbers;

  private void Awake(){
    randomNumbers = new int[ARRAY_SIZE];
    for(int i=0; i<ARRAY_SIZE; i++){
      randomNumbers[i] = Random.Range(0, 1000);
    }

    StartCoroutine( FindMinMax() );
  }

  private IEnumerator FindMinMax() {
    int min = int.MaxValue;
    int max = int.MinValue

    for(int i=0; i<ARRAY_SIZE; i++){
```

```
        if(i % SEGMENT_SIZE == 0){
            print("frame: " + Time.frameCount + ", i:" + i + ",
min:" + min + ", max:" + max);

            // suspend for 1 frame since we've completed
another segment
            yield return null;
        }

        if(randomNumbers[i] > max){
            max = randomNumbers[i];
        } else if(randomNumbers[i] < min){
            min = randomNumbers[i];
        }
    }

    // disable this scripted component
    print("** completed - disabling scripted component");
    enabled = false;
    }
}
```

2. Run the game, and you'll see how the search for highest and lowest values in the array progresses in steps, avoiding undesirable delays between each new frame.

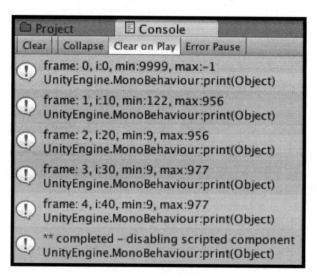

How it works...

The `randomNumbers` array of random integers is created in `Awake()`. Then, the `FindMinMax()` method is started as a coroutine. The size of the array is defined by constant `ARRAY_SIZE`, and the number of elements to process each frame by `SEGMENT_SIZE`.

The `FindMinMax()` method sets initial values for *min* and *max* and begins to loop through the array. If the current index is divisible by the `SEGMENT_SIZE` (remainder 0), then we make the method display the current frame number and variable values and suspend execution for one frame with a `yield null` statement. For every loop, the value for the current array index is compared with `min` and `max`, and those values are updated if a new minimum or maximum has been found. When the loop is completed, the scripted component disables itself.

There's more...

Some details you don't want to miss:

Retrieving the complete Unity log text files from your system

As well as seeing log texts in the **Console** panel, you can also access the Unity editor log text file as follows:

- Mac:
    - `~/Library/Logs/Unity/Editor.log`
    - And access through the standard Console app

- Windows:
    - `C:\Users\username\AppData\Local\Unity\Editor\Editor.log`

- Mobile devices (see the Unity documentation for accessing device log data)

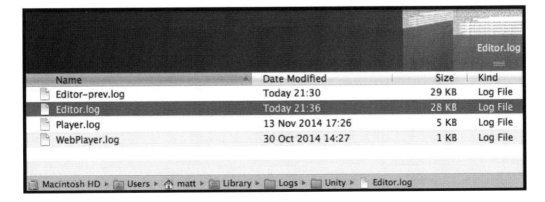

For more information about Unity logs files, see the online manual at `http://docs.unity3d.com/Manual/LogFiles.html`.

See also

Refer to the *Executing methods regularly but independent of frame rate with coroutines* recipe in this chapter for more information.

Evaluating performance by measuring max and min frame rates (FPS)

Optimization principal 4: Use performance data to drive design and coding decisions.

A useful raw measurement of game performance is the maximum and minimum frame rate for a section of a game. In this recipe, we make use of a Creative Commons **Frames Per Second** (**FPS**) calculation script to record the maximum and minimum frame rates for a game performing mathematics calculations for each frame.

Getting ready

For this recipe, we have provided C# script `FPSCounter.cs` in the `1362_11_12` folder. This file is the one we have modified to include the maximum and minimum values based on the **Do-It-Yourself** (**DIY**) frame rate calculation script from Annop "Nargus" Prapasapong, kindly published under Creative Commons on the Unify wiki at `http://wiki.unity3d.com/index.php?title=FramesPerSecond`.

How to do it...

To calculate and record the maximum and minimum FPS, follow these steps:

1. Start a new project, and import the `FPSCounter.cs` script.
2. Add the `FPSCounter` script class to the **Main Camera**.

3. Add the following C# script class `SomeCalculations` to the **Main Camera**:

```csharp
using UnityEngine;
using System.Collections;

public class SomeCalculations : MonoBehaviour {
  public int outerLoopIterations = 20;
  public int innerLoopMaxIterations = 100;

  void Update(){
    for(int i = 0; i < outerLoopIterations; i++){
      int innerLoopIterations =
Random.Range(2, innerLoopMaxIterations);
      for(int j = 0; j < innerLoopIterations; j++){
        float n = Random.Range(-1000f, 1000f);
      }
    }
  }
}
```

4. Run the game for 20 to 30 seconds. On the screen, you should see the current average and the maximum and minimum frame rates displayed.

5. Stop the game running. You should now see in the **Console** a summary message stating the max and min frames per second, as shown in the following screenshot:

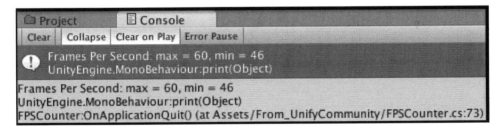

How it works...

The `SomeCalculations` script ensures that we make Unity do something for each frame, in that it performs lots of calculations when the `Update()` method is called for each frame. There is an outer loop (loop counter `i`) of public variable `outerLoopIterations` iterations (which we set to `20`), and an inner loop (loop counter `j`), which is a random number of iterations between 2, and the value of public variable `innerLoopMaxIterations` (which we set to `100`).

The work for the calculations of average **Frames Per Second** (**FPS**) is performed by the FPSCounter script, which runs coroutine method FPS() at the chosen frequency (which we can change in the **Inspector**). Each time the FPS() method executes, it recalculates the average frames per second, updates the max and minimum values if appropriate, and, if the **Display While Running** checkbox was ticked, then a **GUIText** object on screen is updated with a message of the average, max, and min FPS.

Finally, the OnApplicationQuit() method in script class FPSCounter is executed when the game is terminated and prints to the console the summary max/min FPS message.

There's more...

Some details you don't want to miss:

Turn off runtime display to reduce FPS processing

We have added an option so that you can turn off the runtime display, which will reduce the processing required for the FPS calculations. You just have to un-check the **Display While Running** checkbox in the **Inspector**.

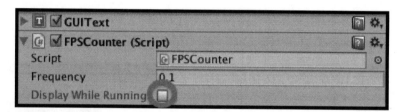

See also

Refer to the following recipes in this chapter for more information:

▸ *Identifying performance bottlenecks with the Unity performance Profiler*

▸ *Identifying performance bottlenecks with Do-It-Yourself. performance profiling*

Identifying performance bottlenecks with the Unity performance Profiler

Optimization principal 4: Use performance data to drive design and coding decisions.

As well as following general asset and code design principals, which we know ought to lead to improved performance, we should be aware that each game is different and that, in reality, the only way to know which design decisions affect performance the most is to collect and analyze runtime performance data. While a raw **Frames Per Second** (**FPS**) measurement is useful, to choose between different decisions having detailed information about the processing requirements for rendering and code execution for each frame is invaluable.

The Unity 5 **Profiler** offers a detailed breakdown of code and rendering processing requirements, as well as processing required by GPU, audio, and both 2D and 3D physics. Perhaps the most useful, it allows programmers to explicitly record data for named code segments. We will name our profile MATT_SomeCalculations and record and examine frame-by-frame processing requirements for our calculations.

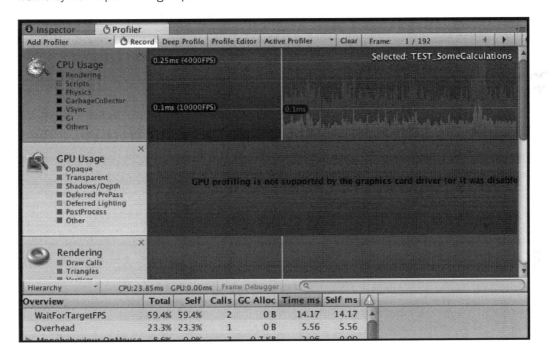

How to do it...

To record processing requirements using the Unity **Profiler**, follow these steps:

1. Start a new 2D project.

2. Open the **Profiler** window from the **Window** menu and ensure that the **Record** option is selected, and that the **Scripts** performance data is being collected, as shown in the following screenshot:

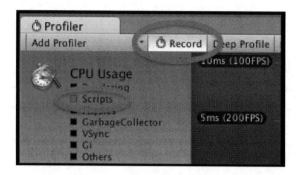

3. Add the following C# script class `ProfileCalculations` to the **Main Camera**:

```
using UnityEngine;
using System.Collections;

public class ProfileCalculations : MonoBehaviour {
  public int outerLoopIterations = 20;
  public int innerLoopMaxIterations = 100;

  void Update(){
    Profiler.BeginSample("MATT_calculations");

    for(int i = 0; i < outerLoopIterations; i++){
      int innerLoopIterations = Random.Range(2,innerLoopMaxIterati
ons);
      for(int j = 0; j < innerLoopIterations; j++){
        float n = Random.Range(-1000f, 1000f);
      }
    }

    Profiler.EndSample();
  }
}
```

4. Run the game for 20 to 30 seconds.

5. Stop the game running. You should now see in the **Profiler** panel details of the breakdown of processing required for the selected frame—each of the jagged lines in the top right of the **Profiler** panel represents the collected data for a frame.

6. View data for different frames by dragging the white line to a different horizontal position—the current frame and the total number of frames are shown at the top right in the form **Frame: frame / totalFrames**.

7. Since we have named a code profile sample, prefixed with **MATT**, we can limit the display of data to only samples containing that word. In the search text box (next to the little magnifying glass,) type MATT, and you should now see just a single row of profile data for our sample **MATT_calculations**. We can see that for frame 83, our code took up 1.2 percent of the processing for that frame.

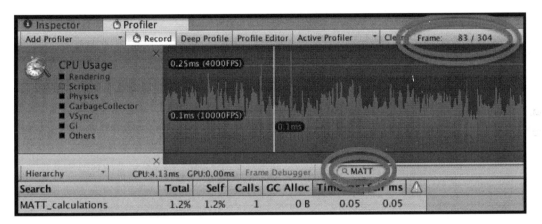

How it works...

The ProfileCalculations script ensures that we make Unity do something for each frame; it does lots of calculations with an inner and outer loop, just like in the previous FPS recipe.

The two important statements are those that mark the beginning and ending of a named code sample to be recorded and presented in the **Profiler**. The Profiler.BeginSample("MATT_calculations") statement starts our named profile and it is ended with the EndSample() statement.

Using an eye-catching prefix allows us to easily isolate our named code profile for analysis, using the search text box in the **Profiler** panel.

See also

Refer to the following recipes in this chapter for more information:

▸ *Evaluating performance by measuring max and min frame rates (FPS)*

▸ *Identifying performance bottlenecks with Do-It-Yourself performance profiling*

Identifying performance "bottlenecks" with Do-It-Yourself performance profiling

Optimization principal 4: Use performance data to drive design and coding decisions.

The Unity 5 performance profiler is great, but there may be times where we wish to have completed control over the code we are running and how it displays or logs data. In this recipe, we explore how to use a freely available script for DIY performance profiling. While it's not quite as fancy as the graphical and detailed profiling of the performance profiler from Unity, it still provides low-level data about the time required for each frame by named parts of scripts, which is sufficient for making code design decisions to improve game performance.

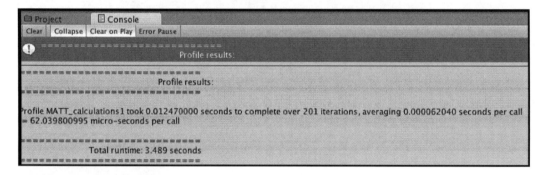

Getting ready

For this recipe, we have provided C# script `Profile.cs` in the `1362_11_14` folder. This is the DIY profiling script from Michael Garforth, kindly published under *Creative Commons* on the Unify Wiki at `http://wiki.unity3d.com/index.php/Profiler`.

How to do it...

To record processing requirements using Do-It-Yourself code profiling, follow these steps:

1. Start a new project, and import the `Profile.cs` script.

2. Add the following C# script class `DIYProfiling` to the **Main Camera**:

```
using UnityEngine;
using System.Collections;

public class DIYProfiling : MonoBehaviour {
  public int outerLoopIterations = 20;
  public int innerLoopMaxIterations = 100;
```

```
void Update(){
   string profileName = "MATT_calculations";
   Profile.StartProfile(profileName);

   for (int i = 0; i < outerLoopIterations; i++){
      int innerLoopIterations = Random.Range(2,innerLoopMaxIterati
ons);
      for (int j = 0; j < innerLoopIterations; j++){
         float n = Random.Range(-1000f, 1000f);
      }
   }

   Profile.EndProfile(profileName);
}


private void OnApplicationQuit() {
   Profile.PrintResults();
}
}
```

3. Run the game for a few seconds.
4. Stop the game running. You should now see in the **Console** a summary message stating total processing time for our named Profile, average time, and number of iterations, and also the total time for which the game was run.

How it works...

As you can see, the script is almost identical to that used with the Unity profiling in the previous recipe. Rather than calling the Unity **Profiler**, we call static (class) methods of Michael Garforth's `Profile` class.

We call `Profile` class methods `StartProfile(...)` and `EndProfile(...)` with the string name for what is to be analyzed (in this example, `MATT_calculations`).

Finally, the `OnApplicationQuit()` method is executed when the game is terminated, calling the `PrintResuls()` method of the `Profile` class, which prints to the console the summary performance information.

The `Profile` class records how many times, and how long between Start and End, each named profile is called, outputting summary information about these executions when `PrintResuls()` is called.

See also

Refer to the following recipes in this chapter for more information:

- ▸ *Evaluating performance by measuring max and min frame rates (FPS)*
- ▸ *Identifying performance bottlenecks with the Unity performance Profiler*

Cache GameObject and component references to avoid expensive lookups

Optimization principal 2: Minimize actions requiring Unity to perform "reflection" over objects and searching of all current scene objects.

Reflection is when, at run time, Unity has to analyze objects to see whether they contain a method corresponding to a "message" that the object has received - an example would be `SendMessage()`. An example of making Unity perform a search over all active objects in a scene would be the simple and useful, but slow, `FindObjectsByTag()`. Another action that slows Unity down is each time we make it look up an object's component using `GetComponent()`.

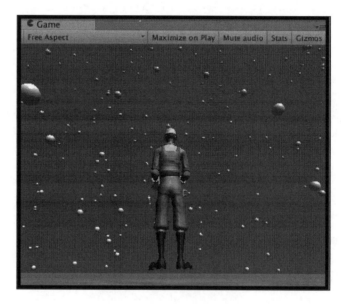

In the olden days for many components, Unity offered *quick component property getters* such as `.audio` to reference the `AudioSource` component of a script's parent **GameObject**, `rigidbody` to reference the **RigidBody** component, and so on. However, this wasn't a consistent rule, and in other cases, you had to use `GetComponent()`. With Unity 5, all these *quick component property getters* have been removed (with the exception of `.transform`, which is automatically cached, so has no performance cost to use). To help game developers update their scripts to work with Unity 5, they introduced *Automatic Script Updating*, whereby (after a suitable warning to have backed up files before going ahead!) Unity will go through scripts replacing *quick component property getters* code with the standardized `GetComponent<ComponentTyle>()` code pattern, such as `GetComponent<Rigidbody>()` and `GetComponent<AudioSource>()`. However, while script updating makes things consistent, and also makes explicit all these `GetComponent()` reflection statements, each `GetComponent()` execution eats up valuable processing resources.

You can read more about Unity's reasons for this (and the alternative *Extension Methods* approach they rejected; a shame—I think we'll see them appear in a later version of Unity since it's an elegant way to solve this coding situation) in this June 2014 blog post and manual page at:

  ▸ `http://blogs.unity3d.com/2014/06/23/unity5-api-changes-automatic-script-updating/`
  ▸ `http://unity3d.com/learn/tutorials/modules/intermediate/scripting/extension-methods`

In this recipe, we'll incrementally refactor a method, making it more efficient at each step by removing reflection and component lookup actions. The method we'll improve is to find half the distance from the **GameObject** in the scene tagged `Player` (a **3rd Person Controller**) and 1,000 other **GameObjects** in the scene tagged `Respawn`.

Getting ready

For this recipe, we have prepared a package named `unity4_assets_handyman_goodDirt` containing the 3rdPersonController handyman and Terrain material `goodDirt`. The package is in the folder `1362_11_15`.

How to do it...

To improve code performance by caching component lookups, follow these steps:

1. Create a new 3D project, importing the provided Unity package `unity4_assets_handyman_goodDirt`.

2. Create a new **Terrain** (size **200 x 200**, located at **-100, 0, -100**) and texture-paint it with **GoodDirt**.

3. Add a **3rdPersonController** at the center of the terrain (that is, **0, 1, 0**). Note that this will already be tagged **Player**.

4. Create a new **Sphere** and give it the tag **Respawn**.

5. In the **Project** panel, create a new empty prefab named **prefab_sphere** and drag the **Sphere** from the **Hierarchy** panel into your prefab in the **Project** panel.

6. Now, delete the **Sphere** from the **Hierarchy** panel (since all its properties have been copied into our prefab).

7. Add the following C# script class `SphereBuilder` to the **Main Camera**:

```
using UnityEngine;
using System.Collections;

public class SphereBuilder : MonoBehaviour
{
  public const int NUM_SPHERES = 1000;
  public GameObject spherePrefab;

  void Awake(){
    List<Vector3> randomPositions =
BuildVector3Collection(NUM_SPHERES);
    for(int i=0; i < NUM_SPHERES; i++){
      Vector3 pos = randomPositions[i];
      Instantiate(spherePrefab, pos, Quaternion.identity);
    }
  }

  public List<Vector3> BuildVector3Collection(int numPositions){
    List<Vector3> positionArrayList = new List<Vector3>();
    for(int i=0; i < numPositions; i++) {
      float x = Random.Range(-100, 100);
      float y = Random.Range(1, 100);
      float z = Random.Range(-100, 100);
      Vector3 pos = new Vector3(x,y,z);
      positionArrayList.Add (pos);
    }

    return positionArrayList;
  }
}
```

8. With the **Main Camera** selected in the **Hierarchy**, drag **prefab_sphere** from the Project panel in **Inspector** public variable `Sphere Prefab`, for script component `SphereBuilder`, as shown in the following screenshot:

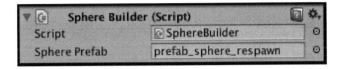

9. Add the following C# script class `SimpleMath` to the **Main Camera**:

```csharp
using UnityEngine;
using System.Collections;

public class SimpleMath : MonoBehaviour {
  public float Halve(float n){
    return n / 2;
  }
}
```

Method 1 – AverageDistance calculation

Follow these steps:

1. Add the following C# script class `AverageDistance` to the **Main Camera**:

```csharp
using UnityEngine;
using System.Collections;
using System;

public class AverageDistance : MonoBehaviour
{
  void Update(){
    // method1 - basic
    Profiler.BeginSample("TESTING_method1");
    GameObject[] sphereArray = GameObject.FindGameObjectsWithTag("
Respawn");
    for (int i=0; i < SphereBuilder.NUM_SPHERES; i++){
      HalfDistanceBasic(sphereArray[i].transform);
    }
    Profiler.EndSample();
  }

  // basic
  private void
HalfDistanceBasic(Transform sphereGOTransform){
```

```
      Transform playerTransform =
  GameObject.FindGameObjectWithTag("Player").transform;
      Vector3 pos1 = playerTransform.position;
      Vector3 pos2 = sphereGOTransform.position;

      float distance = Vector3.Distance(pos1, pos2);

      SimpleMath mathObject = GetComponent<SimpleMath>();
      float halfDistance = mathObject.Halve(distance);
    }
  }
```

2. Open the **Profiler** panel and ensure that **record** is selected and and that the script processing load is being recorded.

3. Run the game for 10 to 20 seconds.

4. In the **Profiler** panel, restrict the listed results to only samples starting with TEST. For whichever frame you select, you should see the percentage CPU load and milliseconds required for **TESTING_method1**.

Method 2 – Cache array of Respawn object transforms

Follow these steps:

1. FindGameObjectWithTag() is slow, so let's fix that for the search for objects tagged Respawn. First, in C# script class AverageDistance, add a private Transform array variable named sphereTransformArrayCache:

    ```
    private Transform[] sphereTransformArrayCache;
    ```

2. Now, add the Start() method, the statement that stores in this array references to the **Transform** component of all our Respawn tagged objects:

    ```
    private void Start(){
      GameObject[] sphereGOArray =
    GameObject.FindGameObjectsWithTag("Respawn");
      sphereTransformArrayCache =
    new Transform[SphereBuilder.NUM_SPHERES];
      for (int i=0; i < SphereBuilder.NUM_SPHERES; i++){
        sphereTransformArrayCache[i] =
    sphereGOArray[i].transform;
      }
    }
    ```

3. Now, in the `Update()` method, start a new **Profiler** sample named **TESTING_method2**, which uses our cached array of games objects tagged with `Respawn`:

```
// method2 - use cached sphere ('Respawn' array)
Profiler.BeginSample("TESTING_method2");
for (int i=0; i < SphereBuilder.NUM_SPHERES; i++){
  HalfDistanceBasic(sphereTransformArrayCache[i]);
}
Profiler.EndSample();
```

4. Once again, run the game for 10 to 20 seconds and set the **Profiler** panel to restrict the listed results to only samples starting with `TEST`. For whichever frame you select, you should see the percentage CPU load and milliseconds required for **TESTING_method1** and **TESTING_method2**.

Method 3 – Cache reference to Player transform

That should run faster. But wait! Let's improve things some more. Let's make use of a cached reference to **Cube-Player** component's transform, avoiding the slow object-tag reflection lookup altogether. Follow these steps:

1. First, add a new private variable and a statement in the `Start()` method to assign the `Player` object's transform in this variable `playerTransformCache`:

```
private Transform playerTransformCache;
private Transform[] sphereTransformArrayCache;

private void Start(){
  GameObject[] sphereGOArray =
GameObject.FindGameObjectsWithTag("Respawn");
  sphereTransformArrayCache = new Transform[SphereBuilder.NUM_
SPHERES];
  for (int i=0; i < SphereBuilder.NUM_SPHERES; i++){
    sphereTransformArrayCache[i] =
sphereGOArray[i].transform;
  }

  playerTransformCache =
GameObject.FindGameObjectWithTag("Player").transform;
}
```

2. Now, in `Update()`, add the following code to start a new **Profiler** sample named **TESTING_method3**:

```
// method3 - use cached playerTransform
Profiler.BeginSample("TESTING_method3");
for (int i=0; i < SphereBuilder.NUM_SPHERES; i++){
```

```
        HalfDistanceCachePlayerTransform(sphereTransformArrayCache[i]);
        }
        Profiler.EndSample();
```

3. Finally, we need to write a new method that calculates the half distance making use of the cached player transform variable we have set up. So, add this new method, `HalfDistanceCachePlayerTransform( sphereTransformArrayCache[i]` `)`:

```
        // playerTransform cached
        private void
        HalfDistanceCachePlayerTransform(Transform sphereGOTransform){
          Vector3 pos1 = playerTransformCache.position;
          Vector3 pos2 = sphereGOTransform.position;
          float distance = Vector3.Distance(pos1, pos2);
          SimpleMath mathObject = GetComponent<SimpleMath>();
          float halfDistance = mathObject.Halve(distance);
        }
```

Method 4 – Cache Player's Vector3 position

Let's improve things some more. If, for our particular game, we can make the assumption that the player character does not move, we have an opportunity to cache the player's **position** once, rather than retrieving it for each frame.

Follow these steps:

1. At the moment, to find `pos1`, we are making Unity find the position `Vector3` value inside `playerTransform` *every time the* `Update()` *method is called.* Let's cache this `Vector3` position with a variable and statement in `Start()`, as follows:

```
        private Vector3 pos1Cache;

        private void Start(){
        ...
        pos1Cache = playerTransformCache.position;
        }
```

2. Now, write a new half-distance method that makes use of this cached position:

```
        // player position cached
        private void
        HalfDistanceCachePlayer1Position(Transform sphereGOTransform){
          Vector3 pos1 = pos1Cache;
          Vector3 pos2 = sphereGOTransform.position;
          float distance = Vector3.Distance(pos1, pos2);
```

```
SimpleMath mathObject = GetComponent<SimpleMath>();
float halfDistance = mathObject.Halve(distance);
}
```

3. Now, in the `Update()` method, add the following code so that we create a new sample for our method 4, and call our new half-distance method:

```
// method4 - use cached playerTransform.position
Profiler.BeginSample("TESTING_method4");
for (int i=0; i < SphereBuilder.NUM_SPHERES; i++){
  HalfDistanceCachePlayer1Position(sphereTransformArrayCache[i]);
}
Profiler.EndSample();
```

Method 5 – Cache reference to SimpleMath component

That should improve things again. But we can still improve things—you'll notice in our latest half-distance method that we have an explicit `GetComponent()` call to get a reference to our `mathObject`; this will be executed *every time the method is called.* Follow these steps:

1. Let's cache this scripted component reference as well to save a `GetComponent()` reflection for each iteration. We'll declare a variable `mathObjectCache`, and in `Awake()`, we will set it to refer to our `SimpleMath` scripted component:

```
private SimpleMath mathObjectCache;

private void Awake(){
  mathObjectCache = GetComponent<SimpleMath>();
}
```

2. Let's write a new half-distance method that uses this cached reference to the math component `HalfDistanceCacheMathComponent(i)`:

```
// math Component cache
private void HalfDistanceCacheMathComponent(Transform
sphereGOTransform){
  Vector3 pos1 = pos1Cache;
  Vector3 pos2 = sphereGOTransform.position;
  float distance = Vector3.Distance(pos1, pos2);
  SimpleMath mathObject = mathObjectCache;
  float halfDistance = mathObject.Halve(distance);
}
```

3. Now, in the `Update()` method, add the following code so that we create a new sample for our *method5* and call our new half-distance method:

```
// method5 - use cached math component
Profiler.BeginSample("TESTING_method5");
for (int i=0; i < SphereBuilder.NUM_SPHERES; i++){
  HalfDistanceCacheMathComponent(sphereTransformArrayCache[i]);
}
Profiler.EndSample();
```

Method 6 – Cache array of sphere Vector3 positions

We've improved things quite a bit, but there is still a glaring opportunity to use caching to improve our code (if we can assume that the spheres do not move, which seems reasonable in this example). At present, for every frame and every sphere in our half-distance calculation method, we are asking Unity to retrieve the value of the `Vector3` position property in the transform of the current sphere (this is our variable `pos2`), and this position is used to calculate the distance of the current sphere from `Player`. Let's create an array of all those `Vector3` positions so that we can pass the current one to our half-distance calculation method and save the work of retrieving it so many times.

Follow these steps:

1. First, add a new private variable and a statement inside our existing loop in the `Start()` method to assign each sphere's `Vector3` transform position in the array `spherePositionArrayCache`:

```
private Vector3[] spherePositionArrayCache =
new Vector3[SphereBuilder.NUM_SPHERES];

private void Start(){
  GameObject[] sphereGOArray =
GameObject.FindGameObjectsWithTag("Respawn");
  sphereTransformArrayCache = new Transform[SphereBuilder.NUM_
SPHERES];
  for (int i=0; i < SphereBuilder.NUM_SPHERES; i++){
    sphereTransformArrayCache[i] =
sphereGOArray[i].transform;
    spherePositionArrayCache[i] =
sphereGOArray[i].transform.position;
  }

  playerTransformCache =
GameObject.FindGameObjectWithTag("Player").transform;
  pos1Cache = playerTransformCache.position;
}
```

2. Let's write a new half-distance method that uses this array of cached positions:

```
// sphere position cache
private void
HalfDistanceCacheSpherePositions(Transform sphereGOTransform,
Vector3 pos2){
  Vector3 pos1 = pos1Cache;
  float distance = Vector3.Distance(pos1, pos2);
  SimpleMath mathObject = mathObjectCache;
  float halfDistance = mathObject.Halve(distance);
}
```

3. Now, in the `Update()` method, add the following code so that we create a new sample for our *method6* and call our new half-distance method:

```
// method6 - use cached array of sphere positions
Profiler.BeginSample("TESTING_method6");
for (int i=0; i < SphereBuilder.NUM_SPHERES; i++){
HalfDistanceCacheSpherePositions(sphereTransformArrayCache[i],
spherePositionArrayCache[i]);
}
Profiler.EndSample();
```

4. Open the **Profiler** panel and ensure that **record** is selected and script processing load is being recorded.

5. Run the game for 10 to 20 seconds.

6. In the **Profiler** panel, restrict the listed results to only samples starting with TEST. For whichever frame you select, you should see the percentage CPU load and milliseconds required for each method (lower is better for both these values!). For almost every frame, you should see how/if each method refined by caching has reduced the CPU load.

Hierarchy ▾	CPU:8.40ms GPU:0.00ms	Frame Debugge Q TEST				
Search	**Total**	**Self**	**Calls**	**GC Alloc**	**Time ms**	**Self ms**
TESTING_method1	18.6%	18.6%	1	7.8 KB	1.56	1.56
TESTING_method2	11.1%	11.1%	1	0 B	0.93	0.93
TESTING_method3	2.9%	2.9%	1	0 B	0.24	0.24
TESTING_method4	2.3%	2.3%	1	0 B	0.19	0.19
TESTING_method5	2.1%	1.2%	1	0 B	0.18	0.10
TESTING_method6	0.8%	0.8%	1	0 B	0.07	0.07

How it works...

This recipe illustrates how we try to cache references once, before any iteration, for variables whose value will not change, such as references to GameObjects and their components, and, in this example, the Transform components and Vector3 positions of objects tagged Player and Respawn. Of course, as with everything, there is a "cost" associated with caching, and that cost is the memory requirements to store all those references. This is known as the **Space-Time Tradeoff**. You can learn more about this classic computer science speed versus memory tradeoff at https://en.wikipedia. org/wiki/Space%E2%80%93time_tradeoff.

In methods that need to be performed many times, this removing of implicit and explicit component and object lookups may offer a measurable performance improvement.

Note: Two good places to learn more about Unity performance optimization techniques are from the *Performance Optimization* web page in the Unity script reference and from Unity's Jonas Echterhoff and Kim Steen Riber Unite2012 presentation *Performance Optimization Tips and Tricks for Unity*. Many recipes in this chapter had their origins from suggestions in the following sources:

> ▸ http://docs.unity3d.com/410/Documentation/ ScriptReference/index.Performance_ Optimization.html
> ▸ http://unity3d.com/unite/archive/2012

See also

Refer to the following recipes in this chapter for more information:

> ▸ *Improving efficiency with delegates and events and avoiding SendMessage!*
> ▸ *Identifying performance bottlenecks with the Unity performance Profiler*
> ▸ *Identifying performance bottlenecks with Do-It-Yourself performance profiling*

Improving performance with LOD groups

Optimization principal 5: Minimize the number of draw calls.

Detailed geometry and high-resolution texture maps can be a double-edged sword: they can deliver a better visual experience, but they can impact negatively on the game's performance. **LOD groups** address this issue by replacing high-quality objects by simplified versions whenever that object takes up a smaller portion of the screen than necessary for a high-quality version to make a significant difference.

In this recipe, we will use a **LOD group** to create a game object featuring two different levels of detail: a high-quality version for whenever the object takes up more than 50 percent of the screen and a low-quality version for the times it takes up less than that amount. We would like to thank Carl Callewaert, from Unity, for his demonstration of the LOD Group functionality, which has informed this recipe in many ways.

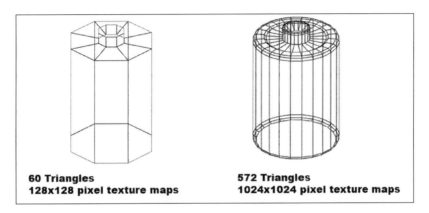

60 Triangles
128x128 pixel texture maps

572 Triangles
1024x1024 pixel texture maps

Getting ready

For this recipe, we have prepared two prefabs for the high- and low-quality versions of the game object. They share the same dimensions and transform settings (position, rotation, and scale), so that they can replace each other seamlessly. Both prefabs are contained within the package named LODGroup, available in the 1362_11_16 folder.

How to do it...

To create a LOD group, follow these steps:

1. Import the **LODGroup** package into your project.

2. From the **Project** view, inside the **LOD** folder, drag the **batt-high** prefab into the **Hierarchy** view. Then, do the same for the **batt-low** prefab. Make sure that they are placed at the same **Position** (**X: 0**; **Y: 0**; **Z: 0**).

3. From the **Create** drop-down menu in the **Hierarchy** view, create a new empty game object (**Create | Create Empty**). Rename it battLOD.

4. Add the **LODGroup** component to **battLOD** (menu **Component | Rendering | LODGroup**).

5. Select the **battLOD** object, and, from the **Inspector** view, **LODGroup** component, right-click on **LOD 2** and delete it (since we'll have only two different LODs: **LOD 0** and **LOD 1**), as shown in the following screnshot:

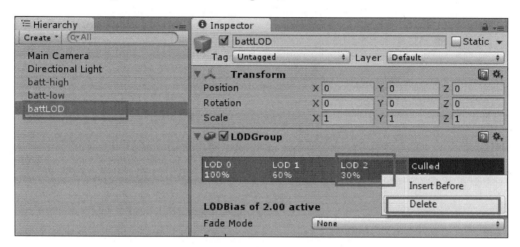

6. Select the **LOD 0** area, click on the **Add** button, and select the **batt-high** game object from the list. A message about reparenting objects will appear. Select **Yes, Reparent**.

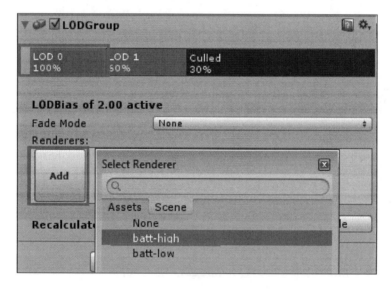

7. Select the **LOD 1** section, click on **Add**, and select the **batt-low** object. Again, chose **Yes, Reparent** when prompted.

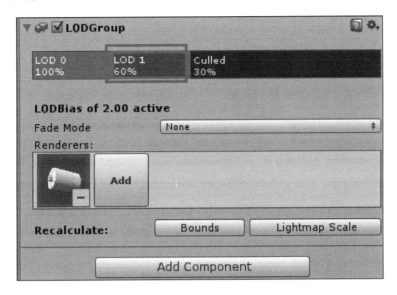

8. Drag the limits of the LOD renderers to set them as: **LOD 0: 100%**, **LOD 1: 50%**, **Culled: 1%.** That will make Unity render **bat-high** whenever it occupies 51 percent to 100 percent of the screen space, **batt-low** when 2 percent to 50 percent, and will not render anything if 1 percent or less.

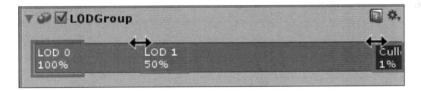

9. Move the scene's camera toward the **battLOD** object and back. You will notice how Unity swaps between the high- and low-definition LOD renderer as it occupies more or less than 50 percent of the screen's space.

How it works...

Once we have populated the LOD renderers with the appropriate models, the **LODGroup** component will select and display the right renderer based on how much of the screen's percentage the object takes up, or even display nothing at all.

There's more...

Some details you don't want to miss:

Adding more LOD renderers

You can add more LOD renderers by right-clicking on an existing LOD renderer and selecting **Insert Before** from the context menu.

Fading LOD transitions

In case you want to minimize the *popping* that occurs when renderers are swapped, you can try changing the parameter **Fade Mode** from **None** to **Percentage** or **Crossfade**.

See also

Refer to the next recipe in this chapter for more information

Improving performance through reduced draw calls by designing for draw call batching

Optimization principal 5: Minimize the number of draw calls.

One way to minimize draw calls is by prioritizing design decisions to qualify objects for Unity's *Static* and *Dynamic draw call batching*.

The more CPU-efficient batching method is Unity's **static batching**. It allows reduction of draw calls for any sized geometry. If that is not possible, then the next best thing is **dynamic batching**, which again allows Unity to process together several moving objects in a single draw call.

Note that there is a cost—batching uses memory, and static batching uses more memory than dynamic memory. So, you can improve performance with batching, but you'll be increasing the scene's memory "footprint." As always, use memory and performance profiling to evaluate which use of techniques is best for your game and its intended deployment device.

How to do it...

In this section, we will learn how to make possible **static batching** and **dynamic batching**.

Static batching

To make possible Unity **static batching**, you need to do the following:

1. Ensure that models share the same material.

2. Mark models as **Static**, as shown in the following screenshot:

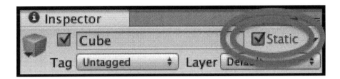

Objects that can be safely marked as **Static** include environment objects that won't move or be scaled.

Many techniques can be used to ensure models share the same material including:

▸ Avoid using textures by directly painting vertices of the model (useful links for this are provided in the *There's more...* section)

▸ Increasing the number of objects textured with exactly the same texture

▸ Artificially enabling objects to share the same texture by combining multiple textures into a single one (texture atlassing)

▸ Maximizing script use of `Renderer.sharedMaterial` rather than `Renderer.material` (since use of `Render.material` involves making a copy of the material and, therefore, disqualifies that GameObejct for batching)

In fact, both static and dynamic batching only work with objects that use the same material, so all methods above apply equally for making dynamic batching possible as well.

Dynamic batching

To make possible Unity **dynamic batching**, you need to do the following:

1. Ensure that models share the same material.

2. Keep the number of **vertex attributes** below 900 for each mesh.

3. Have the group of objects to quality for dynamic batching to use the same transform scale (although non-uniform scaled models can still be batched).

4. If possible, have dynamic lightmapped objects point to the same lightmap location to facilitate dynamic batching.

5. Avoid the use of multi-pass shaders and real-time shadows if possible, since both of these prevent dynamic batching.

To calculate the number of **vertex attributes**, you need to multiply the number of vertices by the number of attributes used by the **Shader**. For example, for a **Shader** using three attributes (vertex position, normal, and UV), it would mean that a model must have less than 300 vertices to keep the total number of attributes below 900 to qualify for dynamic batching.

There's more...

Some details you don't want to miss:

Reduce the need for textures by vertex painting

For more information about this topic, see the following:

- Blender:

  `http://wiki.blender.org/index.php/Doc:2.6/Manual/Materials/Special_Effects/Vertex_Paint`

- 3D Studio Max:

  `http://3dmax-tutorials.com/Vertex_Paint_Modifier.html`

- Maya: free Vertex Chameleon plugin

  `http://renderheads.com/portfolio/VertexChameleon/`

Information sources about reducing textures and materials

For more information about this topic, see the following:

- Unity manual page for Draw Call Batching:

  `http://docs.unity3d.com/Manual/DrawCallBatching.html`

- Paladin Studios:

  `http://www.paladinstudios.com/2012/07/30/4-ways-to-increase-performance-of-your-unity-game/`

- Nvidia white paper on texture atlassing to increase draw call batching opportunities:

  `http://http.download.nvidia.com/developer/NVTextureSuite/Atlas_Tools/Texture_Atlas_Whitepaper.pdf`

- Nvidia free texture tools and Photoshop plug-in:

  `http://www.nvidia.com/object/texture_atlas_tools.html`

See also

Refer to the *Improving performance with LOD groups* recipe in this chapter for more information

Conclusion

In this chapter, we have introduced some extra features and a range of approaches to improve game performance and collect performance data for analysis.

The first three recipes in this chapter provide some ideas for adding some extra features to your game (pausing, slow motion, and securing online games). The rest of the recipes in this chapter provide examples of how to investigate and improve the efficiency and performance of your game.

There's more...

Just as there are many components in a game, there are many parts of a game where processing *bottlenecks* may be found and need to be addressed to improve overall game performance. Some additional suggestions and further reference sources are now provided to provide a launching pad for your further exploration of the issues of optimization and performance, since such topics could take up a whole book rather than just one chapter.

Game audio optimization

Mobile devices have considerably less memory and processing resources than consoles, desktops, or even laptops, and often raise the biggest challenges when it comes to game audio. For example, the iPhone can only decompress one audio clip at a time, so a game may suffer processing spikes (that is, slow down game frame rate) due to audio decompression issues.

Paladin Studios recommend the following audio file compression strategies for mobile games:

- **Short Clips**: Native (no compression)
- **Longer clips** (or ones that loop): Compressed in memory
- **Music**: Stream from disc
- **Files which consistently cause CPU spikes**: Decompress on load

For more information about this topic, see the following:

- Unity manual audio:

  `http://docs.unity3d.com/Manual/AudioFiles.html`

- Paladin Studios:

  `http://www.paladinstudios.com/2012/07/30/4-ways-to-increase-performance-of-your-unity-game/`

- Apple developers audio page:

  `https://developer.apple.com/library/ios/documentation/`
  `AudioVideo/Conceptual/MultimediaPG/UsingAudio/UsingAudio.html`

Physics engine optimization

For some strategies relating to physics, you might consider to improve performance the following:

- If possible, use **geometric primitive colliders** (2D box/2D circle/3D box/3D sphere/3D cylinder):

  - You can have multiple primitive colliders

- You can also have primitive colliders on child objects:

  - As long as you have a rigid body on the root object in the object hierarchy

- Avoid **2D polygon** and **3D mesh** colliders:

  - These are much more processor intensive

- Try increasing the delay between each `FixedUpdate()` method call to reduce physics:

  - Although not to the point where user experience or game behavior is below acceptable quality!

- Wherever possible, start off rigid bodies in sleep mode (so that they don't require physics processing until woken up by code or a collision). See the following Unity script reference pages for making objects go to sleep and wake up:

  - `http://docs.unity3d.com/ScriptReference/Rigidbody.Sleep.`
    `html`
  - `http://docs.unity3d.com/ScriptReference/Rigidbody.`
    `WakeUp.html`

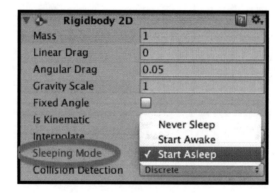

More tips for improving script efficiency

Some code strategies you might consider to improve performance include the following:

- Use **Structs** rather than **Classes** to improve speed up processing.

- Wherever possible, use simple arrays of primitive types rather than **ArrayLists**, **Dictionaries,** or more complex collection classes. A good article about choosing the most appropriate collection in Unity can be found at `http://wiki.unity3d.com/index.php/Choosing_the_right_collection_type`.

- Raycasting is slow, so avoid performing it every frame, for example, use coroutines to only raycast every 3rd or 10th frame.

- Finding objects is slow, so avoid finding objects in `Update()` or inner loops, and you can have objects set up a `public static` variable to allow quick instance retrieval, rather than using a `Find(...)` method. Or you could use the Singleton design pattern.

- Avoid using `OnGUI()`, since it is called every frame just like `Update()`; this is much easier to avoid now with the new Unity 5 UI system.

Sources of more wisdom about optimization

Here are several other sources that you might want to explore to learn more about game optimization topics:

- Unity general mobile optimization page:

  `http://docs.unity3d.com/Manual/MobileOptimisation.html`

- X-team Unity best practices:

  `http://x-team.com/2014/03/unity-3d-optimisation-and-best-practices-part-1/`

- Code Project:

  `http://www.codeproject.com/Articles/804021/Unity-and-Csharp-Performance-Optimisation-tips`

- General graphics optimization:

  `http://docs.unity3d.com/Manual/OptimizingGraphicsPerformance.html`

- Learn more about mobile physics at Unity's iPhone optimization physics page:

  `http://docs.unity3d.com/Manual/iphone-Optimizing-Physics.html`

Published articles that discuss premature optimization

Here are several articles discussing Donald Knuth's famous quotation about premature optimization being "evil":

- ▶ Joe Duffy's blog:

  `http://joeduffyblog.com/2010/09/06/the-premature-optimization-is-evil-myth/`

- ▶ "When is optimization premature?" Stack Overflow:

  `http://stackoverflow.com/questions/385506/when-is-optimisation-premature`

- ▶ *The Fallacy of Premature Optimization*, Randall Hyde (published by ACM), source: Ubiquity Volume 10, Issue 3, 2009:

  `http://ubiquity.acm.org/article.cfm?id=1513451`

Sources of more about Game Managers and the State Pattern

Learn more about implementing the State Pattern and Game Managers in Unity from the following sites:

- ▶ `http://rusticode.com/2013/12/11/creating-game-manager-using-state-machine-and-singleton-pattern-in-unity3d/`

- ▶ `https://github.com/thefuntastic/Unity3d-Finite-State-Machine`

12

Editor Extensions

In this chapter, we will cover the following topics:

- ▶ An editor extension to allow pickup type (and parameters) to be changed at design time via a custom Inspector UI

- ▶ An editor extension to add 100 randomly located copies of a prefab with one menu click

- ▶ A progress bar to display proportion completed of Editor extension processing

- ▶ An editor extension to have an object-creator GameObject, with buttons to instantiate different pickups at cross-hair object location in scene

Introduction

One aspect of game development in general (and inventories as our particular examples in this chapter) is the distinction about *when* we undertake an activity. **Run-time** is when the game is running (and when all our software and UI choices take affect). However, **design-time** is the time when different members of our game design team work on constructing a wide range of game components, including the scripts, audio and visual assets, and the process of constructing each game level (or "scene" in Unity-speak).

In this chapter, we will introduce several recipes that make use of Unity's Editor extensions; these are scripting and multimedia components that enable a game software engineer to make design-time work easier and less likely to introduce errors. Editor extensions allow workflow improvements, thus allowing designers to achieve their goals quicker and more easily; for example, removing the need for any scripting knowledge when generating many randomly located inventory pickups in a scene via a menu choice, or editing the type or properties of pickups being hand-placed in different locations in a level.

While Editor extensions are quite an advanced topic, having someone on your team who can write custom editor components, such as those we illustrate, can greatly increase the productivity of a small team with only one or two members who are confident at scripting.

An editor extension to allow pickup type (and parameters) to be changed at design time via a custom Inspector UI

The use of **enums** and corresponding drop-down menus in the Inspector panel to restrict changes to one of a limited set often works fine (for example, pickup types for a pickup object). However, the trouble with this approach is, when two or more properties are related and need to be changed together, there is a danger of changing one property, for example, pickup type from **Heart** to **Key**, but forgetting to change corresponding properties; for example, leaving the **Sprite Renderer** component still showing a **Heart sprite**. Such mismatches cause problems both in terms of messing up intended level design and, of course, the frustration for the player when they collide with something showing one pickup image, but a different kind of pickup type is added to the inventory!

If a class of GameObject has several related properties or components, which all need to be changed together, then a good strategy is to use Unity Editor extensions to do all the associated changes each time a different choice is made from a drop-down menu showing the defined set of enumerated choices.

In this recipe, we introduce an Editor extension for PickUp components of GameObjects.

Getting ready

This recipe assumes you are starting with project Simple2Dgame_SpaceGirl setup from the first recipe in *Chapter 2, Inventory GUIs*. A copy of this Unity project is provided in a folder named unityProject_spaceGirlMiniGame in the 1362_12_01 folder.

How to do it...

To create an editor extension to allow pickup type (and parameters) to be changed at design-time via a custom Inspector UI, follow these steps:

1. Start with a new copy of mini-game Simple2Dgame_SpaceGirl.

2. In the **Project** panel, create a new folder named EditorSprites. Move the following images from folder Sprites into this new folder: star, healthheart, icon_key_green_100, icon_key_green_32, icon_star_32, and icon_heart_32.

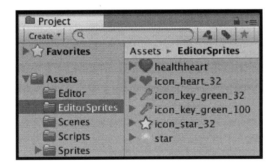

3. In the **Hierarchy** panel, rename GameObject star to be named pickup.

4. Edit the tags, changing tag **Star** to **Pickup**. Ensure the pickup GameObject now has the tag **Pickup**.

5. Add the following C# script PickUp to GameObject pickup in the **Hierarchy**:

```
using UnityEngine;
using System;
using System.Collections;

public class PickUp : MonoBehaviour {
  public enum PickUpType {
    Star, Health, Key
  }
```

```
    [SerializeField]
    public PickUpType type;

    public void SetSprite(Sprite newSprite){
      SpriteRenderer spriteRenderer =
          GetComponent<SpriteRenderer>();
      spriteRenderer.sprite = newSprite;
    }
}
```

6. In the **Project** panel, create a new folder named Editor. Inside this new folder, create a new C# script class named PickUpEditor, with the following code:

```
using UnityEngine;
using System.Collections;
using System;
using UnityEditor;
using System.Collections.Generic;

[CanEditMultipleObjects]
[CustomEditor(typeof(PickUp))]
public class PickUpEditor : Editor
{
  public Texture iconHealth;
  public Texture iconKey;
  public Texture iconStar;

  public Sprite spriteHealth100;
  public Sprite spriteKey100;
  public Sprite spriteStar100;

  UnityEditor.SerializedProperty pickUpType;

  private Sprite sprite;
  private PickUp pickupObject;

  void OnEnable () {
    iconHealth = AssetDatabase.LoadAssetAtPath("Assets/
EditorSprites/icon_heart_32.png", typeof(Texture)) as Texture;
    iconKey = AssetDatabase.LoadAssetAtPath("Assets/EditorSprites/
icon_key_32.png", typeof(Texture)) as Texture;
    iconStar =
AssetDatabase.LoadAssetAtPath("Assets/EditorSprites/
icon_star_32.png", typeof(Texture)) as Texture;
```

```
    spriteHealth100 =
AssetDatabase.LoadAssetAtPath("Assets/EditorSprites/
healthheart.png", typeof(Sprite)) as Sprite;
    spriteKey100 =
AssetDatabase.LoadAssetAtPath("Assets/EditorSprites/
icon_key_100.png", typeof(Sprite)) as Sprite;
    spriteStar100 =
AssetDatabase.LoadAssetAtPath("Assets/EditorSprites/
star.png", typeof(Sprite)) as Sprite;

    pickupObject = (PickUp)target;
    pickUpType = serializedObject.FindProperty ("type");
  }


  public override void OnInspectorGUI()
  {
    serializedObject.Update ();

    string[] pickUpCategories = TypesToStringArray();
    pickUpType.enumValueIndex =
EditorGUILayout.Popup("PickUp TYPE: ",
pickUpType.enumValueIndex, pickUpCategories);

    PickUp.PickUpType type =
(PickUp.PickUpType)pickUpType.enumValueIndex;
    switch(type)
    {
    case PickUp.PickUpType.Health:
      InspectorGUI_HEALTH();
      break;

    case PickUp.PickUpType.Key:
      InspectorGUI_KEY();
      break;

    case PickUp.PickUpType.Star:
    default:
      InspectorGUI_STAR();
      break;
    }

    serializedObject.ApplyModifiedProperties ();
  }
```

```
private void InspectorGUI_HEALTH()
{
  GUILayout.BeginHorizontal();
  GUILayout.FlexibleSpace();
  GUILayout.Label(iconHealth);
  GUILayout.Label("HEALTH");
  GUILayout.Label(iconHealth);
  GUILayout.Label("HEALTH");
  GUILayout.Label(iconHealth);
  GUILayout.FlexibleSpace();
  GUILayout.EndHorizontal();

  pickupObject.SetSprite(spriteHealth100);
}

private void InspectorGUI_KEY()
{
  GUILayout.BeginHorizontal();
  GUILayout.FlexibleSpace();
  GUILayout.Label(iconKey);
  GUILayout.Label("KEY");
  GUILayout.Label(iconKey);
  GUILayout.Label("KEY");
  GUILayout.Label(iconKey);
  GUILayout.FlexibleSpace();
  GUILayout.EndHorizontal();

  pickupObject.SetSprite(spriteKey100);
}

private void InspectorGUI_STAR()
{
  GUILayout.BeginHorizontal();
  GUILayout.FlexibleSpace();
  GUILayout.Label(iconStar);
  GUILayout.Label("STAR");
  GUILayout.Label(iconStar);
  GUILayout.Label("STAR");
  GUILayout.Label(iconStar);
  GUILayout.FlexibleSpace();
  GUILayout.EndHorizontal();

  pickupObject.SetSprite(spriteStar100);
}
```

```
    private string[] TypesToStringArray(){
       var pickupValues =
(PickUp.PickUpType[])Enum.GetValues(typeof
(PickUp.PickUpType));

       List<string> stringList = new List<string>();

       foreach(PickUp.PickUpType pickupValue in pickupValues){
          string stringName = pickupValue.ToString();
          stringList.Add(stringName);
       }

       return stringList.ToArray();
    }
}
```

7. In the **Inspector** panel, select GameObject `pickup` and choose different values of the drop-down menu **PickUp Type**. You should see corresponding changes in the image and icons in the **Inspector** for the **Pick Up (Script)** component (three icons with the name of the type in between). The **Sprite** property of the **Sprite Renderer** component for this GameObject should change. Also, in the **Scene** panel, you'll see the image in the scene change to the appropriate image for the pickup type you have chosen.

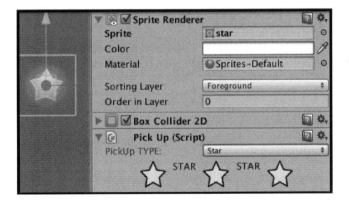

How it works...

Our script class `PickUp` has the enum `PickUpType` with the three values: `Star`, `Health`, and `Key`. Also, there is the variable `type`, storing the type of the parent GameObject. Finally, there is a `SetSprite(...)` method that sets the **Sprite Renderer** component of the parent GameObject to be set to the provided `Sprite` parameter. It is this method that is called from the editor script each time the pickup type is changed from the drop-down menu (with the corresponding sprite for the new type being passed).

The vast majority of the work for this recipe is the responsibility of the script class `PickUpEditor`. While there is a lot in this script, its work is relatively straightforward: for each frame, via method `OnInspectorGUI()`, a dropdown list of `PickUpType` values is presented to the user. Based on the value selected from this drop-down list, one of three methods is executed: `InspectorGUI_HEALTH()`, `InspectorGUI_KEY()`, `InspectorGUI_STAR()`. Each of these methods displays three icons and the name of the type in the Inspector beneath the drop-down menu and ends by calling the `SetSprite(...)` method of the GameObject being edited in the Inspector to update the **Sprite Renderer** component of the parent GameObject with the appropriate sprite.

The C# attribute `[CustomEditor(typeof(PickUp))]` appearing before our class is declared, tells Unity to use this special editor script to display component properties in the **Inspector** panel for **Pick Up (Script)** components of GameObjects, rather than Unity's default **Inspector** which displays public variables of such scripted components.

Before and after its main work, the `OnInspectorGUI()` method first ensures that any variables relating to the object being edited in the Inspector have been updated — `serializedObject.Update()`. The last statement of this method correspondingly ensures that any changes to variables in the editor script have been copied back to the GameObject being edited—`serializedObject.ApplyModifiedProperties()`.

The `OnEnable()` method of script class `PickUpEditor` loads the three small icons (for display in the **Inspector**) and the three larger sprite images (to update the **Sprite Renderer** for display in the **Scene/Game** panels). The `pickupObject` variable is set to be a reference to the `PickUp` scripted component, allowing us to call the `SetSprite(...)` method. The `pickUpType` variable is set to be linked to the type variable of the `PickUp` scripted component whose special **Inspector** editor view makes this script possible— `serializedObject.FindProperty("type")`.

There's more...

Here are some details you don't want to miss.

Offer the custom editing of pickup parameters via Inspector

Many pickups have additional properties, rather than simply being an item being carried. For example, a health pickup may add health "points" to the player's character, a coin pickup may add money "points" to the characters bank balance, and so on. So, let's add an integer `points` variable to our `PickUp` class and offer the user the ability to easily edit this points value via a GUI slider in our customer Inspector editor.

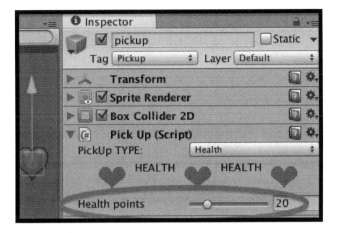

To add an editable points property to our `PickUp` objects, follow these steps:

1. Add the following extra line into C# script `PickUp` to create our new integer `points` variable:

    ```
    public int points;
    ```

2. Add the following extra line into C# script `PickUpEditor` to work with our new integer `points` variable:

    ```
    UnityEditor.SerializedProperty points;
    ```

3. Add the following extra line into the `OnEnable()` method in C# script `PickUpEditor` to associate our new `points` variable with its corresponding value in the `PickUp` scripted component of the GameObject being edited:

    ```
    void OnEnable () {
      points = serializedObject.FindProperty ("points");
      pickUpType = serializedObject.FindProperty ("type");
      // rest of method as before...
    ```

4. Now we can add an extra line into each GUI method for the different PickUp types. For example, we can add a statement to display an **IntSlider** to the user to be able to see and modify the points value for a **Health PickUp** object. We add a new statement at the end of the `InspectorGUI_HEALTH()` method in C# script `PickUpEditor` to display a modifiable **IntSlider** representing our new `points` variable as follows:

    ```
    private void InspectorGUI_HEALTH(){
      // beginning of method just as before...

      pickupObject.SetSprite(spriteHealth100);

    // now display Int Slider for points
      points.intValue = EditorGUILayout.IntSlider
    ("Health points", points.intValue, 0, 100);
    }
    ```

We provide four parameters to the `IntSlider(…)` method. The first is the text label the user will see next to the slider. The second is the initial value the slider displays. The last two are the maximum and minimum values. In our example, we are permitting values from 0 to 100, but if health pickups only offer one, two, or three health points, then we'd just call with `EditorGUILayout.IntSlider ("Health points", points.intValue, 1, 5)`. This method returns a new integer value based on where the slider has been positioned, and this new value is stored back into the integer value part of our `SerializedProperty` variable points.

Note that the loading and saving of values from the scripted component in the GameObject and our editor script is all part of the work undertaken by our calls to the `Update()` method and the `ApplyModifiedProperties()` method on the serialized object in the `OnInspectorGUI()` method.

Note that since points may not have any meaning for some pickups, for example, keys, then we simply would not display any slider for the GUI Inspector editor when the user is editing **PickUp** objects of that type.

Offer a drop-down list of tags for key-pickup to fit via Inspector

While the concept of "points" may have no meaning for a key pickup, the concept of the type of lock that a given key fits is certainly something we may wish to implement in a game. Since Unity offers us a defined (and editable) list of string tags for any GameObject, often it is sufficient, and straightforward, to represent the type of lock or door corresponding to a key via its tag. For example, a green key might fit all objects tagged **LockGreen** and so on.

Therefore, it is very useful to be able to offer a custom Inspector editor for a string property of key pickups that stores the tag of the lock(s) the key can open. This task combines several actions, including using C# to retrieve an array of tags from the Unity editor, then the building and offering of a drop-down list of these tags to the user, with the current value already selected in this list.

To add a selectable list of strings for the tag for lock(s) that a key fits, follow these steps:

1. Add the following extra line into C# Script `PickUp` to create our new integer `fitsLockTag` variable:

```
public string fitsLockTag;
```

2. Add the following extra line into C# script `PickUpEditor` to work with our new integer `fitsLockTag` variable:

```
UnityEditor.SerializedProperty fitsLockTag;
```

3. Add the following extra line into the `OnEnable()` method in C# script `PickUpEditor` to associate our new `fitsLockTag` variable with its corresponding value in the PickUp scripted component of the GameObject being edited:

```
void OnEnable () {
  fitsLockTag =
serializedObject.FindProperty ("fitsLockTag");
  points = serializedObject.FindProperty ("points");
  pickUpType = serializedObject.FindProperty ("type");
  // rest of method as before...
```

4. Now we need to add some extra lines of code into the GUI method for key PickUps. We need to add several statements to the end of method `InspectorGUI_KEY()` in C# script `PickUpEditor` to set up and display a selectable popup drop-down list representing our new `fitsLockTag` variable as follows. Replace the `InspectorGUI_KEY()` method with the following code:

```
private void InspectorGUI_KEY() {
  GUILayout.BeginHorizontal();
  GUILayout.FlexibleSpace();
  GUILayout.Label(iconKey);
  GUILayout.Label("KEY");
  GUILayout.Label(iconKey);
  GUILayout.Label("KEY");
  GUILayout.Label(iconKey);
  GUILayout.FlexibleSpace();
  GUILayout.EndHorizontal();

  pickupObject.SetSprite(spriteKey100);

  string[] tags =
UnityEditorInternal.InternalEditorUtility.tags;
```

```
    Array.Sort(tags);
    int selectedTagIndex =
Array.BinarySearch(tags, fitsLockTag.stringValue);
    if(selectedTagIndex < 0)  selectedTagIndex = 0;
    selectedTagIndex =
EditorGUILayout.Popup("Tag of door key fits: ",
selectedTagIndex, tags);

    fitsLockTag.stringValue = tags[selectedTagIndex];
}
```

We've added several statements to the end of this method. First `tags`, an array of strings, is created (and sorted), containing the list of tags currently available in the Unity editor for the current game. We then attempt to find the location in this array of the current value of `fitsLockTag` — we can use the `BinarySearch(...)` method of built-in script class `Array` because we have alphabetically sorted our array (which also makes it easier for the user to navigate). If the string in `fitsLockTag` cannot be found in array `tags`, then the first item will be selected by default (index 0).

The user is then shown the drop-down list via the `GUILayout` method `EditorGUILayout.Popup(...)`, and this method returns the index of whichever item is selected. The selected index is stored into `selectedTagIndex`, and the last statement in the method extracts the corresponding string and stores that string into the `fitsLockTag` variable.

Note: Rather than displaying all possible tags, a further refinement might remove all items from array 'tags' that do not have the prefix 'Lock'. So the user is only presented with tags such as 'LockBlue' and 'LockGreen', and so on.

Logic to open doors with keys based on fitsLockTag

In our player collision logic, we can now search through our inventory to see if any key items fit the lock we have collided with. For example, if a green door was collided with, and the player was carrying a key that could open such doors, then that item should be removed from the inventory `List<>` and the door should be opened.

To implement this, you would need to add an `if` test inside the `OnTriggerEnter()` method to detected collision with the item tagged `Door`, and then logic to attempt to open the door, and, if unsuccessful, do the appropriate action (for example, play sound) to inform the player they cannot open the door yet (we'll assume we have written a door animation controller that plays the appropriate animation and sounds and when a door is to be opened):

```
if("Door" == hitCollider.tag){
  if(!OpenDoor(hitCollider.gameObject))
    DoorNotOpenedAction();
}
```

The `OpenDoor()` method would need to identify which item (if any) in the inventory can open such a door, and, if found, then that item should be removed from the `List<>` and the door should be opened by the appropriate method:

```
private bool OpenDoor(GameObject doorGO){
  // search for key to open the tag of doorGO
  int colorKeyIndex = FindItemIndex(doorGO.tag);
  if( colorKeyIndex > -1 ){
    // remove key item from inventory List<>
    inventory.RemoveAt( colorKeyIndex );

    // now open the door...
    DoorAnimationController doorAnimationController =
doorGO.GetComponent<>(DoorAnimationController);
    doorAnimationController.OpenDoor();

    return true;
  }

  return false;
}
```

The following is the code for a method to find the inventory list key item fitting a door tag:

```
private int FindItemIndex(string doorTag){
  for (int i = 0; i < inventory.Count; i++){
    PickUp item = inventory[i];
    if( (PickUp.PickUpType.Key == item.type) &&
(item.fitsLockTag == doorTag))
      return i;
  }

  // not found
return -1;
}
```

The need to add [SerializeField] for private properties

Note that if we wished to create editor extensions to work with private variables, then we'd need to explicitly add `[SerializeField]` in the line immediately before the variable to be changed by the editor script. Public variables are serialized by default in Unity, so this was not required for our public `type` variable in script class `PickUp`, although it's good practice to flag ALL variables that are changeable via an Editor Extension in this way.

Learn more from the Unity documentation

Unity provides documentation pages about editor scripts at `http://docs.unity3d.com/ScriptReference/Editor.html`.

An editor extension to add 100 randomly located copies of a prefab with one menu click

Sometimes we want to create "lots" of pickups, randomly in our scene. Rather than doing this by hand, it is possible to add a custom menu and item to the Unity editor, which, when selected, will execute a script. In this recipe, we create a menu item that calls a script to create 100 randomly positioned star pickup prefabs in the Scene.

Getting ready

This recipe assumes you are starting with the project `Simple2Dgame_SpaceGirl` setup from the first recipe in this chapter.

How to do it...

To create an editor extension to add 100 randomly located copies of a prefab with one menu click, follow these steps:

1. Start with a new copy of mini-game `Simple2Dgame_SpaceGirl`.

2. In the **Project** panel, create a new folder named `Prefabs`. Inside this new folder, create a new empty prefab named `prefab_star`. Populate this prefab by dragging GameObject `star` from the **Hierarchy** panel over `prefab_star` in the **Project** panel. The prefab should now turn blue and have a copy of all of GameObject star's properties and components.

3. Delete GameObject `star` from the **Hierarchy**.

4. In the **Project** panel, create a new folder named `Editor`. Inside this new folder, create a new C# script class named `MyGreatGameEditor`, with the following code:

    ```
    using UnityEngine;
    using UnityEditor;
    using System.Collections;
    using System;
    ```

```
public class MyGreatGameEditor : MonoBehaviour {
  const float X_MAX = 10f;
  const float Y_MAX = 10f;

  static GameObject starPrefab;

  [MenuItem("My-Great-Game/Make 100 stars")]
  static void PlacePrefabs(){
    string assetPath = "Assets/Prefabs/prefab_star.prefab";
    starPrefab = (GameObject)AssetDatabase.
LoadMainAssetAtPath(assetPath);

    int total = 100;
    for(int i = 0; i < total; i++){
      CreateRandomInstance();
    }
  }

  static void CreateRandomInstance(){
    float x = UnityEngine.Random.Range(-X_MAX, X_MAX);
    float y = UnityEngine.Random.Range(-Y_MAX, Y_MAX);
    float z = 0;
    Vector3 randomPosition = new Vector3(x,y,z);

    Instantiate(starPrefab, randomPosition,
Quaternion.identity);
  }
}
```

5. After 20 to 30 seconds, depending on the speed of your computer, you should now see a new menu appear, **My Great Game**, with a single menu item, **Make 100 stars**. Chose this menu item and, as if by magic, you should now see 100 new **prefab_star(Clone)** GameObjects appear in the scene!

How it works...

The core aim of this recipe is to add a new menu, containing a single menu item that will execute the action we desire. C# attribute [MenuItem("<menuName>/<menuItemName>")] declares the menu name and the menu item name, and Unity will execute the static method that follows in the code listing, each time the menu item is selected by the user.

In this recipe, the [MenuItem("My-Great-Game/Make 100 stars")] statement declares the menu name as My-Great-Game and the menu item as Make 100 stars. The method immediately following this attribute is the PlacePrefabs() method. When this method is executed, it makes the starPrefab variable become a reference to the prefab found via the Assets/Prefabs/prefab_star.prefab path. Then, a for loop is executed 100 times, each time calling the CreateRandomInstance() method.

The CreateRandomInstance() method creates a Vector3 randomPosition variable, making use of X_MAX and Y_MAX constants. The Instantiate(...) built-in method is then used to create a new GameObject in the scene, making a clone of the prefab and locating it at the position defined by randomPosition.

There's more...

Some details you don't want to miss:

Child each new GameObject to a single parent, to avoid filling up the Hierarchy with 100s of new objects

Rather than having hundreds of new object clones fill up our **Hierarchy** panel, a good way to keep things tidy is to have an empty "parent" GameObject and child a collection of related GameObjects to it. Let's have a GameObject in the **Hierarchy** named **Star-container** and child all the new stars to this object.

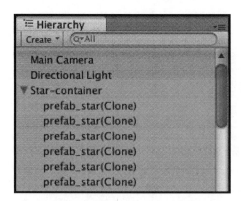

We need a variable that will be a reference to our container object, `starContainerGO`. We also need a new method, `CreateStarContainerGO()`, which will find a reference to GameObject **star-container**, if such an object already exists it is deleted, and then the method will create a new empty GameObject and give it this name. Add the following variable and method to our script class:

```
static GameObject starContainerGO;

static void CreateStarContainerGO() {
  string containerName = "Star-container";
  starContainerGO = GameObject.Find(containerName);
  if (null != starContainerGO)
    DestroyImmediate(starContainerGO);
  starContainerGO = new GameObject(containerName);
}
```

Before we create the prefab clones, we need to first ensure we have created our star container GameObject. So we need to call our new method as the first thing we do when the `PlacePrefabs()` method is executed, so add a statement to call this method at the beginning of the `PlacePrefabs()` method:

```
static void PlacePrefabs(){
  CreateStarContainerGO();

  // rest of method as before ...
}
```

Now we need to modify the `CreateRandomInstance()` method so that it gets a reference to the new GameObject it has just created and can then child this new object to our **star-container** GameObject variable `starContainerGO`. Modify the `CreateRandomInstance()` method so that it looks as follows:

```
static void CreateRandomInstance() {
  float x = UnityEngine.Random.Range(-X_MAX, X_MAX);
  float y = UnityEngine.Random.Range(-Y_MAX, Y_MAX);
  float z = 0;
  Vector3 randomPosition = new Vector3(x,y,z);

  GameObject newStarGO = (GameObject)Instantiate(starPrefab,
randomPosition, Quaternion.identity);
  newStarGO.transform.parent = starContainerGO.transform;
}
```

A progress bar to display proportion completed of Editor extension processing

If an Editor task is going to take more than half a second or so, then we should indicate progress complete/remaining to the user via a progress bar so that they understand that something is actually happening and the application has not crashed and frozen.

Getting ready

This recipe adds to the previous one, so make a copy of that project folder and do your work for this recipe with that copy.

How to do it...

To add a progress bar during the loop (and then remove it after the loop is complete), replace the `PlacePrefabs()` method with the following code:

```
static void PlacePrefabs(){
   string assetPath = "Assets/Prefabs/prefab_star.prefab";
   starPrefab = (GameObject)AssetDatabase.
LoadMainAssetAtPath(assetPath);

   int total = 100;
   for(int i = 0; i < total; i++){
     CreateRandomInstance();
     EditorUtility.DisplayProgressBar("Creating your starfield",
i + "%", i/100f);
   }

   EditorUtility.ClearProgressBar();
}
```

How it works...

As can be seen, inside the `for` loop, we call the `EditorUtility.DisplayProgressBar(...)` method, passing three parameters. The first is a string title for the progress bar dialog window, the second is a string to show below the bar itself (usually a percentage is sufficient), and the final parameter is a value between 0.0 and 1.0, indicating the percentage complete to be displayed.

Since we have loop variable `i` that is a number from 1 to 100, we can display this integer followed by a percentage sign for our second parameter and just divide this number by 100 to get the decimal value needed to specify how much of the progress bar should be shown as completed. If the loop were running for some other number, we'd just divide the loop counter by the loop total to get our decimal progress value. Finally, after the loop has finished, we remove the progress bar with statement `EditorUtility.ClearProgressBar()`.

An editor extension to have an object-creator GameObject, with buttons to instantiate different pickups at cross-hair object location in scene

If a level designer wishes to place each pickup carefully "by hand", we can still make this easier than having to drag copies of prefabs manually from the **Projects** panel. In this recipe, we provide a "cross-hairs" GameObject, with buttons in the Inspector allowing the game designer to create instances of three different kinds of prefab at precise locations by clicking the appropriate button when the center of the cross-hairs is at the desired location.

A Unity Editor extension is at the heart of this recipe and illustrates how such extensions can allow less technical members of a game development team to take an active role in level creation within the Unity Editor.

Getting ready

This recipe assumes you are starting with the project `Simple2Dgame_SpaceGirl` setup from the first recipe in *Chapter 2, Inventory GUIs*.

For this recipe, we have prepared the cross-hairs image you need in a folder named `Sprites` in the `1362_12_04` folder.

How to do it...

To create an object-creator GameObject, follow these steps:

1. Start with a new copy of mini-game `Simple2Dgame_SpaceGirl`.

2. In the **Project** panel, rename GameObject `star` as `pickup`.

3. In the **Project** panel, create a new folder named `Prefabs`. Inside this new folder, create three new empty prefabs named `star`, `heart`, and `key`.

4. Populate the `star` prefab by dragging GameObject `pickup` from the **Hierarchy** panel over `star` in the **Project** panel. The prefab should now turn blue and have a copy of all of the star GameObject's properties and components.

5. Add a new tag `Heart` in the Inspector. Select GameObject `pickup` in the **Hierarchy** panel and assign it the tag `Heart`. Also, drag from the **Project** panel (folder `Sprites`) the **healthheart** image into the Sprite property of GameObject `pickup` so that the player sees the heart image on screen for this pickup item.

6. Populate the `heart` prefab by dragging GameObject `pickup` from the **Hierarchy** panel over `heart` in the `Prefabs` folder in the **Project** panel. The prefab should now turn blue and have a copy of all of the pickup GameObject's properties and components.

7. Add a new tag `Key` in the Inspector. Select GameObject's `pickup` in the **Hierarchy** panel and assign it this tag `Key`. Also, drag from the **Project** panel (folder `Sprites`) image **icon_key_green_100** into the Sprite property of GameObject's `pickup` so that the player sees the key image on screen for this pickup item.

8. Populate the `key` prefab by dragging GameObject `pickup` from the **Hierarchy** panel over `key` in the `Prefabs` folder in the **Project** panel. The prefab should now turn blue and have a copy of all of the pickup GameObject's properties and components.

9. Delete GameObject's `pickup` from the **Hierarchy**.

10. In the **Project** panel, create a new folder named `Editor`. Inside this new folder, create a new C# script class named `ObjectBuilderEditor`, with the following code:

```
using UnityEngine;
using System.Collections;
using UnityEditor;
```

```
[CustomEditor(typeof(ObjectBuilderScript))]
public class ObjectBuilderEditor : Editor{
  private Texture iconStar;
  private Texture iconHeart;
  private Texture iconKey;

  private GameObject prefabHeart;
  private GameObject prefabStar;
  private GameObject prefabKey;

  void OnEnable () {
    iconStar = Resources.LoadAssetAtPath("Assets/EditorSprites/
icon_star_32.png", typeof(Texture)) as Texture;
    iconHeart =
Resources.LoadAssetAtPath("Assets/EditorSprites/
icon_heart_32.png", typeof(Texture)) as Texture;
    iconKey = Resources.LoadAssetAtPath("Assets/EditorSprites/
icon_key_green_32.png", typeof(Texture)) as Texture;

    prefabStar =
Resources.LoadAssetAtPath("Assets/Prefabs/star.prefab",
typeof(GameObject)) as GameObject;
    prefabHeart =
Resources.LoadAssetAtPath("Assets/Prefabs/heart.prefab",
typeof(GameObject)) as GameObject;
    prefabKey =
Resources.LoadAssetAtPath("Assets/Prefabs/key.prefab",
typeof(GameObject)) as GameObject;
  }

  public override void OnInspectorGUI(){
    ObjectBuilderScript myScript =
(ObjectBuilderScript)target;

    GUILayout.Label("");
    GUILayout.BeginHorizontal();
    GUILayout.FlexibleSpace();
    GUILayout.Label("Click button to create instance of
prefab");
    GUILayout.FlexibleSpace();
    GUILayout.EndHorizontal();
    GUILayout.Label("");

    GUILayout.BeginHorizontal();
    GUILayout.FlexibleSpace();
```

```
        if(GUILayout.Button(iconStar)) myScript.
AddObjectToScene(prefabStar);
        GUILayout.FlexibleSpace();
        if(GUILayout.Button(iconHeart)) myScript.
AddObjectToScene(prefabHeart);
        GUILayout.FlexibleSpace();
        if(GUILayout.Button(iconKey)) myScript.
AddObjectToScene(prefabKey);
        GUILayout.FlexibleSpace();
        GUILayout.EndHorizontal();


    }
}
```

11. Our Editor script is expecting to find the three icons in a folder named `EditorSprites`, so let's do this. First create a new folder named `EditorSprites`. Next drag the three 32 x 32 pixel icons from the `Sprites` folder into this new `EditorSprites` folder. Our Editor script should now be able to load these icons for image-based buttons that it will be drawing in the Inspector, from which the user chooses which pickup prefab object to clone into the scene.

12. From the **Project** panel, drag sprite **cross_hairs.fw** into the **Scene**. Rename this gameObject `object-creator-cross-hairs`, and in its **Sprite Renderer** component in the **Inspector**, set **Sorting Layer** to **Foreground**.

13. Attach the following C# script to GameObject `object-creator-cross-hairs`:

```
using UnityEngine;
using System.Collections;

public class ObjectBuilderScript : MonoBehaviour {
  void Awake(){
    gameObject.SetActive(false);
  }

  public void AddObjectToScene(GameObject
prefabToCreateInScene){
```

```
    GameObject newGO =
(GameObject)Instantiate(prefabToCreateInScene,
transform.position, Quaternion.identity);
    newGO.name = prefabToCreateInScene.name;
  }
}
```

14. Select the **Rect Tool** (shortcut key _T_), and as you drag gameObject `object-creator-cross-hairs` and click on the desired icon in the **Inspector**, new pickup GameObjects will be added to the scene's **Hierarchy**.

How it works...

The script class `ObjectBuilderScript` has just two methods, one of which has just one statement—the `Awake()` method simply makes this GameObject become inactive when the game is running (since we don't want the user to see our cross-hairs created tool during gameplay). The `AddObjectToScene(...)` method receives a reference to a prefab as a parameter and instantiates a new clone of the prefab in the scene at the location of GameObject `object-creator-cross-hairs` at that point in time.

Script class `ObjectBuilderEditor` has a C# attribute `[CustomEditor(typeof(ObjectBuilderScript))]` immediately before the class is declared, telling Unity to use this class to control how `ObjectBuilderScript` GameObject properties and components are shown to the user in the **Inspector**.

There are six variables, three textures for the icons to form the buttons in the Inspector, and three GameObject references to the prefabs of which instances will be created. The `OnEnable()` method assigns values to these six variables using the built-in method `Resources.LoadAssetAtPath()`, retrieving the icons from the **Project** folder `EditorSprites` and getting references to the prefabs in the **Project** folder `Prefabs`.

The `OnInspectorGUI()` method has a variable `myScript`, which is set to be a reference to the instance of scripted component `ObjectBuilderScript` in GameObject `object-creator-cross-hairs` (so we can call its method when a prefab has been chosen). The method then displays a mixture of empty text `Label`s (to get some vertical spacing) and `FlexibleSpace` (to get some horizontal spacing and centering) and displays three buttons to the user, with icons of star, heart, and key. The scripted GUI technique for Unity custom **Inspector** GUIs wraps an `if` statement around each button, and on the frame the user clicks the button, the statement block of the `if` statement will be executed. When any of the three buttons is clicked, a call is made to `AddObjectToScene(...)` of scripted component `ObjectBuilderScript`, passing the prefab corresponding to the button that was clicked.

Conclusion

In this chapter, we introduced recipes demonstrating some Unity Editor extension scripts, illustrating how we can make things easier, less script based, and less prone to errors, by limiting and controlling the properties of objects and how they are selected or changed via the **Inspector**.

The concept of serialization was raised in the Editor extension recipes, whereby we need to remember that when we are editing item properties in the Inspector, each change needs to be saved to disk so that the updated property is correct when we next use or edit that item. This is achieved in the `OnInspectorGUI()` method by first calling the `serializedObject.Update()` method, and after all changes have been made in the Inspector, finally calling the `serializedObject.ApplyModifiedProperties()` method. Some sources for more information and examples about custom Editor extensions include:

▶ For more about custom Unity Editors in Ryan Meier's blog, refer to
   `http://www.ryan-meier.com/blog/?p=72`

▶ For more custom Unity Editor scripts/tutorials, including grids and color pickers,
   refer to `http://code.tutsplus.com/tutorials/how-to-add-your-own-tools-to-unitys-editor--active-10047`

Index

About Packt Publishing

Packt, pronounced 'packed', published its first book, *Mastering phpMyAdmin for Effective MySQL Management*, in April 2004, and subsequently continued to specialize in publishing highly focused books on specific technologies and solutions.

Our books and publications share the experiences of your fellow IT professionals in adapting and customizing today's systems, applications, and frameworks. Our solution-based books give you the knowledge and power to customize the software and technologies you're using to get the job done. Packt books are more specific and less general than the IT books you have seen in the past. Our unique business model allows us to bring you more focused information, giving you more of what you need to know, and less of what you don't.

Packt is a modern yet unique publishing company that focuses on producing quality, cutting-edge books for communities of developers, administrators, and newbies alike. For more information, please visit our website at www.packtpub.com.

Writing for Packt

We welcome all inquiries from people who are interested in authoring. Book proposals should be sent to author@packtpub.com. If your book idea is still at an early stage and you would like to discuss it first before writing a formal book proposal, then please contact us; one of our commissioning editors will get in touch with you.

We're not just looking for published authors; if you have strong technical skills but no writing experience, our experienced editors can help you develop a writing career, or simply get some additional reward for your expertise.

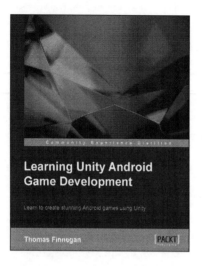

Learning Unity Android Game Development

ISBN: 978-1-78439-469-1   Paperback: 338 pages

Learn to create stunning Android games using Unity

1. Leverage the new features of Unity 5 for the Android mobile market with hands-on projects and real-world examples.

2. Create comprehensive and robust games using various customizations and additions available in Unity such as camera, lighting, and sound effects.

3. Precise instructions to use Unity to create an Android-based mobile game.

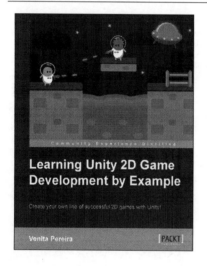

Learning Unity 2D Game Development by Example

ISBN: 978-1-78355-904-6   Paperback: 266 pages

Create your own line of successful 2D games with Unity!

1. Dive into 2D game development with no previous experience.

2. Learn how to use the new Unity 2D toolset.

3. Create and deploy your very own 2D game with confidence.

Please check **www.PacktPub.com** for information on our titles